Berlioz's Orchestration Treatise

A Translation and Commentary

Berlioz's orchestration treatise is a classic textbook which has been used as a guide to orchestration and as a source book for the understanding both of Berlioz's music and of orchestral practice in the nineteenth century. This is the first new English translation of Berlioz's complete text since 1856, and it is accompanied throughout by Hugh Macdonald's extensive and authoritative commentary on the instruments of Berlioz's time and on his own orchestral practice, as revealed in his scores. It also includes extracts from Berlioz's writings on instruments in his *Memoirs* and in his many articles for the Parisian press.

The *Treatise* has been highly valued both for its technical information about instruments and for its poetic and visionary approach to the art of instrumentation. It includes a chapter on the orchestra itself, seen as a giant independent instrument, and on the art of conducting, one of the first documents of its kind. Berlioz was not only one of the great orchestrators of the nineteenth century, he was also the author with the clearest understanding of the art.

HUGH MACDONALD is Avis Blewett Professor of Music at Washington University, St Louis. He has been General Editor of the New Berlioz Edition since its inception in 1967. He has edited *The Selected Letters of Berlioz* (1995) and Volumes IV, V, VI, VII and VIII of the Berlioz *Correspondance générale* (1992–). He is also author of *Skryabin* (1978) and *Berlioz* (1982).

CAMBRIDGE MUSICAL TEXTS AND MONOGRAPHS

General editors: John Butt and Laurence Dreyfus

This series has as its centres of interest the history of performance and the history of instruments. It includes annotated translations of authentic historical texts on music and monographs on various aspects of historical performance and instrument history.

Recent titles

Frontispiece Berlioz, *Grand traité d'instrumentation et d'orchestration modernes*, Paris [1844], title page.

Berlioz's Orchestration Treatise

A Translation and Commentary

HUGH MACDONALD

CAMBRIDGE
UNIVERSITY PRESS

CAMBRIDGE UNIVERSITY PRESS
Cambridge, New York, Melbourne, Madrid, Cape Town, Singapore, São Paulo

Cambridge University Press
The Edinburgh Building, Cambridge CB2 8RU, UK

Published in the United States of America by Cambridge University Press, New York

www.cambridge.org
Information on this title: www.cambridge.org/9780521239530

First published 2002
Reprinted 2004
This digitally printed version 2007

A catalogue record for this publication is available from the British Library

Library of Congress Cataloguing in Publication data
Berlioz, Hector, 1803–1869.
    [Grand traité d'instrumentation et d'orchestration modernes. English]
    Berlioz's orchestration treatise: a translation and commentary / [translation,
commentary by] Hugh Macdonald.
        p.   cm. – (Cambridge musical texts and monographs)
Includes bibliographical references and index.
ISBN 0 521 23953 2
1. Instrumentation and orchestration.   2. Conducting.   I. Macdonald, Hugh,
1940–   II. Title.   III. Series.
MT70 .B4813 2002
781.3′74–dc21   2001052619

ISBN 978-0-521-23953-0 hardback
ISBN 978-0-521-03611-5 paperback

Contents

Illustrations

Preface

Berlioz's *Grand traité d'instrumentation et d'orchestration modernes*, first published in 1844 with a second edition in 1855, is a classic textbook which has been widely read for over a century and a half by students, composers, historians and all who are drawn to Berlioz the musician or Berlioz the man. Like Rameau's *Traité de l'harmonie* it is a remarkable example of a great composer venturing into the world of technical and theoretical exposition and producing a masterpiece which affected the musical thinking of generations. In the nineteenth century Berlioz's *Treatise* (as we shall hereafter call it) was read as a book of instruction; in the twentieth century it became a source book for anyone curious to learn more about the history of instruments and orchestral practice and a revealing exposure of Berlioz's musical thinking. His purpose in writing it was to guide composers towards a more expert and expressive use of instruments and to advise them of pitfalls that the unwary may encounter. This is explained in the book's introduction and again alluded to in the section on 'Other percussion instruments':

> Our purpose in the present work is simply to study instruments which are used in modern music and to seek the laws which govern the setting up of harmonious combinations and effective contrasts between them while making special note of their expressive capabilities and of the character appropriate to each.

The study of an instrument's character and expressive potential was really more important to Berlioz than its range and technical limits, careful though he was to set out the latter in as clear a manner as possible. Practical information was already to be found in other treatises and in the separate 'Méthodes' available for every instrument, so there was a special urgency in conveying his personal understanding of colour and timbre, couched in the notion of continuity and tradition from Gluck through Spontini, Beethoven and Weber to the present day. 'Harmonious combinations and effective contrasts' are treated in the chapter on the orchestra, so that the novice composer may learn the essentials of orchestration from a study of this book, an aspect of his art which was seriously overlooked, as Berlioz kept repeating, at the Paris Conservatoire. In its enlarged second edition the *Treatise* included an essay on the art of conducting, which Berlioz's own experience had taught him to regard, like the complexities of concert organisation and management, as part of the composer's craft.

Unlike so much of Berlioz's music, the *Treatise* was successful both in France and abroad. It has been translated into five languages and has been almost continuously in print to this day. Both his contemporaries and his successors recognised its great virtues. Bizet admired it and recommended it to his pupils,[1] and Saint-Saëns said of it:

> For all its oddities, it's a marvellous book. The whole of my generation was brought up on it, and well brought up, I would say, too. It had that inestimable gift of inflaming the imagination and making you love the art it taught. What it didn't teach it gave you the desire to find out, and one learns best what one learns oneself.[2]

Rimsky-Korsakov tells how Balakirev's circle of composers followed the *Treatise*'s instructions slavishly, even when its teaching, on natural brass instruments for example, was out of date.[3] Mahler, Elgar, Delius, Busoni, d'Indy, Debussy, Puccini and Strauss are all known to have used it. Zola studied the clarinet from it. Ravel, no great admirer of Berlioz's music, kept a copy of the *Treatise* near at hand.[4] Most subsequent orchestration textbooks – by Gevaert, Widor, Rimsky-Korsakov and Kœchlin, for example – are in some measure indebted to it, and Strauss's version, incorporating many examples from Wagner's scores, has been widely read and translated.

A new edition of the *Treatise* must today serve a quite different purpose since one no longer refers to it for information about, say, the range of the trumpet or how to write for the harp. It has been superseded by many more comprehensive textbooks. Its value rests rather on its incomparable record of the instrumental practice of Berlioz's time and on the light it sheds on his music. For him it was the other way round: he used extracts from his scores to support the study of orchestration, while we use his remarks on orchestration to enhance our study of his scores. My purpose in the present edition is therefore fourfold: 1) to provide a new translation for English-speaking readers who have long had to depend on Mary Cowden Clarke's very Victorian version of 1856 or Theodore Front's 1948 translation of Strauss's version, 2) to relate what Berlioz says in the *Treatise* to what he has to say elsewhere about instruments and orchestration, 3) to comment on

[1] 'It's an admirable work, the *vade mecum* of any composer who writes for the orchestra. It's utterly complete, with abundant examples. It's indispensable!' Bizet reported by Hugues Imbert in *Portraits et études* (Paris, 1894), p. 178.
[2] Camille Saint-Saëns, *Portraits et souvenirs* (Paris, 1909), pp. 5–6.
[3] N. A. Rimsky-Korsakov, *My Musical Life* (London, 1924), p. 66.
[4] Ravel's copy of the *Treatise* is still displayed on the piano at his house at Montfort-Lamaury.

the state of instruments and instrumental practice of Berlioz's time and 4) to compare what he advises in his *Treatise* with what he does in his own music. For the most part, of course, his music is an admirable illustration of the technical and artistic principles set out in the *Treatise*, but there are times when he does not practise what he preaches. He greeted certain new developments, for example the harp glissando and the saxophone, with enthusiasm, but then did nothing to promote them in his music. Nor did he use most of the violin double-stops and harmonics he so carefully set out as available to the composer. But since his purpose was to offer technical understanding to other composers he was under no obligation to distinguish between those features which he would wish to use himself and those which were available to composers of different tastes.

We can now see how the task of writing the *Treatise* refined his own orchestral technique in mid-career. His early works, including the *Symphonie fantastique* and *Harold en Italie*, contained 'errors' that he was able to correct by withholding publication until he had sufficient experience of conducting them himself. His intense interest in orchestration in the late 1830s made the *Requiem* and *Roméo et Juliette* particularly rich examples of advanced orchestral technique which he drew upon as models for the instruction of others, and in his later works he remained largely faithful to the practice he expounded in the *Treatise*, occasionally calling for new instruments such as the saxhorns used in the *Te deum* and *Les Troyens*. It was probably writing the chapter on the organ for the *Treatise* that gave him the idea for the magnificent opposition of orchestra and organ we find in the *Te deum*, composed seven years later.

BERLIOZ AND THE ORCHESTRA

From the *Symphonie fantastique*, universally admired for its audacious orchestration, it is clear that Berlioz's interest in this aspect of his art was manifest early in his career. In chapter 15 of his *Memoirs* he gives a vivid account of attending the Opéra in the 1820s with a circle of friends, from which it is plain that his attention was as sharply focused on the personnel and activities of the orchestra as upon the not always more dramatic goings-on on stage. Hiller recalled that 'for a number of years he was constantly at the Opéra, where he followed the performances score in hand and made a note every time he observed some effect of solo or combined instrumentation'.[5] His Irish friend George Osborne, who knew Berlioz in his student days, later recalled in similar vein:

---

[5] Ferdinand Hiller, *Künstlerleben* (Cologne, 1880), p. 103, trans. Michael Rose in *Berlioz Remembered* (London, 2001), p. 18.

It was his constant habit to go into orchestras and sit with the different performers watching them and turning over the pages for them. In this way he learned the capacity of each instrument. Besides which he got several instrumentalists to come to his house where they played together little things which he wrote for them to see what they could accomplish. He also asked both Chopin and myself whether such and such passage could be played on the piano.[6]

When Berlioz had to report on the visit of a German opera company to Paris in 1829 he deplored the state of the Théâtre Italien orchestra man by man:

The eight first and eight second violins are held together by four young men from the Conservatoire having a good working knowledge of the instrument. Of the four violas one is good, one moderate and two are hopeless. Of the three (would you believe it!) cellos only one made any impression, M. Franchomme, a very talented young man with a brilliant career before him. The other two are old men who fortunately sleep more than they play.

All one can say of the seven double basses is that they are neither good nor bad. There is little better to be said of the brass, except that Gallay is the most gifted horn player in Paris, but for reasons of seniority he plays third horn and never gets a solo. The flutes and clarinets are good, which makes the oboes and bassoons even more unbearable. The bassoons cannot play fast and the first oboe is quite without a sense of rhythm. [. . .] The timpanist is reliable enough, but he pays more attention to catching the ladies' eyes than to counting his bars. It is, in a word, one of the worst orchestras.[7]

Berlioz's ability to dissect the workings of an orchestra and to understand its strengths and weaknesses was a key to his success as a conductor and it was also invaluable both to his composing and to his work as a critic. It bore two remarkable but very different literary fruits. The first was the *Treatise*, in which his awareness of the human dimension of the orchestra is never far from view, and the second was *Les soirées de l'orchestre*, a compilation of essays and reviews put together in 1852 and cast as the serious and frivolous exchanges of the players in a theatre orchestra who are often so numbed by the futility of their duties that they exchange gossip, stories and flights of fancy. Although Berlioz had almost no orchestral experience as a player himself, his illustrious career as a conductor was strengthened by his profound understanding of what goes on in an orchestra and how its members individually function. It is as though his physiology classes at the School of Medicine had taught him to think of the orchestra as an

---

[6] George Osborne, 'Berlioz', *Proceedings of the Musical Association*, 5 (1878–9), pp. 60–71, cited in A. W. Ganz, *Berlioz in London* (London, 1950), p. 87.

[7] *Berliner allgemeine musikalische Zeitung*, 27 June 1829; *Cm*, 1, p. 25.

organism made up of limbs, organs, joints, nerves and muscles all serving a larger collective purpose.

Whereas most music critics in France would concentrate on the literary and vocal qualities of an opera, Berlioz often chose to draw attention to instrumental effects in unashamedly technical language. His article on Meyerbeer's *Robert le diable* in the *Gazette musicale* of 12 July 1835, for example, is specifically entitled 'On the instrumentation of *Robert le diable*', and it points out that the huge success of the opera was due in no little part to its resourceful and inventive orchestration, making demands far beyond the capacity of most of the provincial theatre orchestras who were called upon to play it.

THE WRITING AND PUBLICATION OF THE *TREATISE*

Berlioz's consuming passion for instruments and their use was obviously a central feature of his art from the beginning. The *Robert le diable* article might be taken as an early indication that he might also become a teacher of the art of orchestration, not just a superlative exponent. Comfortable in his command of contemporary French instrumental practice and its rapidly advancing technology, Berlioz received a jolt in 1837 when Johann Strauss *père* brought his Viennese musicians to Paris, one of the earliest orchestras to go on tour as a group. There is no mistaking the shock of Berlioz's realisation that the German lands did things differently in this respect. He was principally impressed by Strauss's sense of rhythm (hence the title of his notice in the *Journal des débats*: 'Strauss, his orchestra, and his waltzes. Of the future of rhythm'[8]), but his curiosity about the different instrumental styles of foreign orchestras was aroused, leading eventually to the German tour of 1842–3 when he could study these things for himself.

In the same year as Strauss's visit, 1837, Georges Kastner, a young composer and polymath newly arrived from Strasbourg, published his *Traité général d'instrumentation*. When Berlioz read the book and met the author we do not know, but by 1839 they had become friends. Kastner seems to have been close to Berlioz during the composition of *Roméo et Juliette* in that year,[9] and when Kastner followed up his *Traité* with a second volume, *Cours d'instrumentation*, in 1839, Berlioz gave both books a warm welcome in the pages of the *Journal des débats*.[10] While he applauded Kastner's achievement, he felt he had not gone far enough in defining what the art of instrumentation could truly do:

---

[8] *Jd*, 10 November 1837; *Cm*, 3, pp. 329–35; Condé, pp. 122–8.
[9] *Cg*, 2, p. 576. Kastner was later presented with the autograph manuscript of *Roméo et Juliette* as a gift.
[10] *Jd*, 2 October 1839.

> Instrumentation, according to him, is the 'art of applying appropriate types
> of instruments to a given line of music'. Certainly it is, but it is much else
> besides. It is the art of using instruments to colour the harmony and the
> rhythm; furthermore it is the art of generating emotion by one's choice of
> timbres, independent of any considerations of melody, rhythm or harmony.

Citing numerous examples of apposite instrumentation by Gluck,
Beethoven, Meyerbeer and others, Berlioz is clearly seized by his own consuming interest in the subject, and we may safely guess that the writing of
this review implanted the idea of compiling his own treatise which would
expound the art as he saw it despite the existence of Kastner's very comprehensive handbook.

He did not pursue it, however, for two years. In that time he composed
the *Symphonie funèbre et triomphale*, *Les nuits d'été* and his arrangements of
Der Freischütz for the Opéra. Having promised Schlesinger a series of articles entitled 'De l'instrumentation' for the *Revue et gazette musicale*, Berlioz
evidently had to write them in a hurry for a succession of deadlines.[11]
On 21 November 1841 the first of sixteen articles appeared, with the last
article of the series published on 17 July 1842. These articles make up
the bulk of the later *Treatise*, but they differ greatly from it in their lack
of musical examples, dictated by the format of the journal, and their lack
of technical discussion. The articles contain the discursive, non-technical
matter of the book, with an emphasis on the poetic and expressive character of individual instruments. Berlioz throws in his characteristic asides on
his favourite topics, and he chides modern composers for their persistent
misuse of instruments. His admiration for Gluck, Beethoven, Weber and
certain living masters, very selectively cited, is clear. He also made repeated
criticism of the Conservatoire for failing to give instruction in certain important instruments (such as percussion) and for failing to 'conserve' such
fine historical instruments as the viola d'amore. Not, presumably, out of
deference to the then late director of the Conservatoire, Cherubini, but
more with an eye to a less ephemeral readership, Berlioz removed these
darts and barbs in the *Treatise* itself. The sixteen articles also lack any reference to his own compositions, except in the anonymous form 'a recent
symphony', 'a certain Requiem' and so forth.

Whether he had all along planned to assemble the articles into a larger
volume on the lines of Kastner's two books is unclear, although the serialisation of books was a common publishing practice of the time. Encouraged
perhaps by the publication of the articles in Italian in the *Gazzetta musicale
di Milano*, he proceeded immediately to fashion them into the full-blown
Treatise. He wrote in August 1842:

---

[11] *Cg*, 2, p. 705.

I am just finishing a *Grand traité d'instrumentation* which will be reasonably profitable, I hope. It will fill a gap in instruction books and I have been urged by many people to undertake it. My articles in the *Gazette musicale* only scratched the surface, they were just the bloom on the rose. Now I have to go over it all and do the foundation work, taking care of all the little technical details.[12]

He found a publisher, Georges Schonenberger, who had not published anything by Berlioz before, but who was known rather for his scores of operas by Rossini and Donizetti. Schonenberger offered Berlioz 2500 francs for the book, or 5000 francs if he could get two hundred subscribers in advance, and the last months of 1842 were devoted to putting the finishing touches to the book and attempting to secure simultaneous publication abroad, as well as preparing for his first extended foreign tour. Schonenberger's advance of 2500 francs was essential to pay for the expenses of the tour.[13]

Just before leaving for Germany Berlioz met the great naturalist Alexander von Humboldt, who smoothed the path for his coming concerts in Berlin. It was evidently Humboldt who suggested offering the dedication of the *Treatise* to Friedrich-Wilhelm, King of Prussia. The King did indeed receive Berlioz with enthusiasm, both on this visit and again in 1847, and he rewarded the dedication with a gold snuff-box and a gold medal. Although Berlioz's principal purpose in going to Germany was to take his music to a wider audience, he was also anxious to learn what he could about the state of instrumental playing and teaching. He had also secured from the Minister of the Interior a commission to report on German musical institutions, and his report gave due attention to the state of instrumental playing in different cities.[14] He wrote a series of articles about the trip for the *Journal des débats*, presented in the form of letters to his friends and later assembled in the *Memoirs* under the title 'Travels in Germany I', and these give a great deal of space to the new valve system for brass instruments, Parish Alvars's technique on the harp, the various talents of the Stuttgart orchestra, the sticks used by timpanists, the quality of the cymbals, the scarcity of cors anglais and so on. This section of the *Memoirs* is an essential adjunct to the *Treatise*, being written at a time when his thoughts were full of mutes, embouchures, trills and the latest orchestral gadgets.

---

[12] *Ibid.*, pp. 726–7.

[13] *Cg*, 3, p. 112. *Cg* 3 provides most of the information about the publication of the *Treatise*. In December 1842 (*Cg*, 3, p. 36) Berlioz said he would lose 2500 francs if 200 subscribers were not found, while in February 1844 (*Cg*, 3, p. 163) the figure is 1500 francs, perhaps reduced because publication was nearly a year late. On 2 January 1843 the *Neue Zeitschrift für Musik* reported that Berlioz had sold the *Treatise* for 10,000 francs.

[14] Peter Bloom, 'La mission de Berlioz en Allemagne: un document inédit', *Revue de musicologie*, 66 (1980), pp. 70–85.

1   Letter to Humbert Ferrand of 12 June 1843, seeking subscriptions to the publication of the *Treatise.*

He found, consequently, that on his return to Paris in May 1843 a good deal needed to be changed in the proofs of the *Treatise*, especially in the sections on the harp, the horn, the trumpet and the cornet. Berlioz reported working through six sets of proofs, one of which, now in the Bibliothèque de Grenoble, gives ample evidence of his late revisions to the text.[15] These were no doubt one cause of the delay in publication, together with the necessity to coordinate the German edition (translated by J. C. Grünbaum and published by Schlesinger, Berlin) and the Italian edition (translated by Alberto Mazzucato and published by Ricordi, Milan). The English edition (translated by George Osborne and published by Addison and Beale, London) never materialised, nor did the Russian edition for which Berlioz had hoped.[16] A set of proof pages of the French edition with many autograph corrections was given to Spontini, probably in November 1843, and on the 24th of that month Berlioz gave a copy to Stephen Heller, still bearing some last-minute corrections.[17] On 23 December a clean bound copy was given to Meyerbeer, who was charged with transporting two further copies to Berlin, one for the Berlin Academy and one for the King of Prussia.[18] This first French edition is often referred to as the '1843' edition, but although it was certainly printed in that year Schonenberger did not put it on sale until 1 March 1844, two weeks before the date by which two hundred subscribers were to have been found. Whether that number was reached is not known. It was published with the opus number 10.[19]

The *Treatise* was laid out in large format and execrably printed. An essential part of Berlioz's plan was to include a great number of excerpts in full score by Gluck, Beethoven, Weber and others, and he also printed a number of passages from his own scores, most of them unpublished at the time. While the pages of engraved music are elegant enough, Berlioz's prose is set out on lines over eight inches long with innumerable misprints and typographical blemishes of many kinds. Many of these survive in later issues from the same plates. Paragraphing and layout were crudely executed, and the German edition, which printed both French and German texts in parallel columns, had a distinct advantage in physical make-up over the French edition, even though it included some unauthorised extracts from Haydn and Mendelssohn of which Berlioz did not approve.[20]

---

[15] Bibliothèque de Grenoble, Vh 1036 Rés., is a set of proofs lacking the chapter on voices and heavily corrected by Berlioz. Vh 1960 Rés. in the same library is a copy of the 1844 edition with annotations in many hands (including Berlioz's) evidently prepared for an English translator, perhaps George Osborne or Mary Cowden Clarke.

[16] *Cg*, 2, p. 730.

[17] *Cg*, 3, p. 143. The Spontini copy was formerly in the Cortot collection and has recently been offered for sale; it bears many more autograph corrections than the Heller copy (British Library, Hirsch Collection) and must be earlier by a few weeks.

[18] *Ibid.*, p. 146. Meyerbeer's copy is in the Deutsche Staatsbibliothek, Berlin.

[19] For a list of editions of the *Treatise*, see the Bibliography.

[20] *Cg*, 5, pp. 183–4.

The *Treatise* received very little notice in the press, although the *Journal des débats* published Spontini's official report on the book for the Académie des Beaux-Arts. Its success was to be in the long rather than the short term. But it established Berlioz's reputation as an authority on instruments, reinforced by the thorough attention he gave to instruments shown at the Industrial Exhibitions of 1844 and 1849 and by his espousal of the work of two successful manufacturers, Edouard Alexandre and Adolphe Sax. The latter was at the peak of his brilliant inventive career, and throughout the 1840s was revolutionising the design and manufacture of wind instruments. Berlioz gave his constant support, with enthusiastic articles on the saxophone, the saxhorn, Sax's proposals for reorganising French military bands, and his contribution to the sensational offstage music at the Opéra from 1847 on. Berlioz was happily not drawn into the series of lawsuits that plagued Sax's career. Less controversial but equally successful was the firm of Alexandre et fils, whose keyboard instruments, particularly the 'orgue-mélodium', figured repeatedly in Berlioz's writings. This association seems to have been a direct result of the appearance of the *Treatise* in 1844, and a close friendship with Edouard Alexandre was sustained to the end of Berlioz's life.

In 1848 there appeared five articles under the title 'Voyage musical en Bohème', later to be recast as 'Travels in Germany II' in the *Memoirs*. Within Berlioz's account of his visit to Prague in 1846 he set out his thoughts on the proper curriculum of a conservatoire. Since orchestration was high on his list of priorities, he included an important text which should be read in conjunction with the *Treatise* and which might have served as a preface to its second edition:

> Another subject yet to be included in the syllabus of any existing conservatoire – one which to my mind is becoming more necessary every day – is instrumentation. This branch of the composer's art has made great strides in the last few years and its achievements have attracted the attention of critics and public. It has also served with certain composers as a means of faking inspiration and concealing poverty of invention beneath a show of energy. Even with undeniably serious and gifted composers it has become a pretext for wanton outrages against good sense and moderation, so you can imagine what excesses their example has led to in the hands of imitators. These very excesses are a measure of the practice, or malpractice, of instrumentation, which is for the most part mere whistling in the dark with blind routine to guide it, when it is not sheer accident. For it does not follow that because the modern composer habitually employs a far larger number of instruments than his predecessors he is any more knowledgeable about their character, their capacity and mechanism and the various affinities and relationships that exist between them. Far from it: there are eminent composers so fundamentally ignorant of the science that they could not even tell you the range of some of the instruments. I know from my own experience

of one to whom the compass of the flute was an undisclosed mystery. Of brass instruments and the trombone in particular they have only the most shadowy notion; you can see this from the way most modern scores, just as in the old days, cling to the middle register of these instruments and avoid taking them high or low, simply because the composer, not knowing their exact compass, is afraid of overstepping it; as he has no inkling of what can be done with the notes at either end of the scale, he leaves them strictly alone. Instrumentation today is like a foreign language which has become fashionable. Many affect to speak it without having learnt to do so; consequently they speak it without understanding it properly and with a liberal admixture of barbarisms.[21]

Berlioz was then an obvious choice as a French Government representative on the jury appointed to judge musical instruments at the Great Exhibition in London in 1851, and he served in the same capacity at the Paris Exposition Universelle in 1855. Earlier that year, 1855, when Berlioz was in London for some concerts, he was approached by Alfred Novello with a proposal for an essay on the art of conducting. It was agreed that this would be an extra chapter to be appended to a revised and enlarged edition of the *Treatise* translated into English. He wrote the essay immediately on his return to Paris and sent it to Novello in September 1855 along with a section on new instruments (chapter 13) and some revisions in the main text. The book was translated by Novello's sister, Mary Cowden Clarke, and published by Novello & Co in May 1856. This was a very successful publication, going into a second edition in 1858 and remaining in print well into the twentieth century. The essay on conducting was serialised in Novello's house journal, the *Musical Times*, between May and August 1856.

Berlioz also persuaded Schonenberger to issue a revised second edition in French, with the extra chapters on new instruments and on conducting (chapters 13 and 15), and this appeared at the end of 1855.[22] The chapter on new instruments, which owed much to his friendship with Sax, Alexandre and Kastner, appeared also in the *Journal des débats* on 12 January 1856 as part of Berlioz's report of the Exposition Universelle; indeed it was his work on that jury that gave him the opportunity to study the latest instrumental inventions. The chapter on conducting, 'Le chef d'orchestre: théorie de son art', was serialised in the *Revue et gazette musicale* between 6 January and 2 March 1856, and it was also issued by Schonenberger as a separate booklet. Lemoine et fils, who acquired Schonenberger's catalogue in 1862, have reissued the second edition of the *Treatise* at intervals to this day.

---

[21] *Memoirs*, 'Travels in Germany', II/6.
[22] In a letter of 9 January 1856 Berlioz implied that the second edition of the *Treatise* had been published for some time (*Cg*, 4, p. 239) and it has always been referred to as the 1855 edition. A footnote in the *Rgm* of 6 January 1856, however, says that it is due to appear 'shortly'.

xxiv *Preface*

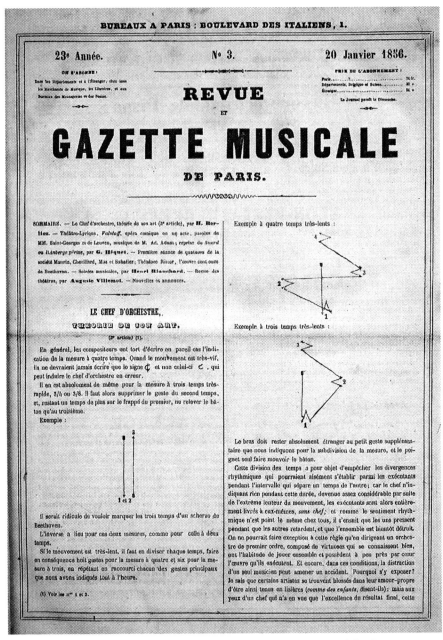

2   *La revue et gazette musicale*, 20 January 1856, the first serialisation of *Le chef d' orchestre*.

Ricordi revised and reissued the Italian edition, and the German translation was similarly revised and reissued by Schlesinger of Berlin; the conducting essay was also separately issued under the title *Der Orchester-Dirigent*. In 1864 Gustav Heinze of Leipzig published a new German translation by Alfred Dörffel under the title *Instrumentationslehre* which includes a preface in German signed by Berlioz but in fact written by Richard Pohl.[23] Numerous editions were issued by Heinze and his successor Peters, and in 1904 Peters issued it with Strauss's additional notes and examples. Strauss's purpose was to study Wagner's orchestration as the natural culmination of Berlioz's work in this sphere, with a few examples also from his own scores. Berlioz himself would have found this wholly unintelligible, since his own sound world was far from Wagner's and since his exposition of the art of orchestration was backward-looking (to Gluck and Beethoven) rather than modern, despite the *Treatise*'s title. Strauss's edition has been reprinted a number of times. It was translated into French by Ernest Closson in 1909, into Russian in 1912, and into English in 1948 by Theodore Front, published in New York by Edwin F. Kalmus and later reprinted by Dover Publications.

OTHER TREATISES

Kastner's and Berlioz's treatises were the most comprehensive textbooks on orchestration that had then been published, but they were not the first.[24] In two articles in the *Gazette musicale* in 1834 (2 and 23 March) Joseph Mainzer declared that he could find no textbook in Germany or France that would give instruction in the ranges of individual instruments or their characters and idiosyncrasies. Pointing out that instrumentation was an important aspect of music with a significant history, he felt the time was ripe for such a textbook and announced that he himself was about to write one in order to spare composers the laborious task of gleaning such information from the numerous tutors and methods published for individual instruments, the product of the Conservatoire's early policy of widening the scope of public musical instruction. In fact there had been several such books, including a useful handbook published in 1813 by Alexandre Choron, the *Traité général des voix et des instruments d'orchestre*, based on Louis-Joseph Francœur's *Diapason général de tous les instruments à vent* of 1772. This was in turn based in part on Valentin Rœser's *Essai d'instruction* of 1764. Rœser was mainly concerned with explaining how to use the two recent additions to the orchestra, the clarinet and the horn, while Francœur's eight chapters discuss in turn the flute, the oboe, the clarinet, the horn, the bassoon, the trumpet, the serpent and the human voice. This last section is an interesting anticipation of Berlioz's chapter

[23] *Cg*, 6, p. 511.
[24] For orchestration treatises before Berlioz, see Adam Carse, 'Text-books on orchestration before Berlioz', *Music and Letters*, 22 (1941), pp. 26–31; and Hans Bartenstein, 'Die frühen Instrumentationslehren bis zu Berlioz', *Archiv für Musikwissenschaft*, 28 (1971), pp. 97–118.

on voices, while the strings are assumed to be too familiar to need any attention. A similar book came from Othon-Joseph Vandenbroek, a Flemish horn player active for many years in the Paris Opéra orchestra. His *Traité général de tous les instrumens à vent à l'usage des compositeurs* (Paris, 1793) gave particular attention to the horn but also covered other wind instruments and timpani too.

Choron's 1813 treatise is likewise principally concerned with wind instruments. He set out the range of each, with useful indications of which notes of the range are weak or difficult or out of tune, which keys suit which instrument, which trills are possible and what kind of phrase has to be avoided at quick tempos. Strings are very briefly summarised, with sections also on keyboard instruments and voices.

It is not certain that Berlioz knew Choron's treatise, but it is probable, for it anticipates many of his principal concerns, even though it was out of date by the time he came to write on the same subject himself. We should expect him, though, to have been familiar with the *Cours de composition musicale* (probably published in 1816–18) by Antoine Reicha, his counterpoint teacher at the Conservatoire. In his *Memoirs* Berlioz said that neither of his teachers, Reicha nor Le Sueur, taught him anything about orchestration and of Reicha he even said that he 'knew the individual scope and possibilities of most of the wind instruments, but I do not think he had more than rudimentary ideas about grouping them in varying numbers and combinations'.[25] In fact part of Reicha's textbook is devoted to orchestration and is far more concerned with orchestral combinations than with the properties of single instruments. His conception of the orchestra as a large instrument upon which the composer plays is so close to Berlioz's own that we have to conclude that Berlioz had never read it, otherwise he would surely have had something more positive to say.[26]

In about 1832 a little handbook appeared, almost unnoticed. This was *Des voix et des instrumens à cordes à vent et à percussion, ouvrage à l'usage des personnes qui veulent écrire la partition et arranger des morceaux en harmonie* by Joseph Catrufo. When Kastner's *Traité général d'instrumentation* appeared in 1837, it did not mention Francœur, Choron or Catrufo, nor did Fétis in his *Manuel des compositeurs, directeurs de musique, chefs d'orchestre & de musique militaire*, which appeared in the same year. Both Kastner's and Fétis's books were designed to equip their readers with a brief but full body of information on the nature and range of instruments. Kastner directed his work especially towards young composers and was the more comprehensive of the two; Fétis had conductors principally in mind. Both writers were voluminously productive on all theoretical and historical aspects of music and these two works exemplify their methods well.

---

[25] *Memoirs*, chapter 13.
[26] David Charlton, 'Orchestration and Orchestral Practice in Paris, 1789–1810' (Ph.D. diss., Cambridge, 1973), pp. 35–6.

Kastner declared he had been urged to undertake the work by Berton and Reicha, and he confirmed his aim of giving with precision and brevity the fundamental information about every instrument, including many oddities for which Kastner obviously felt strong sympathy. Thus, besides the voices and all the standard strings, wind and percussion of his day his treatise lists the 'viola di sparla', the 'décacorde', the 'gussel ou gusli' and the 'aéolodicon', not to mention many other inventors' brainchildren that never even looked like winning admirers or users. Nonetheless his work is precise and painstakingly informative. He makes scarcely any reference to particular examples of instruments' use, but lists all available 'Méthodes' for individual instruments, works from which he had compiled his main information.

Fétis's book is brief but purposeful. No classic or contemporary works are referred to and there is a certain disregard for the niceties of instrumental practice of which Kastner was so fond. His advice to conductors about how to audition, tune, rehearse, arrange and organise an orchestra was timely and characteristic. Berlioz would have allowed himself a smile on reading the chapter 'Du respect du directeur de musique ou du chef d'orchestre pour les œuvres des compositeurs', having roundly lambasted Fétis in *Le retour à la vie* (later named *Lélio*) in 1832 for distorting the works of great composers. Of Berlioz's familiarity with Fétis's book we have no record. It was reviewed in the *Revue et gazette musicale* not by Berlioz but by the violinist Panofka.

Kastner followed up his *Traité* with a companion volume, *Cours d'instrumentation*, in 1839. Its purpose was to show the application of the knowledge set out in the *Traité*, that is to say to give instruction in the choice of instruments for particular effects and occasions. He gives a summary history of the art of instrumentation and statistics on the composition of the best orchestras (Paris, Stuttgart, Darmstadt), and assesses the character of individual instruments with well-known examples of their use by recent composers. The layout of scores and the use of mutes, pizzicato and special effects are also discussed. Half the book gives examples in full score of what Kastner regarded as the best models for a young composer: extracts from operas by Gluck, Mozart, Meyerbeer and Berton, from choral music by Cherubini and Berlioz (the *Requiem*), and from Beethoven symphonies and other works. This is the book which, we may suppose, inspired Berlioz to write his own treatise. Kastner later issued supplements to both his books, both supplements appearing in 1844 at the same time as Berlioz's *Treatise*.

Curiously parallel to Berlioz's *Treatise* is a remarkable and little known publication by a German musician, Ferdinand Gaßner (1798–1851), Hofmusikdirektor of the Baden Kapelle in Karlsruhe. He was a worthy though unremarkable musician at a time when other German cities might claim their musical leadership in the hands of such men as Mendelssohn, Schumann, Hiller or Liszt. Gaßner's preoccupations were similar to

Berlioz's, and his publications were, like his date of birth, just a few years ahead. In 1838 there were published in Karlsruhe the two volumes of his *Partiturkenntnis, ein Leitfaden zum Selbstunterrichte für angehende Tonsetzer oder solche, welche Arrangiren, Partiturlesen lernen oder sich zu Dirigenten von Orchestern oder Militärmusik bilden wollen*, in which the families of instruments and their individual members are set out and discussed in turn, furnished with details of range, tonal variation, flexibility and character, and accompanied by musical examples drawn from the works of Mozart, Boieldieu, Winter, Meyerbeer, Rossini and others. He was much concerned with instrumental colour and character and with matching sound to its expressive purpose, and although his book inevitably lacks Berlioz's wit and strong sense of personal mission, it is certainly as comprehensive and humane as his.

There is no evidence that Berlioz ever met Gaßner or came across his work. Having no German he could not read it (it did not appear in French until 1851). An uncanny parallel is provided by Gaßner's follow-up publication, a book, indeed probably the first book, on the technique of conducting. *Dirigent und Ripienist* was published in Karlsruhe in 1844, an extremely comprehensive handbook on all the practicalities of the conductor's trade: how to select programmes, prepare pieces for performance, organise rehearsals, deal with hostile and incompetent performers, set the orchestra out on the platform and get them tuned up. He then deals with tempo, expression and ensemble, and describes the correct baton movements, though without the diagrams that are such a picturesque feature of Berlioz's conducting essay. Gaßner then appends a series of sixteen diagrams showing platform arrangements adopted by orchestras in different German institutions, a precious guide to the practices of that age.

After Berlioz there continued to appear new textbooks on orchestration. In French the first important example was the *Traité général d'instrumentation* by François-Auguste Gevaert (Ghent, 1863), translated into Russian by Tchaikovsky in 1865 and revised as the *Nouveau traité d'instrumentation* in 1885. Ernest Guiraud's modest volume, *Traité pratique d'instrumentation*, appeared in 1892, the year of his death. Charles-Marie Widor's more substantial and influential textbook, *Technique de l'orchestre moderne*, appeared in 1904 with many subsequent editions. In his preface Widor paid his respects to Berlioz's treatise and claimed to be merely bringing that work up to date: 'The present work is simply a sequel to a work which deserves the most religious respect and to which we do not aspire.' Strauss's *Instrumentationslehre* (1904) was, as we have seen, an adaptation of Berlioz's work for modern German composers, while Rimsky-Korsakov's posthumous treatise *Osnovï orkestrovki* (St Petersburg, 1913) used his own works exclusively as models for imitation. Among the many orchestration textbooks published in the twentieth century those by Cecil Forsyth (1914) and Walter Piston (1955) have been most widely read in the English-speaking world, while French readers have relied mostly on Widor's treatise, Busser's enlargement of Guiraud's *Traité pratique d'instrumentation* (Paris, 1933) and Kœchlin's four-volume *Traité de l'orchestration* (written in 1939–43 but not published until 1954–9).

THEMES AND IDEAS

The *Treatise* is a judicious mixture of technical detail, sometimes set out at length, and personal views about instruments and composers. The technical information has been assembled with great care, the fruit of consulting many *Méthodes* and textbooks and of buttonholing friends whose expertise Berlioz could trust. Surviving letters to the flautist Coche, to the authority on the viola d'amore Johann Kral and to the violin-maker Vuillaume attest to Berlioz's search for authoritative information.[27] The complexity of brass instruments of the day almost certainly required Sax's advice, and his magnificent exposition of the trombone and its uses seems to have had inside help, perhaps from Dieppo, the leading trombonist of the age. He was fully aware of a precept stated clearly twice in the guitar section: that only a player of the instrument can write for it (and, by implication, about it) with competence.

Yet he was capable of error, even when writing about his own instrument, the guitar, and we should approach the sections on the violin and the piano, for example, with caution since he had no personal expertise to draw upon. The violin entry is unusually full, from the technical point of view. It covers tuning, range, trills, double-stopping and chords, tremolo, subdivision, bowing, harmonics, mutes, *sul ponticello*, pizzicato, *sul G*, *sul D* and much else. Yet some of the suggestions about harmonics, for example, would be misleading for a novice composer, and Berlioz was cautious enough not to follow his own advice. His understanding of both piano and organ pedals was seriously adrift, and he sometimes mixes up the right and left hands. He was obsessively concerned with the transpositions of wind instruments and explained the subject, sometimes at extraordinary length, evidently because he found players and composers to be woefully ignorant of it. Since current practice was changing rapidly as he wrote, particularly in the case of the cornet, his advice is sometimes breathless, as if the whole topic was getting too complex for a mere treatise to deal with.

Pursuing his goal to 'study instruments which are used in modern music' he deals comprehensively with all the strings, woodwind, brass and percussion then available in France. Without being sidetracked, as Kastner was, by

[27] *Cg*, 2, p. 706; *Cg*, 5, pp. 134, 137.

the crazy inventions that proliferated at that time, Berlioz gives due space to the most important advances, in particular the double-action harp, the application of valves to brass instruments, the bass clarinet, the tuba and Sax's new families of brass instruments, including the saxophone. He seems not to have been aware of the organ swell-box or of advances in machine-tuned timpani, both of which would probably have been to his liking. He included the concertina even though he cannot possibly have seen it as an orchestral instrument, and he gives space to several obsolescent instruments such as the tenoroon and the bugle for which he never had any use himself; in fact he despised the bugle as fit only to 'lead conscripts out to the parade ground', and even then he feels sorry for any soldier who is subjected to it.

In his choice of excerpts Berlioz is much less forward-looking. The passages that he cites from the *Requiem* and *Roméo et Juliette* illustrate an advanced orchestral style (curiously, he never even mentions *Harold en Italie* or *Benvenuto Cellini*, both of which could have provided abundant illustrations of his points), yet the predominance of passages from Gluck, who had been dead for nearly sixty years when the *Treatise* was written, contradicts his claim to be propounding *modern* orchestration. This is what Saint-Saëns meant when he spoke of it as a 'paradoxical' book. Sacchini and Spontini, whose music was already almost forgotten, are cited with approval. Beethoven and Weber were familiar but no longer modern. Strauss's insertion of extracts from Wagner and from his own works gave the *Treatise* an even more unbalanced air. But Gluck was the model from which Berlioz learnt his orchestral sensibility and this, he would assert, was not subject to the vagaries of fashion or mechanical science. Berlioz's ideal was to apply Gluck's incomparable sense of dramatic aptness to modern instruments, an ideal most clearly embodied in *Les Troyens*, with its very Gluckian dramatic tone and brilliant modern orchestration.

There is another sense in which Berlioz's craft is modern. At certain points in the book he advocates techniques for getting effects from instruments which in practice deceive the listener. Somewhere between the eighteenth century, when orchestration was still the art of part-writing, giving instruments self-contained and intelligible things to do, and the early twentieth century, when, as in Ravel for example, the art of disguising one instrument as another and cleverly dovetailing two lines to sound like one was finely developed, composers began to manipulate instruments as parts in a great machine, not as voices in a choir. The milestone is perhaps the *Symphonie fantastique* and the curious passage at the end of the first movement where Berlioz subdivides the violins for a passage in constant quaver movement played *forte* against the full tutti of the wind. He judged the passagework to be too risky for the players to play all the notes, so he split it into two parts to obtain a more secure performance. But because the first and second violins are seated at opposite sides of the orchestra it would be spatially very uneven to divide this passage between the firsts and seconds. So he divided *both* firsts and seconds; four lines of music thus give the effect of a unison line (see Ex. 25, p. 28). This was certainly a new concept of orchestration, manipulating the allocation of notes to create an effect unperceived by the players themselves. The distribution of the notes of a melody between two or three horns or trumpets crooked in different keys was also a device serving the same end and one which he advocated with enthusiasm and practised widely in his scores.

Although Berlioz's music was regarded as audaciously advanced by many critics of his time, he was never much interested in the concept of modernity for its own sake. His sense of the future was tinged with idealism and impracticable fantasy. He would have liked to assemble, as he explains in the chapter on the orchestra, a huge festival ensemble including thirty pianos, thirty harps and a whole section of violas d'amore. His utopianism here (and in the story 'Euphonia' in *Les soirées de l'orchestre*) presumed that he would have the controlling authority over such vast forces. He was driven to despair by the inefficiency and ill-will of many with whom he had to work (as we read in the last chapters of the *Memoirs*) and an authoritarian strain creeps into his views on conducting. It is hard to imagine an orchestra today taking kindly to his suggestion that players who fail to count their bars should be fined and that a whole section of players should pay for those who habitually offend. On the other hand many conductors will be sympathetic to his view that lazy players who cannot be bothered to do tremolos at the proper speed should be fired.

Behind his idealism and his earnest endeavour to infuse in the reader a proper respect for the high craft of orchestration lies the humour that is never absent from his writings. The *Treatise* is not a funny book on the scale of *Les soirées de l'orchestre*, *Les grotesques de la musique* or even the *Memoirs*, but there are frequent glimpses of Berlioz's habitual humour that raise a smile and lighten the pedagogy. As always, it is tinged with irony, even pain. His evocation of tenth-rate choral conductors (in the chapter on conducting) is absurdly funny, yet for Berlioz it recalled many bitter experiences which he would gladly have done without. Much more appealing are those passages where he finds an excuse for leaping tangentially on to one of his favourite hobby-horses and riding it with fury as far as it will go. Such a passage is the passionate sermon, prompted by his discussion of pedalling in the chapter on the piano, on treating the works of other composers with proper respect. Such a passage is the extraordinary essay on chromatic harmony to be found in, of all places, the section on the concertina; indeed one suspects that Berlioz wrote about the concertina solely in order to be able to air these views. Less surprising is the homily on the proper style of church music to be found in the chapter on the organ.

Berlioz moves us most when he gets carried away by his passion for the subject. The whole *Treatise* betrays a feverish enthusiasm for the art of orchestration as though no one had ever discovered it before. We sense his deep involvement in it similar to the absorption he described when composing works like *Roméo et Juliette* and *Les Troyens.* He gave it an opus number as if it were to be considered one of his musical works and it is no less personal, despite its wealth of technical detail, than they. There are few passages in all his writing to compare with his evocation of the nobility of the trombone, for example, or the miraculous page where the mere thought of how Weber used the clarinet in the overture to *Der Freischütz* draws out an exclamation of admiration so deeply felt that under the stress of emotion the pen seems to fall from his hand. This spirit alone will ensure that the *Treatise* will be read as long as Berlioz's music is played and as long as the music of his age still retains its power to enthrall us.

A note on the edition

Berlioz's text is printed in larger type than the commentary, which breaks into the text at intervals. The text is that of the second (1855) edition, with alternative texts from the 1841–2 articles in the *Revue et gazette musicale* (the '*Rgm* text'), from the 1843 proofs, and from the first (1844) edition shown in the commentary. A full critical edition of the *Treatise* will shortly be published by Bärenreiter-Verlag, edited by Peter Bloom, as Volume 24 of the *New Berlioz Edition*, to which the reader is referred for further textual commentary. The present work has profited greatly from that endeavour and from an abundant exchange of information and ideas with its editor.

An Appendix lists Berlioz's principal writings on instruments and orchestration, and the Bibliography gives details of the *Treatise*'s publication.

The chapters of the *Treatise* were numbered 1–6 as follows:

1   On the families of instruments, from 'Every sounding body . . .'.
2   The violin
3   The viola
4   The viola d'amore
5   The cello
6   The double bass

Thereafter there are no more chapter numbers, although there are headings for the main divisions and for separate instruments. The present edition has divided the *Treatise* into an introduction and fifteen chapters, with subsidiary section headings.

Under the umbrella of translation I have exercised considerable editorial licence in selecting and adapting the many musical excerpts which Berlioz included in the *Treatise*. The commentary makes abundant reference to Berlioz's own works, so I have presumed that the reader has access to his music, preferably in the *New Berlioz Edition*. In many cases I have not included the longer passages from his own works which he printed, nor, for similar reasons, some substantial passages from Beethoven's and Mozart's works. The modern reader has much easier access to scores of

Mozart's operas and Beethoven's symphonies (not to mention recordings) than Berlioz's readers would have had. In the case of Gluck, I have included at least a part of most of the passages he refers to. Many excerpts have been reduced to focus on the orchestral point that Berlioz wished to illustrate. In compensation I have excerpted a number of works, by Sacchini, Spontini and Weber, for example, which Berlioz mentioned but did not print. In some cases where Berlioz seems to have been quoting music from memory I have revised his text to match the composer's. Readers who seek the full texts of the *Treatise* are again referred to Bloom's edition.

The musical examples in the text (some of which amount to fragmentary compositions) have been grouped in sets where there is some advantage in doing so. In many cases where Berlioz used musical notation to indicate the range of an instrument or even individual notes these are here represented with a modified version of Helmholtz's pitch notation, as used in *The New Grove* and the *New Berlioz Edition*: middle C is *c′*, with octaves above as *c″*, *c‴*, etc and octaves below as *c*, *C*, *C′* etc (see 'Abbreviations', p. xxxix). Specific pitches are shown in italic; pitch classes in roman capital letters.

References to Berlioz's music in the commentary are given in the form '*NBE* 9: 26' (i.e. *New Berlioz Edition*, volume 9, page 26) when the work has appeared in the *NBE* series, or in the form '*B&H* 4: 43' (i.e. Breitkopf und Härtel collected edition of Berlioz, volume 4, page 43) when the work has not yet appeared in the *NBE*. The first category includes:

NBE		
	1a–1c	*Benvenuto Cellini*
	2a–2c	*Les Troyens*
	3	*Béatrice et Bénédict*
	5	*Huit scènes de Faust*
	6	Prix de Rome works
	7	*Lélio*
	8a–8b	*La damnation de Faust*
	9	*Grande messe des morts*
	10	*Te deum*
	11	*L'enfance du Christ*
	12a–12b	Choral works
	13	Songs with orchestra
	14	Choral works with keyboard
	16	*Symphonie fantastique*
	17	*Harold en Italie*
	18	*Roméo et Juliette*
	19	*Grande symphonie funèbre et triomphale*
	20	Overtures
	23	*Messe solennelle*

The Breitkopf und Härtel edition is referred to principally for:

B&H   4   Overture *Les francs-juges*
         18   Arrangements

Works which have not yet been published in either series are without reference pages, but the reader will find bibliographical information about their sources in Holoman, *Catalogue*. These include the incomplete operas *Les francs-juges* and *La nonne sanglante*, and Berlioz's orchestration of Meyer's *Marche marocaine*.

A note on the translation

For Berlioz the term 'instrumentation' came more easily to his pen than the newer-sounding 'orchestration', just as 'orchestration' is a more familiar English word than 'instrumentation'. Both appear in Berlioz's title, although he did not expound the difference between them. Mindful of Ravel's insistence that the two terms are entirely different, I have retained 'instrumentation' for 'instrumentation' and 'orchestration' for 'orchestration' throughout.

I have also retained 'pistons' and 'cylinders', since Berlioz was conscious of the difference between them and had no ready generic term for 'valves'. Only in the discussion of the valve trombone have I used this English term, where the distinction between pistons and cylinders is not at issue.

All passages quoted from Berlioz's *Memoirs* are cited in David Cairns's translation, with permission (*The Memoirs of Hector Berlioz*, Cardinal Edition, London 1990).

A translator must labour under Berlioz's repeated rebuke. To Lvov, 1 August 1845: 'Translators are all traitors; the Italian proverb is assuredly true.' To Wagner, 10 September 1855: 'The flower of expression always fades beneath the weight of translation, however delicately it may be done.' In *A travers chants*: 'Translators: the most perfidious people in the world.' To Ferrand, 28 October 1864: 'Translators are such asses!' He even warned the first English translator of the *Treatise*, Mary Cowden Clarke: 'It is very difficult to transfer this into another language with *clarity*.'

Acknowledgments

A great many friends and colleagues have provided information and kindly answered my questions. I would particularly like to thank the following: Anna Amalie Abert, Paul Banks, Hans Bartenstein, Elizabeth Bartlet, Jean-Pierre Bartoli, Diana Bickley, Peter Bloom, Clive Brown, David Cairns, Stuart Campbell, Stewart Carter, David Charlton, Pierre Citron, Donna Di Grazia, Katharine Ellis, Joël-Marie Fauquet, Annegret Fauser, John Eliot Gardiner, Kern Holoman, Wally Horwood, Ian Kemp, Michel Noiray, Kathryn Puffett, Alan Rosenkoetter, Albi Rosenthal, Ian Rumbold, Ken Shifrin, Mary Jean Speare, John Stewart, Robin Stowell, Sue Sutherley, Sue Taylor, Ruzena Wood and Hon-Lun Yang. I am particularly grateful to Richard Macnutt for help with the illustrations. To the Oxford University Orchestra I am indebted for a fine copy of *Le chef d'orchestre* inscribed by Berlioz.

This book is published with assistance from the Dragan Plamenac Publication Endowment Fund of the American Musicological Society.

Abbreviations

B&H	Hector Berlioz, *Werke*, ed. Charles Malherbe and Felix Weingartner (Leipzig, 1900–7)
Cairns, *Berlioz*	David Cairns, *Berlioz, the Making of an Artist* (London, 1989)
Cg, 1–7	Hector Berlioz, *Correspondance générale*, ed. Pierre Citron (Paris, 1972–2001)
Cm, 1	Hector Berlioz, *Critique musicale*, 1 (1823–34) (Paris, 1996)
Cm, 2	Hector Berlioz, *Critique musicale*, 2 (1835–6) (Paris, 1998)
Cm, 3	Hector Berlioz, *Critique musicale*, 3 (1837–8) (Paris, 2001)
Condé	Hector Berlioz, *Cauchemars et passions*, ed. Gérard Condé (Paris, 1981)
Gluck, *Werke*	Christoph Willibald Gluck, *Sämtliche Werke* (Kassel, 1951–)
Gm	*Gazette musicale*
Holoman, *Berlioz*	D. Kern Holoman, *Berlioz* (Cambridge, Mass., 1989)
Holoman, *Catalogue*	D. Kern Holoman, *Catalogue of the Works of Hector Berlioz*, NBE vol. 25 (Kassel, 1987)
Hopkinson	Cecil Hopkinson, *A Bibliography of the Musical and Literary Works of Hector Berlioz 1803–1869*, 2nd edn, ed. Richard Macnutt (Tunbridge Wells, 1980)
Jd	*Journal des débats*
Memoirs	*The Memoirs of Hector Berlioz*, trans. and ed. David Cairns (London, 1969; rev. edn 2002). Because of the great number of editions of this work I cite by chapter only. Readers of Ernest Newman's edition are advised that chapter

	numbers above 51 differ from the French editions and from Cairns's translation.
NBE	*New Berlioz Edition*, ed. Hugh Macdonald (Kassel, 1967–)
Rgm	*Revue et gazette musicale*
Les soirées de l'orchestre	Hector Berlioz, *Œuvres littéraires*, ed. Léon Guichard (Paris, 1968–71)
Les grotesques de la musique	*Ibid.*
A travers chants	*Ibid.*

Pitch notation:

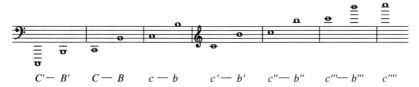

C' — B' C — B c — b c' — b' c'' — b'' c''' — b''' c''''

The Treatise

Introduction

Never in the history of music has so much been said about instrumentation as at the present time. The reason perhaps lies in the very recent development of this branch of the art and perhaps too in the profusion of criticism, discussion and widely differing opinions held and judgments passed, both sane and insane, written and spoken, about even the most trivial works of the obscurest composers.

Much value seems now to be attached to this art of instrumentation, which was unknown at the beginning of the last century, and whose advancement even sixty years ago faced resistance from numerous so-called lovers of music. They now do all they can to raise obstacles to musical progress elsewhere. Things have always been like that and we should not be surprised. At one time music was only permitted as a series of consonant harmonies interspersed with a few suspended dissonances. When Monteverdi tried to introduce the unprepared dominant seventh, scorn and abuse was hurled at him. But once this seventh had been accepted as an addition to the repertory of suspended dissonances, it became a point of honour among those who regarded themselves as musically aware to disdain any composition whose harmony was simple, mild, clear-sounding or natural. They were only content with music stuffed with minor and major seconds, sevenths, ninths, fifths and fourths, applied without any rhyme or reason whatsoever, unless making harmony as unpleasant on the ear as possible can be said to be a reason. These composers had developed a taste for dissonant chords, just as certain animals do for salt or prickly plants or thorn-bushes. It was an over-reaction.

Beneath all these fine sonorities melody disappeared. When it did appear they all said the art had been cheapened and debased, that hallowed rules had been forgotten, etc, etc. All was lost, evidently. But then melody made its way and the reaction in favour of melody was not long in coming. There were fanatical melodists who could not endure anything in more than three parts. Some wanted the solo part to be accompanied most of the time just by the bass line, *leaving the listener the pleasure of guessing the*

3

filling-out notes of the harmony. Others went even further and opposed any kind of accompaniment whatever, declaring harmony to be an uncivilised invention.

Then it was modulation's turn. In the days when modulation was normally just to closely related keys, the first person to shift to an unrelated key was decried. He should have expected that. Whatever effect this new modulation had, his superiors criticised it sharply. It was no good our pioneer saying: 'Listen to it carefully. Notice how it's correctly prepared, well structured, cleverly joined to what precedes and follows it, see what a superb sound it makes!'

'THAT'S NOT THE POINT,' came the reply. 'This modulation is forbidden, so it must not be done.'

But since on the contrary that *is* the point, the *whole* point, modulations to unrelated keys quickly made their appearance in serious music with results as agreeable as they were unexpected. Almost at once a new pedantry was born: people felt it was a disgrace to modulate to the dominant and slipped playfully in the most unassuming little rondos from C to F ♯ major.

Time has restored all these things one by one to their proper place. Force of habit and the reactionary vanity of folly and obstinacy are seen for what they are, and people are now more generally disposed to accept that in harmony, melody and modulation what sounds good *is* good and what sounds bad *is* bad; not even the authority of a hundred old men, not even if they were all 120 years old, would make us regard fair as foul or foul as fair.

For instrumentation, expression and rhythm it is a different matter. Their turn to be discovered, rejected, accepted, imprisoned, freed and exaggerated came much later, so they have not yet reached the stage other branches of the art reached before them. Instrumentation, let me say, is ahead of the other two: it is at the exaggeration stage.

It takes a long while to discover the Mediterraneans of music, longer still to learn to navigate them.

Berlioz's Introduction invokes history and plunges into a résumé of historical trends too coloured by beliefs and prejudices of his own day to be taken seriously as history. A similar historical preface had served to introduce his essay on rhythm provoked by the visit of Johann Strauss *père* to Paris in November 1837. Monteverdi's introduction of the dominant seventh, repeatedly cited by Fétis as the cornerstone of the invention of tonality itself, was also referred to there.[1] The date when the Bohemians 'first permitted the use of the unprepared dominant seventh' is offered as an example of pointless historical enquiry in the *Memoirs*.[2]

[1] *Jd*, 10 November 1837; *Cm*, 3, p. 332.
[2] *Memoirs*, 'Travels in Germany', II/4.

In the *Rgm* version of this passage Berlioz named Rousseau as one who 'opposed any kind of accompaniment' and who declared harmony to be an 'uncivilised invention'.

Every sounding object employed by the composer is a musical instrument. We may thus divide the resources at his disposal in the following way.

1 Strings
    a bowed: violin, viola, viola d'amore, cello, double bass
    b plucked: harp, guitar, mandolin
    c with keyboard: piano
2 Wind
    a with reeds: oboe, cor anglais, bassoon, tenoroon, contrabassoon, clarinet, basset horn, bass clarinet, saxophone
    b without reed: flute, piccolo
    c with keyboard: organ, melodium, concertina
    d brass with mouthpiece: horn, trumpet, cornet, bugle, trombone, ophicleide, bombardon, bass tuba
    e woodwind with mouthpiece: Russian bassoon, serpent
    f voices: men, women, children, castrati
3 Percussion
    a fixed, audible pitch: timpani, antique cymbals, jeu de timbres, glockenspiel, keyboard harmonica, bells
    b indeterminate pitch, making noises of different types: side drum, bass drum, tambourine, cymbals, triangle, tamtam, Turkish crescent

'Every sounding object employed by the composer is a musical instrument.' I wonder if Berlioz would have clung to this maxim if closely questioned on it. He was normally less liberal in his approach to composition and orchestration and did indeed contradict the principle in an essay on imitation in music published in 1837:

Several composers have made fools of themselves imitating certain noises by using the very noises themselves in all their anti-musical reality. An Italian composer, for example, whose name escapes me, wrote a symphony on the death of Werther and decided he could best imitate the suicide's pistol shot by having an actual pistol discharged in the orchestra; this is the height of absurdity. When Méhul and Weber wanted to render gunfire, the one in the overture to *Le jeune Henri*, the other in the infernal hunting scene in *Der Freischütz*, they found the solution in a simple timpani stroke carefully placed without transgressing the rules of their art.[3]

[3] *Rgm*, 1 January 1837; *Cm*, 3, p. 5; Condé, p. 102.

Berlioz himself then called for a 'feu de peloton', a volley of musketry, in his *Marche pour la dernière scène d'Hamlet*, composed in 1844, to represent the salute to the dead (*NBE* 12b: 115). The pistol shot Berlioz referred to was fired by Gaetano Pugnani when conducting a performance of his twenty-two-movement suite on Goethe's *Werther* in Turin in the 1790s. Pugnani, for realistic effect, conducted in his shirtsleeves. The story was told by Blangini in his *Souvenirs*, published in Paris in 1834 and doubtless read by Berlioz. He must also have been aware that Musard used to enliven his Opéra balls with pistol shots.

In the *Rgm* version of this passage the order of the string groups was different, namely: plucked, with keyboard, bowed. The lute was included with the other plucked strings. In the list of wind instruments the *Rgm* omitted tenoroon, bass clarinet, saxophone, bugle, bombardon, bass tuba and all woodwind with mouthpiece; under 2b it included the flageolet. The melodium and concertina were added in 1855. In the list of percussion instruments the *Rgm* omitted the antique cymbals, the jeu de timbres, the glockenspiel and the tambourine (although they were discussed in a later article of the series). The keyboard harmonica was added in 1855.

The use of these various sonorities and their application either to colour the melody, harmony or rhythm, or to create effects *sui generis*, with or without an expressive purpose and independent of any help from the other three great musical resources, this is the art of instrumentation. From the poetic point of view this art can no more be taught than the writing of beautiful melodies or beautiful chord progressions or original or powerful rhythmic patterns. What suits the various instruments best, what is or is not practicable, easy or difficult, muffled or resonant, this can be taught. One can also say that this or that instrument is more suitable than another for producing certain effects or certain feelings. When it comes to combining them in groups, small ensembles or large orchestras, and the art of mixing them in order to modify the sound of one with that of another and produce from the whole a particular timbre unobtainable on any instrument on its own or with another of its own kind, one can only point to the example of great composers and draw attention to the way they did it; their practice will doubtless be altered in a thousand different ways for better or for worse by composers who wish to imitate them.

The purpose of the present work is first, therefore, to show the range and certain essential details of the mechanism of each instrument, and then to examine the nature of the tone, particular character and expressive potential of each – a branch of study hitherto greatly neglected – and finally to consider the best known ways of grouping them effectively. Beyond that we would be stepping into the domain of inspiration, where only genius may make discoveries and where only genius is allowed to tread.

1

Bowed strings

THE VIOLIN

The four strings of the violin are normally tuned in fifths, with the fourth string tuned to *g*, the third to *d'*, the second to *a'* and the first to *e"*. The top string, the *e"* string, is also known as the 'chanterelle'. When the left-hand fingers are not modifying the pitch by shortening the portion of string set in motion by the bow, the strings are termed 'open' strings. Notes to be played open are indicated by an 'o' marked above them.

Certain great players and composers have not felt under any obligation to tune the violin in this way. Paganini tuned all the strings a semitone higher, to *ab*, *eb'*, *bb'* and *f"*, to give the instrument more brilliance. So by transposing the solo part he would be playing in D when the orchestra was in Eb, or in A when they were in Bb, thus keeping most of the strings open with their greater sonority without having to apply the fingers. This would not have been possible with normal tuning. De Bériot often tunes the *g* string up a tone in his concertos; Baillot, on the other hand, used to tune the *g* string down a semitone for soft, low effects. Winter even used *f* instead of *g* for the same purpose.

Paganini's Violin Concerto in Eb, op. 6, was intended to be played on a violin tuned up a semitone; the soloist is thus playing in D (Mozart used the same scordatura for the viola in his *Sinfonia concertante*, K. 364). This scordatura is also found in Paganini's variations on 'Di tanti palpiti' from Rossini's *Tancredi*.

In his *L'art du violon*(1834) Baillot mentions Paganini's scordatura and also de Bériot's tuning, *a–d'–a'–e"*.[1] He explains his own tuning of the *g* string to *f♯* and his trick of tuning it slowly down to *d* while still bowing.

The only composition by Peter von Winter (1754–1825) Berlioz seems to have known is *Marie von Montalban* (Munich, 1800), whose overture he commended in 1841.[2] It does not require any retuning of the *g* string. Not even in his concertos

---

[1] Pierre-Marie-François de Sales Baillot, *The Art of the Violin*, ed. Louise Goldberg (Evanston, 1991), pp. 417–18.
[2] *Jd*, 11 August 1841.

does Winter ever seem to have called for scordatura; Berlioz's claim could be pure hearsay, otherwise the remark remains unexplained.

In view of the great agility which our young violinists display today, the range that the violin in a good orchestra may be expected to cover is from *g* to *c''''*, with all chromatic intervals. The great players add a few more notes at the top of the range, and even in orchestral writing one may obtain much higher pitches by means of harmonics, of which more will be said later.

Berlioz respected *c''''* as the violin's top note (except with harmonics, and except for a high *d''''* in Ex. 41b of this *Treatise*). He reached this on several occasions, for example at bar 472 of the first movement of the *Symphonie fantastique* (*NBE* 16: 40) and throughout the *Septuor* in Act IV of *Les Troyens* (*NBE* 2b: 566–74).

Trills are practicable throughout this vast range of three and a half octaves, although one should have due regard for the extreme difficulty of trills on the top *a'''*, *b'''* and *c''''*. My view is that in orchestral writing it would be prudent not to use them. One should also, if possible, avoid the semitone trill on the fourth string, from open *g* to *ab*, this being harsh and rather unpleasant in effect.

Chords of two, three or four notes which can be struck or arpeggiated on the violin are very numerous and quite different in effect one from another. Two-note chords, produced by what is called 'double-stopping', are suitable for melodic passages, sustained phrases either loud or soft, also for all kinds of accompaniment and tremolo. Three- and four-note chords, on the other hand, produce a poor effect when played *piano*. They only seem rich and strong in *forte*, otherwise the bow cannot attack the strings with enough impact to make them vibrate simultaneously. Do not forget that of these three or four notes two at the most can be sustained, the bow being compelled to quit the others as soon as it has struck them. At a moderate or slow tempo it is therefore useless to write Ex. 1a. Only the upper two notes can be sustained, so it would be better in this case to notate the passage as in Ex. 1b.

Ex. 1

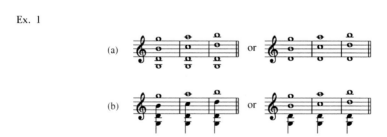

All chords contained between low *g* and *d'* are obviously impossible, since there is only one string (the *g* string) with which to produce two notes. When you need harmony at this extreme end of the range it can only be obtained in orchestral music by dividing the violins, shown by the Italian term 'divisi' or the French terms 'divisés' or 'à deux' written above the notes. The violins then divide so that some play the upper part, the others the lower part, as in Ex. 2.

Ex. 2

Above *d'*, the third string, all intervals of a second, third, fourth, fifth, sixth, seventh or octave are practicable, except that they get progressively harder the further up the top two strings you go:

	easy	progressively harder from
seconds	*c'–d'* up to *g"–a"*	*a"–b"* upwards
thirds	*b–d'* up to *f"–a"*	*g"–b"* upwards
fourths	*a–d'* up to *e"–a"*	*f"–b"* upwards
fifths	*g–d'* up to *e"–b"*	*f"–c'''* upwards
sixths	*g–e'* up to *f"–d'''*	*g"–e"* upwards
sevenths	*g–f'* up to *e"–d'''*	*f"–e"* upwards
octaves	*g–g'* up to *e'–e'''*	*f"–f'''* upwards

The double-stopped unison is sometimes used, but although it can be executed on many other notes it is as well to confine its use to the following three – *d'*, *a'* and *e"* – since only these are sufficiently easy to sound well and produce a variety and strength of sound resulting from the fact that one of the two strings in each case is open (see Ex. 3a). In other unisons, such as *e'*, *f'*, *g'*, *b'*, *c"* and *d"*, there is no open string; they are rather difficult to play and so are very rarely played in tune.

A lower string may cross a higher open string going up the scale while the open string acts as a pedal (see Ex. 3b). The *d'* here remains open while the rising scale is played throughout on the fourth string.

Intervals of a ninth or tenth are feasible but much less straightforward than narrower intervals. It is better not to write them at all in orchestral parts unless the lower string is open, in which case there is no risk (see Ex. 3c). Double-stopped leaps requiring large shifts of the left hand should be avoided, being exceedingly difficult, if not impossible (see Ex. 3d). In general one should not write such leaps unless the upper two notes belong to a four-note chord which could be struck as one. Ex. 3e is feasible because the chords in Ex. 3f can be struck as single four-note chords. In the next example, Ex. 3g, on the other hand, the four notes of each group (except the last) could only be played simultaneously with some difficulty, yet the leap from lower pair to upper pair is actually straightforward, the lower two notes being played open and the other two with the first and third fingers.

Ex. 3

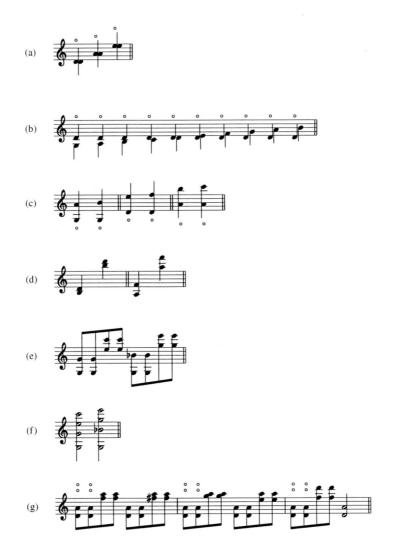

   The best and most resonant three-note and particularly four-note chords are always those containing the most open strings. In my view, in fact, it is better to make do with a three-note chord if no open string is available for a four-note chord. Ex. 4a–c sets out the commonest chords. These are the most resonant and the least difficult. For all chords marked * it is better to leave out the bottom note and make do with three notes. All these chords are straightforward, provided they follow one another in this way.

Ex. 4

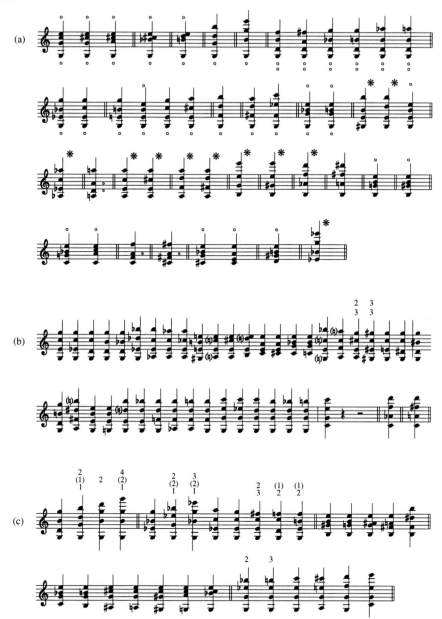

These can be played as arpeggios, that is to say with each note heard in turn, and the result is often very satisfactory, especially *pianissimo* (Ex. 5a); yet there are certain arpeggio passages similar to these whose four notes could not be played simultaneously except with great difficulty, but which are playable as arpeggios by passing the first or second finger across from the fourth string to the first to produce both the bottom and the top note (Ex. 5b).

Ex. 5

If you leave out the top or bottom note of the chord in Ex. 4, you get the same number of three-note chords. In addition there is the series of chords obtained by various pitches on the *e″* string above the two middle strings played open, or by fingering both the *e″* and the *a′* string above an open *d′* (Ex. 6a–b). If you need an isolated chord of d minor or D major, you must not use the form given at * in Ex. 6b, since it is too difficult when not approached by step. Better write it as Ex. 6c, which is easy and more resonant, with its two open strings.

Ex. 6

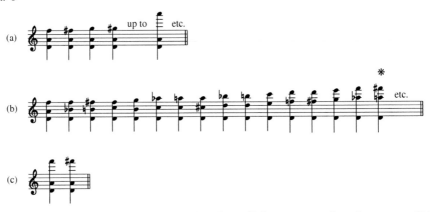

It will be seen from these examples that all three-note chords are possible on the violin provided you take care in cases where no open string is available to separate the notes by an interval of a fifth or a sixth. The sixth can be the upper or lower interval, or both, as in Ex. 7a. Some three-note chords can be set out in two ways. It is always better to choose the one which uses an open string. Ex. 7b is acceptable; Exx. 7c and 7d are better.

Ex. 7

The error shown in Ex. 1a was made by Berlioz in the last bar of the *Resurrexit* in the *Messe solennelle* (*NBE* 23: 186), all three notes of an E♭ chord being marked with a pause.

A prominent use of the device shown in Ex. 3a with two strings playing e'' is found in *Le carnaval romain* (*NBE* 20: 233–4), and at bar 63 of the *Chant des chemins de fer* (*NBE* 12b: 15) all the strings except double basses have a double-string unison d' (or d). In his *Memoirs* Berlioz commended Meyerbeer's introduction of a two-string unison tremolo d' in Gluck's *Armide*, but later added: 'I should not have written that.'[3]

The principle illustrated in Ex. 3b is applied in the viola solo part in bar 72 of the first movement of *Harold en Italie* (*NBE* 17: 15). Ninths and tenths were used by Berlioz only with an open string, as shown in Ex. 3c.

The three sets of quadruple stops, Exx. 4a–c, are none too clearly set out. In the first group Berlioz identifies harder chords with an asterisk, whereas the third group is described as 'easy in moderate tempo'. Chords with no open strings are marked with asterisks, although the first two of these are very hard, the next five are easy; then come two requiring the very difficult octave stretch between third and fourth fingers, then an easy diminished seventh, followed by a much harder stretch with no asterisk. In the third group the pre-penultimate chord (dominant seventh on a) is far harder than the rest and may have the note a misprinted for g.

Berlioz said that he learnt nothing about instrumentation from his teachers,[4] so he must have learnt these chords from a violinist friend (Ernst perhaps?) or from one of the many violin tutors published in France in the early nineteenth century.[5] But the uneven estimate of their difficulty is hard to explain.

It is also odd that Berlioz offered these as 'straightforward' and suggested they might be freely used in orchestral music when he never wrote any quadruple stops himself with the single exception of an A major chord for the second violins in *La damnation de Faust* (*NBE* 8a: 111). Triple stops are frequent and nearly all reasonably easy: the hardest are found in the *Bacchanale* of *La mort d'Orphée*, the Prix de Rome cantata of 1827 (*NBE* 6: 40–53). Double stops are frequent also; Berlioz implies, by the lack of a *divisi* marking, that each player should play both notes, even though it might be wiser to divide and would be more sonorous. A particular case is his writing of double-stopped octaves in orchestral parts, which will almost certainly sound stronger if divided. This is found at bar 78 of the *Scène aux champs* in the *Symphonie fantastique* (*NBE* 16: 78), bar 62 of the *Marche pour la dernière scène d'Hamlet* (*NBE* 12b: 109), bar 108 of Part I of *La damnation de Faust* (*NBE* 8a: 19) and at bar 367 of the *Scène d'amour* in *Roméo et Juliette* (*NBE* 18: 177). In the solo part of *Harold en Italie* (first and third movements) such double-stopped octaves have of course a quite different effect.

Berlioz's use of broken arpeggios of the kind shown in Ex. 5 is found in storm music such as the *Tempête* fantasy in *Lélio* (*NBE* 7: 89) and in the *Chasse royale et orage* in Act IV of *Les Troyens* (*NBE* 2b: 454). A very problematic example is the accompaniment to Mephistopheles's *Sérénade* in Part III of *La damnation de Faust* (*NBE* 8a: 313–24), where the second violin and viola parts combine pizzicato and arpeggio with the instruction 'Arpeggiate by sliding the thumb over the four strings'. This is the only example, too, of Berlioz giving string fingering (apart from open strings on occasion). He evidently underestimated the great difficulty

---

[3] *Memoirs*, 'Travels in Germany', I/8.   [4] *Memoirs*, chapter 13.
[5] For a complete list see Robin Stowell, *Violin Technique and Performance Practice in the Late Eighteenth and Early Nineteenth Centuries* (Cambridge, 1985), Appendix.

of phrases such as Ex. 8a in the violas and Ex. 8b in the second violins (bar 104) at a speed of 72 bars to the minute. In its earlier version in C major this piece was much better laid out for strings (see *NBE* 8b: 505) with greater use of open strings.

Ex. 8

In the *Rgm* text Berlioz had more on the subject of string arpeggios:

> Violin arpeggios are not much used in orchestral music nowadays. The kind written by Grétry and his contemporaries is wretched in design, admittedly, but just because something has been badly done does not mean that it could not be done better. On the contrary, there are most certainly some elegant arpeggios, not too hard to play, which could prove delightful as accompaniment.

He may have been referring to Grétry's *Richard Cœur-de-lion* (revived in Adam's rescoring in 1841), where the violins have arpeggiated variations on Blondel's theme.

One may write double trills in thirds, starting from low *bb* (Ex. 9), but they are harder to play than ordinary trills, and since the same effect is obtained much more neatly by dividing the violins it is on the whole better to refrain from them in orchestral writing.

Ex. 9

A body of violins playing tremolo, either single notes or double-stops, produces many fine effects. On one (or two) of the lower three strings and provided it is not much higher than *bb'*, it expresses distress, agitation or terror depending on whether the dynamic is *piano*, *mezzo-forte* or *fortissimo* (Ex. 10a). Across the top two strings, *fortissimo*, it is stormy and violent (Ex. 10b). High up on the *e''* string, on the other hand, divided into many parts and *pianissimo*, it becomes angelic and ethereal (Ex. 10c).

Ex. 10

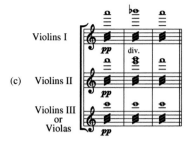

At this point I should say that orchestral violins are customarily divided into two sections, although there is no reason why they should not be subdivided into two or three sub-sections if the composer so desires. One may even sometimes divide them into as many as eight sections with good effect, either by taking eight solo violins playing in eight parts from the main body or by dividing both first and second violins into four equal parts.

Berlioz subdivided his string section in a great variety of ways, into as many as sixteen parts (*Sanctus* of the *Requiem*, *NBE* 9: 122). Part of *Rob Roy* (*NBE* 20: 154) is divided 4–2–2–2–1, and the *Chant de bonheur* in *Lélio* is divided 2–2–2–4–0 (*NBE* 7: 58). The finale of the *Symphonie fantastique* begins with 3–3–2–1–1 (*NBE* 16: 114), and *Absence* with 4–2–2–1–1 (*NBE* 13: 59). Eight violin soloists (four firsts, four seconds) are required in the *Tempête* fantasy in *Lélio* (*NBE* 7: 70); nine soloists (three firsts, three seconds, three violas) are singled out in *Benvenuto Cellini* (*NBE* 1c: 773). More often he calls for four violin soloists, sometimes four firsts, as in the first movement of *Harold en Italie* (*NBE* 17: 11) and the *Sanctus* in the *Requiem* (*NBE* 9: 122), sometimes two firsts and two seconds, as in *Dans le ciel* in *La damnation de Faust* (*NBE* 8a: 438) and the *Duo-nocturne* in Act I of *Béatrice et Bénédict* (*NBE* 3: 187). *La captive* (*NBE* 13: 11) has an optional second string orchestra.

To return to the tremolo, to bring it off effectively it is important that the bow strokes should be rapid enough to produce a true trembling or shuddering. So the composer must notate it precisely, taking the general pace of the movement into account. Orchestral players, who are only too pleased to be spared a type of playing that tires them, miss no opportunity of avoiding it when they can.

So if, in allegro assai, you write a tremolo as in Ex. 11a, producing repeated semiquavers, there is no problem and the tremolo will happen. But if you leave a tremolo indicated as semiquavers in an adagio, the players will do strict semiquavers and instead of a trembling you will get an abominably gross effect. In that case you must write it as in Ex. 11b, and even sometimes, if the tempo is slower than adagio, as in Ex. 11c.

Ex. 11

A tremolo, *fortissimo*, in the lower or middle range on the bottom two strings is much more distinctive if the bow touches the strings close to the bridge. In a large orchestra (when the players take the trouble to do it properly) it produces a noise like a mighty cascade. It requires the indication 'près du chevalet' (near the bridge).

A magnificent example of this kind of tremolo is found in the oracle scene in Act I of Gluck's *Alceste* (see Ex. 12). The shuddering of the second violins and violas is enormously enhanced by the striding, menacing progressions of the bass instruments, the first violins now and then breaking in, the successive entries of the wind, and most of all by the sublime recitative which this orchestral cauldron accompanies. I know nothing else of its kind, so dramatic or so overwhelming.

Ex. 12

(It should be said that the tremolo is not marked to be near the bridge in Gluck's score, and the idea should not be attributed to him. All credit should go to M. Habeneck, who called for this feverish style of playing from the violins, so incontestably appropriate in this passage, when he was conducting rehearsals of this amazing scene at the Conservatoire.)

Certain types of dramatic accompaniment, when the mood is very agitated, can be successfully done with a broken tremolo, either on one string or across two, as in Ex. 13 a–b.

Ex. 13

Finally there is a kind of tremolo now no longer used but which Gluck put to admirable effect in recitative: I call it the 'tremolo ondulé', the wavy tremolo. It consists of repeated notes at a relatively slow speed joined together without taking the bow off the string. In these unmeasured accompaniments the players cannot all play the same number of notes in the bar; some play less, some more, and the result is a kind of fluctuation and indecision in the orchestra, absolutely right in certain scenes for conveying anxiety and distress. Gluck wrote it as in Ex. 14.

Ex. 14

Tremolo is widely used by Berlioz for the purposes he describes. The ethereal type shown in Ex. 10c is illustrated by bars 28–30 of the *Chant sacré* (*NBE* 12a: 271) and by the introduction to the *Septuor* in Act IV of *Les Troyens* (*NBE* 2b: 565–6). Berlioz sometimes reinforces his advice to be clear in the notation, e.g. marking 'tremolo strettissimo' for Mephistopheles's entry in *La damnation de Faust* Part II (*NBE* 8a: 109) and for Aeneas's departure in *Les Troyens*, Act V (NBE 2b: 649, 658), or 'tremolo très serré' in the *Dies iræ* of the *Requiem* (*NBE* 9: 44) and in Tableau I of *Benvenuto Cellini* (*NBE* 1a: 297). In the prologue of *Roméo et Juliette* Berlioz's notation clearly shows even semiquavers, but the printed parts were marked 'tremolo' (*NBE* 18: 35, 371). Berlioz's criticism of *Rienzi* and *Der fliegender Holländer* was that tremolo was abused in those operas: 'A sustained tremolo is of all orchestral devices the one that the ear tires of most quickly. It calls for no invention on the part of the composer when there is no striking idea accompanying it above or below.'[6]

The indication 'sur le chevalet' or 'sul ponticello' is found in the *Dies iræ* of the *Requiem* (*NBE* 9: 44), the scherzo *Reine Mab* in *Roméo et Juliette* (*NBE* 18: 223), the *Chanson de Méphistophélès* in *La damnation de Faust* (*NBE* 8a: 160) – though not in the version in the *Huit scènes de Faust* (*NBE* 5: 75) – , *La captive* (*NBE* 13: 17), *Le spectre de la rose* (*NBE* 13: 45) and Act I of *Les Troyens* (*NBE* 2a: 56). Berlioz never uses a cancelling instruction such as 'naturale'.

Ex. 12 is the opening of a much longer extract from Act I of Gluck's *Armide*, which Berlioz printed to illustrate the tremolo. This includes a number of tremolos of the kind shown as Ex. 13a, which are also found in *Les francs-juges* (*Chœur de soldats*, bar 155) and at the opening of Act II of *Les Troyens* (*NBE* 2a: 203). He presumably intended the bow to change at the same rapid pace as the left-hand fingers, although bar 11 of the *Les Troyens* passage is slurred over a whole bar, casting doubt on his intentions.

Berlioz later pointed out that Gluck used two kinds of tremolo. A wavy line indicates a form of vibrato, while a series of notes with a slur over them (as in Ex. 14) requires 'the strings to repeat steadily the same note in an irregular way, some doing four notes per bar, some eight, some five, some seven or six, producing a host of different rhythms which spread their imprecision right through the orchestra and create a kind of affecting vagueness which is so often dramatically appropriate'.[7]

---

[6] *Memoirs*, 'Travels in Germany', I/5.   [7] *A travers chants*, pp. 188–9.

Berlioz used the wavy line tremolo once himself, in *Herminie* (*NBE* 6: 69, 77). Baillot describes a kind of tremolo, termed 'ondulation', produced by the bow alone.[8]

Bowing is of great importance and has a lot of bearing on the sound and expression of phrases and melodies. It must be carefully marked, depending on what effect is intended, using the following signs: *détaché*, as in Ex. 15a; phrased across the beat in pairs, as in Ex. 15b; long slurs, as in Ex. 15c; staccato or light *détaché* bowing, single or double, to be played all in one bow with a series of little jerks moving the bow as little as possible on each one, as in Ex. 15d and 15e; the *grand détaché porté*, which is designed to draw as much sound as possible from the string by leaving it to vibrate after the bow's attack, especially good for pieces of proud and grandiose character, in a moderate tempo, as in Ex. 15f. Notes repeated two, three or four times, depending on the tempo, give more strength and agitation to the violins' sound and are useful for many orchestral effects at all dynamic levels (Ex. 15g, 15h, 15i). But at a broad tempo and in music of forthright character, single notes played with *grand détaché* bowing are much more effective when they are *not* given any tremolo on each note. Ex. 15j is incomparably nobler and stronger in sound than Ex. 15k, in view of the slow tempo.

Ex. 15

(a)

(b)

(c)

Allegro
(d)

Andante
(e)

(f)

---

[8] See Erich Schenk, 'Zur Aufführungspraxis des Tremolo bei Gluck', in *Anthony van Hoboken: Festschrift zum 75. Geburtstag* (Mainz, 1962), pp. 137–43.

It would be pedantic, in my view, if composers gave bowing indications in their scores, with signs for up and down bows such as are found in violin studies and concertos. But when a passage unequivocally requires lightness, great energy or fullness of sound, it is a good idea to indicate the method of playing with the words 'at the tip of the bow', 'at the heel of the bow', or 'full bow on each note'. The same applies to the words 'on the bridge' and 'on the fingerboard', indicating when the bow should strike the string near or far from the bridge. The metallic, rather harsh sound made by the bow passing close to the bridge is very different from the soft, subdued sound made by letting it cross the fingerboard.

There is a symphonic work depicting the horrible and the grotesque which uses the wood of the bow to strike the strings. This bizarre device should be extremely rarely used and only with proper justification; and it can only be effective in a large orchestra, when the great number of bows cascading on to the strings produces a kind of crackling which would scarcely be heard if there were too few violins, since the sound it produces is so weak and brief.

Berlioz's treatment of bowing is a mere summary of a complex subject widely discussed at the time by authors more expert in violin playing than he. The 'grand détaché porté' was Habeneck's term for a variation of Baillot's *grand détaché*.[9] The phrasing across the beat in Ex. 15b was known as 'Viotti bowing'.[10]

Despite the implication of Ex. 15c, slurs do not necessarily imply bowing in Berlioz's string parts, especially in long phrases where one slur may begin where

[9] F. Habeneck, *Méthode théorique et pratique du violon* (Paris, n.d.).

[10] See Stowell, *Violin Technique*, pp. 166–201; and Clive Brown, 'Bowing styles, vibrato and portamento in nineteenth-century violin playing', *Journal of the Royal Musical Association*, 113/1 (1998), pp. 97–128.

the previous one ends, a notation known as 'slur-elision'.[11] Berlioz regarded the slur as a notation for legato.

The bounced or 'ricochet' bow-stroke is not mentioned by Berlioz, although it was explained by Baillot in his *L'art du violon*. Berlioz used it in the *Reine Mab* scherzo in *Roméo et Juliette* (*NBE* 18: 182), where the second violins, violas and cellos have Ex. 16 marked 'en faisant rebondir l'archet' ('making the bow bounce'). At bar 136 of the same movement the double bass entry is marked 'en frappant l'archet sur la corde' ('striking the bow on the string'), a kind of *fouetté* effect.

Ex. 16

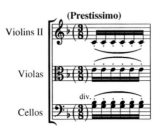

Berlioz never marked up- and down-bows in his scores. The instruction 'a punta d'arco' (at the point of the bow) is found twice in the *Symphonie fantastique* (*NBE* 16: 6, 114). 'Avec le talon de l'archet' (with the heel of the bow) is found in *Cléopâtre* (*NBE* 6: 142) and in all the strings in the *Rex tremendæ* of the *Requiem* (*NBE* 9: 56). 'Full bow on each note' is not found.

For 'près du chevalet' markings, see above, p. 16. The solo viola is marked 'sul ponticello' for the middle section of the *Marche de pèlerins* in *Harold en Italie* (*NBE* 17: 90). 'Sur la touche' ('on the fingerboard') appears once, at bar 77 of *Le jeune pâtre breton* (*NBE* 13: 29). A special string-crossing effect is used in the last Tableau of *Benvenuto Cellini* (*NBE* 1c: 1074), where Ex. 17 is marked 'on two strings'.

Ex. 17

The 'symphonic work' Berlioz refers to is of course his own *Symphonie fantastique* in whose finale, at bar 444, firsts, seconds and violas are instructed: 'frappez avec le bois de l'archet' ('strike with the wood of the bow') (*NBE* 16: 156). *Col legno* was not a widely used technique at the time. Berlioz was certainly ignorant of Mozart's marking 'coll'arco al roverscio' in his Violin Concerto in A, K. 219, and of the 'col' legno d'arco' in Haydn's Symphony no. 67, but he would have known Boieldieu's *Le calife de Bagdad*, which was in the repertory of the Opéra-Comique in the 1820s. Késie's famous air from that opera, 'De tous les pays pour vous plaire', imitates songs from France, Italy, Spain, Scotland, Germany and England. The

---

[11] Hugh Macdonald, 'Two peculiarities of Berlioz's notation', *Music and Letters*, 50 (1969), pp. 25–36.

Spanish section has the strings marked 'avec le dos de l'archet'. A similar effect
is found in Dalayrac's *Une heure de mariage* (1804), which was also often revived.

In a copy of his own *Traité d'instrumentation* Kastner reported that the scherzo of
Berlioz's *Roméo et Juliette* required col legno playing, although no such indication
is found in the score.[12]

Harmonics are produced by touching the strings at points of division
of their length with the fingers of the left hand but without sufficient
pressure to bring them into contact with the fingerboard, as they are in
normal playing. They have a special quality of softness and mystery, and
the extremely high pitch of some of them extends the upper range of the
violin immensely. There are natural and artificial harmonics, the former
produced by lightly touching the open strings at certain points. These
harmonics speak more reliably, with a better sound on all four strings. In
Ex. 18a–d the black notes show the actual pitch of the harmonics, while
the white notes show the positions to be touched on the open strings.

Ex. 18

(a) on the *e″* string

(b) on the *a′* string

(c) on the *d′* string

(d) on the *g* string

Artificial harmonics can sound clearly over the whole range by pressing the first finger firmly on the string, providing a movable nut, while the other fingers touch it lightly. Touching an octave higher gives its unison, a fingering scarcely ever used except on the *g* string because it is so awkward (Ex. 19a). Touching a fifth higher gives its octave, easier than the previous one but harder than the next (Ex. 19b). Touching a fourth higher gives its twelfth (Ex. 19c).

Ex. 19

This last fingering is the easiest of these, and the best for orchestral purposes except for a note a twelfth above an open string, when the fingering with a fifth (Ex. 19b) is preferable. Thus, to produce *b'''* it is better to touch *b''* on the open *e''* string, giving a note an octave higher with greater sonority, than to use a string on which the first finger has to be pressed down, for example fingering *b'* on the *a'* string and touching *e''*, giving the same note *b'''* as before.

Touching the string a major third or minor third higher is very rarely used, the harmonics this produces being much less good. Touching a major third gives a note two octaves higher, pressing with the first finger and touching with the third (Ex. 20a). Touching a minor third higher gives a note a major seventeenth higher (Ex. 20b). Touching a major sixth higher gives a twelfth higher (Ex. 20c). Although this is less often used than the fourth (Ex. 19c), it is quite good and often useful.

Ex. 20

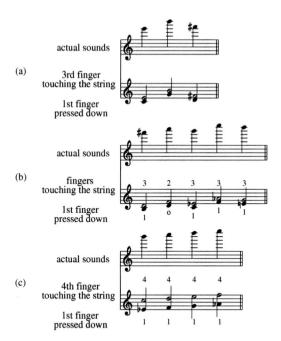

I must repeat that touching the fourth and fifth higher (Exx. 19c and 19b) are much the most highly recommended.

Some virtuosi can play double-stopped harmonics, but this effect is so difficult and so risky that composers would be well advised not to write it.

Harmonics on the *g* string sound rather like a flute, an idea worth using for slow, singing melodies. Paganini used them with extraordinary success in the *Prière* from Rossini's *Moïse*. On the other strings harmonics are purer and thinner the higher up you go. This characteristic, as well as their crystalline timbre, makes them suitable for what I call 'fairy' chords. These are chordal effects which draw the listener into ecstatic dreams and carry the mind away to the imaginary delights of a poetic, make-believe world. Although they are familiar to young violinists today, they should not be used at a quick tempo, or at least one should avoid writing a series of rapid notes, to be certain of their being played correctly.

Berlioz's table gives a comprehensive list of obtainable natural harmonics, but he does not mention that most of them were regarded as the province of virtuosi only and belong more to the realm of theory than of practice. Paganini's playing had revealed an uncharted world of harmonics. These were tabulated by Guhr (whom Berlioz lampooned in his *Memoirs*) in his *Ueber Paganinis Kunst, die Violine zu spielen* (Mainz, 1829), which was translated into French and may have been known to Berlioz. Mazas's *Méthode de violon* (Paris, 1830) and Baillot's *L'art du violon* (1834) also discuss harmonics at length. Of the fifty-one natural harmonics listed here Berlioz himself used only two: the two-octave harmonic obtained by placing the finger lightly on the string a fourth higher than the pitch of the open string, which he used on the *a'* and *e''* strings only. For viola and cello harmonics, see below, pp. 34 and 47.

Ex. 19a shows octave stretches for unison harmonics, but 'awkward' is a gross understatement. This fingering is in effect impossible except by hands of superhuman size. The *g/g'* natural harmonic is commonly used, but the artificial harmonics are virtually unknown. Baillot's treatise shows the octave harmonic on *ab* but more for theoretical completeness than as a practical suggestion; Guhr merely described it as 'difficult, on account of the great extension of the little finger; it becomes easier by holding the fundamental note with the side of the first joint of the forefinger, by which means the little finger can reach the middle of the string'. In practice Berlioz required exclusively the two-octave harmonics shown in Ex. 19c. He wrote them in three works: *Roméo et Juliette* (*Reine Mab* scherzo) (*NBE* 18: 203–7), *Au cimetière* (*NBE* 13: 70–1) and Act V of *Les Troyens* (*NBE* 2b: 639–43). He used only the upper part of the range, from *f'* (sounding *f'''*) up to *g''* (sounding *g''''*). To call the harmonics shown in Ex. 20c 'quite good and often useful' is an exaggeration. The stretch of a sixth from first to fourth fingers is for very large hands only, and the harmonic does not speak easily. Berlioz never found any use for it himself, nor did Guhr or Baillot list it.

Double-stopped harmonics were one of Paganini's many innovations. The Introduction and Variations on 'Dal tuo stellato soglio' from Rossini's *Moïse* was composed in 1818–19 but not published until 1855. Paganini played the piece frequently, although Berlioz appears never to have heard him play. It is notated in C minor, but sounds in Eb minor with the *g* string tuned up to *bb*.

The composer may write harmonics in two, three, or even four parts, according to the number of violin parts he has. Sustained chords of this kind have a truly remarkable effect if they match the subject of the piece and accord with the rest of the orchestration. The first time I wrote them was in the scherzo of a symphony, with three parts sustained over a fourth violin part (not playing harmonics) which trills throughout on the lowest note of the chord. The extreme delicacy of the harmonics in this passage is intensified by the use of mutes. Dampened in this way they sound in the remotest regions of the audible scale, an effect almost unobtainable with ordinary fingering.

When writing chords of harmonics like this, one must be sure, in my view, to use notes of different shape and size placed one above the other to show the note where the finger touches the string and the note of its actual sound. This applies to harmonics made with an open string. With a stopped string one must also indicate the note where the finger stops the string, so that as many as three signs may have to be used for a single sounding note. Without this precision in the notation the performance could become a confused jumble in which the composer would scarcely recognise his own work.

Berlioz always notates violin harmonics with the precision he advocates, using three pitches for every note (or two when an open string is used): the finger to be pressed (or open string), the finger touching the string lightly, and the resultant pitch.

In the *Treatise* he excerpted bars 354–88 of the *Reine Mab* scherzo (*NBE* 18: 203–5) in full score at the point where he referred to 'the scherzo of a symphony'. Kastner used the same passage from *Roméo et Juliette* as an illustration in the Supplément to his *Cours d'instrumentation*, published in 1844 shortly after Berlioz's *Traité*. There he remarks: 'We believe that still better results could be obtained from giving harmonics to the whole string section, including the double basses; we communicated our ideas on this subject to several composers, including MM. Meyerbeer and Berlioz, long before the composition of *Roméo et Juliette*.' When Berlioz says he used harmonics for the first time in *Roméo et Juliette* he is referring to harmonics on the violin; he had written harmonics for the cello in the *Huit scènes de Faust* (see p. 48).

In the *Rgm* Berlioz described it as 'annoying that the profound study of harmonics is not undertaken at the Conservatoire'. In his *Memoirs* he again complained that the subject of harmonics was not taught at the Paris Conservatoire: 'The little that our young violinists have learnt about it they have acquired for themselves since Paganini's appearance.'[13]

Mutes are small wooden devices to be placed on the bridge of stringed instruments in order to weaken the sound, giving at the same time a sad, mysterious and soft character to the instrument. They can be appropriate in any kind of music. Mutes are used principally in slow pieces, but they can be equally effective in light, rapid figures, if it suits the subject of the piece, or in accompaniments with urgent pulse. Gluck demonstrated this in his sublime monologue in the Italian version of *Alceste*, 'Chi mi parla'.

Normally, when mutes are used, the whole string section is muted, yet there are occasions – less rare than one might suppose – when a single section muted (the first violins, for example) will have a special effect on the whole orchestral colour by mixing clear with veiled sound. There are other occasions when the character of the melody is so different from that of its accompaniment that the distinction can be highlighted by the use of mutes. If a composer calls for mutes in the middle of a piece (to be indicated by the words 'con sordini') he must not forget to give the players time to take them off and put them on. He should leave the violins a gap of two bars in common time at moderate tempo or its equivalent. A shorter gap is sufficient for the indication 'senza sordini' for taking them off since that change can be done much more quickly. The sudden switch from this dampened sound of a violin section to the clear, open unmuted sound is sometimes astonishing in its effect.

Without referring to it in his text, Berlioz here inserted the first twenty-eight bars of the *Reine Mab* scherzo (*NBE* 18: 182–3) in full score as an illustration of the use of mutes in 'light, rapid figures' before printing the extract fom the Italian version of *Alceste*, with the repeated rhythm of Ex. 21 in the strings. He discussed the Gluck

---

[13] *Memoirs*, 'Travels in Germany', II/5.

passage in two articles in 1861;[14] he had already regretted its omission from the French version of the opera in an article in the *Gazette musicale* on 8 June 1834.

Ex. 21

A good example of the first violins being muted while the rest of the strings remain unmuted is found in Chorèbe's air 'Mais le ciel et la terre' in *Les Troyens* Act I (*NBE* 2a: 68). Conversely, first violins remain unmuted in *La damnation de Faust* Part I Scene 1 while seconds, violas and cellos are muted (*NBE* 8a: 9). On this occasion, since the seconds and violas have too few rests in which to put on mutes, Berlioz directs them to do it in stages over five bars.

Pizzicato (plucking) is also a widely used device for bowed instruments. The sound produced by plucked strings is much loved by singers for accompaniments since it never covers the voice. It is very effective also in symphonic music, even in energetic orchestral passages, either in all the strings or in just one or two sections.

The slow movement of Beethoven's Fourth Symphony provides a delightful example of pizzicato on second violins, violas, cellos and basses while the first violins play with the bow. In this passage (bars 26–34) the two contrasting sonorities blend in a truly marvellous manner with the clarinet's melodic sighs, and greatly enhance its expression.

Pizzicatos played *forte* should in general not be written too high or too low on the instrument, the very high notes being thin and dry, the low ones being too dull. Against a vigorous wind passage, therefore, you would get a very good pizzicato effect by giving all the strings a figure such as Ex. 22.

Ex. 22

Plucked chords of two, three or four notes are also useful in *fortissimo*. This is done by crossing the strings so rapidly with the one finger violinists always use that they seem to be struck all at once and to vibrate almost simultaneously. Soft accompanying figures, pizzicato, are always graceful in effect; they relax the listener and if not overused provide some variety in orchestral texture. Violinists do not regard pizzicato as an integral part of violin technique and have therefore scarcely studied it at all. At present they have only developed the technique of using the thumb and forefinger, so they cannot manage runs or arpeggios faster than semiquavers

---

[14] *Jd*, 26 March and 23 November 1861.

in common time at a very moderate tempo. Instead of which, if they put down their bows and use the thumb and three fingers, resting the little finger on the body of the violin to support the right hand as if playing the guitar, they would quickly develop the skill of plucking passages like Exx. 23a–c, which are unplayable today (the numbers indicate the right-hand fingers which pluck: T stands for thumb). The double and triple repetition of the upper notes in Exx. 23b and 23c becomes extremely easy if the forefinger and middle fingers are alternated on the same string.

Ex. 23

Slurred grace notes are also practicable in pizzicato. Ex. 24, a passage from the scherzo of Beethoven's Fifth Symphony which includes some, always comes off very well.

Ex. 24

Some of our younger violinists have learnt from Paganini how to do rapid plucked descending scales, tearing the fingers of the left hand away from the neck of the fiddle; also how to do left-hand pizzicatos alternating with bowed notes or even accompanying a tune played with the bow. These various techniques will doubtless be familiar to all players eventually; then it will be possible for composers to make use of them.

In the *Rgm* version of the paragraph on pizzicatos played *forte* Berlioz added: 'A very loud pizzicato on the bottom string of the double bass is the only one to work well – when well judged.' The highest pizzicato Berlioz ever wrote is a violin *a'''*, which occurs many times in the *Tempête* fantasy in *Lélio* (NBE 7: 144, etc) and is also found in a rejected passage of the *Scène d'amour* in *Roméo et Juliette*

(*NBE* 18: 410). A high pizzicato *g'''* in the *Roi Lear* overture (*NBE* 20: 111) was said by Strauss to represent the collapse of the old king's sanity.[15]

On pizzicato training the *Rgm* version has: 'It is not taught at the Conservatoire, wrongly, in my view', and in the *Memoirs* Berlioz names the lack of pizzicato study as the main deficiency of violin teaching at the Conservatoire.[16]

The guitar hold was advocated as a legitimate pizzicato technique by such authoritative writers as Baillot and Spohr. The only occasion Berlioz specified the use of the thumb is in Mephistopheles's *Sérénade* in *La damnation de Faust*, where the second violins and violas are instructed to 'arpeggiate by drawing the thumb across the four strings'. He does not specify the guitar hold, although that is implied (for the left-hand problems of this piece, see above, pp. 13–14). Other rapid pizzicato passages are found in *La damnation de Faust* Scene 10, for the first violins (*NBE* 8a: 260), and in the *Christe, rex gloriæ* of the *Te deum* (*NBE* 10: 74–7), itself a borrowing from the *Messe solennelle* of 1824 (*NBE* 23: 132).

In the *Rgm* version Berlioz credited Beethoven with being the first to write pizzicato grace notes.

Today's violinists can play (with the bow) nearly anything one asks of them. They can play in the extreme upper register almost as easily as in the middle range; neither rapid figuration nor bizarrely angular lines alarm them. In a large enough orchestra what one player cannot manage is covered by the others, so that the effect obtained is what the composer intended without any noticeable shortcomings. But if the rapidity, complexity or high register of a passage make it insecure, or if the performance needs to be clean and safe, the passage should be broken up, with the violin section divided: one fragment is given to some, the rest to the others. Thus each part is dotted with little silences, unnoticed by the listener, which allow the players to breathe, so to speak, give them time to shift to difficult positions and consequently attack the string with the necessary conviction and vigour (Ex. 25).

Ex. 25

[15] Richard Strauss, *Instrumentationslehre von Hector Berlioz* (2 vols., Leipzig, 1904), 1, p. 46.
[16] *Memoirs*, 'Travels in Germany', II/5.

dividing, since the figuration presents no difficulty; fragmentation would simply weaken the body of

violin tone without any benefit.

Here the fragmentation

is helpful.

To get all the violins to play a passage like this, or harder, it is always better to subdivide the first violins into first and second players – and the seconds similarly so that they double the two lines of the firsts – than have all the firsts play one fragment and all the seconds play the other. This is because the wide separation of sound sources would break the evenness of the passage and make the seams too obvious, whereas if the division is made on both sides within the two bodies of violins between the two players at each desk, one playing the first part, the other the second, the divided lines are so close to each other you cannot tell that the figure has been broken up; the listener will think it is played by all the violins together (Ex. 26).

Ex. 26

This procedure applies also to all sections of the orchestra which share the same sonority and agility. It should be followed whenever a passage is too difficult to be played right by a single instrument or a single group.

Although not identified, Ex. 25 is the first violin part of bars 410–39 of the first movement of the *Symphonie fantastique* (*NBE* 16: 34–8). In practice this division of the line between two sub-sections does not necessarily strengthen it, and it can create rhythmic difficulties. A more powerful effect is obtained from a good section, arguably, when all the players play all the notes. Other examples of this technique are found in the *Francs-juges* overture (*B&H* 4: 46), the finale of the *Symphonie fantastique* (*NBE* 16: 121–2), the *Tempête* fantasy (*NBE* 7: 157) and the *Évocation* in *La damnation de Faust* (*NBE* 8a: 278).

Berlioz's concern for the wide separation of sound sources that should be integrated derives from the universal practice in the nineteenth century of seating first and second violins opposite each other on either side of the conductor. Many passages require this seating arrangement for their proper effect, for example the second subject of the *Waverley* overture (*NBE* 20: 20). On seating arrangements, see below, pp. 323–6.

In orchestral writing I believe that more could be made than has been hitherto of phrases on the *g* string and, for some melodies, high on the *d'* string. When a particular string is required in this way, you must mark clearly how long that string is to be used, otherwise the players will be certain to yield to habit and convenience by crossing over to play the phrase in the ordinary way (Ex. 27).

Ex. 27

These examples are invented, not drawn from existing pieces. Berlioz's instructions to stay on the *g* or *d'* strings are rare, being found only in the *Marche pour la*

dernière scène d'Hamlet (*NBE* 12b: 100) and in *Les Troyens* Act I (*NBE* 2a: 65). The highest he takes the player on the *g* string is to *bb'*, in Herod's air in *L'enfance du Christ* (*NBE* 11: 31); an adjacent phrase going up to *c"* is marked to be played on the *d'* string.

The first violins are often doubled an octave lower by the seconds to give a passage more power. But if it is not too high it is much better to double it in unison. The effect is then incomparably stronger and finer. The overwhelming brilliance of the close of the first movement of Beethoven's Fifth Symphony is due to the violins' unison. On such occasions, with the violins in unison like this, one may wish to increase their volume even more by adding the violas an octave lower. But this lower doubling is too weak because of the disproportionate strength of the upper line and makes a pointless rumbling sound which obstructs rather than reinforces the violins' higher notes. If the violas cannot be given a distinctive line it is preferable to use them to augment the sound of the cellos, taking care to keep them in unison and not an octave higher, so far as the lower range of the instrument permits. Ex. 28 shows how Beethoven did it.

Ex. 28

Despite Berlioz's advice the doubling of the first violins by the second violins an octave lower has always (since Mozart) been an accepted and effective source of power. The 'error' of giving the violas a line an octave below unison violins is committed in *L'enfance du Christ*, at the end of Herod's air (*NBE* 11: 42). The violins are supported by cellos an octave lower in melodies in the overtures *Roi Lear* (*NBE* 20: 74) and *Benvenuto Cellini* (*NBE* 1a: 10). The rarest octave doubling in Berlioz's music is the three-layered melody with first violins, second violins and cellos each an octave apart; it is found in *La damnation de Faust*, soon after Marguerite's first entrance (*NBE* 8a: 263), an unusually rich effect suggesting a later operatic style first adopted by Gounod. For violas and cellos in unison see below, p. 41.

Ex. 28 shows the string parts only.

Violins sound brighter and are easier to play in keys which allow the use of open strings. The key of C seems to be an exception to this rule in that its sonority is evidently weaker than those of A and E even though it uses four open strings, while A has only three and E only two.

The quality of different keys on the violin can be characterised as follows, with an indication of their relative facility:

Major keys:

C	Easy	Grave, but dull and subdued
C♯	Very difficult	Less subdued, more refined
D♭	Difficult, but less so than C♯	Majestic
D	Easy	Gay, noisy, rather vulgar
D♯	Almost impracticable	Dull
E♭	Easy	Majestic, quite sonorous, gentle, grave
E	Not too difficult	Bright, stately, noble
F♭	Impracticable	
F	Easy	Energetic, vigorous
F♯	Very difficult	Bright, incisive
G♭	Very difficult	Less bright, more tender
G	Easy	Quite gay, slightly vulgar
G♯	Almost impracticable	Dull but noble
A♭	Not too difficult	Gentle, veiled, very noble
A	Easy	Bright, refined, joyful
A♯	Impracticable	
B♭	Easy	Noble, but without brilliance
B	Not too difficult	Noble, sonorous, radiant
C♭	Almost impracticable	Noble, but not very sonorous

Minor keys:

c	Easy	Dark, not very sonorous
c♯	Quite easy	Tragic, sonorous, refined

db	Very difficult	Dark, not very sonorous
d	Easy	Gloomy, sonorous, rather vulgar
d♯	Almost impracticable	Dull, subdued
eb	Difficult	Very subdued and sad
e	Easy	Shrill, inclined to vulgarity
fb	Impracticable	
f	Rather difficult	Not very sonorous, dark, violent
f♯	Less difficult	Tragic, sonorous, incisive
gb	Impracticable	
g	Easy	Melancholy, quite sonorous, gentle
g♯	Very difficult	Not very sonorous, sad, refined
ab	Very difficult, almost impracticable	Very dull, sad, but noble
a	Easy	Quite sonorous, gentle, sad, quite noble
a♯	Impracticable	
bb	Difficult	Dark, dull, harsh, but noble
b	Easy	Very sonorous, wild, rough, sinister, violent
cb	Impracticable	

The argument that open strings contribute to the brightness of keys on the violin collapses almost at once when Berlioz realises that C is weaker than A or E. If he had added F, which also has four open strings, the point would scarcely have been worth making.

The facility of each key is measured as much by ease of notation as by ease of playing: hence the distinction between, for example, C♯ and Db major. Bb is 'easy', while A♯ is 'impracticable', literally, in that there would be no practical purpose in composing in that key.

The character of each key is derived from its sound on the violin, although elements of general key characteristics, a common preoccupation of the period, must play their part here. Many of the extreme keys, such as C♯ major, D♯ major, G♯ major, Cb major, db minor, d♯ minor, g♯ minor and ab minor, were not used by Berlioz. Some, such as B major, F♯ major and Gb major, are rare (*Le spectre de la rose, Absence* and the duet in Act IV of *Les Troyens*, respectively).

Bowed instruments, known collectively as the 'strings', are the basic and fundamental element of every orchestra. In their hands resides the greatest expressive power and an unrivalled variety of colour. Violins in particular can display a host of seemingly incompatible nuances. In a body they can show strength, lightness, grace, melancholy and joy, reverie and passion. One has only to learn how to make them speak. There is no need to worry about the length of a held note and to give an occasional rest, as one must for wind instruments. They will certainly not run out of breath. Violins are faithful, intelligent, energetic and indefatigable servants.

Slow, tender melodies tend today to be given too often to the wind, but in fact they cannot be better rendered than by a section of violins.

There is nothing like the telling sweetness of twenty e'' strings activated by twenty well controlled bows. This is the orchestra's truly feminine voice, at once passionate and chaste, heart-rending and gentle, able to weep and moan and wail, or sing and implore and dream, or break out in joy as no other instrument can. A slight movement of the arm, an imperceptible nuance of feeling which would have no visible effect in the hands of a single violinist, these can generate a magnificent and irresistible flow of feeling when multiplied by a cluster of unisons, and strike to the heart of one's very being.

THE VIOLA

The four strings of the viola are normally tuned in fifths like those of the violin and at a pitch a fifth lower, to the notes c–g–d'–a'. Its usual range is at least three octaves, from c to c''' with all chromatic intervals. Its music is written on the alto clef, using the treble clef when it goes into its higher register. What we said in the previous section about trills, bowing, sustained and arpeggiated chords, harmonics and so on, applies equally to the viola, treating it as a violin tuned a fifth lower.

The only occasions Berlioz wrote as high as c''' for the violas is the final note of the *Quartetto e coro dei maggi* (*NBE* 12a: 305) and in Ex. 10c in the section on violins of this *Treatise*. He avoided the note in a passage in the *Huit scènes de Faust* (*NBE* 5:11). Although the original draft of *Harold en Italie* took the soloist up to high g''' (*NBE* 17: 220), b'' (twice) is the summit in the final version (*NBE* 17: 14, 192), and also in the orchestral violas in the overture to *Béatrice et Bénédict* (*NBE* 3: 14–15). In practice Berlioz did not require the same agility and effects from the viola as he did from the violin, except of course in the solo part of *Harold en Italie*. It is curious that that work is nowhere mentioned here or anywhere else in the *Treatise*, despite the great advancement it gave to the status of the viola. Nor does he mention his first treatment of the viola as a soloist, in *Le roi de Thulé* in the *Huit scènes de Faust*. He showed implicit faith in the viola, too, by opening both *Roméo et Juliette* and *La damnation de Faust* with exposed fugato entries for the section.

For the use of tremolo, 'sur le chevalet' and mutes, see above under the violin, pp. 14, 16 and 25. The soloist in *Harold en Italie* has an extensive passage 'sul ponticello' in the *Marche de pèlerins* (*NBE* 17: 90–5), a passage which also offers fine examples of arpeggiated chords. Berlioz wrote artificial harmonics for the viola only in *Au cimetière* (*NBE* 13: 70–1), and one natural harmonic, the final note for the soloist in the *Marche de pèlerins* in *Harold en Italie* (*NBE* 17: 99), a note whose meaning has been widely misunderstood. Berlioz originally wrote it as Ex. 29a, which sounds e'''. The autograph was then revised to Ex. 29b, but the '8va' indication was omitted from the printed scores. The engraved solo part includes a few fingerings, probably provided by Urhan, the first exponent of the solo part, including a '4' for this note, indicating a natural harmonic on the a' string.

Berlioz clearly indicated the note *e'''*, played as a harmonic, but may have realised that his suggestion of an artificial harmonic on the *c* string was less good than the natural harmonic played on the *a'* string. Most performances follow the printed score and give the harmonic an octave too low, producing the note *e"* as a natural or artifical harmonic on the *c* string.

Ex. 29

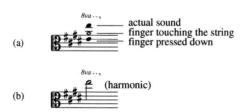

(a)   actual sound
finger touching the string
finger pressed down

(b)   (harmonic)

In the original draft of the following movement, *Sérénade*, Berlioz wrote a six-bar section marked 'sons harmoniques', notating the notes *g'*, *e'* and *c'* (*NBE* 17: 217). If they were meant to sound two octaves higher it does not say so; if they were to sound at pitch, the *e'* is unobtainable.

Of all orchestral instruments the one whose admirable qualities have been most persistently misunderstood is the viola. It is as agile as the violin, the sound of its lower strings has a particular pungency, its high notes have an especially sad and passionate character, and its profoundly melancholy tone makes its general character quite distinct from that of other stringed instruments. Yet it was long neglected or given the obscure and pointless duty, as often as not, of playing an octave above the bass line.

There are many reasons for the inequitable treatment of this noble instrument. First, most composers of the last century had no use for it since they only rarely worked four real parts, and when they could think of no immediate filling notes of the harmony they just wrote the fatal 'col basso', sometimes so carelessly that the result is a doubling of the bass line an octave higher in contradiction to the harmony or the melody or both. Second, it was unfortunately impossible at that time to write distinctive parts for the violas requiring any normal performing skill; players of the viol (the former name for the viola) were always drawn from discarded violinists. When a player could not manage to keep his place as a violinist he went over to the viola, with the result that viol players could play neither the violin nor the viol. I have to say that this prejudice against the viola has not entirely vanished to this day; there are still some viola players in the best orchestras who are no better at the viola than the violin. But the trouble this easy-going attitude can cause is more widely recognised every day, so that the viola will gradually come to be entrusted only to competent hands, like other instruments.

In referring to the careless doubling of the bass line, Berlioz is no doubt objecting to the mishap of allowing the violas to reach above the violins, yet still in octaves with the basses (an example is found at bars 15–16 of the first movement of Haydn's Symphony no. 49 in F minor). In stating that the viol was the former name for the viola, Berlioz is confusing the two separate families of string instruments. He was doubtless unaware of the viol's continued use (especially in France in the eighteenth century) long after violas, constructed like larger violins, had been developed by Italian craftsmen. The inferior status of viola players had been noted (and mocked) before, for example by Quantz in his *Versuch einer Anweisung die Flöte zu spielen* (1752). Wagner was also to complain of too few genuine violists in his *Über das Dirigieren* of 1869. Of the many violists who played the solo part in *Harold en Italie* in Berlioz's lifetime most were known, even celebrated, as violinists (Ernst and Joachim, for example). It also attracted the attention of specialist viola players such as Heissler, who played it under Berlioz in Vienna in November 1845, and Henry Hill, who did the same in London in February 1848.[17] Berlioz admired Hill's fine instrument made by Barak Norman.[18]

In the *Memoirs* Berlioz bewailed the lack of a viola class at the Paris Conservatoire.[19]

The viola's sound attracts and holds attention so readily that it is not needed in such numbers as the second violins, and the expressive quality of its sound is so striking that on those rare occasions when early composers gave it prominence it never failed to come up to expectation. The profound impression it always makes in the scene in Gluck's *Iphigénie en Tauride* when the exhausted Orestes, gasping for breath and overcome with remorse, falls into a slumber with the words 'Le calme rentre dans mon cœur!' is well known (Ex. 30); the orchestra, with muffled agitation, depicts sobbing and convulsive moans, pervasively dominated by the persistent horrifying mutterings of the violas. Even though this incomparable inspiration contains no note in either the voice or the instruments anything

Ex. 30

---

[17] For a complete list of *Harold en Italie* soloists in Berlioz's lifetime see *NBE*, 17, Appendix IV.
[18] *Les soirées de l'orchestre*, p. 313.   [19] *Memoirs*, 'Travels in Germany', II/5.

less than sublime, one must acknowledge that the fascination it exercises over its listeners and the sensation of horror with which many pairs of eyes open wide and brim with tears are mainly due to the viola part, the timbre of its *g* string, its syncopated rhythm and the curious unison which arises from the violas' tied *a* being sharply interrupted by another *a* in the cellos and basses on a different rhythm.

In the overture to *Iphigénie en Aulide* (Ex. 31) Gluck used them again to sustain, alone, the lowest voice of the harmony, not this time to exploit their special tone quality but to accompany the first violins' melody as softly as possible and to make the entry of the cellos and basses, when they come in *forte* after many bars' rest, more powerful.

Ex. 31

Sacchini has also given the bass line to the violas on their own in Œdipe's air 'Votre cœur devint mon azyle' in *Œdipe à Colonne*, but without any intention of preparing an explosive entry (Ex. 32). On the contrary, this scoring of the accompaniment gives the melody a ravishing freshness and tranquillity.

Ex. 32

Melodies on the upper strings of the viola are marvellously effective in religious and classical scenes. Spontini first hit on the idea of giving them the melody at certain points in his admirable prayer scenes in *La vestale* (Ex. 33a–b).

Ex. 33

Méhul was so struck by the kinship between the sound of violas and the dreamy character of Ossianic poetry that in his opera *Uthal* he used them constantly, even to the complete exclusion of the violins. The result, according to the critics of the day, was an intolerable monotony which ruined the opera's chances of success. This is what prompted Grétry to exclaim: 'I'd give a louis d'or for the sound of an E string!' This viola sound is precious when well used and deftly contrasted with the sound of violins and other instruments, but it quickly grows wearisome. It has too little variation and is too imbued with sadness to serve any other function.

The accentuation of the viola part in Ex. 30 is not Gluck's. The 1779 Paris score of *Iphigénie en Tauride* has the *sforzando* on the first note of each bar, not the second.[20] But Berlioz preferred it his way. In a letter to Liszt of 9 May 1847 he spoke of a 'nervous trembling that seizes me, with my heart beating in the rhythm [of Ex. 30] and I must yield to it'.[21] Berlioz's admiration for this scene was implanted in childhood from reading the Gluck article in Michaud's *Biographie universelle*, published in 1816.[22]

In the overture to *Iphigénie en Aulide* (Ex. 31), which, like the following three examples, Berlioz did not print in the *Treatise*, the violas are not in fact alone, but supported in unison by a bassoon, perhaps a pair. The bassoon even drops to a lower octave for part of the passage. In Wagner's version of the overture the cellos are required to reinforce the violas.

Sacchini's *Œdipe à Colonne* (1786, Ex. 32) was a work in the Gluckian tradition which Berlioz greatly admired.[23] The passages from Spontini's *La vestale* (Ex. 33a–b) are from Act I no. 3, the *Marche*, where divided violas share the melody with flutes and clarinets, and from Act III no. 19, the *Chœur de femmes* 'Vesta, nous t'implorons', where the violas are again divided and the violins are silent.

In Méhul's *Uthal*, which Berlioz never heard, the violas are divided throughout; it was first performed in 1806, the year before *La vestale*. The Grétry story was widely circulated, though the sum on offer varied from six francs to a louis d'or.

The viola section is now often divided into firsts and seconds. In orchestras like that at the Opéra, where there are enough of them, this presents no difficulty; but everywhere else, where there are no more than four or five violas, dividing can only weaken a section already below strength which is constantly drowned by other sections. It should also be said that few violas in use in our French orchestras today have the requisite dimensions; they have neither the size nor, consequently, the sonority of true viols, being little more than violins fitted with viola strings. Conductors should refuse to tolerate these hybrid instruments whose weak sound dilutes one of the most interesting elements in the orchestra, depriving it of much of its energy, especially on low notes.

[20] Gluck, *Werke*, 1/9, p. 351.   [21] *Cg*, 3, p. 425.
[22] Cairns, *Berlioz*, p. 425.   [23] *Memoirs*, chapter 15.

Throughout Berlioz's career the Opéra orchestra contained eight violas (against twenty-five violins, ten cellos and eight double basses). Berlioz normally called for at least ten violas in his orchestral works, with more for larger works: eighteen in the *Te deum* and twenty in the *Requiem*. Yet the only piece which has two sections of violas throughout is the third movement of *Harold en Italie*. They are divided into four for the *Sanctus* and the *Agnus dei* of the *Requiem* (*NBE* 9: 115–22, 132–4), and four solo violas are required in Act IV of *Les Troyens* (*NBE* 2b: 565–6).

Berlioz seems here to contradict his earlier remark that the viola 'is not needed in such numbers as the second violins'. It was widely suggested in the nineteenth century that violas should be made larger (as they had been in the early eighteenth century) if they were to match the sonority of the violin a fifth lower. Vuillaume made such a viola in 1855, and a number of other large violas anticipated the famous 'Tertis' model first introduced in 1937.

When the cellos take a melody it is sometimes excellent to double them with the violas in unison. This gives considerable roundness and purity to the sound of the cellos without affecting their predominance. An example is the theme of the Adagio of Beethoven's Fifth Symphony (Ex. 34).

Ex. 34

Such a doubling of a cello melody by violas is found in the *Messe solennelle* (*NBE* 23: 141) and in *L'enfance du Christ* to introduce Herod's air (*NBE* 11: 30). More usually Berlioz added bassoons to this combination, as in the *Scène aux champs* (*Symphonie fantastique*, *NBE* 16: 77), *Le cinq mai* (*NBE* 12a: 371–7) and the *Entrée des matelots* (*Les Troyens*, *NBE* 2b: 345–8).

A viola function which Berlioz does not mention is that of accompanist to the wind section. He very often gave the violas a lengthy tremolo against melodic wind parts, as for example in the *Francs-juges* overture (*B&H* 4: 14–15), at the beginning of the *Scène aux champs* (*Symphonie fantastique*, *NBE* 16: 72–3), against wind chords in the *Reine Mab* scherzo in *Roméo et Juliette* (*NBE* 18: 221) and in the *Menuet des follets* (*La damnation de Faust*, *NBE* 8a: 293). An unusual combination of melodic violas with melodic wind is found in the final movement of the *Te deum* (*NBE* 10: 151–5). A single viola note sustained under a pause introduces two scenes in *La damnation de Faust*, one for the entry of Marguerite, one to join her Romance to the *Invocation à la nature* (*NBE* 8a: 325, 382).

The violist who gave the first performance of *Harold en Italie* in 1834 and played it many times subsequently was Chrétien Urhan (1790–1845), principal violin in the Opéra orchestra and enthusiastic exponent of both the viola and the viola d'amore. Despite his rare qualities and remarkable character Berlioz had very little to say about him in the *Memoirs*.

THE VIOLA D'AMORE

This instrument is a little larger than the viola. It has almost entirely gone out of use; but for M. Urhan, the only musician in Paris who plays it, it would now be known to us only by name.

It has seven strings made of gut, with the three lowest covered with silver wire like the *c* and *g* strings of the viola. Below the neck and passing under the bridge are seven more strings, of wire, tuned in unison with the first seven to vibrate in sympathy with them and thus give the instrument a second resonance full of sweetness and mystery. It used to be tuned in all sorts of bizarre ways, but M. Urhan has adopted the following tuning in thirds and fourths as the simplest and most rational: *d–f♯–a–d'–f♯'–a'–d''*.

The range of the viola d'amore is at least three and a half octaves, from *d* chromatically up to *a'''*, notated on the two clefs, alto and treble, like the viola.

It is clear from the set-up of the strings that the viola d'amore is well equipped to play chords of three, four or more notes, either arpeggiated or struck simultaneously or sustained, and especially for playing double-stopped melodies. Yet in writing chords for the instrument one must observe a different practice from that of violins, violas and cellos (which are tuned in fifths) and take care in general not to separate the notes of chords by more than a third or a fourth unless the lower string is played open. Thus the note *a'* allows the *d''* above it to extend upwards a full octave, as in Ex. 35.

Ex. 35

I need hardly point out that chords of a minor third or second at the bottom of the range, such as *d–f* or *d–e*, are impossible, since both constituent notes in each case would have to be played on the bottom *d* string. A little thought will show that there are similarly impossible chords on the lowest strings of all bowed instruments.

The effect of harmonics on the viola d'amore is excellent. They are obtained in exactly the same way as on the violin and the viola, except that with its seven strings tuned to a perfect major chord the viola d'amore can easily play rapid arpeggios of D major one or two octaves above the stopped note (Exx. 36a and 36b), of A major a twelfth above (Ex. 36c) and of F♯ major a seventeenth above (Ex. 36d).

Ex. 36

From these examples it may be seen that if you wish to use these delightful viola d'amore arpeggios, the keys of D, G, A, F♯ and B are the ones which provide the most scope. Since three arpeggio chords would doubtless be inadequate for accompanying a freely modulating melody throughout, there is no reason why one should not have a section of violas d'amore variously tuned, in C, for example, or in D♭, depending on which chords the composer needs. For the exquisite delight of these arpeggiated harmonics on open strings it is well worth going to any length to obtain them.

The tone of the viola d'amore is weak and soft; it has a seraphic quality akin to the viola or to harmonics on the violin. It is very well suited to dreamy melodies in legato style, and for expressing ecstatic religious feeling. M. Meyerbeer has felicitously used it in Raoul's *Romance* in Act I of *Les huguenots* (Ex. 37). In this passage it plays a solo. Imagine the effect of a large section of violas d'amore singing some lovely *prière*, andante, in several parts, or providing a sustained accompaniment for a melody on violas or cellos or cor anglais or horn or flute (in its middle register), supported by harp arpeggios!!! It would truly be a great pity if this precious instrument were to disappear; any violinist could learn to play it in a few weeks.

Ex. 37

The viola d'amore survived perilously through the nineteenth century. Urhan had persuaded Kreutzer and Kreubé to write a part for it in their opéra-comique *Le paradis de Mahomet* in 1822; so did Schneitzhoeffer in his *Zémire et Azor* in 1824. Berlioz probably first encountered it in the benefit concert he arranged for Harriet Smithson on 2 April 1833, when Urhan played a *Fantaisie* for viola d'amore. In *Les huguenots* the solo Berlioz refers to is clearly intended for the viola d'amore even though it is headed 'un alto solo' in the full score. In the main part of the *Romance* which follows Ex. 37, the solo is quite unsuited to the viola d'amore, and it goes below its range to *c*♯; it was traditional at the Opéra for the opening recitative to be played on the viola d'amore and for the player to switch to the viola and back later for some more D major arpeggios.[24]

Berlioz incorrectly notated the harmonics shown in the last three bars of this passage on the alto clef. The harmonics shown in Ex. 37 are especially effective because of the viola d'amore's great number of open strings.

Yet Berlioz never wrote for the instrument himself; he would have been hard pressed to assemble the whole section of violas d'amore he dreamed of (see p. 329). It is true that the Meyerbeer solo could be played by any competent violinist with access to an instrument, but Urhan was the only player in Paris to take it seriously. Wilhelm Mangold, whom Berlioz had known as a student in Paris and whom he met again in Darmstadt in 1843, played the viola d'amore in his brother Carl-Amand Mangold's opera *Tanhauser* (Darmstadt, 1846). In 1855 Berlioz wrote to Johann Kral, the eminent player of the viola d'amore from Prague, to consult him for the second edition of the *Treatise*.[25] Kral's *Anleitung zum Spiele der Viole d'amour* was published in Leipzig in 1870.

The viola d'amore enjoyed a resurgence at the turn of the century when it found a place in compositions by Charpentier, Massenet, Puccini, Loeffler, Pfitzner and others. Janáček's interest in the instrument amounted almost to an obsession, and it reached Hollywood in Bernard Herrmann's score for the film *On Dangerous Ground* (1951).

In the *Rgm* text of this entry Berlioz added: 'Here's another instrument being allowed to disappear! It's pathetic! The Conservatoire is a poor conservator.' He then added a brief comment on the baryton: 'The baryton, the instrument so loved by Prince Esterhazy for which Haydn wrote so many charming pieces, was to the cello what the viola d'amore is to the viola. No one plays it any more and it has quite disappeared.'

THE CELLO

The cello's four strings are tuned in fifths, exactly an octave below the four strings of the viola: *C–G–d–a*. Its range can extend, even in orchestral music, to three and a half octaves, from *C* to *g″* with all the chromatic intervals. The great virtuosi can play even higher, but in general these very high notes are only pleasing at the end of slow passages and are not often used with normal fingering; they are usually obtained by means of harmonics, which speak more easily and have much better quality.

It would be wise before proceeding further to warn the reader of the two meanings attached to the treble clef in cello music. At the beginning of a piece, or immediately after a bass clef, it implies an octave lower than the written pitch. Both Exx. 38a and 38b sound as in Ex. 38c. It only has its real meaning when it follows the tenor clef, the only occasion when it represents actual sounds and not the octave below. Ex. 38d sounds as in Ex. 38e.

---

[24] Paul Garnault, 'Les violes', in *Encyclopédie de la musique*, ed. Lavignac and Laurencie (Paris, 1925), part 2, pp. 1725–8.

[25] *Cg*, 5, p. 134.

Ex. 38

This quite unjustifiable practice leads to errors all the more frequently since certain players ignore it and use the treble clef for its actual meaning. To avoid misinterpretation we shall use it here only after a tenor clef or when that clef would require too many leger lines; in those circumstances the treble clef will always mean actual pitches, as in Ex. 38d.

The highest note Berlioz ever wrote for the cello is the *g″* in the *Chants de la fête de Pâques*, no. 1 of the *Huit scènes de Faust* (*NBE* 5: 15). This four-bar passage is the only occasion on which he used the treble clef for the cello, its notation being an octave higher than its sound. Thereafter he used only the bass and tenor clefs, probably to avoid the confusion he describes. This confusion persisted through the nineteenth century, since the old treble clef usage is still found as late as Bruckner, Dvořák and even Mahler.[26] Berlioz was sufficiently confused himself to write 'above' for 'below' in the phrase 'the only occasion when it represents actual sounds and not the octave below'.

In his mature music Berlioz was cautious in the cello's upper range, going no higher than *e″* (*Roméo et Juliette*, *NBE* 18: 44). Although there is a *d″* in *Harold en Italie* (*NBE* 17: 88) and another in Tableau 1 of *Benvenuto Cellini* (*NBE* 1a: 335), he noticeably avoids a *c″* in the opera's overture (*NBE* 1a: 70).

What we said about double-stopping, arpeggios, trills and bowing for the violin applies equally to the cello. One must never forget that its strings are longer than violin strings and that it requires a considerably wider stretch of the left hand; thus passages of tenths in double-stops can be played on the violin or viola but not on the cello, and one must strike an isolated tenth only if the lower note is an open string, e.g. *d–f′*, *G–b* or *C–e*. Tenths such as *e–g′*, *c–e′* or *A–c* would be impossible. Furthermore, in view of its low pitch and the size of its strings, the cello cannot share the great agility of the violin and viola.

Berlioz is very cautious in his use of cello double-stops and rarely goes beyond a two-note chord with an interval of a third, fourth, fifth or sixth. Octaves, with the

26 Norman Del Mar, *Anatomy of the Orchestra* (London, 1981), pp. 109–11.

lower string open, are quite frequent. The last three bars of the first movement of the *Symphonie fantastique* (*NBE* 16: 43) have a chord of a tenth, *C–e*. Berlioz seems to imply a double-stopped octave *g–g'* (with no open string) in the finale of *Roméo et Juliette* (*NBE* 18: 314). There are no triple or quadruple stops.

Natural and artificial harmonics, frequently used on the cello in solo music, are obtained by the same method as on the violin or viola. The length of the strings makes very high natural harmonics, produced near the bridge, much easier to obtain and much finer in quality than on the violin. Ex. 39 shows the table of the best harmonics on the *a* string.

Ex. 39

harmonics'
sounding
pitch

fingers
touching
the open
a string

The best way to obtain artificial harmonics is to apply the first finger or thumb to make a movable nut and touch the string lightly a fourth higher, as in Ex. 40a. This is almost the only practicable fingering on the cello. Touching the string a fifth higher can really only be used in the upper range of the string since distances and proportions are much smaller here than lower down and the left hand is required to stretch less far; the fourth finger can thus touch a fifth higher while the thumb serves as a nut, as in Ex. 40b (the sign ♀ means the placing of the thumb transversely across the strings). An example of a scale in both natural and artificial harmonics is given in Ex. 40c.

Ex. 40

(a)

harmonics'
sounding
pitch

(b)

harmonics'
sounding
pitch

(c)

harmonics'
sounding
pitch

Chords made up of harmonics on cellos would certainly be a charming effect in a soft, slow orchestral piece, but it is easier, and so less hazardous, to obtain the same result with divided violins playing muted, high on the *e″* string. The two sounds are so similar that it is almost impossible to distinguish one from the other. The effect shown in Ex. 41a can be obtained more easily with ordinary notes on violins, as in Ex. 41b.

Ex. 41

The only occasion on which Berlioz called for cello harmonics was the closing section of the *Concert de sylphes* in the *Huit scènes de Faust* (*NBE* 5: 66–7). Four solo cellos play sustained chords made up of notes ranging from *a′* up to *d‴*, all easily obtainable on the *d* and *a* strings using natural and artificial harmonics. This passage disappeared when the music was revised for *La damnation de Faust*.

Although Berlioz showed Ex. 39 four times over, once for each string, we have here omitted three of them. They are identical except that in the case of the C string the last note is not shown.

The preferred fingering for artificial harmonics on the cello is thumb and third finger; Berlioz shows both third and fourth fingers for this purpose.

In the orchestra the cellos are normally given the double bass part, doubling it an octave higher or in unison. But there are a multitude of occasions when it is good to separate them, either giving them a melody or melodic outline to sing on the upper strings, or writing them *below* the double basses to take advantage of an open string or to produce a special harmonic effect, or, lastly, making their part similar to that of the double basses but giving them rapid notes which the latter cannot easily play, as in Ex. 42. The cello part here is more agitated and active, but it plays more or less the same notes as the double basses and follows their outline almost throughout.

Ex. 42

In the example from my *Requiem* (Ex. 43), on the other hand, the cellos are quite separate from the double basses and are sounding beneath them. This is to get the terrifying dissonance of a low minor second with the raw vibration of the open bottom *C* of the cellos, while the double basses grind their *b♮* against the upper *c*, sounding it strongly on their top string.

Ex. 43

One must never without very good reason – without being sure of its effectiveness, in other words – separate the cellos from the double basses completely; nor must they ever be written two octaves apart, as some composers have done. The effect of this is greatly to weaken the sound of the lowest notes of the harmony. The double bass part, abandoned by the cellos, sounds muffled, raw and extremely heavy, and it blends poorly with the upper parts, since they are too far from the extremely low bass notes.

If you wish to produce soft string harmony, it is often good to omit the double basses and give the lowest part to the cellos. That is what Weber does in the accompaniment to the andante section of Agathe's sublime air in *Der Freischütz* Act II (Ex. 44). It should be noted that in this example the violas start off as the bass, beneath violins in four parts. The cellos enter later and double the viola part.

Ex. 44

A cello section of eight or ten players is, essentially, a body of singers. Their sound on the top two strings is one of the most expressive in the orchestra. Nothing is so voluptuous and melancholy, nothing is better for tender, languorous themes than a group of cellos playing in unison. They are also excellent for melodies of a religious character. The composer must then indicate which strings the phrase must be played on. The bottom two strings, *C* and *G*, especially in keys which give many opportunities for them to be played open, have a deep, unctuous quality very well suited to such things, but their very lowness scarcely allows them to be given anything but bass lines, however melodic, the true singing phrases being reserved for their upper strings. Weber, in the overture to *Oberon*, has his cellos singing in their upper register with rare felicity while two unison clarinets in A play below them in their bottom register. It is very original and striking (Ex. 45).

Ex. 45

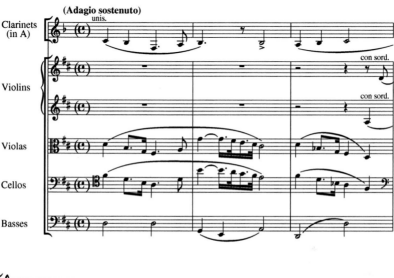

Although our cellists today are very skilled and can perform all kinds of intricacies without difficulty, it is very rare for fast passages in the low register of the cello not to sound messy. As for passages with high notes in thumb positions, one should expect even less. They are not very sonorous and always hard to play in tune. Phrases in those registers are clearly better suited to the violas or second violins. In the better-off modern orchestras which have plenty of cellos, the section is often divided into firsts and seconds, the firsts playing a special part either melodic or harmonic, while the seconds double the double basses either at the octave or in unison.

For accompaniments of a veiled, mysterious character one may sometimes leave the bottom line to the double basses alone, with two different cello parts above them and the violas completing a low-register four-part string sound. This layout is not often fully justified; care must be taken not to misuse it (see the opening of the *Scène d'amour* in my *Roméo et Juliette* (*NBE* 18: 145)).

Double-stopped tremolos and arpeggios, *forte*, are well suited to cellos. They greatly enrich the harmony and add to the general sonority of the orchestra.

At the beginning of the overture to *Guillaume Tell* Rossini has written a quintet for five solo cellos accompanied by the other cellos divided into firsts and seconds playing pizzicato. These low, homogeneous timbres are most effective and they heighten the effect of the brilliant orchestration of the following Allegro.

Ex. 42 is an extract from Berlioz's *Requiem*, though he does not say so. It comes from bars 48–51 of the *Rex tremendæ*, immediately preceding the passage quoted as Ex. 43.

Berlioz divided the cello section into two on many occasions, especially in *Roméo et Juliette*, where there are virtually two cello sections throughout. The second cellos often double the bass line, as in the *Fête chez Capulet* (*NBE* 18: 75–81). He was perhaps following Le Sueur's practice, which he described in 1837 as follows: 'The cellos are often divided into two halves, one doubling the violas, the other the basses. Or sometimes the cellos are divided into two unequal bodies, the larger playing the lower part, the smaller – consisting perhaps of two or at the most four cellos – doubling the melody at the octave.'[27] The section divides into three for Priam's blessing of Astyanax in *Les Troyens* Act I (*NBE* 2a: 119–20), and into four for the chords in harmonics in the *Huit Scènes de Faust* mentioned above, for the Pope's entrance in *Benvenuto Cellini* (*NBE* 1c: 853), and again in the *Tibi omnes* of the *Te deum* (*NBE* 10: 28, 34–5). A passage in the *Waverley* overture for cellos in four parts was later reduced to two parts (*NBE* 20: Appendix I). Divided cellos often combine with divided double basses (see below, p. 62).

In the *Guillaume Tell* overture the five solo cellos are accompanied by 'Basses ripiennes' divided into two staves, intended by Rossini to be played by the remainder of the cello section playing in two parts.

The cello pizzicato cannot be very rapid, and the method we have proposed for improving its execution on the violin does not apply here because

---

[27] *Rgm*, 15 October 1837; *Cm*, 3, p. 307; Condé, p. 159.

of the size and tension of the strings and their distance from the finger-board. With the current level of expertise one cannot much exceed pluck-ing eight quavers in a bar of alla breve in allegro non troppo (Ex. 46a) or twelve semiquavers in arpeggio in a bar of six-eight andantino (Ex. 46b).

Ex. 46

Ex. 46a is comparable to the rapid pizzicatos in the *Christe, rex gloriæ* of the *Te deum* (*NBE* 10: 74–7), where the metronome mark requires plucking at a rate of 304 per minute; Ex. 46b is similar to the passage for cellos in *Roméo seul* in *Roméo et Juliette* (*NBE* 18: 67), where the rate is 348 per minute.

Although Berlioz does not discuss mutes for cellos, he requires them freely, if less frequently than for violins. One curious instruction is to put on 'sourdines à petits grelots' (mutes with little bells) in the Act I finale of *Benvenuto Cellini* (*NBE* 1a: 311). These are clearly not meant to dampen the instrument in a noisy finale, but must be little bells to be attached to the bridge, or perhaps to the bow. Unfortunately Berlioz gave no further instruction and never called for them else-where. These 'mutes with bells' were originally required in the violins and violas also.

Berlioz's regard for the cello was sympathetic but perhaps not as passionate as that of some composers; he was a more persuasive advocate of the viola. He was evidently mistrustful of the solo cello. The third version of *La captive* has an optional accompaniment for solo muted cello. A solo cello is given prominence in the *Invitation à la valse* orchestration (*B&H* 18: 58, 97), but elsewhere it is rarely audible on its own. In the stable scene in *L'enfance du Christ* (*NBE* 11: 80–1) it is covered by violins in unison and a flute an octave above; in *Le spectre de la Rose* (*NBE* 13: 39–40) it blends with sustained string harmony; and in Héro's air in *Béatrice et Bénédict* (*NBE* 3: 76) it shares a melody with oboe and clarinet.

Yet the cellos clearly bear an important message in *Roméo et Juliette*, impersonat-ing Romeo himself on several occasions. In the *Strophes* in the same work six cellos in unison have a prominent and expressive counterpoint to the contralto soloist. The cellos are given an important exposed role in the first part of the *Waverley* overture (*NBE* 20: 5–11). And in Dido's scene 'Va, ma sœur' in Act V of *Les Troyens* (*NBE* 2b: 679–84) the full section of cellos offers the most poignant commentary on her tragic fate.

The *Rgm* text has additionally at the end of the cello entry: 'The cellos are, with the violins, the members of the string family to have taken over the most intelligent role in the last twenty years not only in symphonies and opera, but also in ballet.' The paragraph which follows the discussion of Agathe's air in *Der Freischütz* was then applied to refer to ballet.

Berlioz counted a number of cellists among his friends, the closest being Batta and Desmarest; Franchomme and Hainl were also to be numbered, the latter eventually pursuing a career as a conductor. He met Dotzauer in Dresden in 1843 and Cossmann in Weimar in 1855; Servais participated in his Paris concerts in 1850, Piatti in his London concerts in 1852; and in 1861 he spoke rapturously of Jacquard's great talent on the cello.[28]

THE DOUBLE BASS

There are two kinds of double bass: with three or with four strings. The three-string bass is tuned in fifths, written *G–d–a*, the four-string bass in fourths, written *E–a–d–g*. Both sound an octave lower than their written pitch. Their orchestral range is two octaves and a fourth, from *E* to *a'* with the chromatic intervals, or, in the case of the three-string bass, from *G* to *a'* with the chromatic intervals.

In my view the four-string bass is preferable to the other, firstly because it is easier to play, its tuning in fourths not requiring a shift to play a scale, secondly because of the great value of the three bottom notes *E*, *F*, and *F♯*, lacking on the bass tuned in fifths; this gap constantly spoils the shape of the best bass lines by compelling the player to make a rapid and clumsy transposition into the upper octave. This applies even more to English double basses, which are tuned in fourths but which have only three strings, *A–d–g*. A well-equipped orchestra should have several four-string basses tuned with one third and three fifths, i.e. to *E–G–d–a*, so that with the other basses tuned in fourths you would get an alternation of open strings which greatly helps the sound, thus:

tuned in thirds and fifths: o   o   o   o

                                 E F G A B c d e f g a

tuned in fourths: o   o   o   o

Berlioz preferred the four-string bass, but most players in France played three-string basses, as Mendelssohn reported in 1832.[29] Berlioz deplored the persistence of this preference.[30] In the *Rgm* text in 1841 he described the four-string tuning as the 'practice of almost all of Germany', but he omitted that comment in the *Treatise* after visiting Germany; presumably it was untrue. Similarly, the sentence about English double basses was added to the 1855 edition after visiting England several times.

Some passages in Berlioz's early music suggest that he regarded *G* as the basses' bottom note. Examples are found in the *Francs-juges*'s *Hymne* (bar 30), *La mort d'Orphée* (*NBE* 6: 9), the finale of the *Symphonie fantastique* (*NBE* 16: 137, 146), *Lélio* (*NBE* 7: 114–17) and four times in *Harold en Italie* (*NBE* 17: 41, 63, 81, 104). Yet the fourth bar of *Harold en Italie* has an *E*, and there are low *E*s in the *Duo* of

[28] *Jd*, 24 April 1861.   [29] *Briefe aus den Jahren 1830 bis 1847* (Leipzig, 1899), p. 250.
[30] *Le rénovateur*, 12 October 1835; *Cm*, 2, p. 310.

Les francs-juges, the *Scène héroïque* (*NBE* 12a: 82) and the *Huit scènes de Faust*. In the latter case they are explained by Berlioz's footnote to an *F* in the first movement: 'Although this low *F* cannot be obtained on the three-string double basses which are used in France, I have written it nonetheless, since it is probable that the four-string double bass will eventually come into general use, as it has been for some time in several cities in Germany' (*NBE* 5: ix). Yet in the same work he has a low *D* in the *Concert de sylphes* (*NBE* 5: 59) and a low *C* a few bars earlier (*NBE* 5: 51). Other low notes include *E♭* in the *Marseillaise* (*B&H* 18: 4), *D* in *Rob Roy* (*NBE* 20: 149), *C♯* in *Cléopâtre* (*NBE* 6: 163) and *C* in *Herminie* (*NBE* 6: 70).

The scores thus provide confusing evidence. After 1834, however, Berlioz clearly expected the basses to reach *E* and made special provision for tuning down to *D* when it was required. This occurs in *La captive* (*NBE* 13: 11) for one note, and in Act V of *Les Troyens* (*NBE* 2b: 639–43) for the appearance of the ghosts; the section is advised to tune down at the beginning of the act and to tune back up after the scene. A low *D* in the *Marche pour la dernière scène d'Hamlet* (*NBE* 12b: 108), however, has no such instruction.

As for the upper range, Berlioz observed his precept and treated *a'* as the upper limit, a note reached on several occasions. In *Le carnaval romain* (*NBE* 20: 234) he avoided a *b♭'*. His avoidance of *a'* in *Un bal* (*Symphonie fantastique*, *NBE* 16: 47) is unexpected.

In the orchestra the double basses carry the lowest notes of the harmony. In the preceding section I set out the occasions on which they may be separated from the cellos. The basses' weakness thus exposed may be covered, within limits, by doubling them at the octave or the unison with bassoons, basset horns, bass clarinets or ordinary clarinets (in their lowest register), but I detest the practice of some composers of using trombones or ophicleides for this purpose; their timbre is neither similar nor sympathetic to that of the double basses and consequently blends very poorly with them.

It is not impossible that an occasion might arise when double basses could successfully use harmonics. The high tension of the strings, their length and their elevation from the fingerboard forbid the use of artificial harmonics, but natural harmonics sound well, especially the first octave situated at the midpoint of the string. These are the same as on the cello, but an octave lower.

More on the practice of using a trombone to reinforce the orchestral bass line is found in the section on the trombone, below.

Berlioz never used double bass harmonics. When saying that the double bass octave harmonics are an octave lower than those on the cello, he refers to the three-string bass, whose open strings lie an octave below open strings on the cello. He was wrong about the tension: the tension of bass strings is of course lower than that of other stringed instruments.

One can, if necessary, write chords and arpeggios for the double bass, so long as only two or three notes at the most are used; only one should be stopped, as shown in Ex. 47.

Ex. 47

An interrupted tremolo is very easily done, thanks to the elasticity of the bow which allows it to bounce on the strings after a single sharp attack, as in Ex. 48a. Ex. 48b is quite different and can only be done with considerable difficulty. The continuous tremolo stroke, activating the strings with the end of the bow, is lacking in force and makes little sound. Yet a continuous tremolo on the double bass, less rapid than in Ex. 48b, has an excellent dramatic effect. Nothing gives the orchestra a more menacing quality. But it must not last too long or the fatigue players suffer in doing it properly (those players who trouble to do it properly) would soon exhaust them. When the depths of the orchestra need to be disturbed like this for a long passage, it is better to divide the basses and instead of a true tremolo give them rapid strokes, staggered in rhythm, while the cellos play a real tremolo, as in Ex. 48c. With the semiquavers only coinciding with the triplet quavers on each beat, it produces a dull murmuring sound like a tremolo, for which this is a good substitute. I find there are many occasions when these simultaneous different rhythms are to be preferred.

Ex. 48

Double-stops for double basses are rare in Berlioz's scores. When cellos and double basses are notated on the same stave, it is not always clear whether two simultaneous notes are to be treated as double stops by both instruments or divided between them. In this category fall the octave *d–d'* and the tenth *d–f♯'*

found in the *Messe solennelle* (*NBE* 23: 3, 4). An octave *d–d'* is found in the *Scène héroïque* (*NBE* 12a: 116), an octave *G–g* in the *Sextuor* in *Benvenuto Cellini* (*NBE* 1c: 910) and a fifth *d–a* in *L'enfance du Christ* (*NBE* 11: 67).

An example of the 'tremolo intermittent' is found in violas, cellos and basses in *Les Troyens* Act II (*NBE* 2a: 249–50).

Berlioz usually required the double basses to tremolo at half the speed of the other strings, or perhaps in triplets, as in Ex. 48c. This is often misprinted in published scores, as for example at bar 43 of the Introduction to *Roméo et Juliette* (*NBE* 18:11), where all earlier printed scores give the double basses repeated sextuplets on *a'* (the basses' highest permitted note); Berlioz's autograph shows double bass quavers against sextuplets in violas and cellos.

An interesting application of this principle is found in *Harold en Italie* (*NBE* 17: 56), where the basses lead off a fugato in triplets, followed by cellos in quadruplets and then violas in sextuplets, all superimposed.

In an article on *Iphigénie en Tauride* in 1834 Berlioz praised Gluck's choice, in Thoas's Air 'De noirs pressentiments', of a tremolando accompaniment for double basses while the rest of the orchestra marks a different rhythm.[31] This effect, he says, was later used by Mozart for the entry of the statue in *Don Giovanni*. Gluck in fact notated repeated semiquavers for cellos and basses under a steady dotted rhythm in the upper strings. Mozart has the same dotted rhythm in all the strings, so perhaps in the Opéra performances of 1834 a tremolando bass line was substituted.

Rapid diatonic scales four or five notes long are often very effective and are very satisfactory to play provided the phrase includes at least one open string, as in Ex. 49a. The last two of these phrases are harder on the bass tuned in fifths, since they include no open strings. Ex. 49b is harder to play because of the descending figure. If it is absolutely necessary to give the double basses long rapid scale figures it is best to divide them in the manner I have indicated for violins (see above, p. 28), making sure that the first basses are not separated from the second (see Ex. 49c).

Ex. 49

These short rapid rising figures in the cellos and basses, as shown in Ex. 48a, are very characteristic of Berlioz's style, derived from Gluck and Spontini. Many examples could be given. His advice to allow for open strings is most flagrantly ignored in the *Duo* in Act I of *Les Troyens*, 'Quitte-nous dès ce soir' (*NBE* 2a: 72–7, 82–4), where he wrote a succession of rising five-note runs of this kind for cellos and basses in the key of B major. Thus only the low E string can be played open. The division of a longer passage on the lines of Ex. 48c is not found in Berlioz.

Modern composers are wrong to give the heaviest of all instruments passages of such rapidity that even the cellos have difficulty with them. The result is a considerable nuisance since idle players, or those incapable of tackling such difficulties, give up at once and take it upon themselves to *simplify* the passage. But since one man's idea of simplification differs from that of the next, having various estimates of the harmonic importance of individual notes in the passage, the result is horrible confusion and disorder. Such buzzing bedlam, full of strange noises and hideous grunting, is made yet worse by other, keener players with more confidence in their own ability who exhaust themselves in pointless attempts to play the passage exactly as it is written.

Composers must therefore take care not to ask more of double basses than is possible or more than can be played with safety. At the same time it must be said that the old system of *simplifying* bass parts, as generally cultivated by the old school, with its attendant dangers as I have described, is now quite discredited. If the composer writes only what the instrument can comfortably manage, the player must play it, no more, no less. When the fault is the composer's, he and the audience must bear the consequences; the player cannot be held responsible for them.

In 1813 Choron's advice to composers was: 'Bass parts are the same as cello parts except for rapid passages which are left out. Composers do not bother to do this reduction themselves; they leave it to the players, who are used to it.'[32] But Berlioz scorned the practice. Attending the Opéra in the 1820s, he would point out to his friends: 'That big red-faced man over there is the leader of the double basses, old Chénié. A very lively old boy despite his age. He's as good as four ordinary basses, and you can be sure his part will be played exactly as the composer wrote it; he's not one of your simplifiers.'[33] In his 1835 article on *Robert le diable* he wrote:

> This is what simplifiers do. When a note is repeated eight times in a bar as eight quavers, they just play four crotchets. If there are four crotchets written, they play two minims. And if there is a semibreve or a single note to hold for a whole bar they begin the note and then drop the bow after one beat as if their strength had suddenly deserted them. If you expect an

---

[32] Alexandre Choron, *Traité général des voix et des instruments d'orchestre* (Paris, 1813), p. 84.
[33] *Memoirs*, chapter 15.

energetic scale rising an octave, don't count on it, since it will almost always be transformed into four notes chosen at will by the player from the eight notes of the scale. Did you write a tremolo? Since this is a bit tiring on the right arm the simplifying bassist will offer you a few clumsy notes, and you'll be lucky if he doesn't reduce it to a simple held note, turning feverish agitation into dull placidity. God preserve us from thieves and simplifiers! [...] Simplifiers are almost always poor in spirit, and since, as the Gospel tells us, theirs is the kingdom of heaven, I often think they ought to get there as quickly as possible.[34]

Berlioz returns to the same theme in the chapter on conducting (see below, p. 361).

In a rapid passage in the *Messe solennelle* (*NBE* 23: 170) Berlioz instructs the first bassist to play all the notes and the rest of the section to play the simplified version. A good example of a simplified double bass part is also found in the *Marche* in the *Te deum* (*NBE* 10: 143–5).

In the *Rgm* text Berlioz had originally written: 'When I spoke out just now against complicated figures on the double bass, I did not mean that groups of rapid notes *in a narrow range* should be avoided; on the contrary, five or six diatonic notes before or after the true bass note are not at all hazardous to play and the effect can be extremely satisfactory.'

Grace notes written small before the main note (Ex. 50) are played by sliding rapidly along the string, without worrying about the accuracy of intermediate notes, and the effect can be extremely satisfactory.

Ex. 50

The furious jolt given by the double basses to the orchestra in the Hades scene in *Orphée* (Ex. 51) is well known, with a high *f'* preceded by four grace notes *b–c'–d'–e'* to the words

> A l'affreux hurlement
> De Cerbère écumant
> Et rugissant!
> (at the horrible howling of foaming, raging Cerberus)

This raucous barking, one of Gluck's greatest inspirations, is here all the more powerful because the composer has placed it on the third inversion of a diminished seventh (F–G♯–B–D) and because he has given his idea the maximum prominence and force by doubling the basses at the octave not only with the cellos but also with the violas and both sections of violins.

---

[34] *Gm*, 12 July 1835; *Cm*, 2, pp. 209–13.

Ex. 51

Beethoven has also turned these brief hurried notes to good account, but the other way round to the previous example, placing the accent on the first note of each group, not the last. An example is found in the Storm movement of the Pastoral Symphony, which gives such a fine effect of violent wind and rain and the dull rumble of gusty squalls (Ex. 52). In this passage, as in many others, Beethoven has given the basses low notes which they cannot play, from which we must conclude that the orchestra he wrote for included double basses going down to bottom *C* an octave below the cellos, which are no longer found nowadays.

Ex. 52

Sometimes, for a fine dramatic effect, one may give the cellos the true bass, or at least the notes which determine the harmony and are struck on the first beat of the bar. Beneath them runs a separate double bass line with regular rests, allowing the harmony to rest on the cello line. Beethoven, in the superb scene in *Fidelio* where Leonora and the gaoler are digging Florestan's grave, has shown how mournful and sombre this style of instrumentation can be (Ex. 53). In actual fact he has given the true bass here to the double basses.

Ex. 53

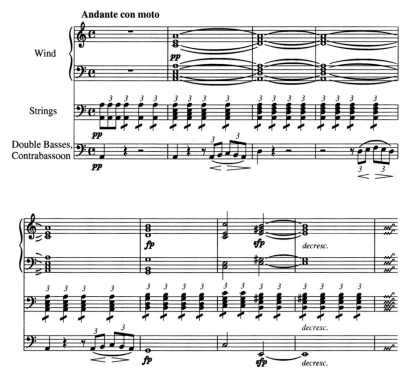

In the *Treatise* Berlioz printed much more of the passages from the Sixth Symphony and *Fidelio* than shown here. He appears to have had this scene in mind when scoring the 'Sinon' scene in Act I of *Les Troyens* (*NBE* 2c: 875–86). Bars 119–46 of that scene have repeated chords in the upper parts and mobile triplets low in the bass. Only a piano reduction has survived.

In order to express a sombre silence in one of my cantatas, *Le cinq mai*, I tried dividing the double basses into four parts with long chords held *pianissimo* while the rest of the orchestra has a diminuendo above them (Ex. 54).

Ex. 54

Berlioz printed much more of *Le cinq mai* in the *Treatise*, but Ex. 54 shows how the double basses are divided into four parts (*NBE* 12a: 387–8). This passage is one of the most effective of many occasions when Berlioz divided his double bass section. The first example is a passage of seven bars in the *Huit scènes de Faust* (*NBE* 5: 47–9) where they play syncopated chords in three parts against different figuration in the other strings. The four-part pizzicato chords at the start of the *Marche au supplice* (*Symphonie fantastique, NBE* 16: 91–2) are well known. Pompeo dies to six-part chords on cellos and basses both divided into three (*Benvenuto Cellini, NBE* 1b: 672). For Herod's account of his dream in *L'enfance du Christ* (*NBE* 11: 47–8) a low five-part texture is produced from violas, cellos in two parts, and double basses in two parts, a sound heard again to accompany Cassandra's gloomy confessions in *Les Troyens* Act I (*NBE* 2a: 37). The *Entrée des laboureurs* in *Les Troyens* Act III (*NBE* 2b: 349–52) has continuous three-part harmony provided by half the cellos and divided double basses, a texture he achieved elsewhere by dividing the cellos over a separate double bass line, as in *Le roi de Thulé* in *La damnation de Faust* (*NBE* 8a: 265–72) and Narbal's Air in *Les Troyens* (*NBE* 2b: 483–7). In the *Légende* in *La nonne sanglante* the two halves of the double bass section are directed to play from opposite sides of the orchestra.

The double bass pizzicato has a good sound, either loud or soft, in the high register at least, but it changes in character according to the harmony above it. Thus the famous pizzicato *A* in the overture to *Der Freischütz* acquires its heavy sense of supernatural menace simply from the chord of the diminished seventh (F♯–A–C–E♭) forming a first inversion and falling on the weak beat of the bar. If it were a tonic major or dominant chord, plucked *mezzo-forte* in a similar context, this *A* would lose all its strangeness.

Mutes are used on double basses as on other string instruments, but the effect has no particular character. They simply reduce the instrument's sonority a little, making it more sombre and colourless.

A player from Piedmont, M. Langlois, who played in Paris about fifteen years ago, gripped the top string between his thumb and forefinger instead of pressing it against the fingerboard, and by going up high near the bridge he obtained some extraordinary high notes of incredible power. If one wanted to get an orchestra to make the sound of a woman shrieking, no instrument could render it better than the double bass played in this fashion. I doubt if our players know M. Langlois's trick for high notes, but they could quickly learn it.

In the *Rgm* text Berlioz described the sound of double bass pizzicato as 'excellent', but changed it in the *Treatise* to 'good'. In referring to the *Freischütz* overture (which he did not print in the *Treatise*) he does not point out that the marking is *pianissimo*, on which his observation partly depends.

On mutes the *Rgm* had instead: 'Mutes and harmonics on the double bass seem to me to be of little use. Nothing remarkable has yet been done with them.' There are many occasions when Berlioz gives instructions for the rest of the strings to mute, but not the double basses. On the other hand he also has them muted occasionally. He seems to have had no firm rule in this regard. Two movements require the double basses to be muted throughout: the *Méditation religieuse*, and the *Duo-nocturne* in *Béatrice et Bénédict*.

A performance by the Piedmontese double bass virtuoso Luigi Anglois (1801–72) was reported in the *Revue musicale* on 8 May 1829. As 'Langlois', his name is also found in Hanslick's report of Bottesini's playing in Vienna in 1866, where the thumb-and-forefinger technique is likened to the sound of a 'howling witch escaping from a chimney-flue'.[35] Despite this imaginative detail it seems likely that Hanslick took his information from the *Treatise*. It was from Berlioz's description of Anglois, too, that Strauss took the idea of using a solo double bass, with the string pinched between thumb and forefinger on the note *bb′*, to accompany the beheading of Jokanaan in *Salome*. A footnote in the score says that the sound 'resembles a woman's stifled groans'.

Berlioz heard the three great double bass virtuosi of his time: Dragonetti, who led the basses for the Beethoven celebrations in Bonn in 1845; August Müller, whom he met in Darmstadt in 1843 and warmly admired;[36] and Bottesini, who appeared in Berlioz's concerts in London on 24 March 1852 and 30 May 1853. He reviewed Bottesini's Paris appearances in January 1853 and April 1861 and referred, in a letter of 1 June 1853, to his 'usual extraordinary ability'.[37]

[35] Hanslick, *Geschichte des Concertwesens in Wien*, part 2 (Vienna, 1870), p. 396.
[36] *Memoirs*, 'Travels in Germany', I/10. [37] *Cg*, 4, p. 324.

2

Plucked strings

THE HARP

This instrument is essentially anti-chromatic, that is to say, movement by semitone steps is almost forbidden. We will explain this in a moment.

Its range used to be only five octaves and a sixth, from F' to d'''' on a scale of E♭, the key in which all harps were in fact tuned. Then the clever harp-maker Erard, trying to overcome the limitations of this system, thought up the mechanism which has provided a solution. He proposed tuning the harp in C♭, the system now adopted by almost all harpists.

On the old harp chromatic intervals can only be obtained by the use of seven pedals operated by the player's foot *one by one*. Each pedal raises the note to which it belongs by a semitone, not just one note at a time but throughout the range. Thus the F pedal cannot sharpen an F without sharpening all the other Fs over the whole range at the same time. As a result, any chromatic scale (except at extremely slow tempos), any chord progression which moves chromatically or involves different keys, and the majority of ornaments which include appoggiaturas with accidentals or little chromatic notes, are impracticable or, in exceptional cases, extremely difficult. They are also horrible to listen to. On the E♭ harp there are even four major seventh chords and four minor ninth chords which are completely impossible and are therefore excluded from its harmonic vocabulary. They are set out in Ex. 55 a–h.

Ex. 55

As will be seen, any chord with a C♭ in it at the same time as a B♭ is impossible, since the harp, tuned in E♭, has pedals which only raise each string a semitone; it cannot therefore produce C♭ except by applying the B♭

pedal, which thereby removes all the Bbs in the range. The same happens with Db, obtained by raising the C, and Gb, obtained by raising the F.

Since with the pedal mechanism of the Eb harp the three flattened notes of the scale (Bb, Eb and Ab) can only be naturalised and four others (F, C, G and D) can only be sharpened, it can only operate in eight keys, viz: Eb, Bb, F, C, G, D, A and E. Flat keys can only be reached by enharmonics and by the instant application and release of one or several pedals. In Ab, for instance, Db is just the enharmonic of C♯, so the player must release the C♯ pedal as soon as it has been applied, otherwise he will have no C♮, the major third of the key. In addition he has to skip over one string (the D) when moving diatonically, which is sufficiently awkward to recommend the avoidance of such keys altogether.

This inconvenience and difficulty is doubly worse in Db and Gb, keys which are almost inaccessible except for a few chords. Furthermore the key of Gb, like that of Cb, presents a new difficulty in that the player has to make an actual transposition for some notes of the scale, since he has to pluck the F♯ string when the desired note is Gb, the B♮ string when the note is Cb, and the C♯ string when the note is Db. The key of Cb is less inaccessible if it is written in its other form, as B♮, but with all the pedals applied one still has to overcome for this key (just as for Ab major) the awful difficulty of skipping one string and then releasing a pedal and pressing it again immediately for the leading note (enharmonic) and the tonic, both requiring the same string.

It is clear that in order to play a two-octave chromatic scale, as in Ex. 56a, one must move five pedals in very quick succession for the first octave and then release them all promptly in order to allow the sharpened notes to fall back to their original pitch. These are required in the second octave, and the pedals must be applied once more as in the first octave. This kind of scale is thus impossible *on all harps*, even at a moderate tempo.

If you need a series of chords in different keys their impossibility will be even more obvious, since there will be several pedals to apply either simultaneously or in turn (Ex. 56b).

Ex. 56

(a)

(b)

Certain appoggiaturas and ornaments with chromatic details can in fact be played after a fashion, but the great majority of these ornaments are, as

I say, scarcely practicable. Such exceptions as there are are poor because of the distortion of the string's sound produced by the pedal being applied and released immediately after. Exx. 57a and 57b are possible; Ex. 57c is better. Ex. 57d, on the other hand, is almost impossible, like any others which include semitones close together in quick tempo.

Ex. 57

It must now be explained that the harp is plucked by both hands and is therefore written on two staves. The lower stave normally uses the bass clef and the upper stave the treble clef. If the bass notes are high or the top notes are low the treble or bass clefs can be found on both staves at once. On the E♭ harp this use of two hands clearly makes many more passages unplayable, since a phrase which is easy for the right hand becomes impossible if the left hand needs certain notes in the accompaniment which have been altered by a pedal for the melody but which would normally be unaltered for the harmony, as in Ex. 58. The two chords marked * cannot be played, since they include an F♮, already sharpened in the upper part. In such cases one or other part must omit the note which is required to do double duty. In this example it is better to spoil the left-hand chord and leave out the *f♮'*.

Ex. 58

When a melody is played first by other instruments and is then repeated by the harp, and when it contains chromatic passages that are impossible or even just dangerous, it must be subtly modified by replacing one or two chromatic notes by others which belong to the harmony. Thus instead of giving the harp Ex. 59a, as it has just been played by the violins, the composer had to write it as in Ex. 59b. The mechanical limitations of the harp required this sacrifice of four semitones in a row in the third bar.

Ex. 59

Berlioz has thus far discussed the single-action harp, invented in about 1720 and an extremely popular domestic instrument in France since about 1770. It proved adequate for diatonic music and for the accompaniment of romances, but the need felt by virtuosi for a fully chromatic harp led to the invention and patenting in 1810 by Sébastien Erard of the double-action harp. This new instrument was manufactured in great numbers in the next few years. The single-action harp gradually gave way in popularity to its more advanced successor and to competition from the piano as a domestic instrument.

Berlioz wrote his harp parts on the assumption that players would use a double-action instrument, at least from *Harold en Italie* onwards, although he wrote for them mostly in sharp keys and avoided awkward chromaticisms. When writing in D♭ for the final scene of *La damnation de Faust* he felt obliged to advise players with single-action harps to tune the D and G strings to D♭ and G♭ (*NBE* 8b: 460). His harp parts can usually be managed, if with difficulty, on the single-action harp. Indeed, Ex. 59 is an extract from the *Symphonie fantastique* (*NBE* 16: 59–60), implying that *Un bal* was written with a single-action harp in mind. The one harp part which can barely be played on either single- or double-action harp is his first, *Le montagnard exilé* (*B&H* 16: 162), published in 1823. This song accompaniment is stated to be for piano or harp, yet it is much too chromatic for the latter instrument.

Struck by the serious problems I have outlined, M. Erard some years ago worked out the mechanism from which harps have acquired the name of 'double-action' instruments. This is how it works and how it allows the harp to play, if not chromatic scales, at least in all keys and to pluck or arpeggiate all chords.

The double-action harp is tuned in C♭. Its range is six octaves and a fourth from C♭′ up to f♭′′′′. Its seven pedals allow the player to raise each string by either a tone or just a semitone. As each pedal is adjusted by a semitone in turn, the C♭ harp is set first in G♭, then D♭, A♭, E♭, B♭, F and finally C. By next raising each string a further semitone (by a further depression of the pedals) the seven notes of the white-note scale will be sharpened since the pedals now produce F♯, C♯, G♯, D♯, A♯, E♯ and B♯, giving the harp the keys of G, then D, A, E, B, F♯ and C♯.

Thus all the keys are available. Minor keys can be fixed only if the rising and descending scales are treated as the same, without allowing for the common practice of adjusting the sixth and seventh notes of the scale. If this is desired, then the two pedals must be applied on the ascending scale and released on the descending scale. If the interval of an augmented second between the sixth and seventh notes is chosen, the minor scale can be fixed and the additional use of the pedals will not be required, a considerable advantage which should be enough to give preference to the harmonic minor scale.

As for chords which are forbidden on the E♭ harp, we can see that the double action makes them possible. To produce the chord shown as Ex. 55a nothing is simpler, since all four notes fall within the scale of the C♭ harp. Ex. 55b requires two pedals raised by a semitone (D♮, F♮); Ex. 55c requires two also (F♮, C♮); Ex. 55d requires three (C♮, E♮, G♮), Ex. 55g just one (F♮), and Ex. 55h three (F♮, A♮, C♮). All these are easily done. Ex. 60a, which seems to require C♮ and C♭ at the same time, can also be done: the *d*♭♭′ (or *c*♮′) is played by raising the *c*♭′ a semitone, and the *c*♭″ is obtained by raising the *b*♭′ a semitone; the *a*♭♭′ comes from the *g*♭′ raised a semitone, and the *f*♭′ requires no pedal change, being in the scale of C♭. This chord, described thus, would therefore be played in the unusual form shown as Ex. 60b, from which it follows that it would be better to write it in C major as Ex. 60c.

Ex. 60

If one had to use double-action harps in an orchestral piece written in B major, it would be incomparably better for the sonority and ease of performance to transpose the part into their key of C♭, as in Ex. 61.

Ex. 61

When writing for harps composers should take care to give advance warning of changes the player has to make and of the pedal he has to depress by placing the following words a few bars before the point of modulation: 'Prepare G♯', 'Prepare C major', etc.

Berlioz's lowest note for the harp is an E♭′ in *Le montagnard exilé* (*B&H* 16: 179), probably intended for the piano. In his orchestral works he reached *G*′ several times, notated as *F*×′ in *Les Troyens* Act II (*NBE* 2a: 281). At the upper end the harp's highest note is a fivefold *e*′′′′ in *Les Troyens* Act IV (*NBE* 2b: 550).

The explanation of how to play the chords in Ex. 55 on the double-action harp omits two, Exx. 55e and 55f, for no apparent reason, although both are easily managed. His explanation of how to achieve a major seventh chord on *d*♭♭′ seems curiously clumsy for a chord and a key for which few composers, least of all himself, could have much use, at least in that notation.

Two Berlioz works in B major employ the harp. In the first, *Le spectre de la rose* (*NBE* 13: 39), he notated the harp part in B; in Act IV of *Les Troyens* (*NBE* 2b: 497–500) he notated the orchestra in B and the harps in C♭, as recommended in Ex. 61.

Berlioz's advice to give advance warning of pedal changes is never observed in his scores, with one solitary and inexplicable exception: 'La♮' is found in the finale to Act I of *Les Troyens* (*NBE* 2a: 191).

Having explained the nature of the instrument, we will now discuss its fingering, wrongly confused by many composers with piano fingering, with which it has nothing in common. Each hand can strike four-note chords whose outer notes fall within an octave, as in Ex. 62a. By stretching the thumb and little finger, however, one can reach chords of a tenth, and this allows chords to be spaced as in Ex. 62b. But this spacing is less comfortable and less natural, so it sounds weaker since each finger cannot attack the string with as much strength as in the ordinary position.

Let us note in passing that chords at the lower end of the instrument, such as Ex. 62c, having no sonority, produce muddy harmony and should be avoided. These low notes are only useful for doubling a bass line with a lower octave, as in Ex. 62d.

Ex. 62

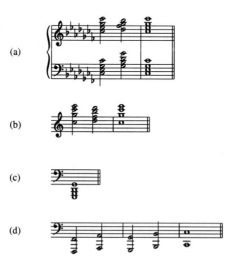

(a)

(b)

(c)

(d)

Berlioz refers to stretching the little finger, though it is not normally used on the harp, as he later acknowledges. The widest stretches, including tenths, are executed with thumb and fourth finger. He wrote a chord of a tenth only once: in the *Fête* in *Roméo et Juliette* (*NBE* 18: 115).

The playing of successive notes of a chord, going up or down, is well within the harp's natural capacity, in fact it is its Italian name 'arpa' which gives these harmonic patterns the name 'arpeggio'. In general they should not exceed an octave in range, especially in quick tempo, otherwise they will need an extremely difficult change of position. Ex. 63a is easy, whereas Ex. 63b is almost impossible. Notes beyond the range of the octave should only be written at the end of a phrase, as in Ex. 63c. The next example, Ex. 63d, is very easy because the change of position from low to high will require neither the use of the little finger, which is hardly ever used, nor the playing of two consecutive notes with the fourth finger.

Ex. 63

In general one must take care not to write the two hands too close together but keep them at least an octave and a sixth apart, otherwise they get in each other's way. Furthermore, if the two hands have arpeggios a third apart, the finger on one hand has to pluck a string just after it has been plucked by the other hand, so it has no time to vibrate and its sound is strangled at birth. Ex. 64a is very bad, while Ex. 64b is very good, because of the separation of the two hands.

Ex. 64

(a)

(b)

Any progression that requires the same finger to jump from one string to another can only be used at a very moderate tempo. If a rapid succession of diatonic octaves is needed, they should normally be written for two hands. The same applies to successions of sixths. They can actually be played by one hand, like scales in thirds, but only descending, enabling the thumb to slide from one upper note to the next while the lower notes are taken by the other three fingers. Ex. 65a is difficult because of the stretch between the thumb and the other fingers. Ex. 65b and Ex. 65c are less difficult. As an exception to what we said before about keeping the parts separate, these same scales in thirds (Ex. 65c) can be played by two hands because in diatonic movement the problem of a string played by one finger and then taken by another is much less acute, the intermediate note giving it a little more time to vibrate. It is preferable, nonetheless, either to write these chains of thirds for two harps, giving the upper part to one and the lower part to the other, or, if you have only one harp and you want plenty of sound, to separate the parts by an octave and write them as a series of tenths, as in Ex. 65d.

Ex. 65

(a)

(b)

(c)

(d)

If a rapid arpeggio exceeding an octave in range, up or down, is required, one must divide it up rather than write it in two parts, and give one fragment to one hand while the other changes position, and vice versa. The passage is then written as in Ex. 66a. Doubled at the octave, as in Ex. 66b, it is impracticable, at least at a fast tempo, though possible at a slow tempo.

Ex. 66

The harp trill exists, but its effect is tolerable only on high notes. The reiteration (*martellement*) of the same note is unpleasant and difficult on old harps because of the slight buzz of the string being plucked by one finger immediately after another, interrupting its vibration (Ex. 67a). But it is easy and sonorous on new harps, since the double action allows a neighbouring string to be raised a whole tone and the *martellement* to be played on two unison strings, as in Ex. 67b.

Ex. 67

A *martellement* in two or four parts, sometimes a very useful orchestral device, can be obtained by using two or more harps and by writing alternations which present no difficulty to the player (Ex. 68a) and produce exactly the desired effect. The listener hears it as Ex. 68b.

Ex. 68

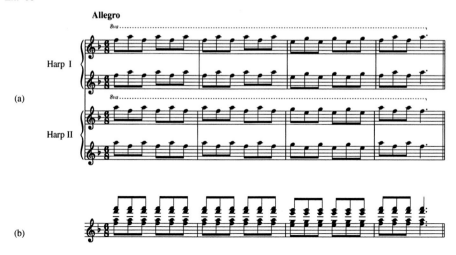

A good example of the technique illustrated in Ex. 66a is found in Act V of *Les Troyens* (*NBE* 2b: 743–4). Earlier in his career Berlioz had written similar passages for harps without any direction about hand-over technique (see the *Symphonie fantastique, NBE* 16: 44–5).

Berlioz did not use *martellement*, as shown in Exx. 67a and 67b, although Ex. 67b resembles a passage from one of his own scores, the *Reine Mab* scherzo from *Roméo et Juliette* (*NBE* 18: 222–7), where only the right hand of each player is engaged. Nor did he require trills, although a two-note tremolo for the right hand is called for both in *Le spectre de la rose* (*NBE* 13: 45–6) and in Act IV of *Les Troyens* (*NBE* 2b: 548). His harp writing usually calls for abundant arpeggios in the right hand and chords in the left hand. Scale passages such as those illustrated in Ex. 65 are rare.

Unless they are to be heard in close intimacy in a salon, harps are more effective the greater number you have. Notes, chords and arpeggios projected across an orchestra or chorus are exceptionally splendid. Nothing matches the spirit of poetic celebration or religious ceremony better than the sound of a large section of harps carefully used. On their own, or in groups of two, three or four, they are also felicitous in effect combined with the orchestra or accompanying vocal or instrumental solos. Of all known timbres it is odd that horns, trombones and brass instruments in general blend best with harps. The harp's lower strings (except the slack and dull strings at the very bottom), with their veiled, mysterious and beautiful sound, have hardly ever been used except as an accompanying bass line in the left hand. This is wrong. Admittedly no harpist is ever keen to play whole pieces in a register so far from his body that he has to lean forward and stretch his arms in an awkward posture and then maintain it for some time, but this argument should not sway composers unduly. The truth is, they have not thought of exploiting this special timbre. Ex. 69 produces a beautifully sweet sound from the bass strings.

Ex. 69

The strings of the top octave have a delicate, crystalline sound and a delicious freshness which makes them suitable for graceful, fairy effects and for letting tender melodies whisper their innermost secrets, provided always that they are not attacked roughly by the player, otherwise they make a hard, dry sound rather like breaking glass – unpleasant and painful.

Berlioz's attachment to a large section of harps has sometimes been ridiculed, especially his call for thirty harps (with thirty pianos) in an ideal festival orchestra (see below, p. 330). But on those rare occasions when twelve harps have been assembled to play, for example, the *Marche* at the end of the *Te deum*, his judgment has been proved right. Like violins, harps need to be multiplied in order to be heard against the rest of the orchestra, and although he wrote for harps normally in one or two parts, their numbers may be freely multiplied. In the *Symphonie fantastique* he called for 'at least four', in *Roméo et Juliette* and *La damnation de Faust* he recommended eight or ten, in *Les Troyens* six or eight. He was doubtless influenced by Le Sueur's *Ossian* (1804), with its two sections of six harps each. He was shocked at the audience's laughter when four harps were carried on stage for a cantata by Ruolz: 'They see seven or eight harps at the Opéra every day without laughing.'[1]

The blend of harps with brass instruments recommended by Berlioz is best illustrated by two operatic scenes, both of which approximate to the notion of 'religious ceremony': the entry of the Pope in *Benvenuto Cellini* (*NBE* 1c: 853) and the blessing of Astyanax by Priam in *Les Troyens* (*NBE* 2a: 119–20).

Ex. 69 is part of the accompaniment of the *Strophes* in *Roméo et Juliette* (*NBE* 18: 38) with the lower left-hand octave added. This accompaniment was in fact first conceived for the guitar (see *NBE* 18: 387).

In the *Rgm* text of the last sentence Berlioz had yet another pejorative description for high notes insensitively played: besides unpleasant and painful, 'extremely prosaic'.

For the positioning of harps within the orchestra, see below, p. 323.

Harp harmonics, especially on several harps in unison, are even more magical. Solo harpists often use them for cadenzas in fantasies, variations and concertos. But there is nothing like the mysterious sonority of these notes against chords on flutes and clarinets in the middle register. It is truly remarkable that only once (and that only three years ago) has anyone made use of this combination and exploited their poetic affinity.

[1] *Rgm*, 9 April 1837; *A travers chants*, p. 442.

The best harmonics, in fact almost the only kind used on the harp, are obtained by touching the middle of the string with the fleshy lower part of the hand and plucking with the thumb and first two fingers of the same hand. This produces the octave above the normal pitch of the string. Harmonics can be played with either hand. The effect of Ex. 70a is shown in Ex. 70b. It is even possible to produce two or three harmonics at once with the same hand, though in that case it would be wise not to give the other hand more than one note (Ex. 70c).

Ex. 70

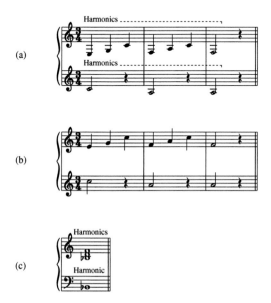

Not all harp strings are conducive to harmonics; one should only use the lowest-but-one and lowest-but-two octaves, i.e. from *F* up to *f'*, these being the only strings long enough to be divided in the middle and taut enough to produce clear harmonics.

In standard harp practice only the left hand produces harmonics by touching the 'fleshy lower part' of the hand in the middle of the string, and so only the left hand can play more than one harmonic at a time. The right hand plays harmonics by pressing the index finger joint against the middle of the string. Although Ex. 70c proposes a chord of three harmonics for the right hand, in his music Berlioz only wrote chords of harmonics for the left hand: a single case in *Roméo et Juliette* (*NBE* 18: 206–7). In *Les Troyens* Act IV (*NBE* 2b: 497–500) the effect of three-note chords is achieved by three harps playing one harmonic each.

The phrase 'three years ago', which first occurred in the *Rgm* text in 1841 and remained unaltered in the 1855 edition of the *Treatise*, refers to *Roméo et Juliette*. Berlioz identified Ex. 70a in a footnote. This example presents something of a textual crux, since confusion has always reigned over whether Berlioz indicated harp harmonics by the string to be played ('string pitch') or by the sounding pitch of the harmonic ('sounding pitch'), and some uncertainties remain.[2] In contrast to violin harmonics, he never specified either in manuscript or in printed scores which he meant, yet it is clear that he wrote the sounding pitch of harmonics in his earliest music and the string pitch in his later works. This leaves an intermediate group of works composed in the 1830s where two interpretations are possible.

His first use of harp harmonics, composed three years after their first orchestral appearance in Boieldieu's *La dame blanche* (1825), was in the *Huit scènes de Faust* (*NBE* 5: 30, 66–7), where he requires a range of more than two octaves from *d* up to *f♯″*. Although these bottom notes are unusually low, there can be no doubt that the sounding pitch is intended since in the same year, 1828, he inserted some harp harmonics in the *Resurrexit* ranging from *g* up to *g‴* (*NBE* 12a: 395, 404), which can only be played at sounding pitch.[3] In *Lélio* the harmonics were originally notated at sounding pitch but later (1855) rewritten an octave lower at string pitch (*NBE* 7: 64, 200).

But the harmonics in *Harold en Italie* (*NBE* 17: 99, 119–22) and *Benvenuto Cellini* (*NBE* 1c: 917–19) are confined to the range between *g* and *a′*, which could imply either sounding pitch or string pitch. The single harmonic at the end of the *Marche de pèlerins* was revised in the autograph from *b″* (evidently sounding pitch) to *b* (an octave too low), then *b′* (string pitch). The harmonics in the *Sérénade* are rather low as sounding pitch and sound better as string pitch, and since this passage was not revised when the score was published in 1847 there is a good case for regarding these notes as string pitch, in accordance with modern practice, not sounding pitch. This would accord with the clear implications of string pitch in *La damnation de Faust* (*NBE* 8a: 206, range *A* up to *b♭′*) and *Les Troyens* (*NBE* 2b: 497–500, range *B♭* up to *c♭″*).

The passage in *Roméo et Juliette* which Berlioz cites as Ex. 70 is nonetheless puzzling (*NBE* 18: 205–7, 437). In the autograph he originally wrote it at the upper pitch (with one part per harp, not two). He later pencilled '8va bassa', although this instruction was carried out neither in the printed scores and parts nor in the extract printed earlier in the *Treatise* to illustrate string harmonics. It was only shown at the lower pitch at this point in the *Treatise* (Ex. 70). This seems to imply that the harmonics in the score of *Roméo et Juliette* are written at sounding pitch. His practice seems to have changed in the period 1840–3, probably in the course of writing the *Treatise* and between the composition and publication of both *Harold en Italie* and *Roméo et Juliette*.

> If the tempo of a composition and the pattern of its instrumentation require a sudden transition in the harp part from one key to another remote from it (from E♭ to E♮, for example), it cannot be done on the same instrument. You then have to have a second instrument tuned in sharps to follow immediately after the other playing in flats. If the transition is not so rapid and there is only one harp available, then the composer must give the player time to make all the pedal changes needed for the modulation.

---

[2] This problem is discussed in Tom S. Wotton, *Hector Berlioz* (London, 1935), pp. 110–11, and Hans Bartenstein, *Hector Berlioz' Instrumentationskunst* (2nd, expanded edn, Baden-Baden, 1974), p. 106.
[3] The recommendation of *NBE*, 5, p. ix is evidently incorrect.

When there are numerous harps as integral members of the orchestra, not just accompanying a vocal or instrumental solo, they are normally divided into firsts and seconds in separate parts, with considerable enrichment of their effect. A greater number of separate parts could doubtless be fully justified, even essential, as we have just seen, when a sudden shift of key has to be achieved without a break in the harps' music.

The bas-reliefs at Thebes, with their precise representation of ancient harps, prove that they had no pedals and therefore never modulated. The no less ancient harps still used by Welsh and Irish bards have several ranks of strings, which evidently provide a more or less effective method of achieving a chromatic style, with modulation.

The *Rgm* text had, in addition: 'This fine instrument, whose origin is lost in the mists of time, seems to have played a considerable role in Egypt in the solemn ceremonies in honour of Isis.' The wall-paintings of harps found in the tomb of Ramses III in Thebes were made known to European musicians by the English explorer James Bruce (1730–94), whose lengthy description was printed by Burney in the first volume of his *A General History of Music* (1776). Burney also reproduced one of Bruce's drawings. Berlioz may have known the writings of the French Egyptologist G.-A. Villoteau (1759–1839), whose extensive study of ancient Egyptian music was first published in 1812. For Berlioz the 'Theban harp' was the harp of the ancient world: in *L'enfance du Christ* the young Ishmaelites entertain the Holy Family with such an instrument (*NBE* 11: 179) and in *Les Troyens* the poet Iopas is accompanied by a 'Theban harpist in Egyptian religious costume', according to the stage direction (*NBE* 2b: 546).

Berlioz's interest in the harps of Wales and Ireland was more literary than practical. The harp is a recurrent image in Thomas Moore, whose song 'The Origin of the Harp' Berlioz set for voice and piano in 1829. He probably had no first-hand knowledge of the Welsh triple harp or other chromatic harps without pedals.

When speaking earlier of *martellement*, I mentioned the advantage offered by the new harps being able to tune two strings in unison, on, say, two C♭s, by the double action of the pedals. One of the C♭s is produced by the C♭ string, the other by the B♭ string raised a semitone. Or for two E♭s, one E♭ is produced by the E♭ string, the other by the D♭ string raised by two semitones. It is truly incredible what possibilities today's great harpists can exploit from these double notes, which they call 'synonyms'. M. Parish Alvars, possibly the most extraordinary virtuoso of the harp ever heard, plays figures and arpeggios which appear at first sight to be absolutely impossible but whose difficulty exists solely in the ingenious use of the pedals. He plays passages like Ex. 71, for example, with extraordinary rapidity. The ease of this passage becomes obvious when one realises that the player has only to slide with three fingers from the top strings downwards, without fingering individual notes and as fast as he pleases, since by using synonyms the instrument is tuned in a complete series of minor thirds, producing a chord of a diminished seventh. Instead of a descending scale of Cb major, it has Cʮ–Cʮ–Aʮ–Gb–Gb–Eb–Eb–Cʮ–Cʮ. Notice that the Aʮ alone cannot be doubled and therefore cannot be struck twice. Four synonyms at once are impossible since there are only seven notes in the scale; four synonyms would require eight strings. In addition, remember that the Aʮ can only be obtained on one string, the Ab string, and cannot be reached by its neighbour, Gb, which has only two positions of the pedal to raise it to and can thus rise only two semitones, only as far as Ab. This problem is also encountered on two other strings, the Cb and Fb. There are thus three synonyms unobtainable on the harp: Dʮ, Gʮ and Aʮ. But this defect – and it is a serious one – will vanish when harp-makers are prepared to apply triple action to three of the strings (Cb, Fb and Gb), as M. Parish Alvars has suggested, allowing these strings to be raised by three semitones.

Ex. 71

M. Erard would be ill-advised to allow such an omission on this instrument to persist. It would be characteristic of such an able manufacturer to be the first to fill the gap. Clearly if one does not want to use all the synonyms at once there are other chords available besides diminished sevenths; and these various combinations, which anyone can use making due allowance for the action of the pedals on the strings, will be greatly increased in number when triple action on the Cb, Fb and Gb strings gives the harp the three synonyms which it presently lacks.

Berlioz heard the English harpist Elias Parish Alvars in Dresden and Frankfurt in 1843. 'I give you my word of honour that he is the most prodigious harpist there has ever been', he wrote, 'he is a phenomenon. He is the Liszt of the harp!'[4] His works for the harp are some of the most difficult ever written. It was certainly the encounter with Parish Alvars on that German tour that caused Berlioz to omit a passage about the inadequate potential of the harp when he revised the *Rgm* text for the *Treatise,* and perhaps also to enlarge the technical description of the instrument and its uses.

Despite his admiration for enharmonics, Berlioz never used them himself and remained relatively unadventurous in his harp writing. The illustration of

---

[4] *Cg,* 3, pp. 86–7, and *Memoirs,* 'Travels in Germany', I/5, where Berlioz expounds the use of enharmonics.

enharmonics in Ex. 71 is in fact incorrect in the left-hand part, where the $g\flat'$ should be repeated and the $a\natural$ played only once. Parish Alvars also exhibited the harp glissando, which Berlioz does not mention. Curiously enough he had already written a harp glissando, though he never did so again. This is found in the fragmentary score of *Sardanapale* (1829, *NBE* 6: 218), where a rapid descending D major scale from a''' down to e' is marked 'passing the finger rapidly against the strings'. This was probably intended for a single-action harp.

The triple-action harp, proposed by Parish Alvars and heartily endorsed by Berlioz, was never produced. At the time of writing, the M. Erard he referred to was Sébastien's nephew Pierre.

Other harpists Berlioz heard and admired were Mlle Claudius, a pupil of Parish Alvars, who played in *Roméo et Juliette* in Prague in 1846, and Johanna Pohl, wife of Richard Pohl of Weimar. Berlioz owned a harp in his later years, but its origin is unknown.[5]

Berlioz found, to his dismay, that many German orchestras possessed no harp, so he was often forced to accept a piano as substitute. Täglichsbeck played the harp part in the *Symphonie fantastique* on the piano in Hechingen in 1843. Montag did the same in Weimar on the same tour, and Mendelssohn likewise in Leipzig. When Berlioz conducted the *Marche de pèlerins* from *Harold en Italie* in Lyons in 1845, George Hainl, a cellist, volunteered to learn the harp sufficiently well to play the two notes that movement requires.[6]

Berlioz's most ambitious writing for the harp is found in the Trio for two flutes and harp in *L'enfance du Christ* (*NBE* 11: 180–7). This contains the direction 'étouffez le son', not found elsewhere in his harp parts. Other prominent harp parts are found in the *Symphonie fantastique*, *Harold en Italie*, the *Ariette d'Arlequin* in *Benvenuto Cellini*, the *Strophes* in *Roméo et Juliette*, and the finale of Act II and Iopas's air in Act IV of *Les Troyens*.

Berlioz acknowledged the 'vague feeling of ideal romantic love' he experienced at the sight of a fine harp: 'whenever I saw one I wanted to go down on my knees and embrace it'.[7] Also: 'If I love the harp so, the look of the instrument has a great deal to do with it.'[8] Paired with a cor anglais two harps represent the purest ideal of beauty in the *Ariette d'Arlequin* in *Benvenuto Cellini* (*NBE* 1b: 635–8). A harp also accompanies the cor anglais in a melody in the *Rob Roy* overture, which doubtless embodies a remote romantic love (*NBE* 20: 153);[9] in *Harold en Italie* the same theme pairs the harp with the solo viola. It was appropriate to accompany the *Strophes* in *Roméo et Juliette*, a song about young love, on the harp (*NBE* 18: 38–45).

Other connotations which Berlioz gave the harp include ceremonial (as he points out earlier in the chapter), the modern ballroom and primitive music-making, especially from the ancient world. The combination of flute and harp, made famous by Gounod's *Sapho* in 1851, came to stand for an idealised representation of classical or exotic music: the Trio for two flutes and harp in

---

[5] *Correspondance inédite de Berlioz*, ed. Daniel Bernard (2nd edn, Paris, 1879), p. 56.
[6] *Les grotesques de la musique*, pp. 290–1. [7] *Memoirs*, chapter 59. [8] *Cg*, 4, p. 283.
[9] Roger Fiske speculated that the passage for cor anglais and harp in *Rob Roy* depicted 'a girl singing an old Scotch song to harp accompaniment' and pointed out that although no such scene is found in the novel *Rob Roy*, there is one in *Waverley*. See *Scotland in Music* (Cambridge, 1983), p. 105.

L'enfance du Christ belongs to this incipient vogue. And in *Dans le ciel*, at the end of *La damnation de Faust*, the harps serve their eternal function as the music of Heaven.

Berlioz also shared the Romantics' widespread fascination with the Aeolian harp, but merely as a symbol, not as a real instrument. Its image is found in the *Tableau musical* at the end of *La mort d'Orphée*, when the breeze draws fragmented sounds from Orpheus's broken harp (*NBE* 6: 59). As *La harpe éolienne* the passage recurs with the same imagery in *Lélio*. In the '2ᵉ soirée' of *Les soirées de l'orchestre* a strolling harpist recounts his experiences and experiments drawing sounds from his harp by letting it rest motionless in the wind.

THE GUITAR

This is an instrument suitable for accompanying the voice and for participating in less noisy instrumental pieces, and also for playing solo pieces of varying levels of complexity and in several independent parts. In the hands of a true virtuoso such pieces can give real delight.

It has six strings tuned in fourths and thirds as follows: *e–a–d'–g'–b'–e''*. The following tuning is sometimes used, particularly for pieces in the key of E: *e–b–e'–g♯'–b'–e''*.

The three lowest strings are made of silk covered in silver wire, the upper three of gut. The guitar is a transposing instrument written on the treble clef an octave above its actual pitch, with a range of three octaves and a fifth from *E* (written as *e*) chromatically up to *a''* (written as *a'''*). Major and minor trills can be performed throughout the range.

It is almost impossible to write well for the guitar unless one is a player oneself. Yet most composers who use it are far from any familiarity with it and write things of unnecessary difficulty with no sonority or effect. Nevertheless we will attempt to show how simple accompaniments on the guitar should be written.

In the normal position of the right hand the little finger rests on the body of the instrument, the thumb is assigned to pluck the bottom three strings (*e*, *a* and *d'*), the index finger the *g'* string, the middle finger the *b'*, and the ring finger the top, *e''*, string. Thus if chords of more than four notes are desired the thumb has to slide across one or two of the lower strings while the three other fingers strike the upper three strings directly. In four-note chords each finger plays just the string assigned to it; these fingers change strings only when plucking low chords like those in Ex. 72.
Ex. 72

Since the guitar is above all a harmonic instrument, it is very important to know the chords and hence the arpeggios it can do. Here is a selection in various keys.

We begin, in Ex. 73, with the easiest, namely those which do not need the bar ('barrage'), the method of placing the left index finger transversely across the neck over two, three or four strings as an artificial nut. (The nut is the small transverse section on the neck across which the strings lie and which determines their vibrating length.) Any selection of these is possible. The chords marked * are difficult, the chord marked ** is harder still.

Ex. 73

Flat keys are far more difficult, and they all need the bar. The easiest of these chords are shown in Ex. 74a–b (the chord marked * is difficult).

Ex. 74

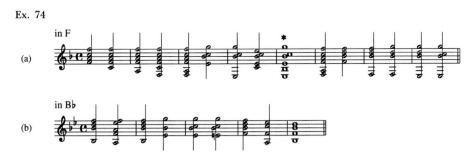

In all chords one must avoid using the first (lowest) and third strings at the same time *without the second,* since the thumb would have to jump over this second string to pass from the first to the third. Such chords are shown in Ex. 75a. It is impossible to strike these chords. But if you add the second string, as in Ex. 75b, they become easy. One must also avoid dominant sevenths in root position with three superimposed thirds such as Ex. 75c since they are almost impossible. Ex. 75d is difficult but possible because of the open *g'.* Ex. 75e is the only such chord which is very easy and sonorous, because of the open *e″*. The chords in Ex. 75f are easy and make a good sequence in any key such as F♯, G, A♭ etc., as in Ex. 75g–j. These chords could clearly sometimes have more than four notes in them in keys which allow a low open string to be added, in A for example, or E or G or F, any key in fact in which one can use one of the three notes *e, a* or *d′* as a bass.

Ex. 75

The sequence in Ex. 76a, which requires a four-string bar, is possible anywhere on the lower two thirds of the fingerboard. This can be taken up in semitones as far as Ex. 76b, the highest point where this fingering can be used.

Ex. 76

(a)

(b)

The arpeggios in Exx. 77a and 77b are extremely effective on the guitar. The two slurred notes at the top in Ex. 77b are played by hooking the top string with the little finger of the left hand. Downward arpeggios (Ex. 77c) are rather awkward, though quite manageable. The same arpeggios in the opposite direction, on the other hand, are very easy. Because of the reversing movement of the thumb on the two lowest notes, Ex. 77d is much more difficult and less effective.

Ex. 77

(a)

(b)

(c)

(d)

Scales slurred in pairs with one note repeated each time (Ex. 78a) are elegant and quite full in sound, especially in the instrument's brighter keys. Scales in thirds are hard at the upper and lower extremities but can be played at moderate tempo; in Ex. 78b the last bar and the second half of the third bar are difficult. The same applies to successions of sixths and octaves.

Ex. 78

(a)

(b)

The repetition of a note two, three, four, even six or eight times can easily be done. Prolonged tremolos on the same note are really only good on the top string, or at any rate on the top three strings, as in Exx. 79a and 79b. The notes marked T are plucked with the thumb, the others with the first and second fingers in alternation. For tremolos the thumb must alternate with the first and second fingers on the same string (Exx. 79c and 79d, which is easier).

Ex. 79

(a)

(b)

(c)

(d)

Harmonics sound very well on the guitar and they are often used to good effect. The best ones are produced by touching the string at the octave, the fifth, the fourth and the major third above the open string. As was explained before in the chapter on bowed strings (see p. 22), touching the string an octave above produces this same octave.

Touching the six open strings at different places produces the following actual sounds: touching the octave produces the octave (Ex. 80a), touching the fifth produces the twelfth (Ex. 80b), touching the fourth produces the fifteenth (Ex. 80c), touching the major third produces the seventeenth (Ex. 80d), and touching the minor third produces the nineteenth, an octave above the twelfth (Ex. 80e). The last group of harmonics, Ex. 80e, is the least sonorous and is hard to produce. It must be understood that the term 'actual sounds' refers to the guitar's pitch, not to actual pitch. In absolute terms, of course, these 'actual sounds' are an octave lower than written, like all guitar notes.

One can also get chromatic and diatonic scales on each string by means of artificial harmonics. For this the left-hand finger presses the note whose upper octave you require; then touch the middle of the string with the right-hand index finger and pluck behind the index finger with the right thumb (Ex. 80f).

Ex. 80

On the *d'* string   On the *g'* string   On the *b'* string On the *e"* string

I must emphasise again that one cannot write guitar pieces in several parts, full of passagework and using all the instrument's capabilities without playing it oneself. To get a good idea of what the great players can do in this sphere one must study the compositions of famous guitarists such as Zani de Ferranti, Huerta, Sor and others.

Since the piano's appearance in all households with the slightest musical pretensions the guitar has become relatively rare everywhere except Spain and Italy. Some great players have cultivated it as a solo instrument (and still do), drawing both fascinating and original sounds from it. Composers scarcely call for it at all, neither in church music nor in the theatre nor in the concert hall. The reason for this is doubtless its weak sonority, which prevents it combining with other instruments or groups of voices of normal strength. Yet its dreamy, melancholy character could be heard more often; its charm is real, and it is not impossible to write for it in such a way as to make that evident. Unlike most instruments the guitar loses by being used in a group; the sound of a dozen guitars in unison is really absurd.

The guitar was Berlioz's own instrument, which explains and excuses his insistence that only those who play it can write for it effectively. He expounds its technicalities with the insight of his own experience. He first studied the guitar in 1819 under Dorant, a local teacher at La Côte-St-André, and a number of transcriptions of romances and airs for voice and guitar survive from that period.[10] No compositions by Berlioz for solo guitar survive, since the variations on Mozart's 'Là ci darem', published in 1828, have disappeared, along with some studies for guitar which are thought to have existed.[11]

In 1829 Berlioz taught the guitar in a girls' orthopædic institution. His experiences were recalled in an article of 1855 entitled 'My way of teaching the guitar':

> In 1829 I had the honour to teach the guitar (I have always been attracted to terrible instruments) in a well-known school for young ladies in the Marais. Three times a week I would emerge from my garret in the Rue de Richelieu and wend my weary way along endless boulevards to near the Place de la Bastille to teach Carulli's *Divertissements*.[12]

He had a guitar with him in Italy in 1831–2, although it is doubtful if he ever played it much thereafter. An instrument from the workshop of Grobert (c. 1794–1869), now in the Musée de Musique, Paris, bears Berlioz's signature, but it came into his possession later. It was loaned by Vuillaume to Paganini (who has also signed it), then returned to Vuillaume, who gave it to Berlioz, who in turn presented it to the Paris Conservatoire. A guitar was among his effects

---

[10] Holoman, *Catalogue*, pp. 4–15; *NBE*, 22b.
[11] They were mentioned by Philip Bone in his *The Guitar and Mandolin* (London, 1914), p. 35.
[12] *Jd*, 8 June 1855.

at his death.[13] An anonymous drawing of the period supposedly shows Berlioz playing the guitar.[14]

He employed the guitar occasionally in his larger works. The eighth of the *Huit scènes de Faust*, Mephistopheles's *Sérénade*, is for guitar and voice. The final six-note chord of each stanza Berlioz marks 'very loud, with the thumb alone; dampen the sound with the arm' (*NBE* 5: 98). When adapted for *La damnation de Faust* the accompaniment was re-scored for pizzicato strings.

In *Benvenuto Cellini* at least four guitars in two parts accompany the maskers in Act I (*NBE* 1a: 136–64) and two or four guitars accompany the workmen's song 'Bienheureux les matelots' in the last Tableau (*NBE* 1c: 1013–24). This was based on a melody Berlioz had heard sung in Italy to the accompaniment of a mandolin, and the strumming 3/8 rhythm of the guitars' accompaniment in the opera may also resemble what he heard then.[15] The first guitar plays two-note chords only: first and second fingers take the repeated notes of the top line, the thumb takes the lower line (on the g' and b' strings). The second guitarist is instructed to remove his e'' string and strike the remaining five strings with the fingernails to produce a strumming effect.

Berlioz next wrote for the guitar in *Roméo et Juliette*. The *Strophes* for contralto solo were originally scored with a guitar accompaniment (*NBE* 18: 387), in figuration like an inverted version of Ex. 77a. Before the first performance, though, the guitar was replaced by a harp (see Ex. 69). The guitar was used again in *Béatrice et Bénédict*, both for the *Improvisation et chœur à boire* and for the *Chœur lointain* (*NBE* 3: 195–207, 253–4), the former employing the same strumming rhythm as that in *Benvenuto Cellini*, the latter approaching closest of all his guitar music to the 'dreamy, melancholy character' he ascribes to the instrument.

All his guitar music (except the transcriptions) is in the key of E or G. Precedents for his use of the guitar in opera are found in Grétry's *Le rival confident* (1788), Cherubini's *Les abencérages* (1813) and Weber's *Abu Hassan* (1811) and *Oberon* (1826).

Berlioz's instructions in the *Treatise* are not free of error. Exx. 75a and 75g are both printed incorrectly there, and the small difference between Exx. 76a and 76b suggests an inconsistency. The chords he marks as 'difficult' in Exx. 73c, 73d and 74a in fact hold no terrors for guitarists. Although he suggests that the slurred notes in Ex. 77b should be played with the little finger, the third finger would in practice be more likely to be used. And the extensive table of harmonics, none of which he ever wrote himself, belongs more to the realm of theory, especially in Exx. 80d and 80e, than of practice.

Berlioz names three celebrated guitarists as worthy models. Marco Aurelio Zani de Ferranti (1800–78) was a pupil of Paganini whom Berlioz met in Brussels in 1842.[16] He wrote copious criticism, always enthusiastic about Berlioz's music. Don A. Trinidad Huerta y Katurla (1804–75) spent a few years in Paris in the early 1830s. He played in two of Berlioz's concerts in 1833 before returning to

---

[13] Peter Bloom, 'Berlioz's furniture: a closer look', *Berlioz Society Bulletin*, 153 (1995), p. 9.

[14] It is reproduced in Jacques Barzun, *Berlioz and the Romantic Century* (Boston, 1950), 2, facing p. 278, and in Holoman, *Berlioz*, p. 121.

[15] *Memoirs*, chapter 38.   [16] *Ibid.*, chapter 51; *Cg*, 3, p. 28; *Jd*, 18 February 1859.

Spain. Berlioz reviewed a return visit to Paris in the *Journal des débats* on 16 February 1840. Fernando Sor (1778–1839) had been settled in Paris since 1826. He played in Berlioz's concert on 6 June 1833. Berlioz may also have heard two celebrated Italian guitarists, Ferdinando Carulli (1770–1841) and Matteo Carcassi (1792–1853), and a Spaniard, Dionysio Aguado (1784–1849), all of whom settled in Paris. He might even have heard Paganini play the guitar.

The question whether Berlioz's experience on the guitar affected his harmonic style has been the subject of considerable debate so well summarised elsewhere that we need not encroach upon it here.[17]

THE MANDOLIN

The mandolin is today almost obsolete, which is a pity, since its timbre, for all its thin nasal quality, is rather piquant and original with many possible applications. There are several kinds of mandolin. The most common has four double strings, that is to say four pairs of unison strings, tuned like the violin in fifths to g–d'–a'–e''. It is written on the treble clef. The e'' strings are made of gut, the a' of steel, the d' of brass and the g of gut covered with silver wire. The range of the mandolin is almost three octaves, from g chromatically up to e'''. It is a melodic instrument rather than a harmonic one. Since its strings are set in motion by a quill or bark plectrum held in the player's left hand, it can certainly manage four-note chords such as those in Ex. 81, obtained by passing the plectrum rapidly across the strings.

Ex. 81

But the effect of these simultaneous groups of notes is pretty wretched. The mandolin's true character and capabilities are only to be found in melodic accompaniments of the kind written by Mozart in Act II of *Don Giovanni*. The mandolin is so neglected today that whenever *Don Giovanni* is staged there is always embarrassment about performing this serenade. Even though any guitarist, or ordinary violinist even, could find his way round the mandolin's fingerboard in a matter of days, the intentions of the great masters are generally held in so little regard (ever since the old ways became subject to every kind of misrepresentation) that almost every theatre, even the Paris Opéra, the last place on earth where such liberties should be taken, presumes to play the mandolin part in *Don Giovanni* on

---

[17] The matter is fully summarised by Julian Rushton in *The Musical Language of Berlioz* (Cambridge, 1983), pp. 56–60. See also Paul J. Dallman, 'Influences and use of the guitar in the music of Hector Berlioz' (MA thesis, University of Maryland, 1972).

pizzicato violins or guitars. The timbre of these instruments has none of the finesse or bite of what they are replacing; Mozart knew perfectly well what he was doing when he chose the mandolin to accompany his hero's sensuous song.

Since the plectrum is always held in the right hand, 'left hand' must be a simple slip of the pen.

Berlioz encountered the mandolin in Italy. Chapter 38 of the *Memoirs* describes a peasant serenade at Subiaco sung to the accompaniment of 'an immense mandolin, a bagpipe, and a small iron instrument like a triangle which they call *stimbalo*'. He never used the instrument himself. He may have known that Grétry's *L'amant jaloux* (1778), as well as *Don Giovanni*, requires a mandolin, although in his notice of a revival of that opera in 1850 he makes no mention of it.[18] When a mandolin player was needed for *Don Giovanni* at the Odéon in 1827, Berlioz was impressed that Seghers, a violinist, learned the instrument within a week expressly for those performances; why could the Opéra not do the same?[19]

The *Rgm* entry on the mandolin is followed by a further section on the lute:

> As for the lute I have never yet seen an artist who can play the passage where Sebastian Bach has used it in his Passion Oratorio, and I very much doubt if one could be found in Paris. Is that not a shame? Should such agreeable instruments be allowed to disappear, especially when they have been given famous parts by the greatest composers? The purpose of the Conservatoire is surely to conserve!

It is remarkable that Berlioz was familiar with the instrumentation of the *St John Passion,* which has a part for a lute. Its full score had been published in 1834 but it was not performed in France until 1902. He heard part of the *St Matthew Passion* in Berlin in 1843.

[18] *Jd*, 25 September 1850.   [19] *Rgm*, 16 May 1841.

3

Strings with keyboard

THE PIANO

The piano is a keyboard instrument with metal strings set in vibration by hammers. Its present range is six octaves and a fourth from C' chromatically up to f''''''. It is written on two different clefs at once: the bass clef is assigned to the left hand and the treble clef to the right hand. Sometimes the low or high range of a passage given to one or other hand requires the use of two bass clefs or two treble clefs. Trills are possible on all notes of the range. Either hand can strike chords of four or even five notes, provided they are as compressed in range as possible (Ex. 82a). They can also be arpeggiated in different ways. Stretches of a tenth are possible, but they are easier if the third and perhaps the octave are left out. They then look like Ex. 82b.

Ex. 82

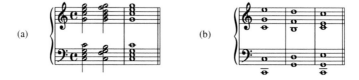

(a)   (b)

One may write for the piano in four or even five real parts if care is taken not to let the outer notes in either hand range wider apart than an octave, or at most a ninth. Alternatively one may use the sustaining pedal, which raises the dampers and allows the sound to be sustained without the player's finger remaining on the note, thus allowing the parts to be more widely separated. Ex. 83a is in four parts, not requiring the pedal; Ex. 83b does require the pedal.

Ex. 83

(a)

(b)

The sign * indicates the reapplication of the dampers by releasing the pedal. It is normally marked at the moment of harmonic change to prevent the vibration of notes in the previous chord continuing through the next one. In view of the excessive prolongation of each sound, one must avoid altered appoggiaturas and passing notes in the middle range when requiring the sustaining pedal, for such notes are sustained like the rest, causing intolerable discords in the harmony where they do not belong. Only at the upper extremity of the keyboard, where the very short strings resonate less, are these melodic decorations acceptable.

One sometimes requires the hands to cross, either passing the right hand under the left or the left hand over the right, as in Ex. 84.

Ex. 84

Largo

The number of combinations of this kind exploiting the piano's various possibilities is very considerable. It would be quite impossible to show them all here. One can form a fair idea of the point which the art of piano playing has reached today by studying the compositions of the great virtuosi, those of Liszt especially. These reveal that the frontiers of the instrument are unknown and that new prodigies achieved every day by its exponents seem to push them further back.

As with the harp there are times when it is better not to let the hands come too close together, in arpeggios for example. An arpeggio like the one in Ex. 85a would be rather awkward. It is far better to write it as in Ex. 85b.

Ex. 85

Diatonic and chromatic scales for two hands in thirds, on the other hand, are easy (Ex. 86a). These two-part scales can be played by a single hand, though they are difficult at a fast tempo. Furthermore one can write chains of six-threes in three parts for both hands, as long as the keys have few sharps or flats (Ex. 86b).

Ex. 86

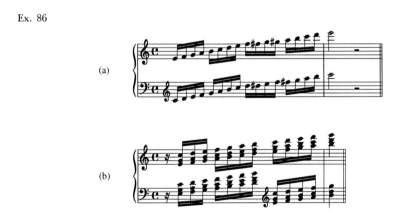

To expound the technique of the piano was, as Berlioz freely acknowledged, an impossible task. Of all instruments it was the most played, the most admired and the most rapidly developing at the time he was writing. So he confined himself almost entirely to the disposition of the hands, omitting all discussion of fingering or touch. He was doubtless conscious of his precept applied to the guitar: that only players of the instruments can write for it well, and he was no pianist. Nevertheless he wished to instruct composers how to write for it, especially if, as he goes on to propose, they wish to use it as an orchestral instrument.

There are some shortcomings in his instruction, however. The chords in Ex. 82b are not well laid out and are hardly to be recommended, especially the right-hand tenths. He wrote no right-hand tenths himself. *Au cimetière* (*B&H* 17: 170) requires a wide left-hand tenth *E-B-g♯*, although elsewhere such stretches are shown arpeggiated, as for example in *Le matin* and *Petit oiseau* (*B&H* 17: 233, 236). Ex. 83 suggests that he viewed the sustaining pedal merely as a means of liberating the fingers for leaps, not as an aid to general sonority or for creating a sense of legato. His own piano music contains pedal markings, but they are sparingly used and confined to the support of chordal harmony. He suggests hardly any pedalling at all in Ex. 84, for example, although most players would use it. They would also cross the right hand over the left to play it, not under, as he suggests. Hand-crossing appears only once in his music, in *La belle voyageuse* (*B&H* 17: 20). The error shown in Ex. 85a was made in the first version of *La tempête* (*NBE* 7: 218), where both pianists have their hands too close together; this was corrected in the revised version. The same early text of *La tempête* has a chromatic scale in thirds similar to Ex. 86a (*NBE* 7: 223).

In view of the degree of perfection achieved by our ingenious manufacturers nowadays one may regard the piano in two ways: either as an orchestral instrument or as itself a complete little orchestra. Only once has it ever been thought appropriate to use it in the orchestra on the same terms as other instruments, that is to say contributing to the ensemble those qualities which belong to it and to it alone. Certain passages in Beethoven's concertos should have drawn the attention of composers in this direction, for they have doubtless all admired in the Fifth Piano Concerto the marvellous effect of slow broken chords in both hands in octaves in the piano's upper range against the theme on flute, clarinet and bassoon and the off-beat chords of the strings. With this accompaniment the piano's sonority is quite enchanting, full of freshness and calm, the very model of grace.

The function of the unique case I mentioned just now is quite different. For a chorus of airy spirits the composer has used two pianos (four hands) to accompany the voices. The lower hands play a rapid upward arpeggio in triplets, answered in the second half of the bar by another arpeggio, this time descending, on piccolo, flute and clarinet in three parts, over which the two upper hands on the piano flutter a double trill in octaves. No other known instrument could produce this kind of harmonious chirruping which the piano can do easily and which the sylph-like character of the piece here requires (Ex. 87).

Ex. 87

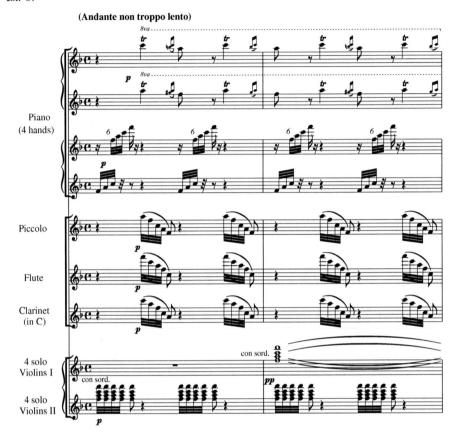

The *Rgm* section on the piano, reproduced intact in the *Treatise,* does not name the work shown in Ex. 87; it is only the heading on the example printed in full score which informs the reader that is from the Fantasy on the *Tempête* from *Lélio.* In writing the *Rgm* text, too, he seems to have been relying on his memory: the descending arpeggio is on the second beat, not the second half of the bar; the upper two hands flutter in thirds, not octaves. He speaks also of two pianos, while the musical example shows only one. This was always a matter of confusion, since he designed the work with two piano parts and normally referred to them ambiguously as 'deux pianos à quatre mains'.[1]

It was almost certainly from Berlioz's first hearing of Beethoven's Fifth Piano Concerto that the idea of using the piano as an orchestral instrument came to him. This was on 1 November 1829, played by Hiller. The Overture (later Fantasy) on *La tempête* was composed a year later, when he was in thrall to the pianist Camille Moke, previously attached to Hiller. 'When she amuses herself flitting over the keyboard you would think an army of fairies was dancing on the keys.'[2] The opening passage of *La tempête* evokes Ariel (Berlioz's name for Camille) and her airy spirits.

[1] See *NBE,* 7, pp. xvi–xvii.   [2] *Cg,* 1, p. 359.

Berlioz was right to claim this as the first orchestral piece to use the piano in this way, although we should remember that the *Symphonie fantastique* always (or nearly always) employed either one, two or 'several' pianos to represent the bells in the last movement and that Berlioz was frequently compelled to accept the piano as a substitute for the harp. But it was new to require the piano for the sake of its sonority. Before the piano came into its own as an orchestral instrument in the twentieth century, there were one or two rare examples by French and Russian composers. Gounod, for example, used a piano in *Philémon et Baucis* (1860) as part of the orchestral texture accompanying an offstage chorus, 'Filles d'Athor, folles bacchantes', although Berlioz, in his notice of the opera, regrettably had no comment on this.[3] Saint-Saëns, who arranged the piano reduction of *Lélio* for publication, has a curious entry for two pianists in his Third Symphony. Duparc used a piano to evoke the bell in his orchestral song *La vague et la cloche* (1871). The piano has a recurrent role in Russian opera, usually to evoke the gusli, the bandura, or bells (Glinka in *Ruslan i Lyudmila*, Musorgsky in *Boris Godunov* and Rimsky-Korsakov in *May Night* and *Snegurochka*).

But as soon as the piano tries to get away from gentle effects and battles with the orchestra, it disappears completely. It must accompany or be accompanied, unless it is used in large numbers, like harps. Such an idea is not to be lightly dismissed, I am convinced, although there would always be great problems getting a dozen grand pianos to play with a large orchestra because of the space they need.

Considered as a small self-contained orchestra the piano should have its own instrumentation. It does already, in fact, and this art is part of the pianist's equipment. It is often the pianist who has to judge whether to bring out certain parts while others remain in the background, whether to play a middle voice loud while upper decorations are treated lightly and the bass line is subdued; he has to judge the advantage of changing fingers or the suitability in a particular melody of using just the thumb. By writing for his own instrument he knows when to compress or thin out the harmony, the various degrees of spread an arpeggio can have and the different sonorities they offer. He has to learn above all how to use the pedals only when they are needed. On this topic we should say that leading composers for the piano have never failed to indicate with care and precision the places where the sustaining pedal is to be applied and released. It is therefore quite wrong when virtuosi, including some of the most able, persist in taking no notice of these markings, keeping the dampers raised almost throughout and forgetting that this results in incompatible harmonies being sustained against each other in the most discordant fashion. This is the deplorable abuse of an excellent thing. This is noise and confusion, not music. It is, moreover, the natural result of an unacceptable tendency for virtuosi great and small, singers and instrumentalists, always

---

[3] *Jd*, 23 February 1860.

to put what they take to be the interest of their personality first. They have scant regard for the inviolable deference owed by every player to every composer and for the tacit but real undertaking, made by the former to his audience, to transmit the thoughts of the latter intact, whether he is honouring a mediocre composer by acting as his interpreter or whether he is privileged to render the immortal thoughts of a genius. In both cases the player who obeys the whim of the moment and lets himself run in the face of the composer's intentions should remember that the composer of whatever work he is playing has probably given a hundred times more thought to the placing and duration of particular effects, to the indication of this or that tempo, to the final design of a melody or a rhythm, and to the choice of chords or instruments, than he, the player, has to contradicting it all. One cannot protest too strongly, in whatever circumstances, against this stupid arrogance too often displayed by instrumentalists, singers and conductors. Such bad habits are not only in themselves ridiculous, they are likely, if care is not taken, to lead art into unspeakable disorder and to bring on disastrous consequences. It is up to composers and critics to get together and refuse to put up with it.

A pedal used much less frequently than the one that raises the dampers is the 'una corda' pedal, treated with enchanting effect by Beethoven and others. Not only does it provide an excellent contrast with the normal sound of the piano and with the grand effect of the sustaining pedal, it is also especially useful for vocal accompaniment when the singer has a weak voice or, more often, to give the performance a character of gentle intimacy. It is indicated by the words 'pédale unicorde' or in Italian 'una corda'. It works by preventing the hammers from striking two of the three strings that sound in unison for each note, as all good instruments are built today. Only the third string then vibrates, reducing the sound by two thirds and changing its character in a remarkable way.

For Berlioz's proposals to assemble thirty pianos in an orchestra, see below, p. 330.

'Una corda' markings are common in Berlioz's piano music, especially in the songs, always cancelled by 'tre corde', '3 cordes', or 'ôtez la pédale'. The autograph of the *Tempête* fantasy has the indication 'pédale céleste' on the first piano part, referring to the 'moderator' pedal device that dampened the sound by inserting a cloth or felt between the hammer and the string.

Berlioz's regard for the piano was at best equivocal. 'The piano! At the thought of that terrible instrument my hair stands on end and I feel a tingling in my toes; just in writing the word I am entering volcanic terrain,' he wrote in 1855 after the experience of judging over ninety pianos a day for several weeks at the Exposition Universelle.[4] A story about a piano playing the Mendelssohn G minor Concerto

[4] *Les grotesques de la musique*, pp. 71–80.

of its own accord after a whole day of examinations at the Conservatoire is told in *Les soirées de l'orchestre*.[5] Piano manufacturers and pianists exasperated him, although a number of virtuosi, notably Hiller, Liszt and Heller (not to mention Camille Moke), were his close friends, and he was a habitué of the Erard circle. He admired Erard's pianos above all and possessed a fine rosewood grand, a gift of the Erards.[6] A friend from Berlioz's first years in Paris recalled his having a 'terrible harpsichord' in his room, which may or may not be true.[7] At all events he possessed a piano in the late 1820s, having not learnt it in his youth. 'My father would not let me take up the piano; otherwise I should no doubt have turned into a formidable pianist in company with forty thousand others... I can only offer up my gratitude to chance, which taught me perforce to compose freely and in silence and thus saved me from the tyranny of keyboard habits.'[8]

There is no music by Berlioz for solo piano, but there are nearly forty songs and choruses with piano accompaniment and he made his own piano arrangements of some larger works. For the four-hand arrangement of the overture to *Les francs-juges* he acknowledged help from pianist friends, including Chopin. In general he disliked four-hand arrangements of symphonic works and preferred solo transcriptions for their clarity.[9] He made the piano reductions of *Les Troyens* and *Béatrice et Bénédict* and may also have done so for *La damnation de Faust* and parts of *Benvenuto Cellini*. His piano writing is in general simple, broad and lacking in mechanical figurations and 'brillante' passagework, although he was extremely fond of tremolos and came close to a true virtuoso style in one or two songs, notably the *Chant guerrier*, the *Chanson à boire* and the *Elégie* from the *Neuf mélodies* of 1829.

The *Rgm* text on the piano was preceded by a passage on the dulcimer ('tympanon'):

Of the instruments whose strings are struck, the piano is the only one in current use, not counting that kind of dulcimer fitted with iron or copper strings like a piano and struck with small hammers. It is quite often to be heard in Paris; destitutes and vagrants still play it in public squares, more to show off their skill in running the hammers over the strings than to attract listeners to an instrument whose harsh nasal sound carries only a short distance.

[5] 'Le piano enragé', in *Les soirées de l'orchestre*, pp. 271–81.   [6] *Cg*, 4, pp. 65, 73.
[7] Adolphe Laferrière, *Mémoires*, 1st series (Paris, 1876), p. 54.
[8] *Memoirs*, chapter 4.   [9] *Cg*, 5, p. 266.

4

Wind: introduction

Before we study the individual members of this large family of instruments, we must define our musical terms as clearly as possible, as far as they relate to the different tessitura of certain instruments, the transpositions that these differences necessitate, the traditional way of writing for them, and the classifications they come under.

We must first establish a demarcation line between those instruments whose pitch is given by the musical notation and those whose pitch is higher or lower than the written note. This distinction gives the following two categories:

Non-transposing instruments (sounding at notated pitch)	Transposing instruments (sounding at other than the notated pitch)
Violin	
Viola	
Viola d'amore	
Cello	Double bass
Flute	All non-standard flutes
Oboe	Cor anglais
Clarinet in C	All other clarinets
Bassoon	Tenoroon
Russian bassoon	Contrabassoon
Horn in high C	All other horns
Cornet in C	All other cornets
Trumpet in C	All other trumpets
Alto trombone	Alto valve trombone
Tenor trombone	
Bass trombone	
Ophicleide in C	All other ophicleides
Bombardon	Serpent
Bass tuba	

Harp	Guitar
Piano	
Organ	
Voices (when they are written on their respective clefs, not when they use the treble clef at the wrong octave)	Tenors and basses (when they are written on the treble clef, sounding an octave lower)
Timpani	
Bells	
Antique cymbals	
Jeux de timbres	
Glockenspiel	
Keyboard harmonica	Steel-bar keyboard

It will be seen from this table that if all non-transposing instruments designated 'in C' sound at the written pitch, then those that have no key indication, such as the violin, oboe or flute, are in exactly the same category. From the composer's point of view they are like instruments in C. The classification of some wind instruments by the natural resonance of the tube has had the most singular and absurd consequences: it has made writing for transposing instruments a most complicated business and deprived musical terminology of all logic. So we must go into this practice here and attempt to bring order where little has prevailed hitherto.

Players sometimes refer to the tenor trombone as the 'Bb' trombone, the alto trombone as the 'Eb' trombone, and, most commonly, the standard flute as the 'flute in D'. These terms are correct insofar as the tubes of these two trombones with the slide in first position give, for the one, the notes of a Bb chord, and for the other the notes of an Eb chord; the standard flute with its holes and keys all closed similarly plays the note D. But since players pay no heed to the resonance of the tube and actually produce the written pitch (a tenor trombone's C is a C and not a Bb, an alto trombone's C is a C, not an Eb, a flute's C is a C, not a D), it is clear that these instruments are not, or are no longer, in the category of *transposing* instruments and that they belong therefore to the category of *non-transposing* instruments; they are deemed to be in C, like oboes, C clarinets, C horns, C cornets and C trumpets, and they need no key designation, not even that of C.

With this in mind, it will be seen how important it is not to call the standard flute a flute in D. The other, higher flutes, being classified according to the difference between their pitches and that of the ordinary flute, instead of being called simply 'tierce flute' or 'ninth flute', which would at least have avoided any confusion of terminology, have come to be called 'flute in F' and 'flute in E♭'. See what that leads to! In a full score the little E♭ clarinet, whose written C sounds E♭, can play the same part as a tierce flute, said to be 'in F', and these two instruments bearing the label of different keys are actually in unison. One of them is incorrectly described, is it not? And is it not absurd to adopt a system of nomenclature and key systems just for the flutes, different from the practice adopted by all other instruments?

From this there follows a principle which I put forward to prevent any misunderstanding: the key of C is the point of reference to be taken when specifying the keys of transposing instruments. The natural resonance of the tube of wind instruments should never be taken into account. Every instrument which does not transpose or which transposes by an octave, whose written C gives a sounding C, is considered as being in C.

Consequently, if an instrument of the same family is pitched above or below the pitch of the standard member of the family, this difference will be defined by the relationship between it and the key of C. Thus the violin, the flute and the oboe, which play in unison with the C clarinet, the C trumpet and the C horn, are *in C*, and if one uses a violin, a flute or an oboe pitched higher than the standard instruments of that name, such a violin, flute or oboe, playing in unison with D clarinets or D trumpets, is *in D*.

From this I conclude that the old-fashioned way of designating members of the flute family must be abolished, no longer calling the tierce flute 'flute in F', but 'flute in E♭' instead, since its C gives E♭; and not calling the ninth flute and minor second flute 'flute in E♭', but 'flute (or piccolo) in D♭', since its C gives D♭; and so on for the other keys.

Berlioz might have been expected to introduce the family of wind instruments with some historical or organological background, making the distinction between those with reeds and those without, those with mouthpieces and those without, and so on, but he concentrates instead on the question of transposing instruments, with some heat. This was evidently generated by exasperating personal experience, almost certainly in his performances of the *Grande symphonie funèbre et triomphale*, which, between 1840 and the publication of the *Treatise*, he had conducted a number of times, in Brussels and Dresden as well as in Paris, and it was published only a few months earlier than the *Treatise* itself. This is the only work in which Berlioz called for tierce flutes in E♭ and piccolos in D♭, both being common in French military bands of the time. The printed parts have, on the piccolo part, 'incorrectly called flute in E♭', and on the tierce flute part 'incorrectly called flute in F' (see *NBE* 19: XI).

At the equivalent point in the *Rgm* articles, written in 1841 before he had been to Germany, a quite different introduction is found:

Wind instruments, made of wood, leather or brass, with or without reeds, with keys, pistons or cylinders, constitute large families which are nearly all incomplete in the present state of orchestras today, thanks partly to the many gaps in the Conservatoire's teaching. In Paris we lack not only a host of individual instruments which could easily be introduced at no great cost but also some which are found in Germany, some which we know, some which the great composers have acknowledged and used in their masterpieces, and some no self-respecting orchestra should ever be without. But let us not jump ahead. This will become all too evident as we proceed with our examination of these various groups.

To the lists of transposing and non-transposing instruments Berlioz made some late additions in proof in 1843: Russian bassoon, bombardon, tuba and keyboard harmonica in the former category, the simple cornet, serpent and steel-bar keyboard ('clavier à barres d'acier') in the latter: the simple cornet was removed from the 1855 edition.

It is odd to read that basses, as well as tenors, were accustomed to reading from the treble clef; this practice is not found in any of Berlioz's own publications.

5

Wind with reeds

There is a distinction between the families of double-reed and single-reed instruments. The first has five members: oboe, cor anglais, bassoon, tenoroon and contrabassoon.

THE OBOE

The oboe's range is two octaves and a sixth from b chromatically up to f'''. It is written on the treble clef. The two highest notes, e''' and f''', must be used with great caution, the f''' especially being risky when approached abruptly. Some oboes have a low $b\flat$, but since this note has not been widely adopted, it is as well to avoid it. The Boehm system will overcome all the fingering problems in the present-day oboe, including rapid passages between $c\sharp''$ and $d\sharp''$ (or $d\flat''$ and $e\flat''$) and between $f\sharp'$ and $g\sharp'$. Trills using these intervals, and some others, are therefore impossible, or very difficult and ineffective; those in Ex. 88a are difficult, those in Ex. 88b are impossible, including all trills higher than the last of Ex. 88b.

Ex. 88

The oboe, like any other instrument, is much happier in keys without too many sharps or flats. It should not be given melodies outside the range from g' up to e'''. Notes below or above this range are either flabby and thin or harsh and shrill, and all of poor quality. Rapid figures, whether chromatic or diatonic, can be played well enough on the oboe, but they are awkward in effect and can be almost comic; arpeggios are the same. The need for such writing must be exceedingly rare, and we have never experienced it, we admit. Whatever virtuosi may attempt in their fantasias and variations scarcely proves the contrary. The oboe is above all a melodic instrument; it has a rustic character, full of tenderness, of bashfulness even.

In a tutti the oboe is always employed without regard for its special timbre, since it is lost in the overall sound and its distinctive expressive quality cannot be heard. The same applies, it must be said at once, to most other wind instruments, the only exceptions being those which are too noisy or whose timbre is strikingly unusual. Such instruments cannot simply be treated as ordinary members of a wind band without riding roughshod over art and common sense. I refer to trombones, ophicleides, contrabassoons and, often, trumpets and cornets.

Berlioz used the oboe's full range from b to f''' in his scores, although there were occasions when he avoided the extremes. In *Le roi Lear* (*NBE* 20: 92) the second oboe avoids c' even in a *fortissimo*, although bottom b is freely used in his later works. In adapting *Cléopâtre* for the *Chœur d'ombres* in *Lélio* Berlioz added a low b for the oboe where little else was changed (*NBE* 6: 167 and 7: 11). His normal top note is e''', although f''' is occasionally found, sometimes 'approached abruptly', as in the *Fête* in *Roméo et Juliette* (*NBE* 18: 119, 123), or in a hectic series of high figurations in the *Marche marocaine*.

The instrument's mechanism was undergoing such rapid development at the time he wrote the *Treatise* that many of the trills he designated as 'difficult' or 'impossible' became possible almost immediately. But he had already asked for the 'difficult' $c''-d''$ trill in the *Symphonie fantastique* (*NBE* 16: 156–7) and the 'difficult' $e''-f\sharp''$ trill in *Benvenuto Cellini* (*NBE* 1a: 121) and *Roméo et Juliette* (*NBE* 18: 12–14). A very exposed example of this latter trill is found in the *Chasse royale et orage* in *Les Troyens* (*NBE* 2b: 444), suggesting that by 1857 it no longer carried any risks. An expressive phrase dwelling on $f\sharp'-g\sharp'$ in Act III of *Les Troyens* (*NBE* 2b: 367) suggests that that interval held no more terrors either. Trills above $c\sharp'''$ ('impossible') are found in *Roméo et Juliette* (*NBE* 18: 12), *Le chasseur danois* (*NBE* 13: 93) and the *Marche marocaine*.

Following his precept, Berlioz is more likely to give arpeggios and rapid figures to flutes and clarinets than to oboes; good examples are the opening section of *La tempête* in *Lélio* (*NBE* 7: 70–86) and the *Chant des chemins de fer* (*NBE* 12b: 48–9). On the other hand the *Te deum* has the oboes playing arpeggios with the rest of the wind (*NBE* 10: 28), and the *Évocation* in *La damnation de Faust* (*NBE* 12b: 277–9) requires angular figuration for its burlesque effect. A curious case is *L'île inconnu* (*NBE* 13: 87), where flute, oboe and bassoon take turns to assist the second clarinet in a series of arpeggios.

A glissando is required of the oboe in the last movement of the *Symphonie fantastique* (*NBE* 16: 116–17, 119), descending from c''' to c''.

The *Rgm* text gives 'basset horns', not 'cornets' (in the final sentence).

The oboe's special characteristics convey candour, naive grace, senti-mental delight, or the suffering of weaker creatures. It expresses this mar-vellously well in cantabile. It has the capacity to express agitation to a certain degree, but one should be careful not to stretch it as far as cries of passion or the splutter of rage or threats or heroics, since its little bitter-sweet voice becomes quite ineffective and absurd. Some great composers, including Mozart, have made this mistake. Their scores contain passages whose passionate and martial character contrasts strangely with the sound of the oboes that play them, and the result is not just a misjudged effect but a shocking misalliance between stage and orchestra and between melody and instrumentation. A march melody, however direct, however beautiful, however noble, loses its nobility, its directness and its beauty when given to the oboes. It would lose a little less if given to the flutes and would lose almost nothing if played by clarinets. If it is absolutely unavoidable to use oboes in such a piece as I have described, to give more body to the wind section and more strength to the group of wind instruments already play-ing, they must at least be written for in such a way that their timbre, which is at odds with this kind of style, is completely covered by that of other in-struments and is indistinguishable in the ensemble. The oboe's low notes, which are most unpleasant when exposed, can be appropriate in strange, mournful harmonies, coupled with the bottom notes of the clarinet and the low d', e', f' and g' of flutes and cors anglais.

Gluck and Beethoven had a wonderful understanding of this precious instrument; both owe the profound emotion generated by some of their finest pages to the oboe. For Gluck I need only mention the oboe solo in Agamemnon's air in *Iphigénie en Aulide*, 'Peuvent-ils ordonner qu'un père' (Ex. 89a). Could those innocent cries, those endless pleas, growing ever more intense, belong to any other instrument but the oboe?... And the famous ritornello to the air in *Iphigénie en Tauride*, 'O malheureuse Iphigénie!' (Ex. 89b). And the childlike cry of the orchestra when Alceste, in the middle of her outpouring of heroic devotion, is suddenly seized by the memory of her young sons and breaks in with the phrase 'Eh! pourrai-je vivre sans toi?' The heartrending exclamation 'O mes enfants!' is her response to this touching instrumental plea (Ex. 89c). Then the dissonance of a minor second in Armide's air, to the words 'Sauvez-moi de l'amour' (Ex. 89d). All these are sublime, not just for the dramatic conception, the profundity of expression or the grandeur and beauty of the melody, but also for the instrumentation and for the composer's unerring choice of the oboes from among a crowd of other instruments quite incapable of producing such effects.

Berlioz printed only two of these examples in his *Treatise*, namely Exx. 89a and 89d. Of Ex. 89a he asks: 'Could this be played by anything other than an oboe?'

Ex. 89

(a)

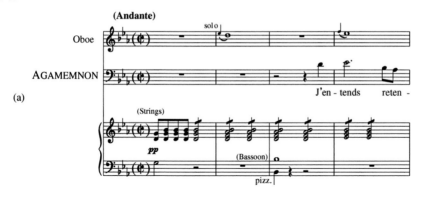

tir   dans mon sein   le   cri   plain- tif   de la na - tu - re

(b)

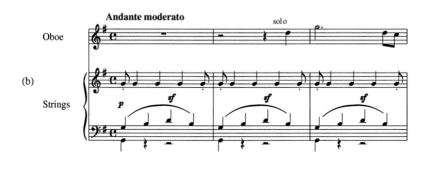

Yet all the Gluck sources give these entries to a flute and an oboe in unison.[1] Similarly Berlioz recalled the passage from *Alceste* (Ex. 89c) as an oboe entry, even though many sources give it to oboes and clarinets in unison.[2]

Beethoven preferred the oboe's joyful sound: witness the solo in the scherzo of the Pastoral Symphony, the one in the scherzo of the Ninth Symphony, the one in the first movement of the Fourth Symphony, and so on. But he was just as successful when he gave it sad or desolate music. This can be observed of the solo in the minor in the second reprise of the finale of the 'Eroica', and above all in the aria in *Fidelio* where Florestan,

[1] Gluck, *Werke*, 1/5b, p. 588.   [2] Gluck, *Werke*, 1/7, pp. 114, 424.

dying of starvation and delirious with suffering, believes he has his weeping family around him; his cries of pain mingle with the broken wailing of the oboe (Ex. 90).

Ex. 90

Berlioz accepted a pair of oboes wholeheartedly as a part of the modern orchestra, although he felt free to omit them on occasions, most strikingly in the cantata *Le cinq mai*, and also in the *Méditation religieuse* and the *Chanson de brigands* (in *Lélio*). A number of orchestral songs require only one oboe, as does *Un bal*, the second movement of the *Symphonie fantastique*.

The *Treatise* suggests a number of characterisations which Berlioz's scores illustrate. The rustic quality of the oboe is found in *Paysans sous les tilleuls* in the *Huit scènes de Faust* (altered in *La damnation de Faust*), in the *Scène aux champs* in the *Symphonie fantastique*, and in the music of the Abruzzi peasants in *Harold en Italie*. The on-stage 'flûtes antiques' in Act I of *Les Troyens*, being both rustic and ancient, are represented by oboes. Tenderness and shyness may be attributed to some of Berlioz's heroines depicted by oboe solos: Teresa's cavatina in *Benvenuto Cellini*, Héro's air in *Béatrice et Bénédict*, and perhaps Cordelia (if it is she) in the introduction of *Le roi Lear*. Both rusticity and tenderness are expressed by the oboe in the stable scene in *L'enfance du Christ* and for the arrival of the Holy Family in Saïs in the same work. 'Weaker creatures' depicted by the oboe include lambs and birds in *Les Troyens* (*NBE* 2a: 70) and insects in *Béatrice et Bénédict* (*NBE* 3: 175).

The heartrending pathos of the oboe in *Iphigénie en Aulide*, as shown in Ex. 89a, was perhaps the model for two passages in *Les Troyens*: one where Chorebus supports the fainting Cassandra, 'Pauvre âme égarée!' (*NBE* 2a: 62–5); the other where Andromache walks slowly away from the silent onlookers (*NBE* 2a: 122). The close of the *Rex tremendæ* in the *Requiem*, 'Salva me' (*NBE* 9: 64–5), is of the same order.

The nearest Berlioz came to using the oboe for agitation was in the *Course à l'abîme* in *La damnation de Faust* (*NBE* 8a: 401), where the oboe line slightly resembles that in the *Fidelio* scene he cites as Ex. 90, even though the image is horror, not joy. A type of use for which he seems to make no allowance in the *Treatise* is in a noble, expressive melody for a solo oboe such as that found in the first movement of the *Symphonie fantastique* (*NBE* 16: 30), in *Le roi Lear* (*NBE* 20: 54), in the overture to *Benvenuto Cellini* (*NBE* 1a: 36, 94) and in the *Fête* of *Roméo et Juliette* (*NBE* 18: 67).

Evil is suggested by the frequent use of a low oboe to accompany Mephistopheles in *La damnation de Faust*. Frivolity is the tone of Anna's response to Narbal, supported by an oboe, in Act IV of *Les Troyens*. And the caricature of comic figures is entrusted to the oboe, first for the Cabaretier in *Benvenuto Cellini*, and second for Somarone in *Béatrice et Bénédict*, with his excruciating *agréments* for the oboe, a scene which recalls Berlioz's scorn of a Dresden oboist in 1843 who ornamented his part despite Berlioz's vigorous instructions not to.[3]

Berlioz was not particularly close to the three notable French oboists of his time, Vogt, Brod and Triébert, although they played in his concerts and taught at the Conservatoire. He wrote a theme from *Roméo et Juliette* in Vogt's autograph album,[4] and told an anecdote about Brod in *Les grotesques de la musique*.[5] The oboist he probably knew best was Barret, a French player who was principal oboe at Covent Garden at the time of Berlioz's visits to London.

In the *Journal des débats* of 28 May 1839 Berlioz wrote about the 'harmoniphon or keyboard-oboe', made by M. Paris, which was

> destined to replace oboes and cors anglais in provincial orchestras where these instruments are very little and very badly studied. For this reason it is a most useful invention. The harmoniphon's keyboard has thirty keys rather smaller than piano keys set out in the same way. Its range is from middle c' up to e'''. It is played by blowing down an elastic tube with the mouthpiece held between the teeth, while the fingers play the keyboard. Pressing the keys simply allows the sound to come out; expression is done with the mouth, so that the player's breathing controls nuances of piano, forte and crescendo, not normally possible on instruments of this kind.

THE COR ANGLAIS

This instrument is an alto oboe, as it were, with the same range. It is written on the treble clef as if it were an oboe in F, in other words a fifth higher than its actual sound. Its range is written on the treble clef from b chromatically up to f''', sounding e up to bb''. Some cors anglais have a low bb also. If the orchestra is playing in C, the cor anglais must be written in G; if it is in D, the cor anglais will be written in A, and so on. What we said above about

[3] *Memoirs*, 'Travels in Germany', I/5.   [4] Pierpont Morgan Library, New York.
[5] *Les grotesques de la musique*, p. 271.

fingering difficulties on the oboe for certain successions of sharps and flats also applies to the cor anglais, with even greater problems in rapid passagework.

Berlioz observed *e‴* as the cor anglais's top note and *b* as its bottom note (reached twice in *La damnation de Faust* and twice in *L'enfance du Christ*). In the *Prière* in *Benvenuto Cellini* he revised a very high passage for cor anglais and gave it to the flute (*NBE* 1c: 756). In the *Requiem* (*NBE* 9: 104) and *Roméo et Juliette* (*NBE* 18: 262) he seems to have avoided its lowest notes. The mention of a low *b♭* was added in the 1855 edition. The instrument is not normally given rapid figuration of any kind, but the 'difficult' *c″–d″* trill is found in *La damnation de Faust* (*NBE* 8a: 172).

Its timbre, being less piercing but deeper and more veiled than that of the oboe, does not lend itself in the same way to merry rustic tunes. Nor can it convey the agony of wailing; the expression of sharp pain is almost beyond it. It is a melancholy, dreamy voice, dignified too, with a retiring, remote quality which makes it superior to every other instrument when it comes to arousing images and feelings of the past, or when the composer wants to pluck the secret string of memory. M. Halévy had a happy inspiration when he used two cors anglais in the refrain of Eléazar's air in Act IV of *La juive* (Ex. 91).

Ex. 91

Berlioz himself used two cors anglais as early as the *Chants de la fête de Pâques* in the *Huit scènes de Faust*, and did so again on three occasions: in the *Requiem*, in *Benvenuto Cellini* (*Prière*), and in *Dans le ciel* in *La damnation de Faust*.

In the Adagio of one of my symphonies the cor anglais first repeats an oboe's phrases an octave lower, like a young country boy in dialogue with his girl, then at the end of the movement recalls these fragments over a muffled accompaniment of four timpani against the rest of the orchestra's silence. The feeling of absence, of oblivion, of bitter loneliness evoked in the hearts of some listeners by this desolate melody would not have a quarter of its impact were it sung by any other instrument but the cor anglais.

The symphony referred to is the *Symphonie fantastique*, whose third movement, the *Scène aux champs*, features the off-stage oboe in dialogue with the cor anglais (*NBE* 16: 72, 89).

The blend of the cor anglais's low notes with the bottom register of the clarinets and horns over a double bass tremolo produces an unusual and also novel effect appropriate for creating an atmosphere of fear and anxiety through its feeling of menace. This effect was unknown to Mozart, Weber and Beethoven, but there is a magnificent example in the duet in Act IV of *Les huguenots*. I believe M. Meyerbeer is the first to have used it in opera (Ex. 92).

Ex. 92

In a piece whose general mood is that of melancholy the frequent use of a cor anglais in the middle of an instrumental ensemble is exactly right. In such a case you write just one part for oboe and replace the second oboe with a cor anglais. Gluck used it in his Italian operas *Telemaco* and *Orfeo*, but without any striking purpose and without making much of it. He never used it in his French scores. Neither Mozart nor Beethoven nor Weber ever used it, I don't know why.

The *Rgm* text here had, in addition: 'Most cors anglais are made of leather, some are made of wood. The tone of the former seems better to me, its character is more definite.' The following week he wrote: 'Before going any further I must hasten to point out an ill-judged expression in my last article which could lead to error. Cors anglais which I indicated as being made of leather are only covered in leather; the body of the instrument is in fact of wood. These are cors anglais of curved shape.' The modern design of cor anglais with the body of the instrument straight and a curved crook to carry the reed was first introduced by Brod in 1839.

In both *Telemaco* and *Orfeo ed Euridice* Gluck used two cors anglais, although the authenticity of their part in *Telemaco* has been questioned.[6] There is also one in the Italian *Alceste*. Berlioz knew all three operas well, although he was unaware that Haydn required a pair of cors anglais in a number of works in the 1760s including the Symphony no. 22 ('The Philosopher'), that Mozart used a pair in *La finta semplice* and in *Il ré pastore*, and that Beethoven had written a trio for two oboes and cor anglais op. 87 in 1795. In Gluck's time the instrument was known in Vienna but not in Paris, where it came into use in the scores of Catel, Cherubini, Spontini and Reicha.[7] Berlioz was later to complain that it was familiar in Paris but apparently rare in Germany; the lack of cors anglais is a constant lament in the *Memoirs'* chapter on his German visits. In Leipzig in 1843 the cor anglais 'was of such poor quality and in such bad condition [...] that we had to entrust the solo to the first clarinet'. The same thing occurred in Weimar, and in Brunswick the part was arranged for an oboe. There exist arrangements by Berlioz of the cor anglais solos in both *Harold en Italie* and *Le carnaval romain* for oboe, presumably for concerts in Germany where no cor anglais was available (see *NBE* 17: 206 and 20: 312).

With the exception of the *Requiem*, where two oboes and two cors anglais all have independent parts, Berlioz always expected the cor anglais to be played by one or both of the two oboists in the orchestra. In his early music it was normally the first oboe who would take it, a reflection of the likely expertise of the principal player, in particular that of Vogt, principal oboe at the Opéra and the Société des Concerts and the leading exponent of the cor anglais in Paris. Berlioz evoked his playing in chapter 5 of the *Memoirs*. The solo in the third movement of *Harold en Italie* is for the first oboist to take, whereas in the *Symphonie fantastique*, *Roméo*

[6] Gluck, *Werke*, 1/2, p. 392.
[7] R. M. Longyear, 'The English horn in classic and early romantic music', *Miscellanea Musicologica*, 9 (1977), pp. 128–44.

et Juliette and most other works neither player is specified. In the overture *Le carnaval romain* and in *Les Troyens* the second oboe doubles the cor anglais, although in a letter Berlioz suggested that in *Le carnaval romain* the first player should do it.[8]

Whoever played the second instrument, there were sometimes extremely rapid changes from one to the other: just a few seconds are allowed in the third movement of *Harold en Italie* (*NBE* 17: 102) and twice in *Le carnaval romain* (*NBE* 20: 203, 211); an instantaneous change is required in *Les Troyens* (*NBE* 2b: 353).

L'enfance du Christ is scored almost throughout for one oboe and one cor anglais, the latter taking the oboe only for *L'adieu des bergers*. In the autograph of *La fuite en Egypte* the cor anglais part is marked 'oboe di caccia ossia corno inglese', as if to heighten the archaism of the music.

Of all wind instruments it was the cor anglais on which Berlioz bestowed his most eloquent solos. Its part in Marguerite's *Romance* in the *Huit scènes de Faust* and *La damnation de Faust* is one of the noblest solos in the whole repertory of the instrument, true to Berlioz's precept of using it to evoke longing or nostalgia. The *Symphonie fantastique* adds a rustic dimension to the feeling of distance and yearning, a symbolisation encouraged by the cor anglais solo in Rossini's *Guillaume Tell* overture. Its other notable solo exposure is found in the overture *Rob Roy* (showing a contrast of moods, both melancholy and lively), in the third movement of *Harold en Italie*, and in the *Ariette d'Arlequin* in *Benvenuto Cellini*, where accompanied by the harp it is charged to express the soul of beauty itself. There is a prominent solo in the overture *Le carnaval romain*.

In his later music Berlioz was inclined to couple the cor anglais with another instrument an octave above or below. In the trio section of the scherzo *La reine Mab* in *Roméo et Juliette* (*NBE* 18: 203–7) it has a flute above it; in the *Entrée des laboureurs* in Act III of *Les Troyens* (*NBE* 2b: 349) it divides the melody, alternating with an oboe an octave above and a bassoon an octave below; in the *Pas d'esclaves nubiennes* one act later (*NBE* 2b: 536) it has a flute one octave above and a piccolo two octaves above. More rarely it shares a unison line with another instrument: with the cellos in the *Lacrimosa* of the *Requiem* (*NBE* 9: 74), and with an oboe in the *Danse cabalistique* in *L'enfance du Christ* (*NBE* 11: 50). As a support to voices the cor anglais plays an important part in the *Quid sum miser* in the *Requiem* (*NBE* 9: 49), and in two contrasting duets in *Les Troyens*: 'Nuit d'ivresse' for Dido and Aeneas in Act IV, and 'Par Bacchus!' for the two sentinels in Act V (*NBE* 2b: 575, 615).

THE BASSOON

This is the bass version of the oboe. It has a range of over three octaves, from Bb' chromatically up to eb'', written on the bass and tenor clefs. The

---

[8] Letter of 23 February 1853 (*Cg*, 4, p. 282).

top third from c'' to eb'' is dangerous, so it is prudent (to say the least) not to take it above top bb'. It is nowadays equipped with keys giving the low $C\sharp$ and $B\natural'$ which used to be unobtainable. Its fingering is the same as for the flute.

Many trills at both ends of the range are impossible, for example on Bb', $B\natural'$, C and $C\sharp$, also the semitone trill on D and the whole-tone trills on Eb, $E\natural$ and $F\sharp$. The whole-tone trill on D and semitone trills on Eb, $E\natural$ and F are difficult. The whole-tone trill on f is difficult and on $f\sharp$ impossible; other difficult trills are the whole-tone on $c\sharp'$, semitone on d' and f', whole-tone on f' and $f\sharp'$. All trills above $f\sharp'$ are poor or impossible.

This instrument leaves much to be desired as far as intonation is concerned and will perhaps profit more than any other wind instrument from the application of Boehm's system.

Berlioz normally kept the bassoon within the range Bb' to bb', exceeding this upper limit only in the *Fête* in *Roméo et Juliette* (*NBE* 18: 101), where a high c'' is found. In the *Huit scènes de Faust* he avoided a $b\natural'$ (*NBE* 5: 46); in *Benvenuto Cellini* he avoided bb' (*NBE* 1a: 333). He made free use of both the low $B\natural'$ and $C\sharp$ throughout his work; keys for these two notes had been added by the bassoon-maker Simiot of Lyons in about 1808. In *Lélio* he was not afraid to write a pianissimo low Bb' (*NBE* 7: 22).

Five of the 'difficult' trills are found: $D\sharp$–E, E–F, and F–Gb all occur in the opening scene of *Benvenuto Cellini* (*NBE* 1a: 143), while f–g and f'–g' are both found in the finale of the *Symphonie fantastique* (*NBE* 16: 124, 156–7); the f–g trill is also found in the *Fête* of *Roméo et Juliette* (*NBE* 18: 109). Two of the 'impossible' trills are found: a'–b' in the *Symphonie fantastique* (*NBE* 16: 157), and E–$F\sharp$ in *Benvenuto Cellini* (*NBE* 1a: 228).

The application of Boehm's system to the bassoon was not achieved until the 1850s, when Triébert and Marzoli in Paris constructed such an instrument. But the complexity and cost of its mechanism militated against its general adoption and a simpler system prevailed in France at least until the recent dominance of German Heckel models. It is more than a little misleading for Berlioz to say that the bassoon's fingering is the same as that of the flute.

In the orchestra the bassoon is very useful on a multitude of occasions. Its tone is not very loud and its timbre completely lacking in brightness and nobility; allowance must always be made for its propensity to sound grotesque when exposed. Its low notes make an excellent bass to the full woodwind section. Bassoons are normally written in two parts, but since large orchestras are always equipped with four bassoons they may be written in four separate parts, or better still in three, with the bottom part doubled an octave lower to reinforce the bass. The character of its top notes is rather painful and dolorous, I might even say miserable, which can sometimes be put to most surprising effect either in a slow melody or in an accompaniment figure. For example the curious little clucking noises heard in the scherzo of Beethoven's Fifth Symphony, towards the end of the decrescendo, are produced simply by the rather pinched sound of the high a♮′ and g′ of the bassoons in unison.

On the other hand, when M. Meyerbeer wanted a pale, cold, cadaverous sound in his scene of the resurrection of the nuns in *Robert le diable,* it was from the flaccid notes of the middle register that he got it (Ex. 93a).

Rapid legato passages can be effective. They sound better in the instrument's favourite keys, such as D, G, C, F, B♭, E♭, A and their relative minors. The scales in the bathing scene in Act II of *Les huguenots* have an excellent effect (Ex. 93b).

Ex. 93

Most of Berlioz's scores require four bassoons even when they play in only two parts. He does not always bother to specify their number. The *Requiem, Symphonie funèbre et triomphale, Te deum* and *L'impériale* all call for eight bassoons, though only in four parts in the first of these, in two parts in the others. The division of bassoons into four parts is a very characteristic feature of his scoring of special effects. The finest example is the *Ecot de joyeux compagnons* (Brander's Song) in the *Huit scènes de Faust* (*NBE* 5: 68), adopted unchanged in *La damnation de Faust.* Low four-part bassoon chords accompany the Cabaretier in *Benvenuto Cellini*, and many other four-part passages are found. A single bassoon is required in some of the orchestral songs: *La belle voyageuse, Le jeune pâtre breton,* and *Villanelle.*

A persistent riddle lies in determining which of the four players play which notes in a four-part layout. '1^{rs} bassoons' refers to the two who play the upper part in two-part music, but when divided into four parts there is evidence to show that these two players play the first and third parts, the principal '2^d bassoon' being always on the second part, even in four parts. The four separate parts in the *Marche de pèlerins* in *Harold en Italie* are laid out in this way (see especially *NBE* 17: 85). But there is little consistency in the manuscript and printed orchestral parts of the period; every orchestra and every copyist may have developed their own practices. It is not a problem that Berlioz appears to have concerned himself with. But the regular doubling of players also suggests that the marking '1° solo' may sometimes imply two players, not one.

Because of the bassoon's 'complete lack of brightness and nobility' Berlioz very rarely treated it as a solo instrument. It sometimes accompanies humble persons such as the Père de famille in the last part of *L'enfance du Christ* and Iopas in Act IV of *Les Troyens*. In Act III of *Les Troyens* bassoons are in unison with violas and cellos to represent sailors (*Entrée des matelots*) and in octaves with a cor anglais to represent labourers (*Entrée des laboureurs*). They also accompany the sentinels' duet in Act V. The bassoon's lack of class, in Berlioz's view, is confirmed by the fact that there are apparently bassoons neither in Heaven (end of *La damnation de Faust*) nor in Bethlehem (Parts I and II of *L'enfance du Christ*). None are admitted to the fashionable ball in the *Symphonie fantastique*. Very occasionally a melancholy, wailing line is given to a solo bassoon, as in the opening bars of *Harold en Italie*. Four bassoons in unison have a curious long descending line in the *Chœur d'étudiants et de soldats* at the end of Part II of *La damnation de Faust*, although the character this is intended to convey is not clear.

There are some striking countermelodies for unison bassoons in both the fourth and fifth movements of the *Symphonie fantastique* (*NBE* 16: 95, 123), deliberately evoking the grotesque quality Berlioz warns against. Bassoons on their bottom note provide part of the picturesque snore in the scherzo *La reine Mab* in *Roméo et Juliette* (*NBE* 18: 223). To portray comic characters the bassoon is much used in *Benvenuto Cellini*, prominently supporting Balducci, Fieramosca and the Cabaretier. An extreme grotesquerie is found in the opening scene of the opera when Balducci's absurd trills are accompanied by four bassoons trilling on a low-pitched diminished seventh (*NBE* 1a: 143). The bassoons imply that Balducci is both comic and socially dubious.

The running bass figures shown in Ex. 93b, from *Les huguenots*, are found similarly deployed in *L'île inconnue* (*NBE* 13: 76), with bassoons in unison with cellos.

Berlioz did not count bassoon players or makers among his friends. In *Les soirées de l'orchestre* he commends Villent, a French bassoonist (Willent-Bordogni), and Beauman (or Baumann), a Belgian living in London, but he apparently had very little personal contact with either.

THE TENOROON

The tenoroon ('basson quinte') is a smaller version of the preceding, pitched a fifth higher. It has almost the same compass and is similarly written on two clefs, but it is a transposing instrument. Its range is chromatic between the written notes Bb' and bb', producing actual sounds from F up to f''. The tenoroon has the same relationship above the bassoon as the cor anglais has below the oboe, the cor anglais being written a fifth higher than its actual pitch and the tenoroon being written a fifth lower. The tenoroon will thus be playing in F when the bassoons are in C, or in G when they are in D, and so on.

This instrument is not found in most orchestras, since the cor anglais has the advantage of the superiority of its top two octaves. Its tone, being less sensitive but louder than that of the cor anglais, would serve admirably in military bands. It is ridiculous and annoying that the tenoroon has been almost completely excluded from wind bands when a large body of bassoons great and small would considerably soften the harshness of their sound.

The tenoroon was a very rare instrument in the nineteenth century. Berlioz never wrote for it himself. His hope that it might be adopted in wind bands was disappointed, and in orchestras the superiority of the cor anglais did, as he realised, efface any possible use for a tenor bassoon. He may have been aware that in about 1833 in Bordeaux, where cors anglais were not available, a tenoroon played the lower part in Halévy's *La juive* (Ex. 91) while the upper part was played on the oboe. The bassoonist Eugène Jancourt played some solos on a tenoroon in Eb in Paris between 1838 and 1840.[9]

THE CONTRABASSOON

This is to the bassoon what the double bass is to the cello, that is, its sound is an octave lower than the written pitch. It is not normally written outside the range of Bb' chromatically up to f', which produces the actual sounds Bb'' up to f. The bottom two notes are hard to produce and ineffective because they are so low.

I need hardly add that this instrument, being extremely cumbersome, is only suitable for broad massed effects and for the bass line at moderate tempos. Beethoven used it in the finales of his Fifth and Ninth Symphonies. It is a very valuable member of a large wind band, yet few players learn to play it. Sometimes an ophicleide is used as a substitute, but its sound

[9] Lyndesay G. Langwill, *The Bassoon and Contrabassoon* (London, 1965), p. 107.

lacks that extreme depth since it plays at the same pitch as the ordinary bassoon rather than at the octave below, and its tone moreover bears no resemblance to that of the contrabassoon. My view is that it is usually better to do without it than make such a substitution as that.

Berlioz called for a contrabassoon only twice: in the revised version of the overture to *Les francs-juges* (1834) and in the *Symphonie funèbre et triomphale*. In both works he is reluctant to use its lower range and descends no lower than written *E* in the overture and *D♯* in the symphony. He exceeded the specified upper limit, on the other hand, rising to written *g♭'* in the first movement of the symphony (*NBE* 19: 23). It is never heard on its own but simply supports the bassoons in heavier passages.

His reason for making so little use of it was undoubtedly the scarcity of instruments and players both in France and abroad. The contrabassoon was familiar in Vienna and thus available to Mozart and Beethoven, but not required in French scores until Isouard's last work, *Aladin ou la lampe merveilleuse*, whose première in 1822 was more famous for the introduction of gas lighting at the Opéra than for the introduction of the contrabassoon. But it evidently did not catch on until the end of Berlioz's career. His addition of a contrabassoon part to the overture to *Les francs-juges* is a mystery, unless he was preparing for performances abroad. It is clear that no contrabassoon figured in the 1840 performances of the *Symphonie funèbre et triomphale* (see *NBE* 19: 109).

The statement in the *Rgm* in 1841 that 'no one in Paris plays it; it is not taught at the Conservatoire' was modified in the *Treatise* in 1843 to 'few players learn to play it'. By the time the symphony was published in 1843 an optional part for one or two contrabassoons had been added to the score, perhaps as a result of encountering the instrument in Germany.

THE CLARINETS

Instruments with single reeds such as clarinets and basset horns make up a family whose relationship to the oboe family is not as close as one might suppose. The main difference is in the sound. Clarinets in their intermediate register have a fuller, purer and more limpid voice than double-reed instruments, whose sound is never free of a certain sharpness or bitterness which players conceal with varying degrees of success according to their ability. Only in the top octave above *c'''* does the clarinet share some of the oboe's louder tone quality, while the character of its lowest notes is close to certain notes on the bassoon because of its coarser vibration pattern.

The clarinet is written on the treble clef and its compass is three and a half octaves or more, from *e* chromatically up to *b♭'''*; *a'''* and *b♭'''* are difficult, while $b\natural'''$, c'''' and d'''' are extremely hazardous. The clarinet has four registers – bottom, chalumeau, intermediate and extreme; the first is from e up to e', the second from f' to bb' (usually muted in quality), the third goes from $b\natural'$ to c''', and the fourth takes the rest of the range from d''' up to d''''.

At the top of the clarinet range Berlioz used written f''' and g''' quite frequently and the 'difficult' a''' once only: in the *Fête* in *Roméo et Juliette* (*NBE* 18: 126). In Act I of *Les Troyens* he appears to avoid using the notes e''' and f''' (*NBE* 2a: 123).

He was confused about the clarinet's registers. The correct names of the registers are, in rising succession, chalumeau ('chalumeau'), throat or intermediate ('médium'), clarinet or clarino ('clairon'), and extreme or acute ('aigu'). In the *Rgm* articles he referred to three, not four, registers – 'chalumeau', 'médium' and 'suraigu' – but he revised this in the *Treatise*, not by adding 'clairon' between 'médium' and 'suraigu', but by placing the 'lowest register' ('les sons les plus graves') at the bottom. Thus 'intermediate' register, in the third sentence of this section, is incorrect, while he calls the awkward register across the break the 'chalumeau', which should correctly apply to the characteristic low octave of the instrument. A passage in the *Symphonie fantastique* (*NBE* 16: 40) has clarinets sustained in the low register, although the autograph gives them an octave higher with the marking 'chalumeau'. In *Cléopâtre* two clarinets playing a' and $f\sharp'$ are marked 'chalumeau' (*NBE* 6: 144), which may be an instruction to play an octave lower, since he knew that 'chalumeau' referred to the bottom octave; in 1835 he exclaimed with delight about the clarinets' 'chalumeau' entry in the Adagio of Weber's *Oberon* overture.[10] 'Chalumeau' and 'intermediate' hereafter in the text should therefore be interpreted as Berlioz used them in the *Treatise*, not according to standard usage.

He makes no mention of the chalumeau as an instrument except when quoting from Gluck's *Alceste* (in the section on violins, Ex. 21), where a footnote remarks: 'This obsolete instrument is quite unknown today.' In the autograph of *L'adieu des bergers* in *L'enfance du Christ* the two clarinet parts are designated 'chalumeaux or clarinets in A', an archaism parallel to the marking of the cors anglais as 'oboi da caccia' (see above, p. 112).

A considerable number of diatonic figures, arpeggios and trills which used to be impracticable are no longer so, thanks to the ingenious mechanism of keys applied to the instrument, and will even be made quite easy when Sax's system is adopted by all makers. Nevertheless it is wise, so long as these improvements remain little known, not to write passages such as those in Ex. 94 except at very slow tempos.

---

[10] *Cm*, 2, p. 61.

Ex. 94

There is a full range of major and minor trills playable on the clarinet. The insecure ones are shown in Ex. 95 divided into difficult (Ex. 95a), very difficult (Ex. 95b) and impossible (Ex. 95c).

Ex. 95

For Sax and the clarinet's mechanical advances, see below under 'Improvements in the clarinet family'. Berlioz cannot seriously have thought that the passages shown in Ex. 94 could only be played 'at very slow tempos'; his scores are full of highly active clarinet parts similar to these, many of them to be played fast, although for the most part he did avoid the more extreme keys in which many of these are set.

Many of the 'difficult' trills (Ex. 95a) are found in Berlioz's scores, especially in the finale of the *Symphonie fantastique* (*NBE* 16: 156–7). But in his early works he was probably not sufficiently familiar with the instrument to appreciate the difficulty, and in his later works (for example an exposed *e″–f♯″* trill in the *Chasse royale et orage* in *Les Troyens* (*NBE* 2b: 444)) he could have expected the player to have an up-to-date instrument on which the difficulty no longer existed.

The clarinet's preferred keys are C, F and G, in the main, followed by B♭, E♭, A♭ and D major, with their relative minors. As clarinets are made in different keys, one can always select them appropriately so as to avoid asking the player to play in keys with many sharps or flats like A, E, B, D♭, G♭ major and their relative minors.

There are four sizes in general use today. The little E♭ clarinet is best given a range of just three octaves and two notes, from *e* up to *g‴*. It is a minor third higher than the clarinet in C and is written as a transposing instrument, so that to obtain Ex. 96a you must write Ex. 96b.

Ex. 96

The other three – the C clarinet, the B♭ clarinet and the A clarinet – all
have the same compass, the last two being respectively a tone and a minor
third lower than the C clarinet. They are consequently written a tone and
a minor third above their pitch, as in Ex. 97.

Ex. 97

The expressions 'good', 'bad' and 'fair' refer here not to the degree of
difficulty in playing the phrase shown in the examples, but simply to the
aptness of the key in which they are written. I should also add that quite
difficult keys like A major and E major do not have to be avoided at all
costs, in simple phrases at slow tempo. It is clear that regardless of their
individual tone-quality (to which I shall return in a moment) different

clarinets are extremely useful from the player's point of view. It is a matter of regret that there are not more. Clarinets in B and in D, for example, which are occasionally found, could enormously enlarge the resources open to composers on a great number of occasions.

The little clarinet in high F, once widely used in military bands, has been supplanted almost entirely by the E♭ instrument, which is rightly held to be less screechy and at the same time adequate for the keys usually found in wind music. Clarinets lose their purity, sweetness and individuality the higher they are pitched above B♭, one of the best keys for this instrument. The C clarinet is harsher than the B♭, with a less appealing tone. The little E♭ clarinet makes a piercing noise above a'' which can sound vulgar. In a recent symphony, moreover, it was used to parody, degrade and (if the word may be pardoned) brutalise a curious transformation demanded by the dramatic meaning of the work. The little F clarinet tends to be even more pronounced in this characteristic. The lower the instrument is pitched, on the other hand, the more veiled and melancholy its sound.

Players should in general use only the instrument specified by the composer. Since each one has an individual character, it is at least probable that he chose one rather than another from a preference for this or that tone-quality, not out of caprice. To play everything on the B♭ clarinet, transposing into that key, as certain notable players insist on doing, is therefore almost always inauthentic practice. This infidelity is even more obvious and heinous if it is supposed to be a clarinet in A, for example. The composer may have chosen it in order to get the low e, sounding $c\sharp$. What will the player of a B♭ clarinet (whose bottom note e sounds only d) then do? He will transpose it up an octave and ruin the effect the composer wanted – an intolerable state of affairs!

Berlioz called for clarinets in five of the keys he mentions. The highest, the clarinet in F, is required in the second (1833) version of the *Scène héroïque* with wind accompaniment. At least four players were provided for by the copyist. It rises to d''', sounding g'''. It had been used by Beethoven and Cherubini but was confined in Berlioz's time to military bands.

The E♭ clarinet has a celebrated role in the finale of the *Symphonie fantastique* (the symphony to which Berlioz modestly refers), being given the distorted version of the *idée fixe* (NBE 16: 123) and rising as high as f''', sounding $a\flat'''$. Either of the two orchestral clarinettists is permitted to take the part. Five E♭ clarinets are required in the *Symphonie funèbre et triomphale*, again rising to f'''. Berlioz was breaking new ground in 1830 by transporting the instrument from its military home into the symphony orchestra.

The standard three clarinets, in C, B♭ and A, are all extensively used in Berlioz's scores. Although the *Messe solennelle* requires A clarinets for one movement, his first orchestral music is almost exclusively for C clarinets. Even the first movement of the *Scène héroïque*, which is in A major, calls for C clarinets. But his larger works, from the opera *Les francs-juges* (1826) up to the *Te deum* (1849), normally require all three instruments. In his late works he abandoned the C clarinet, either because it was no longer necessary to allow for the player's comfort, or because the instrument was becoming scarce, or because he did not like its sound.

In general, as one would expect, he used the B♭ clarinet in flat keys and the A clarinet in sharp keys. Music in the intermediate keys, C and G, is equally served by all three. In his late music he felt less need to call for a change of instrument when the music changed key, so one finds quite long stretches on the 'wrong' instrument, the third part of *L'enfance du Christ*, for example, where A clarinets are retained even after flat keys have been well established. Similarly, for the *Cérémonie funèbre* in Act V of *Les Troyens* (*NBE* 2b: 713) B♭ clarinets continue to play music in C♯ minor perhaps in anticipation of more music in B♭ at the end of the opera. The finale of *Roméo et Juliette* is surprising in retaining B♭ clarinets when the music is predominantly in B minor/major and D major.

When such remote keys are called for, Berlioz usually notated the clarinet part with no accidentals in the key signature. *Benvenuto Cellini*, for example (*NBE* 1a: 228), has B♭ clarinets playing music in B major but showing no key signature. A very odd case is the finale of Act III of *Les Troyens* (*NBE* 2b: 417), where the music is in B major, the clarinets are in B♭, and the key signature has a single meaningless flat.

Certain pieces where the clarinet selected is not in the key closest to that of the music imply that tone-quality was the main consideration. The more strident character of the C clarinet is clearly intended in the 'Amen' chorus in *La damnation de Faust*, where the key is D major. The same applies to the *Marche marocaine* arrangement. C clarinets for music in A major are even more obviously chosen for their timbre: see the *Hymne à la France* and *La nonne sanglante*. Clarinets in C, not B♭, play the raucous B♭ *Marche au supplice* in the *Symphonie fantastique*.

Conversely, the A clarinet seems deliberately chosen for the subdued and gentle *Roi de Thulé* in *La damnation de Faust* when the key is F, a key normally served by the B♭ clarinet. The use of B♭ clarinets in the *Menuet des follets* in the same work, where the key is D, is baffling. A passage in the *Tempête* fantasy in *Lélio* (*NBE* 7: 115–17) takes the clarinets briefly into B♭ (from C) for the Caliban episode even though the change is not required by the key or the pitch of the passage. For Chorebus's music in Act I of *Les Troyens*, similarly, the clarinet (the first only) has to change to the B♭ instrument for a prominent solo passage (*NBE* 2a: 67) while the second player remains in A.

The A clarinet is sometimes called upon to provide its extra low note regardless of the key of the music. It was usually sufficient to require only the second player to take the lower instrument. This occurs in the *Chanson de Méphistophélès* in both the *Huit scènes de Faust* and *La damnation de Faust*, where the first player is in B♭, and in the introduction to the *Waverley* overture and the duet in *La nonne sanglante*, where the first player is in C. (*Waverley* was originally scored for four clarinets, two in C and two in A.) In the overture to *Benvenuto Cellini* the two clarinets change from C to B♭ for the Larghetto passage both to obtain the low *e* and for the more expressive quality of the music. Later, in the chapter on the conductor, Berlioz warns about lazy clarinettists who do not bother to change instruments when instructed to do so.

As with the oboe and cor anglais the change from one instrument to another often had to be effected in very little time. Instantaneous changes required in *Benvenuto Cellini* (*NBE* 1b: 348) and *La damnation de Faust* (*NBE* 8a: 150) are the result of revision and reorganisation of the score, but there are occasions in *La damnation de Faust* (*NBE* 8a: 273) and *Les Troyens* (*NBE* 2b: 497) where only a few seconds are provided for the change. In the overture to *Benvenuto Cellini* the first clarinet has to change to bass clarinet in five seconds (*NBE* 1a: 13, 73), while in the *Te deum* (*NBE* 10: 123) one of four clarinets has to change to bass clarinet 'as quickly as possible' while the music continues.

The *Rgm* text remarked of the A clarinet: 'The A clarinet, though excellent in many ways, perhaps lacks a purity in the intermediate register as perfect as that of the B♭ clarinet. This difference is even more pronounced in the low G clarinet, which is very like the basset horn, as we shall see.' Berlioz used neither this G clarinet nor the clarinets in B and D which the *Treatise* text mentions. The B clarinet, used by Mozart, was described by Choron in 1813 as 'one of the most successful clarinets', which may be why Berlioz first drafted the *Gratias* in the *Messe solennelle* (*NBE* 23: 74) for B clarinets before replacing them with A instruments. The B clarinet was already rare, according to Kastner's *Traité* of 1836. In the 1855 edition of the *Treatise* Berlioz inserted a remark about the D clarinet: 'The D clarinet is not well known, although it should be. Its tone is pure, with a distinct pungency, and it could be extremely useful on many occasions.' He had probably come across these instruments in Germany, where they were much more common than in France. He advocated the teaching of a wide range of clarinets,[11] including the smaller members of the family in E♭, F and high A♭, but it is nonetheless odd that he should have regarded it as 'a matter of regret that there are not more' when players were already under the obligation to equip themselves with at least three instruments for normal use. The survival of two versions of the clarinet in everyday use today is a strange anachronism in the light of its mechanical fluency, achieved in Berlioz's lifetime.

We mentioned earlier that the clarinet has four registers. Each of these registers also has its distinctive tone-quality. The extreme register is rather piercing and should only be used in an orchestral *fortissimo* (although some very high notes can be sustained *piano* when they are carefully approached) or in the extrovert passagework of a brilliant solo. The intermediate and chalumeau registers are suitable for melodies, arpeggios and passagework. The bottom register is ideal for those icily menacing effects, those dark expressions of repressed fury which Weber ingeniously hit upon, especially in long held notes.

---

[11] *Memoirs*, 'Travels in Germany', II/5.

If you wish to use the piercing shrieks of the very top notes in a striking fashion, and if you are not sure of the player's ability to make a clean attack on a difficult note, you must disguise the clarinet entry under a loud chord by the full orchestra which can break off as soon as the sound has had time to establish itself cleanly and then leave it on its own without danger (Ex. 98). Opportunities for making appropriate use of these high sustained notes are rather rare.

Ex. 98

The character of the clarinet's intermediate register, marked by a certain haughtiness with intimations of tenderness and nobility, equips it well for the expression of the most poetic thoughts and feelings. Only frivolity – and perhaps naive joy too – seems to suit it not at all. The clarinet is not made for the *idyllic*, it is an instrument of the *epic*, like horns, trumpets and trombones. Its voice is the voice of heroic love, and if the massed brass in large military bands bring to mind a regiment in shining armour marching to glory or to death, massed clarinets in unison playing with them seem to evoke the loved ones, wives and sweethearts, whose proud eyes and earnest passions exult to the sound of arms, who sing as they enter the fray and who crown their conquering heroes or die with the defeated. I have never been able to hear the distant sound of military bands without being profoundly moved by this feminine quality in the clarinets and filled with images of this kind, as from reading the epic poetry of the ancients. This beautiful instrumental soprano, so richly evocative and so penetrating when employed in the mass, gains, when played solo – in delicacy, elusive nuances and mysterious sensibility – what it loses in force and brilliance. There is nothing so virginal or so pure as the shades of colour bestowed on certain melodies by the tone of the intermediate register of the clarinet in the hands of a skilful player.

Of all wind instruments it is the one most able to begin, swell, diminish and stifle its sound, which accounts for its precious capacity to produce distant effects or echoes, or echoes of echoes, or half-shades of sound. I could cite no more admirable example of the application of some of these effects than the dreamy phrase on the clarinet over a string tremolo in the middle of the allegro section of the *Freischütz* overture!!! Is this not the lonely virgin, the huntsman's fair bride, her eyes upturned to heaven, mingling her passionate plaint with the roar of the storm-wracked forest? . . . Oh Weber!!! . . . (Ex. 99).

Ex. 99

This imagery of the clarinet solo in the *Freischütz* overture representing Agathe was put forward in Berlioz's review of the Opéra production published on 13 June

1841 and echoed in the *Rgm* clarinet article six months later. The review was later reprinted in *A travers chants.*

Berlioz's own music for large wind forces illustrates the heroic image very well, with prominent clarinets in many cases, especially in the *Symphonie funèbre et triomphale.* His identification of the clarinet's voice as feminine is borne out by those passages in *Roméo et Juliette* (especially in the movement *Roméo au tombeau des Capulets*) in which Juliet is evidently portrayed by a solo clarinet.

The clarinet's usefulness for distant effects and echoes is illustrated by a number of passages: the *Tableau musical* in *La mort d'Orphée* (*NBE* 6: 59–60, later adapted as *La harpe éolienne* in *Lélio*), the ***pppp*** 'écho' in the *Scène aux champs* in the *Symphonie fantastique* (*NBE* 16: 82), the '***ppp*** aussi doux que possible, presque rien' at the beginning of *Harold en Italie* (*NBE* 17: 10), and the ***pppp*** 'sons d'écho' at the end of the *Ballet des sylphes* in *La damnation de Faust* (*NBE* 8a: 212). No other wind instrument could achieve this quintessentially romantic effect so well. The longing and spleen associated with distance and absence often fall to the clarinet to evoke, especially in the *Symphonie fantastique*, where the clarinet is several times singled out for the related function of evoking the *idée fixe* as a memory (see, for example, *NBE* 16: 66, 112).

I will take the liberty of again quoting from my monodrama *Lélio*, where the effect of a clarinet melody is, if not similar, at least analogous: the broken fragments of melody, interspersed with silences, are also accompanied by tremolos on some of the strings while the double basses' occasional low pizzicatos make a kind of heavy pulsation beneath the harmony and a harp sketches out a few broken arpeggios. But here, to give the clarinet sound as indistinct and distant a quality as possible I had the instrument enclosed in a leather bag as a substitute for a mute. This desolate murmuring and the half-stifled sound of the solo recalling a melody already heard in another piece have always made a deep impression on an audience. This ghostly music produces an effect of desolation and brings tears to the eyes as no other expression of sorrow could do; it wrings the heart as much even as the trembling harmonies of the Aeolian harp itself (Ex. 100).

Ex. 100

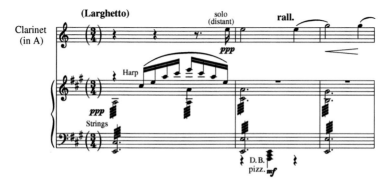

In its original form as the *Tableau musical* at the end of the cantata *La mort d'Orphée* this passage was a semitone lower, in A♭ with a B♭ clarinet marked '*ppp* lointain' but with no mention of a mute. A footnote explains that it represents a shepherd from the mountains of Thrace trying to recall Orpheus's song on a flute. The autograph of *Lélio* has the instruction to wrap the clarinet in a leather (later changed to cloth) bag, but although the muting instruction is shown here in the *Treatise* extract, allowing either leather or cloth, the full score of *Lélio* published in 1857 omitted the muting instruction. One of the fragmentary pages in the autograph of *Les francs-juges* has the note: 'clarinets with their bells wrapped in a [?] bag', either 'leather' or 'cloth' having been torn away. The idea of muting clarinets came from Act III of Spontini's *Fernand Cortez*, where both oboes and clarinets are instructed to enclose their bells in leather bags.

When Beethoven wished to reflect the noble and melancholy character of the A major theme in the immortal Andante of his Seventh Symphony and to express every ounce of passionate regret in the phrase, he entrusted it of course to the intermediate register of the clarinet (Ex. 101a). In Gluck's *Alceste*, for the ritornello of Alceste's air 'Ah! malgré moi mon faible cœur partage' (Ex. 101b), the composer first wrote for a flute, but then observing no doubt that this instrument's tone was too weak and lacked the nobility necessary for the projection of a theme imbued with such desolation and such profound melancholy, he gave it to the clarinet. It is again clarinets that support the voice in Alceste's other air of doleful resignation, 'Ah! divinités implacables!' (Ex. 101c).

Ex. 101

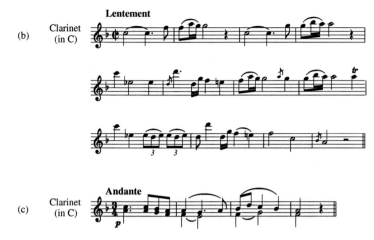

The slow movement of Beethoven's Seventh Symphony is an Allegretto, not an Andante. For the air 'Ah, malgré moi' from *Alceste*, Gluck's autograph and the printed score give the part to a flute, but a set of parts in the Bibliothèque de l'Opéra, Paris, shows that a Bb clarinet played the solo in that theatre, not a flute. Whether the change was made by Gluck himself is not certain.[12]

A different kind of effect is achieved by three slow notes for clarinets in thirds in the air 'Votre cour devint mon azile' from Sacchini's *Œdipe à Colonne* (Ex. 102). At the end of the theme Polinices breaks off, turns to Theseus's daughter, then adds, with his eyes on her: 'Je connus, j'adorai la charmante Eryphile.' The two clarinets descend softly in thirds before the entry of the voice just at the moment when the two lovers exchange tender glances and make an admirable dramatic point with exquisitely musical effect. The two instrumental voices are here a symbol of love and purity. One can almost see Eryphile chastely lowering her eyes at the sound. Superb! Put oboes here in place of the two clarinets and the whole effect is ruined. In point of fact this wonderful orchestral effect is not found in the printed score of Sacchini's masterpiece, although I have noticed it too often in performance to have any doubt about my memory.

Ex. 102

The clarinets are indeed missing from the printed score of 1787, but by 1822, when Berlioz probably first heard it, someone, not necessarily Sacchini himself,

---

[12] Gluck, *Werke*, 1/7, p. 441.

must have added them. *Œdipe à Colonne* was performed at the Opéra thirty-three times between 1822 and 1825 and remained in the repertory until 1830. Berlioz would have heard it many times over; he claimed in 1826 to know it from memory.[13]

Neither Sacchini nor Gluck nor any of the great composers of that period made use of the instrument's low notes. I have no idea why not. Mozart seems to have been the first to use them, for accompaniments of sombre character such as the trio of maskers in *Don Giovanni*. It was left to Weber to discover just what terror the tone of these low notes can inspire when used to support sinister harmony. In such cases it is better to write for the clarinets in two parts than have them in octaves or unisons. The more notes there are in the harmony the more striking the result. If one had three clarinets available for the chord *c♯–e–b♭*, for example, and if it were appropriate, properly prepared and scored in this way, the diminished seventh would take on a horrifying aspect made still more sombre if a low *G* were added on a bass clarinet (Ex. 103).

Ex. 103

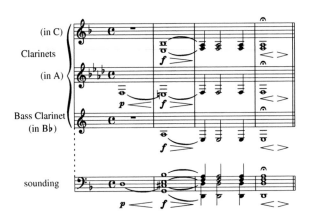

Low clarinets are extensively used in Berlioz, too frequently to need listing in full. The examples of Mozart and Weber clearly supplied the model. Low sextuplet arpeggios like those in Mozart's trio of maskers are found in the *Quartetto e coro dei maggi* (*NBE* 12a: 302), where a bassoon has a parallel figure a third below, and also in the *Sérénade* in *Harold en Italie* (*NBE* 17: 103), a movement that has other parallels with Mozart's Act I finale. Of many low sustained clarinet notes, those in the *Chanson de Méphistophélès* in the *Huit scènes de Faust* (*NBE* 5: 72) – and in *La damnation de Faust* – may have been directly prompted by *Der Freischütz*, while those in Herod's scene in Part I of *L'enfance du Christ* (*NBE* 11: 33) reflect a more mature and penetrating use of a unique orchestral resource. In *La captive* (*NBE* 13: 12) low clarinets in thirds support tremolo strings to fine effect. *Au cimetière*'s despondent character is largely the effect of low clarinet colour.

---

[13] *Memoirs*, chapter 12.

Out of Berlioz's enormous admiration for the great Weber clarinet solo in the overture to *Der Freischütz* came the similar plaintive solo at the end of *Sardanapale* (*NBE* 6: 221). In most of his music, however, the clarinet's versatility is constantly at the service of orchestral effect, with all registers variously used; yet the clarinet, like the bassoon and the flute, is not often heard on its own for more than a bar or two at a time. A very characteristic Berlioz sound is created by giving a flute and a clarinet a melody in octaves such as that found at the opening of *Le spectre de la rose* (*NBE* 13: 39), or more usually a running accompaniment figure as at the beginning of the *Symphonie fantastique* (*NBE* 16: 8). Octave grouping with oboes and bassoons is also common. A more unusual coupling, with the cellos, is a striking feature of *Villanelle* (*NBE* 13: 36). Between the *Mort d'Orphée* / *Lélio* solo and Andromache's *Pantomime* in Act I of *Les Troyens* (*NBE* 2a: 115), one of the greatest clarinet solos in the whole repertory, the only substantial clarinet solo in Berlioz's work is the accompaniment of Herod's narration of his dream to the soothsayers in Part I of *L'enfance du Christ* (*NBE* 11: 47). After the *Scène d'amour* in *Roméo et Juliette* Berlioz made more and more use of a pair of clarinets, usually in thirds, prominently featured. A leading example is the *Duo-nocturne* at the end of Act I of *Béatrice et Bénédict* (*NBE* 3: 187), with its magical close over a gently swaying low clarinet. Two closely clinging clarinets accompany Dido's 'D'un malheureux amour' at the end of *Les Troyens* (*NBE* 2b: 730). Two clarinets also accompany Hylas's song at the beginning of that act, and, with two bassoons, assume a more debased character in the sentinels' duet, a few pages later.

In 1857 Berlioz invited Leroy, principal clarinettist at the Opéra and one of the leading players of his day, to run through the solo for Andromache's scene in *Les Troyens*. He described his playing as 'cold', his phrasing as 'almost', and his response 'lukewarm'; it was a bitter experience made worse by the fact that Arban had played the same solo on a cornet just before and played it so sensitively that Berlioz was deeply moved.[14] He never heard that scene, with its incomparable clarinet solo, performed in public.

THE ALTO CLARINET

This is simply a clarinet in low F or low E♭, in other words a fifth below the C clarinet or the B♭ clarinet, with the same compass. It is written therefore as a transposing instrument either a fifth or a minor sixth above its actual pitch. The alto clarinet in F is written from *e* up to *g'''*, giving actual pitches *A* up to *c'''*. The alto clarinet in E♭ is written from *e* up to *g'''*, giving actual pitches *G* up to *bb''*. It is a very beautiful instrument which ought to take its place in all well established orchestras.

The alto clarinet (sometimes also called the tenor clarinet) has always been confined to military bands since its invention in about 1808 by Iwan Müller. Berlioz never wrote for it.

[14] *Cg*, 5, p. 428.

THE BASS CLARINET

Still lower than the preceding, this is an octave lower than the B♭ clarinet. There is one in C also (an octave lower than the C clarinet) but the B♭ one is much more widely used. Since it is still the same instrument as the ordinary clarinet but constructed to larger dimensions, its compass is more or less the same. Its reed is a little softer and thicker than that of the other clarinets. The bass clarinet's role is clearly not to take the place of the higher-pitched clarinets in its upper register but simply to extend their range downwards. There are some very fine effects to be obtained however by doubling the upper notes of the B♭ clarinet an octave lower on a bass clarinet. It is written on the treble clef like the other clarinets, with a range from *e* up to *g'''* giving actual pitches from *D* up to *f''*. Its best notes are its lowest notes, but in view of their slow rate of vibration they must not follow on too quickly one after the other. M. Meyerbeer has assigned an eloquent monologue in the trio in the last act of *Les huguenots* to the bass clarinet (Ex. 104).

Ex. 104

Depending on how it is written for and how well it is played, this instrument in its low register can take on the uncouth tone of the ordinary clarinet's bottom notes or the calm, solemn, priestly strain of certain organ registrations. So it may often be aptly used. Furthermore, if four or five are used in unison in wind bands the bass line acquires an admirably unctuous quality.

In the proofs of the 1844 edition of the *Treatise* Berlioz added at the end of this section: 'The best bass clarinets are evidently those made in Paris by the able manufacturer Adolphe Sax, who plays it himself with remarkable skill.' He deleted this before publication.

Of the two bass clarinets Berlioz used exclusively the B♭ version. The first time was in *Benvenuto Cellini*, composed in 1836, the year of the bass clarinet's celebrated first appearance in *Les huguenots*. It accompanies the Pope in a 'solemn, priestly strain' (*NBE* 1c: 853) and features also therefore in the papal music in the overture.

A bass clarinet is offered as an alternative to play the trombone solo in the second movement of the *Symphonie funèbre et triomphale* (*NBE* 19: 108); that work has a part throughout for two bass clarinets, which should perhaps aspire to the 'admirable unctuous quality' he mentions, since they mostly play the bass line. In the *Rgm* text of this passage Berlioz wrote: 'Certain German military bands owe the unctuous sound of their low instruments in soft passages to the numerous bass clarinets they have. We have this instrument at the Opéra, introduced by M. Meyerbeer, but none anywhere else.' At the time of writing (1841) he had not yet visited Germany.

In the *Chant sacré* (1843) Berlioz required two clarinets and two bass clarinets, each with its own part, although he allowed the substitution of clarinets if bass clarinets were not available. He knew this was the case in Marseilles where it was first performed.[15] The instrument plays an important part in *La damnation de Faust* in Mephistopheles's scene with the 'follets'; a third player is required here, although in other works the bass clarinet is to be taken by one of the two clarinets, or, in the last two movements of the *Te deum*, one of the four clarinets. Its greatest part in Berlioz's music is in the last act of *Les Troyens*, where it has a considerable supporting part in Dido's monologue 'Je vais mourir' (*NBE* 2b: 706). It is also used to evoke the ghosts earlier in the act, and in the *Prologue Lamento* to *Les Troyens à Carthage*.

Its highest note is a *b″* reached in *Benvenuto Cellini* (*NBE* 1c: 881) and in *Les Troyens* (*NBE* 2b: 707).

THE BASSET HORN

This would differ from the alto clarinet in low F only by the addition of the little brass bell which extends its lower end but for its ability to go chromatically down to *c*, a third below the bottom note of the clarinet. Its range is from *c* chromatically up to *g‴*, giving actual pitches from *F* up to *c‴*. Notes above this range are exceedingly hazardous; there is really never any good reason why they should be used when there are higher clarinets to produce them with less difficulty and greater purity.

Like those of the bass clarinet the bottom notes of the basset horn are the finest and most individual. It should simply be observed, however, that all the notes below *e* (that is to say, *eb–d–db–c*) can only be produced at a slow pace with one note detached from the next. A figure like Ex. 105 would not be practicable.

Ex. 105

15 *Cg*, 3, p. 140.

Mozart used this fine instrument in pairs to darken the harmonic colour of his *Requiem*, and gave it some important solos in his opera *La clemenza di Tito*.

In the *Rgm* text Berlioz had added: 'In Paris we cannot play these masterpieces in the composer's instrumentation since our orchestras have no basset horns at all and since this fine instrument is not taught at the Conservatoire!!!' In 1848 Berlioz wrote his 'Voyage musical en Bohème'[16] in which the basset horn is again discussed:

> The omission of the basset horn from the syllabus of students of the clarinet [at the Paris Conservatoire] was until recently a serious error, for it meant that a great deal of Mozart's music could not be performed properly in France – an absurd state of affairs. But now that Adolphe Sax has perfected the bass clarinet to the point where it can perform everything that lies within the range of the basset horn and more (it can play a minor third lower), and since its timbre is similar to the basset horn's but even more beautiful, the bass clarinet should be studied in conservatoires alongside the soprano clarinet and the smaller clarinets in E♭, F and high A♭.

Berlioz had heard Mozart's *Requiem* in Naples in 1831 and written a comparison of it and Cherubini's *Requiem* in March 1834.[17] He knew at least parts of *La clemenza di Tito* from their adaptation in Lachnith's travesty of *Die Zauberflöte* called *Les mystères d'Isis*, still in the repertory of the Opéra in the 1820s. He never wrote for the basset horn in any of his scores.

IMPROVEMENTS IN THE CLARINET FAMILY

The manufacture of the clarinet, which remained in its infancy for so long, is today on the verge of making valuable progress. Good results have already been achieved by the clever and intelligent instrument maker, M. Adolphe Sax of Paris. By a small extension of the body of the clarinet down towards the bell he has given it an extra semitone at the bottom so that it can now play the *e♭* (or *d♯*). The *b♭'* in the intermediate register – a poor note on the old clarinet – is one of the best notes on the new one. The trills *a–b*, *e'–f♯'*, *b♭'–c♭"* and *b♭'–c"*, the rapid alternation of *f'–f"*, and a host of other unplayable passages, have become easy and effective. Top notes are a well-known bugbear for composers and players, who venture to use them only rarely and with the greatest caution. Thanks to a small key placed very near the mouthpiece, M. Sax has made these notes as pure, as mellow and almost as easy as the intermediate register. Thus high *b♭'''*, which normally one would scarcely dare write, speaks on Adolphe Sax's clarinets without

---

[16] Later reprinted as *Memoirs*, 'Travels in Germany', II/5.
[17] *Le rénovateur*, 30 March 1834; *Cm*, 1, p. 203.

requiring any preparation or effort on the part of the player. It can be tongued *pianissimo* without any danger and it is at least as soft as on the flute.

To solve the problem of wooden mouthpieces being affected by dryness on the one hand and humidity on the other depending on whether the instrument has gone several days without being played or has at the other extreme been too long in use, M. Sax has made a clarinet mouthpiece of gilt metal which brightens the sound and suffers none of the variability of wooden mouthpieces. This clarinet has a greater range, a more equal tone, is easier to play and is more in tune than the old model without any change in fingering except for a small number of simplifications.

M. Sax's new bass clarinet is even more advanced. It has twenty-two keys. The features which really mark it off from the old one are its perfect intonation, its even temperament throughout the chromatic scale and its stronger sound. Since the bore is very long the bell is practically touching the ground with the player standing up. This would have an appalling dampening effect if the resourceful inventor had not devised a concave metal reflector which being placed beneath the bell prevents the sound getting lost, directs it wherever one may choose and considerably increases its volume. Adolphe Sax's bass clarinets are in Bb.

This section did not appear in the 1841 *Rgm* articles on the clarinets, in which Adolphe Sax's name was not mentioned (the mention of Sax in the section on the clarinet that precedes Ex. 94 was added for the *Treatise* in 1843). It is derived from an article in the *Journal des débats* of 12 June 1842 devoted to Sax, who had recently arrived in Paris from Brussels, and his innovations. Berlioz became one of his most ardent admirers. He praised his work on innumerable occasions in the press and advocated the introduction of his instruments wherever he could. The clarinet was in fact undergoing rapid advances in two Parisian workshops simultaneously, that of Sax, and that of Klosé and Buffet, whom Berlioz never mentioned, but whose adaptation of Boehm's flute mechanism for the clarinet was ultimately to win universal acceptance by clarinet players. Sax's model, successful enough in its time, led to the 'simple system' now used only by beginners.

Sax took out patents for the addition of two semitones to the bottom end of the clarinet, *e*b and *d*, with the advantage that Bb clarinets could now play anything written for the A clarinet. More important, the overblown twelfths, *b*b' and *a*', were now of good quality rather than subject to the weakness of the break. None of Sax's innovations – the extra low notes, the second speaker-key, and the gilt-metal mouthpieces – survive in use today.

His bass clarinet, on the other hand, had lasting success, even though a Boehm mechanism would eventually supplant his own. The article in the *Journal des débats* differs somewhat here. The passage on the bass clarinet is:

Sax's new bass clarinet has replaced everything except its name. Its holes have been done away with and replaced by keys adjusted to nodal points of vibration. It has twenty-two keys. Its special qualities are its perfect intonation and an even temperament throughout the chromatic scale. Its enlarged diameter produces a stronger sound without inhibiting or restricting the performance of octaves and fifths. This advantage is also the result of drilling a speaker-key near the instrument's mouthpiece. Its range is three octaves and a sixth. But it is not the immense compass that makes it so valuable, since the bass clarinet has little role to play in the upper register. The beauty of its low notes alone gives it its great value.

He adds the description of the reflector-plate and then goes on to discuss the saxophone (see below, p. 296).

6

Wind without reeds

For a long period this instrument was most imperfect in many respects, but it is now, thanks to the skill of certain makers and to the method of manufacture adopted by Boehm following Gordon's discovery, as comprehensive, as accurate in tuning and as even in sound as one could wish.

The same will soon be true, moreover, of the whole woodwind family. Their intonation could clearly never be anything near irreproachable since the holes had always been bored to accommodate the natural spacing of the player's fingers and not in accordance with the rational division of the resonating tube, a division based on the laws of resonance and determined by the nodes of oscillation. Gordon, followed by Boehm, began by boring wind instruments at the precise positions on the tube required by the physics of resonance without any regard for the facility or even the possibility of placing fingers over each hole. They were confident that they could then make it possible by one method or another.

Once the instrument was bored according to this procedure and made in tune, they worked out a mechanism of keys and rings placed where the player's fingers could easily reach and designed to open or close those holes that lie beyond the reach of the fingers. The old fingering has thus had to be changed and players have had to develop new ways of practising. But once this difficulty had been overcome the new instruments soon offered such compensating advantages that at the present time we are convinced by their gradual acceptance that within a few years all new woodwind instruments will be made according to the Gordon–Boehm system, to the complete exclusion of the old models.

This passage was written at a time when bitter controversy raged over the respective contributions of Gordon and Boehm to the development of the flute; Berlioz seems to distance himself from the dispute by not taking sides. A member of Charles X's Swiss guard, Captain William Gordon spent the years 1826 to

1830 in Paris, where he was a pupil of Drouet and Tulou. Fleeing the 1830 Revolution he went to London, where his new ideas on the mechanism of the flute were taken up by a number of flautists and where he first met Boehm. Theobald Boehm (1794–1881) was trained both as a goldsmith and as a flautist. After hearing the flautist Charles Nicholson in London and the encounter with Gordon, Boehm produced an improved flute in his Munich workshop in 1832, the basis of his many advances in flute design. Gordon's work was brought to an end by his mental collapse and death in Lausanne about 1838, and his claims to be the originator of Boehm's innovations were vigorously upheld by the flautist Victor Coche and by the historian of the flute R. R. Rockstro. Although Boehm's flute reached its definitive form in 1847, Berlioz did not revise the chapter on the flute for the 1855 edition of the *Treatise*. He did, however, write a report on the Boehm flute as a member of the jury at the Great Exhibition in 1851:

> The true inventor of this system was called Gordon. But the ingenious application M. Boehm has made of it, especially on the flute, deserves the attention given to his work by players and public. M. Boehm makes most of his flutes of silver. Their sound is soft and crystalline but less full and loud than that of wooden flutes. The new system has the advantage of making the intonation of wind instruments almost perfect and of allowing players to play easily in keys which were almost impossible on the old instruments.
>
> The fingering of M. Boehm's instruments is essentially different from that used on other types, hence the resistance by many players to the introduction of the new system. It would cost them too much to relearn their instrument, and it is easy to see that the example of MM. Dorus and Brunot, who did not hesitate to start their flute studies over again, has few imitators even among young players. We are convinced, however, that the Gordon–Boehm system will soon prevail.[1]

Just a few years ago the flute had a range that went only from d' chromatically up to a'''. To this compass there have been added in turn two semitones at the bottom and three at the top, giving three full chromatic octaves from c' up to c'''' (this top note is very harsh). But since not all players have the low c' attachment (the little tuning extension which gives the flute the low $c\sharp'$ and c'), it is best in most cases to avoid these two notes when writing for the orchestra. The top two notes b''' and c'''' should likewise not be used in *pianissimo* because of the difficulty of getting the notes to sound and because of their rather harsh quality. High $b\flat'''$, on the other hand, is easily produced and can be held as softly as one wishes without any danger. The number of practicable trills was rather limited on the old flute, but thanks to the keys fitted to the new flute major and minor trills are practicable over a great part of its chromatic range. Exceptions are shown in Ex. 106; difficult trills are shown as Ex. 106a, very difficult trills

---

[1] *Jd*, 12 January 1856. See Philip Bate, 'The Boehm–Gordon controversy', in his *The Flute* (2nd edn, London, 1979), pp. 246–50, and *Encyclopédie de la musique*, ed. Lavignac and Laurencie (Paris, 1925), Part 2, pp. 1495–1503.

as Ex. 106b and impossible trills as Ex. 106c. On flutes constructed on the Boehm model trills are practicable all the way from $d\flat'$ up to top c'''', even at the very top end of the range, and in addition they are far better in tune.

Ex. 106

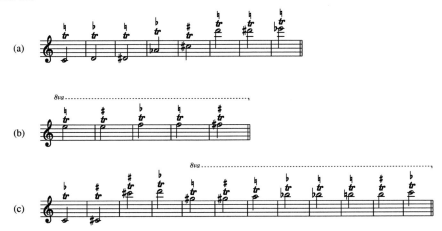

Berlioz treated the flute's upper limit as $b\flat'''$ in his earliest works. After *Rob Roy* (*NBE* 20: 121) the limit was raised to $b\natural'''$, avoiding c'''' in the *Symphonie fantastique* (*NBE* 16: 36) and *Le roi Lear* (*NBE* 20: 75, 81). After the *Corsaire* overture (*NBE* 20: 294) the top flute note is treated as c''''. Some printed scores of *Le roi Lear* show a high d'''' at bar 589 (*NBE* 20: 111), but this is an octave too high, a misreading of an indistinct autograph.[2]

At the lower end of the instrument he used d' freely and frequently. The transposition of *Le roi de Thulé* (in *La damnation de Faust*) down from G to F gave the second flute a number of sustained and exposed passages on the note c', calling for a footnote to advise transposing the part up an octave on instruments which lack the c' keys (*NBE* 8b: 459). A low c' is found also in *Au cimetière* (*NBE* 13: 72) with no footnote.

Berlioz's remarks on trills seem to apply only to older instruments, and his later works may have been expected to enjoy the advantages of Boehm's improvements. On the basis of Ex. 106 some passages in the *Symphonie fantastique* might have been 'very difficult' at the time (*NBE* 16: 106 – triplets $e\natural''''-f\sharp''''$) or even 'impossible' (*NBE* 16: 106 – triplets $g\sharp''''-a''''$). In *Benvenuto Cellini* the rapid alternation $g\flat'''-a\flat'''-g\flat'''$ is avoided (*NBE* 1c: 883).

The flute is the most agile of wind instruments, equally at home in rapid passagework, whether diatonic or chromatic, legato or detached, in arpeggios, or even wide intervals, as in Ex. 107a, or repeated notes like a violin staccato, obtained by 'double-tonguing', as in Ex. 107b.

Ex. 107

[2] The error is in the scores published by Catelin, Richault and Eulenburg. The autograph is in the Koch Collection at the Beinecke Rare Book Library at Yale University.

The keys of D, G, C, F, A, E, B♭, E♭ and their relative minors are the flute's favourite keys; the rest are much harder. On the Boehm flute, on the other hand, D♭ is almost as easy as D♮.

The style of Ex. 107a, typical of flute concerto writing, is not found in Berlioz's music, but Ex. 107b is very similar to a passage in the slow movement of the *Symphonie fantastique* (*NBE* 16: 87), a type of flute writing Berlioz never used again. A technical feature he does not mention or explain is the glissando descending from *c'''* to *c''* in the last movement of the *Symphonie fantastique* (*NBE* 16: 116–17, 119).

The sound of the instrument is soft in the middle register, rather piercing at the top and very individual at the bottom. The tone in the middle and top registers has no specially distinct character. These registers may be used for melodies or a variety of expressive purposes, but they can never match the oboe's naive gaiety or the clarinet's noble tenderness. The flute in fact seems to be an instrument almost lacking in expression; because of its facility in playing rapid notes and in sustaining high notes which an orchestra needs to fill in the upper parts of the harmony, it is constantly called upon in every kind of circumstance. In general this is true. But if you study it carefully you will recognise its characteristic expression and grasp its capacity to render certain states of mind in a way no other instrument can. If for example you need a desolate – but also humble and resigned – tone for a sad melody, the weak notes in the flute's middle register, especially in the keys of C minor or D minor, will certainly produce the right nuance. One composer alone has made something of this pale colouring, in my view, and that is Gluck. If you listen to the ballet in D minor in the scene in the Elysian Fields in *Orphée*, you will see at once that only a flute could play the melody. An oboe would have been too childlike and its voice would not seem sufficiently pure; the cor anglais is too low and serious; a clarinet would have done better, no doubt, except that certain notes would have been too loud; not even its softest notes could fade to the frail, stifled, veiled *f''* and *bb'*, notes which give the flute such a sad quality in this key of D minor, a key in which they occur frequently. In fact neither the violin nor the viola nor the cello, either in solo or in a section, would suit the depiction of this thousand-fold sublime wailing of a suffering, despairing shade of the departed; it needed precisely the instrument the composer chose. And Gluck's melody is conceived in such a way that the flute lends itself to all the vicissitudes of this eternal grief, still imprinted with the scars of passion from life on earth. At first it is a scarcely audible voice that seems afraid to be heard; then it begins to wail softly, rising to a reproach, then to profound grief, then to the cry of a heart rent by an incurable wound, and then falls back little by little to the lamentation, the wailing and the bitter sob of a soul resigned . . . What a poet!

Berlioz's low opinion of the flute's capacity for expression is confirmed by the scarcity of flute solos in his music. In 1834 he called the flute 'the most idiotic instrument of all'.[3] Apart from the trio for two flutes and harp in *L'enfance du Christ* (where local colour is the object), there is no passage in any work that features the flute in a prominent solo role, the nearest being the scene in Part III of *La damnation de Faust*, where Faust examines Marguerite's chamber (*NBE* 8a: 261). This passage conforms with Berlioz's prescription of a 'desolate – but also humble and resigned – tone for a sad melody' on 'the weak notes in the flute's middle register', and is in the key of C minor, one of the keys he suggests for this effect.

Melodies in which the flute plays with other woodwind in unison or an octave above are common. A flute supported by a clarinet an octave lower is a very characteristic Berlioz timbre. Less usual is the combination with a bassoon an octave lower, as in *Le roi Lear* (*NBE* 20: 77), and the doubling of a single flute with the first violins, used memorably in the *Symphonie fantastique* for the main melodies of both first and third movements. In the latter case the original scoring of the melody was for violins and clarinet, not flute, as in the *Gratias agimus* of the *Messe solennelle*.

Although he admired Gluck's use of the solo flute and often praised the great solo in Act II of *Orphée*, he was less enthusiastic about Beethoven's. He once dismissed the famous flute solo in the overture *Leonora no. 3* as 'unworthy of the rest'.[4]

An effect of remarkable sweetness is the combination of two flutes playing successions of thirds in the middle register in E♭ or A♭, keys which especially favour the instrument's velvety sound. There are some fine examples in the Priests' Chorus in Act I of Sacchini's *Œdipe à Colonne*, 'O vous que l'innocence même' (Ex. 108a), and in the cavatina in the duet in *La vestale*, 'Les dieux prendront pitié' (Ex. 108b). The notes *b♭″–a♭″–g″–f″–e♭″* on flutes have much the same sound as a harmonica in this spacing (Ex. 108c). Thirds on oboes, cors anglais or clarinets would be altogether different.

Ex. 108

(a)

[3] *Cm*, 1, p. 225.   [4] *Jd*, 19 May 1860.

(b)

LICINIUS

Les dieux prendront pi - tié   du   sort   qui nous ac-

Flutes

- ca - ble. Ils   ont   jeté sur nous   un re - gard fa - vo-

pp

- ra - ble.

(c)   Flutes

It was perhaps this sound that he meant to evoke in Act I of *Les Troyens* (*NBE* 2a: 46) when Cassandra 'falls into a tender reverie' and gives out Chorebus's name to the notes $bb'-ab'-g'$, echoed by a pair of flutes in thirds.

The flute's low notes have been used badly or not at all by the majority of composers; yet Weber, in a host of places in *Der Freischütz*, and before him Gluck, in the *Marche religieuse* in *Alceste*, have shown just what can be done with them in moods of gravity or reverie (Ex. 109a). These low notes, as I have already said, blend very well with the low range of the cor anglais and the clarinet: they lend a darker shade to soften the expression. See also Ex. 109b, from Weber's *Der Freischütz*. There is something wonderfully entrancing about those two flutes holding low notes for Agathe's melancholy prayer; her eyes scan the treetops silvered by the light of the stars. Modern composers generally write too persistently in the high register of the flute; they seem to be afraid that it will not be heard distinctly over the main body of the orchestra. The result is that it is too prominent, instead of blending into the ensemble, and the instrumentation becomes shrill and harsh instead of sonorous and harmonious.

Ex. 109

Berlioz's attachment to the special sound of low flutes in the march from *Alceste* was formed early, as we can tell from the *Memoirs'* record of his remarks before performances at the Opéra:

> The conductor ought to keep an eye on Guillou, the first flute, who's coming in now. He takes extraordinary liberties with Gluck: the *Marche religieuse* in *Alceste*, for instance, where the composer has written for the bottom register of the flutes, precisely because he wants the special effect of their lowest notes. That doesn't suit Guillou. He has to dominate, his part has got to be heard – so he transposes the flute line up an octave, destroying the composer's intention and turning an imaginative idea into something feeble and obvious.[5]

Despite his liking for the sound of low flutes, Berlioz found little place for them in his scores. In *La mort d'Orphée* there is a striking combination of two low flutes in unison with a solo horn and a solo viola (*NBE* 6: 8). For special effects an accented low flute is sometimes used over a clarinet (*Sara la baigneuse*, *NBE* 12a: 330) or horns (*Le cinq mai*, *NBE* 12a: 387), and the combination with low clarinets in *Le roi de Thulé* has already been mentioned. Low flutes are briefly but tellingly exposed in the final scene of *Les Troyens* (*NBE* 2b: 728) when Dido utters the words 'Je sens rentrer le calme dans mon cœur', a line borrowed from Gluck's *Iphigénie en Tauride*.

Flutes have a family, like oboes and clarinets, and just as extensive. The flute we have just described is the most common. In normal orchestras one generally writes two flute parts; nevertheless soft chords held by three flutes would make a marvellous effect. There is a delightful sound to be had by combining one solo flute in the high register with four violins, making a sustained high harmony in five parts. Despite the custom of always giving the first flute the top notes of the harmony, which is reasonable enough, there are many occasions when the opposite can be done to advantage.

Berlioz's discussion of the flute family follows after the next section on the piccolo.

There are some departures from the usual practice of writing for two flutes in his music. A single flute is required in the three orchestral songs *La belle voyageuse*, *Le jeune pâtre breton* and *Zaïde*. A section of three flutes is required in *La damnation de Faust*, primarily to provide flexibility in combination with one, two or three piccolos, but also for the sonority of three flutes in harmony, used both in the *Chant de la fête de Pâques* and the final scene *Dans le ciel*. Four flutes are required in both the *Requiem* and the *Te deum*. The *Hostias* in the former work includes the famous passage where chords on three high flutes are supported by eight low unison trombones (*NBE* 9: 113) and the *Agnus dei* calls for four-note chords on four flutes (*NBE* 9: 133). In the *Te deum* the four flutes play in four parts only in the final *Marche*. The mention of 'one solo flute in the high register with four violins' refers to the *Sanctus* in the *Requiem* (*NBE* 9: 115), where that very combination provides a celestial accompaniment for the solo tenor two octaves below the flute line. A similar use of the solo flute is found in the third movement of *Harold en Italie* (*NBE* 17: 119–22), where a high flute with harp harmonics an octave below sings out the *Harold* theme in long notes over the brisker rhythms of the *Sérénade*.

Berlioz's suggestion that the flute need not take the upper line in the harmony is not often taken up in his scores. There are some brief passages in *L'enfance du Christ* where this disposition is found: for the close of the soothsayers' counsel (*NBE* 11: 60) and the opening of the scene in the stable at Bethlehem (*NBE* 11: 80). The second flute part in the *Messe solennelle* is often rather ineffectively placed an octave below the first. In *Sara la baigneuse* Berlioz tried the odd effect of placing the second flute two octaves below the first, below oboes and clarinets and in the middle of the texture (*NBE* 12a: 314).

Berlioz's skimpy treatment of the flute in his music is strange since it was the only orchestral instrument (apart from the percussion) that he had any skill or experience at playing. The flute played a significant part in his earliest steps as a musician. At the age of about twelve he found an old flageolet at the back of a drawer and soon persuaded his father to allow him to progress to the flute. This he studied with the aid of Devienne's *Méthode de flute théorique et pratique*, published in 1795, and he soon learnt to play Drouet's concertos. Three of his earliest compositions (now all lost) had important parts for flute: the *Potpourri concertant* of 1817–18 and the two quintets for flute and string quartet that followed soon after. In 1819 he acquired a new flute 'made of red ebony, with eight keys of silver, slide ditto and a foot-joint in C',[6] and in his early years in Paris he must have been playing this instrument keenly if in 1826 he considered finding a flute vacancy in an orchestra and even played a concerto in a suburban concert.[7] He probably abandoned the instrument soon thereafter.

Although the flageolet is not discussed in the *Treatise*, the *Rgm* text on the flute began as follows:

> I have little to say about flageolets. Despite the really remarkable talent of certain virtuosi and the pleasure a well-played flageolet solo can sometimes give, it is a fact that no masters of the art have ever used this silly little instrument, and they were right not to include it in their orchestras. In bright, sprightly dance pieces it is not out of place, however, though this is the only exception I would make in its favour. Its tone is rather cheap and common, quite incompatible with any piece at all elevated in style; its range is scarcely more than two octaves; and with the exception of the three or four top notes it has a rather weak sound.

Berlioz once called the flageolet 'that leper of modern music'.[8] The *Rgm* text goes on: 'Flutes, on the other hand, are almost indispensable in instrumentation even though they are often featured in pieces where it would be better if they weren't.'

For Berlioz, as for many composers of the time, the flute had associations with antiquity, even more so in association with the harp. Two flutes and a harp are

---

[6] Cairns, *Berlioz*, p. 86.   [7] *Ibid.*, pp. 190, 531.   [8] *Jd*, 1 May 1836; *Cm*, 2, p. 457.

the domestic instruments in the Ishmaelite household (in *L'enfance du Christ*), and the autograph of *La fuite en Egypte* specifies a 'flûte douce' (ordinary flute in the published score). In the opening scene of *Les Troyens* three 'antique double flutes' are seen on stage, their sound represented by three oboes. Berlioz would have known Virgil's references to this instrument and also Kastner's illustration of it in his *Manuel général de musique militaire* (1848).[9]

THE PICCOLO

The piccolo is an octave higher than the flute. Ex. 110a has the effect shown in Ex. 110b. It has the same compass with the exception of top *c''''*. This note is very hard to get and sounds almost unbearable; one must take care not to write it. Even top *b'''* is extremely harsh and can only be used in a full orchestral *fortissimo*. For the contrary reason it is hardly any good writing for the notes of the bottom octave; they are scarcely audible. So barring some special reason for wanting their weak tone, it is better to substitute the corresponding notes in the flute's second octave.

Ex. 110

Berlioz did not himself use the piccolo's top two notes, *b'''* and *c''''*, the highest note in his scores being the *bb'''* found in the *Tempête* fantasy and several times in the finale of *Harold en Italie*. He used the lowest octave quite freely, the lowest note being *d'*. The overture to *Béatrice et Bénédict* has the piccolo play a scale of G major from *d'* up to *a'''* (*NBE* 3: 6). A notable use of low piccolo notes can be heard in the final bars of the first movement of the *Symphonie fantastique* (*NBE* 16: 43).

Piccolos are curiously misused these days, like all instruments whose vibrations yell or shriek or flash. For pieces of joyful character the second octave (written *d''* to *d'''*) can be very appropriate at all dynamic levels. The top notes (written *e'''* up to *b'''*) are excellent, *fortissimo*, for effects of violence or agony; for a storm, for example, or in a scene of ferocious, satanic character. Thus the piccolo is exactly right in the fourth movement of Beethoven's Pastoral Symphony, sometimes on its own exposed high above the tremolo of the violas, cellos and basses and imitating the whistling of a tempest whose full might is not yet unleashed, sometimes with the full orchestral tutti on even higher notes. In the storm in *Iphigénie en Tauride* Gluck got the top notes of the two unison piccolos to squeak even more harshly, writing them at the top of parallel 6/3 chords a fourth above the

[9] Ian Kemp, *Hector Berlioz: Les Troyens* (Cambridge, 1988), p. 204.

first violins. With the piccolos sounding an octave higher the result is a succession of parallel elevenths with the first violins and an asperity which is here wholly justified.

In the *Chœur des Scythes* in the same opera two piccolos double the violins' turns an octave higher. These shrill notes, combined with the baying of the savage horde and the incessant rhythmic clatter of cymbals and small drum, have a terrifying effect.

Everyone is familiar with the demonic sneering of the two piccolos in thirds in the drinking song in *Der Freischütz*, one of Weber's happiest orchestral inspirations (Ex. 111).

Ex. 111

It was Spontini, in the magnificent *Bacchanale* he wrote for Salieri's *Les danaïdes* (which later became an orgiastic chorus in *Nurmahal*), who first thought of coupling a brief piercing cry on the piccolos with a cymbal clash. The unique relationship thus established between two such dissimilar instruments had not been suspected before. It causes an instantly lacerating, stabbing sensation, like a swordthrust. This is a very characteristic effect even if only the two instruments in question are used. But with a staccato entry of the timpani and a short chord on all the other instruments its force is greatly increased (Ex. 112).

Ex. 112

Berlioz cited bars 68–76 of the opening of *Iphigénie en Tauride*, giving a *c♮‴* for flute and piccolos at the midpoint of the seventh bar of the excerpt, although this is not supported by any Gluck source. When Salieri's *Les danaïdes* was revived at the Opéra in 1817, Spontini provided some additional music, the composer being too old to travel from Vienna. A *Grande bacchanale* composed for this occasion was used again in *Nurmahal* (Berlin, 1822), an opera which Berlioz never saw. Ex. 112 seems to be an illustration invented by Berlioz. The combination of piccolo and cymbals appears several times in Berlioz's work, most notably in the *Francs-juges* overture (*B&H* 4: 42–5) and in *La damnation de Faust* for the appearance of Mephistopheles (*NBE* 8a: 109). In a letter to Ferrand of 28 June 1828 Berlioz wrote out the passage from the *Francs-juges* overture with the words 'coup de poignard' at the point where the *fortissimo* shriek on piccolo and cymbals occurs.[10] A characteristic of these 'satanic' shrieks is the grace note (or notes) on the piccolo, as in Exx. 111 and 112. A similar use of two piccolos is found for the death of *Cléopâtre* (*NBE* 6: 195), but without cymbals.

These various examples – and many others I could mention – strike me as admirable from every point of view. Beethoven, Gluck, Weber and Spontini have made ingenious, original and sensible use of the piccolo. But when I hear it used to double a baritone singing three octaves lower, or to cast its shrill voice into a religious solemnity, or to reinforce and sharpen the orchestral top line from one end of an opera to the other simply for love of noise, I cannot help regarding this type of instrumentation as of a platitude and idiocy only too worthy of the melodic style to which it is applied.

The piccolo can be very effective in soft passages; it is a fallacy to think it can only play very loud. Sometimes it serves as a continuation of the top range of the flute, taking over at the point where the latter runs out of notes. The take-over from one instrument to the other can be handled by the composer without any difficulty in such a way that it sounds like a single flute with an extraordinary range, as in Ex. 113a. There is a delightful

Ex. 113

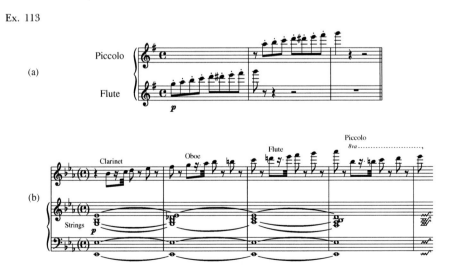

10 *Cg*, 1, pp. 198–9, incorrectly transcribed.

example of this device in Act I of Auber's opera *Le dieu et la bayadère*, in a phrase played *pianissimo* over a low held chord on the strings (Ex. 113b).

Ex. 113a is Berlioz's invention; Ex. 113b is not shown in the *Treatise*.

Berlioz used the piccolo freely and frequently. In many works one or other of the two flutes, usually the second, is required to double on the piccolo. In the *Symphonie fantastique* Berlioz seems to have been indifferent as to which player it was, giving the part to the first flute in two of the movements and to the second in a third.[11] Sometimes both flutes are required to double on piccolos, as in the *Francs-juges* overture, *Cléopâtre* and *La mort d'Orphée*. Berlioz seems to have planned *Benvenuto Cellini* originally for three players, then reverted to two, but he did expand the section to three players in *Roméo et Juliette*, then in *La damnation de Faust*, the orchestral version of *Sara la baigneuse*, and *Les Troyens*. This enabled him to score for two piccolos and one flute (as in the *Menuet des follets*) or even for three piccolos (as in the *Évocation* in Part III of *La damnation de Faust*). The original version of *Waverley* required four players in all, playing two flutes and two piccolos. Two piccolos (with no flutes) are required in *Paysans sous les tilleuls* in the *Huit scènes de Faust* (to suggest rustic piping) and in the wind-band version of the *Scène héroïque*.

The piccolo never has melodic material on its own, although it is often grouped with other woodwind such as flutes and clarinets. In the third movement of *Harold en Italie* it is coupled with an oboe an octave lower to suggest the Abbruzzi peasant's pipe.

A curious feature of Berlioz's piccolo writing is his habit of treating the first flute as the melodic line even when a piccolo is playing above it. The piccolo part is often simply a second flute part played an octave higher. His autographs place the second flute (or the piccolo) on the second stave down, which may be an explanation for this voicing procedure. *Benvenuto Cellini* provides many examples of this practice.

In the finale of the *Symphonie fantastique* (*NBE* 16: 116–17, 119) the piccolo is twice required to execute a glissando descending from c''' to c''. Berlioz provided no explanation of how this is to be done.

OTHER FLUTES

Three other flutes which are useful in military bands could be a considerable asset in ordinary orchestras also. They are:

1 The *flûte tierce* (or 'flute in F'), whose C sounds E♭ and which is thus to be classed with transposing instruments in E♭ in accordance with what we said in chapter 4. It is exactly a minor third higher than the normal flute, from which it differs only in this respect and in its more bell-like sound. Ex. 114a sounds as in Ex. 114b.
2 The minor ninth piccolo ('petite flûte neuvième mineure' or 'piccolo in E♭'), whose C sounds D♭ and which is thus to be classed with

---

[11] *NBE*, 16, p. xiv.

transposing instruments in D♭. It is a semitone higher than the piccolo and it should be treated in a similar manner. Ex. 114c sounds as
in Ex. 114d.

3   The tenth piccolo (or 'piccolo in F'), whose C sounds E♭ and which we
call tenth piccolo ('petite flûte dixième') in E♭. It is an octave higher
than the *flûte tierce* and a tenth higher than the normal flute. Ex. 114e
sounds as in Ex. 114f. It should not be taken above *a′′′*, and even this
exceedingly piercing note is hard to get.

Some orchestras have a 'minor second flute', whose C sounds D♭ and
which should be called the 'flute in D♭'. Its pitch is just a semitone above
the normal flute. Ex. 114g sounds as in Ex. 114h.

Ex. 114

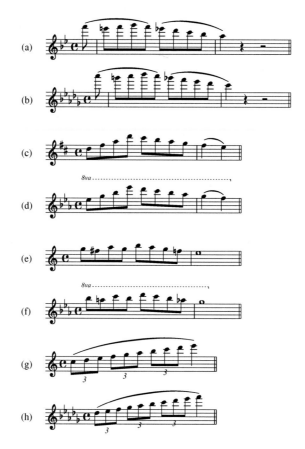

The explanation of why these members of the flute family are pitched in particular keys but referred to incorrectly as if they were pitched a whole tone higher
is found in chapter 4.

A group of five *flûtes tierces* is required in the *Symphonie funèbre et triomphale*. They
are notated in E♭, with the 1843 orchestral part marked 'incorrectly named flute
in F'. The *Rgm* text has here, in addition:

The tone of the *flûte tierce*, moreover, is not quite like that of the normal flute. It is an asset for bright, joyful melodies. So it's a pity they don't make a *flûte quinte* in G to stress the expressive possibilities of the high flutes without having to fall back on the often too piercing sound of the flutes' top notes. In sharp keys, which are generally chosen for lively pieces, this middle-sized flute, playing with one less sharp than the rest of the orchestra (in D instead of A, in A instead of E, etc.) would do wonders, in my opinion.

A group of four Db piccolos is required in the *Symphonie funèbre et triomphale*. In the 1843 orchestral parts they are described as 'incorrectly named flute in Eb'. In 1846 Berlioz suggested transposing the piccolo part of the last movement of the *Symphonie fantastique* for Db piccolo, although this was never done.[12] The piccolo in Eb and the flute in Db are not found in Berlioz's scores.

All these flutes serve to extend the upper limits of the instrument and have variously individual tone qualities. They are useful, furthermore, for making playing easier and for safeguarding the flute's sonority by allowing it to play in one of its brighter keys when the orchestra is playing in one of its duller keys. In a piece in Eb it is obviously better to choose the minor ninth piccolo in Db than the normal piccolo, since it can then play in the key of D, a much easier and more resonant key for it.

It is a pity that the *flûte d'amour* has fallen into disuse. Its pitch was a minor third lower than the normal flute, in the key of A therefore. Ex. 115a sounds as in Ex. 115b. It would complete the lower end of this family (which could be as numerous as the clarinet family if one wished), and its soft, mellow tone could be excellent either to contrast with the tone of higher flutes and oboes, or to give more body and colour to those remarkable harmonies made up of the bottom notes of flutes, cors anglais and clarinets.

Ex. 115

The *flûte d'amour* is not found in Berlioz's scores. It was in use in the eighteenth and early nineteenth centuries but was in effect extinct by Berlioz's time. This passage appeared in the *Rgm* text as follows:

One may add an extension to the flute called a 'C key' which gives low *c'* and *c♯'* at the bottom of its range. This would not be necessary if we had the

---

[12] *Ibid.*

flûte d'amour whose pitch is a minor third lower than the ordinary flute, in the key of A in other words. Its soft, mellow tone quality could produce some delightfully different effects. Unfortunately it is almost unknown. By forming whole families of wind instruments one would get results of which the organ's *jeu de flûtes* and *jeu d'anches* can give only a feeble impression. This will come about in due course.

Berlioz's optimism was justified, although it was eventually the alto flute in G not the *flûte d'amour* in A that found a place in the orchestra.

7

Wind with keyboard

This is a keyboard instrument with wooden and metal pipes set in vibration by wind blown by bellows.

The greater (or smaller) the number of ranks of pipes of different materials and different dimensions an organ has, the greater (or smaller) the choice of stops by means of which the organist can change the tone, dynamic and range of the instrument. The mechanism by which the organist gets this or that rank to sound, drawing out a small piece of wood, is called a stop (*registre*).

The range of the instrument is not fixed. It depends on its size, normally determined by the length in feet of its largest pipe giving the lowest note on the keyboard. Thus one speaks of a 32-foot organ, or a 16-foot, or 8-foot, or 4-foot organ. If an instrument possesses the lowest rank, called 32-foot open flute, as well as the 16-foot open flute, the 8-foot open flute, the 4-foot *prestant* or open flute, and the *doublette* which sounds an octave higher than that, it has an immense range of eight octaves. The 32-foot range is from C'' up to c', the 16-foot from C' up to c'', the 8-foot from C up to c''', the *prestant* or 4-foot from c up to c'''', and the *doublette* from c' up to c''''', all these being chromatic. These five ranks thus have four octaves each, although many of those we mention below have only three or even two. Organ builders nowadays add five notes at the top of the keyboard; the top of the range is thus extended chromatically to f'''.

A full organ normally has five manuals one above the other. The one nearest to the organist is the *positif*, the next the *grand orgue*, the third the *bombarde*, the fourth the *récit*, the fifth the *écho*. There is a sixth keyboard arranged in such a way that it can be activated by the player's feet and therefore known as the pedalboard. It is responsible for the organ's lowest sounds. It has just two octaves at the very bottom and sometimes even has certain notes left out. Several ranks, such as the 8-foot for example, which are used on as many as three keyboards – the *grand orgue*, the *positif*, and the pedals – can be duplicated or triplicated.

Organ stops are divided into flue pipes ('jeux à bouche') and reed pipes ('jeux d'anche'). The former are named after a kind of open mouth at one end which helps produce the sound; the latter are named after the little brass tongue also placed at the end of the pipe, which produces a special tone. Flue stops are divided into foundation stops, or 'octave' stops, and 'mutation' stops. Foundation stops are open or stopped; the stopped pipes, known as 'bourdons', sound an octave lower than open pipes of the same length. Mutation stops are odd in that they sound the third, fifth, tenth, twelfth etc. above each note in such a way as to make up the aliquots, or harmonics, of larger pipes by the operation of several smaller pipes. Organ-builders and organists are unanimous in admiring the effect of this multiple resonance, which actually causes several different keys to sound at once. 'It would be unbearable if one could pick out the two upper notes', they say, 'but they are *inaudible*, absorbed by the sound of the bottom note.' The problem is to know how something inaudible can make a good impression on the ear. At all events this unusual scheme will always tend to give the organ the very harmonic resonance which they are always desperately trying to avoid on large grand pianos and which in my view is one of the most severe drawbacks of the sound that modern improvements have brought to that instrument.

Among mutation stops are:

1 The *gros nazard*, sounding a fifth above the 8-foot open flute.
2 The *grosse tierce*, sounding a fifth above the *prestant*.
3 The *onzième de nazard*, in unison with the *doublette*.
4 The *tierce*, sounding a third above the *doublette*.
5 The *fourniture*, or *plein jeu*, made up of three ranks of pipes and seven ranks of pipes aliquot one to another.
6 The *cymbale*, the same as the *fourniture* except that the pipes are smaller.
7 The *cornet*, a very bright stop of two octaves' range and five ranks of pipes; it has only the treble register. Large organs have three *cornet* stops, one on the *positif*, one on the *grand orgue*, and a third on the *récit*.

Of the reed stops we will list only the following:

1 The *bombarde*, a stop of great power played on a separate manual or on the pedals. Its first pipe is of 16-foot length. It is in unison with the 16-foot open stops.
2 The *trompette*, sounding in unison with 8-foot stops, thus an octave higher than the *bombarde*.
3 The *clairon*, an octave higher than the *trompette*.
4 The *cromorne*, at the same pitch as the *trompette* but less noisy. It is always played on the *positif*.

5 The *voix humaine*, sounding at 8-foot pitch and played on the *grand orgue*.
6 The *hautbois*, in unison with the *trompette*. It normally has only the top octaves, but is complemented by the *basson* taking care of the other two octaves.

These various stops more or less resemble the instruments whose names they bear. Some organs have many more, such as *cor anglais, trombone* etc.

Every organ has to have a stop which provides the principal sonority, covering the whole keyboard, and for this reason it is called the *principal*.

The sentence reporting the extension of the upper range of organ keyboards up to f''' was added in the 1855 edition.

Berlioz's technical description of the organ is incomplete and inaccurate in a few particulars. Only the largest organs, for example, had five manuals. The pedalboard in Berlioz's time was already extending above (and below) the two-octave compass. The *gros nazard* is an octave lower than the more usual *nazard*, which is not mentioned and which sounds the twelfth. The *grosse tierce* sounds a third, not a fifth, above the *prestant*. The *onzième de nazard* is more usually termed the *quarte de nazard*, sounding the fifteenth, i.e. an eleventh above the *gros nazard*. The definition of *fourniture*, a complex and variable mixture stop, is not at all clear, the term 'aliquot' referring to the mathematical ratios of different ranks of pipes. Both *fourniture* and *cymbale* had from three to six ranks, usually four. The *voix humaine* is in fact more often found on the *récit* than on the *grand orgue*. *Principal* is not the usual French term for the organ's principal sonority, although it is sometimes found; the normal 8-foot stop of this kind is the *montre*, with the 4-foot *prestant*.

Berlioz's dislike of mutation stops was based more on logic than on experience, which has long established the richness that non-octave overtones can give to organ tone. He returns to this topic in the section on the melodium (see pp. 311–12). In 1844, when the new organ at St-Eustache was destroyed by fire, he reacted thus:

> If the fire had destroyed just those horrible mutation stops which play every-thing in three keys at once, mixing major and minor and creating harmonies fit to drive donkeys mad, hallowed by tradition and likely to be perpetuated by organists and organ-builders until the end of time, there would be cause for rejoicing. But the whole thing! That's a terrible loss.[1]

Organ fingering is the same as on the piano, except that since notes sound less instantaneously on the organ, they cannot be played in such rapid succession; moreover the organ's keyboard mechanism requires much heavier pressure on the keys. This instrument has the faculty of sustaining notes for as long as one desires, so it is therefore better suited than any other to the legato style, that is to say the style in which the

---

[1] *Jd*, 29 December 1844.

harmony is often built on suspensions and stepwise movement. But this is not, in my opinion, a good reason for confining it exclusively to that style.

One sometimes writes for the organ on three staves, the two upper staves being for the hands and the lowest stave for the pedals.

Berlioz notated all his organ parts on two staves, following standard practice in orchestral and operatic organ parts; three staves are found only in solo organ music at that time. But in the *Te deum* his indications of which notes are to be played on the pedals are thoroughly misleading.[2] The music is notated as low as C' – for example at bars 208–10 of the *Judex crederis* (*NBE* 10: 136–7) – giving the actual pitch required. But the marking *Péd.* is given when, and only when, the lowest note goes below C, as if Berlioz regarded the pedals as mere extensions of the manuals, useful only when the latter could not reach the required notes. He must have been aware of the pedals' independent sonority and their role in providing the organ's main bass line, but a strict observance of his pedal markings would produce a disturbingly unbalanced effect and would require the transposition of the bottom line up an octave at least. This misunderstanding of organ pedals is a curious parallel to his misunderstanding of piano pedals (see above, p. 93).

Like the piano – indeed, much more so than the piano – the organ seems to have two identities in the hierarchy of instruments: as an addition to the orchestra, or as a full and independent orchestra on its own. Doubtless it is perfectly possible to combine the organ with the various constituent groups of the orchestra; it has been done many times. But it is a strange degradation to reduce this majestic instrument to such a secondary role. Besides, it must be recognised that its even, equal, uniform sound never fully blends with individual orchestral timbres and that there seems to be a secret hostility between these two musical powers. The organ and the orchestra are both kings; or rather, one is Emperor and the other is Pope. Their missions are not the same, their interests are too wide and various to be interlocked. So on almost every occasion when this unique fusion is attempted, either the organ heavily outweighs the orchestra, or the orchestra, reinforced to massive strength, almost swamps its adversary.

Only the softest organ stops seem suitable for accompanying voices. In general the organ is made for absolute domination; it is a jealous and intolerant instrument. It seems to me that only one circumstance would allow it to mix with chorus and orchestra without loss of authority, and that would be on the sole condition that it remained strictly separate. For example, if a large body of voices placed in the choir of a church at a great distance from the organ breaks off singing from time to time to allow the organ to repeat its phrases either in whole or in part, or if in a ceremony of mournful character the choir is accompanied by the antiphonal wailing of

---

[2] *NBE*, 10, p. xi, and Denis McCaldin, 'Berlioz and the organ', *The Organ Yearbook*, 4 (1973), pp. 3–17.

orchestra and organ coming from opposite points of the building with the organ answering the orchestra like a mysterious echo of its lamentation, this would be a type of instrumentation capable of tremendously sublime effects. But even here the organ would not really blend with the other instruments; it would respond to them, it would pose them questions; there would simply be an alliance between the two rival powers all the more sincere in that neither would suffer loss of face. Every time I have heard an organ playing at the same time as an orchestra it has struck me as a detestable noise, detracting from the orchestra rather than adding to it.

This passage formed the opening section of Berlioz's article on the organ published in the *Rgm* on 24 April 1842. It is strikingly prophetic of Berlioz's conception of the *Te deum*, which he first mentioned in 1846 and composed mostly in 1849. In a letter of May 1847 to V. V. Stasov Berlioz wrote: 'As for the organ, it can be put to good use in certain kinds of sacred music by playing in dialogue with the orchestra. But I don't think it can be effective if they are both employed simultaneously.'[3] In a notice preceding the performance of the *Te deum* in 1855 Berlioz wrote:

> In this work the organ is not reduced to the role of accompanist. It is rarely heard at the same time as the orchestra and is in dialogue with the voices and the other instruments. It puts forward the theme that the rest have to develop, or at other times it supplies a weighty conclusion at the end of a movement, or utters a kind of musical reflection when the other performers at the far end of the church are silent.[4]

Berlioz was familiar with one or two notable uses of the organ in opera, but he does not mention them. The organ makes a striking entry in the last act of *Robert le diable* and at the opening of *La juive*, both for church scenes, and although in his lengthy article on the instrumentation of *Robert le diable* Berlioz says nothing about the organ,[5] his notice of *La juive* included the following:

> Ever since *Robert le diable* it has been forbidden to write an opera of any significance without using the organ. Not even Musard could refrain from this majestic support for his contredanses. The introduction of the organ in a style so incompatible with religious dignity would once have been regarded not only as scandalously blasphemous but also as an act of barbarism in terms of art. But today we have no more prejudices of that kind. 'Tout est dans tout', M. Jacquotot has told us, which is why the public adores a duet for organ and flageolet; the supremely grand, noble and religious with the supremely small, wretched and frivolous; Handel and Collinet.[6]

Berlioz was more amused than impressed by Spontini's attempt in *Agnes von Hohenstaufen* to imitate an organ using wind instruments.[7]

[3] *Cg*, 3, p. 430.   [4] *NBE*, 10, p. 194.   [5] *Gm*, 12 July 1835; *Cm*, 2, p. 209.
[6] *Le rénovateur*, 1 March 1835; *Cm*, 2, p. 76. Collinet was Musard's star flageolettist.
[7] *Les soirées de l'orchestre*, pp. 221–2.

As for working out how to write for the organ on its own, treating it as a complete orchestra, this is not the place to embark on that. We have assuredly not set ourselves the task of giving a series of tutors for individual instruments but simply of studying how they can contribute to the musical ensemble in combination. The science of the organ, the art of registration and of contrasting one stop with another, these make up the organist's skill, assuming that he is able to improvise, as most are. If not – that is, if he is simply an expert player who undertakes to play the written notes – he must strictly abide by the indications of the composer, who is therefore required to know the special capabilities of the instrument he is writing for and how to use them well. But these capabilities being so vast and various, a composer can never get to know them well, I believe, unless he is himself a skilled organist.

Berlioz says no more than this on the subject of registration. In the *Te deum* the following registrations are indicated: *grand jeu, flûtes, jeux de flûtes, jeu de trompettes* and *bombardes.* The *Hymne pour la consécration du nouveau tabernacle* has the indi- cation *jeux de flûtes.* For registrations on the melodium, see below, p. 311.

If one composes a piece combining the organ with voices or other instru- ments, one must not forget that its pitch is a tone lower than present-day orchestral pitch and that it must therefore be treated as a transposing instrument in B♭. (The organ of St Thomas's, Leipzig, on the other hand, is the only one whose pitch is a tone higher than orchestral pitch.)

In 1855 Berlioz added a footnote to this paragraph: 'This only applies to old organs; organ-builders now tune their instruments to orchestral pitch.' The re- mark is generous since only a few months earlier, at the performance of the *Te deum* at St-Eustache in April 1855, he had had a 'cruel experience' since the organ was tuned a quarter-tone lower than orchestral pitch, with the result that 'even by extending the whole orchestra's sounding tubes it was still impossible to bring the orchestra in tune with the new organ built scarcely three years [in fact one year] before'.[8]
French classical organs were generally low in pitch, as Berlioz points out, often below $a' = 390$, while some German baroque organs were high. The observation about St Thomas's, Leipzig, was added to the *Treatise* in proof after Berlioz's visit to Leipzig in February 1843. Berlioz had a great deal more to say on the subject of pitch in 1858–9 when he sat on a government commission set up to study the question.[9] But if, as Peter Williams has said, 'the whole subject [of the pitch of French organs] is a quagmire into which I think it unjustifiable to lead the reader',[10] let us not enter that quagmire any further here.

The organ can produce soft, noisy or threatening sounds, but it is not in its nature to produce them in quick succession; it cannot switch

[8] *A travers chants,* p. 315.   [9] *Ibid.,* pp. 305–17.
[10] Peter Williams, *The European Organ* (London, 1966), p. 310.

suddenly from *piano* to *forte*, as an orchestra can, or from *forte* to *piano*. By means of certain recent advances in organ-building it can produce a kind of crescendo by adding different stops in cumulative succession, and thus also make a decrescendo by closing them in the same order. But graduated increases and decreases in the volume of sound by this ingenious method do not pass through those intermediate nuances which give so much power to the dynamics of an orchestra. One is always conscious to some degree of an inanimate mechanism at work. Only Erard's instrument known as the 'orgue expressif' can truly increase and diminish the sound, but it is not yet in use in churches. Serious persons who are otherwise wholly sensible have forbidden its use on the grounds that it would destroy the organ's character and sacred function.

Berlioz seems to have been ignorant of the device of the swell-box, introduced into France in the early nineteenth century and used by Cavaillé-Coll, one of whose many achievements was the even gradation of dynamics, as a result of which 'the player could produce a general crescendo with an even timbre through the whole dynamic range without removing his hands from the keyboards'.[11] Berlioz does not even recognise the organ's capacity to make sudden changes of dynamic by moving from one manual to another. His attachment to Erard's 'orgue expressif' and later to Alexandre's 'orgue-mélodium' (see below, p. 311) kept him from a true appreciation and understanding of the church organ.

Berlioz's chapter on the organ has been the subject of criticism and even ridicule arising from his supposed ignorance of an instrument he did not play and cannot have known at all well.[12] But his English critics have been largely misled by Mary Cowden Clarke's translation. His purpose was clearly to consider the organ in the context of the orchestra and as an accompaniment to voices, not as a solo instrument or as an aid to worship, and his technical errors are not grievous. He displayed little interest in French or foreign instruments on his travels. He was not close to the leading Parisian organists of his day, Benoist and the Lefébures (father and son), and conceived the important organ part in his *Te deum* without any player in mind. In planning the performance of that work, he considered a number of possible soloists: Liszt, Hesse, Lemmens and the younger Lefébure ('that pretty little organist with rings, cameos and a gold-knobbed cane, who prettifies the tunes he plays and is called Lefébure-Wely...'[13]). Henry Smart was asked to play, so was Saint-Saëns, but it was eventually Edouard Batiste, organist at St-Eustache where the performance took place, who played.

But his feuilletons betray a greater interest in the organ than one might suppose. Since the greater part of his article on instruments in the 1839 Exhibition of Industry was devoted to the organ, it should be quoted at length:

French organ-building has recently made extraordinary progress, coinciding with an increasing interest in the conservation of ancient religious

[11] *The New Grove Dictionary of Music and Musicians*, ed. Stanley Sadie (20 vols., London, 1980), 4, p. 19.
[12] D. Batigan Verne, 'Berlioz versus the organ', *Organ*, 6 (1927), pp. 171–8, and Guy Warrack, 'Hector, thou sleep'st', *Musical Times*, 104 (1963), pp. 896–7.
[13] *Cg*, 4, pp. 553–4.

monuments. The repair of all the fine old organs built before the Revolution is now generally in hand. New organs are being built, and in this way the benefits of harmony are brought to the humblest villages. Students in primary and high schools are now studying music, the piano and the rudiments of harmony in order to become organists. There is much to hope from all this for the dissemination of music in France. What is unfortunately missing is a supply of good organ builders to respond to this demand and this taste for organs which is evident everywhere. For lack of qualified people provincial churches have been taken over by ignorant workers in whom the clergy have blindly put their faith in getting them to repair – or rather wreck – some of the very finest instruments. The cathedral organ at Nevers was ruined by the caretaker of the bishop's palace. At Orléans the cathedral organ has been put in the charge of a blind man and the interesting old organ at St-Paterne has been repaired by the prison gaoler. Elsewhere there are Alsatian and Lorrainian workers going about France and damaging organs of great value.

There are no more than three or four builders today who can be trusted to repair or build an organ of any worth. Of these, M. Callinet and M. John Abbey are the leading figures. Both have exhibited organs which allow us to appreciate their talents.

The organ exhibited by the firm of Callinet and Daublaine and built in consultation with M. Danjou, the excellent organist of St-Eustache, is one of the most remarkable organs to be built for a very long time. Apart from the Beauvais organ (the work of a magistrate, M. Hamel) and the organ built for the royal chapel by M. Erard, there is no instrument with a finer quality of sound, greater variety of stops or better mechanical layout than the organ by Daublaine and Callinet. Several new stops should be mentioned: very accurate imitations of the bassoon and the clarinet, and some delightful viola da gamba stops not used before in France.

The special distinction of this organ lies in the purity of its sound and the variety of its stops. This variety is especially necessary in France, where the organist alternates with the choir and plays a great number of different pieces in the course of a service, while in Germany and England the organ is always accompanying and only plays a few preludes on its own. In addition German and English organs have great power, but very little variety in registration.

The organ exhibited by M. John Abbey is also a very fine instrument, but it suffers from this fault of having too little variety in the choice of stops.

The other organs on show do not merit any mention and are all marred by the poor quality of their sound. Some organs, which come from Mirecourt in the Vosges, are mechanically well laid out but their sound is harsh and unpleasant. The jury was not particularly critical, so that a number of instruments seemed really unfit to appear in this exhibition of the marvels of our industry. Under the name of 'Milacor organ' there is an invention which seems ingenious at first sight, but which could be very damaging. This consists of a keyboard placed over the organ manual by means of which a man with no knowledge of music can produce chords by touching numbered notes with one finger. When applied to plainchant this device produces a series of mostly hideous chords, always characterless, which can never replace the organist's fingers. It would be better to have no organ in a church than to use something like this. It is important to warn the clergy against this invention, which is being actively promoted.

Of the expressive organs, Muller's deserve particular mention, as always. The 'poikilorgue' by MM. Cavaille, Coll [*sic*], is also an attractive instrument.[14]

Berlioz was thus familiar with the work of Daublaine, Callinet and Abbey (an English builder established in Paris since 1826, who built the Opéra organ for *Robert le diable*), as well as Alexandre Muller and Cavaillé-Coll, father and son, the greatest French organ builders of their time. In 1841 he wrote briefly about the new Cavaillé-Coll organ at St-Denis, singling out the *jeu de cor anglais* for praise.[15] He thought the *voix humaine* less good than that at Fribourg, although the St-Denis organ in general was, he said, better. He evidently felt no compunction about mentioning organs he could never have heard – English and German organs, for example. He had probably never heard the organs in Beauvais, Nevers and Orléans. He had certainly never heard the organ in Fribourg, built by Aloys Mooser in 1834, but its *vox humana* stop was famous[16] and he may have had a first-hand report of it from Liszt, who played it in September 1836, an occasion recorded in George Sand's *Lettre d'un voyageur*.[17]

A later comment on Cavaillé-Coll's work is equivocal in tone: 'M. Cavaillé-Coll is a skilled artist who has made a powerful contribution to the advance of organ-building both by his own improvements and by the felicitous application of other builders' inventions. His organ in the church of St-Vincent-de-Paul is a masterpiece.'[18] A lesser builder, Ducroquet, was one of the sponsors of the 1855 performance of the *Te deum*, being the builder of the new St-Eustache organ which was prominently featured.

Berlioz had a cousin, Jules Berlioz, who tried his hand at organ-building. He wrote to his uncle Victor, Jules's father, in 1848:

> What's Jules up to? Has he finished his organ? The creator of such a work evidently has the makings of a master and the elements of a fortune if things are on his side. I see more merit in building this little instrument in the conditions that Jules has to work in than there was in Cavaillé's making of the organ at St-Denis with all those workmen and all the money he had at his disposal. But overcrowding is as obvious in this business as it is in every part of scientific industry; going to North America to exploit it is about the only way to find the vein of gold it promises. Protestants are mad about organs and chorales and a new church goes up in the United States every day. It's worth considering.[19]

Apart from the *Te deum*, Berlioz composed only smaller pieces that require the organ. The lost *Salutaris* of 1828–9 had an accompaniment for organ or piano.

---

[14] *Jd*, 28 May 1839.   [15] *Jd*, 19 October 1841.   [16] *The New Grove*, 12, p. 552.
[17] *Revue des deux mondes*, 15 November 1836.   [18] *Jd*, 12 January 1856.   [19] *Cg*, 3, p. 590.

Three choral works from the end of his career also have organ accompaniment: the *Hymne pour la consécration du nouveau tabernacle, Le temple universel* and the Couperin arrangement *L'invitation à louer Dieu*. The first of these offers the piano as an alternative.

Without broaching the large and much-discussed question of the appropriateness of expression in sacred music (a question which plain unprejudiced common sense would resolve at once), we will take the liberty nevertheless of drawing the attention of advocates of *plain* music, of *plainchant*, and of the *inexpressive* organ (as if loud and soft stops with their different tone qualities had not already furnished the organ with variety and expression), we will take the liberty, I say, of drawing their attention to the fact that they are the first to exclaim with admiration when the performance of a choir in sacred music shines out with expressive nuances like crescendo, decrescendo, light and shade, notes swelling, sustained and fading, in fact every device that the organ lacks and that Erard's invention would give it. They evidently contradict themselves over it, unless they argue (and they are quite capable of doing so) that expressive nuances which are perfectly appropriate, holy and catholic in the human voice suddenly become unholy, heretical and blasphemous when applied to the organ. It is also strange – if I may be forgiven the digression – that these very critics, guardians of orthodoxy in the matter of sacred music who rightly wish to be inspired by the purest religious feeling (while forbidding any expression of nuances of that feeling), should never have condemned the practice of writing fast-tempo fugues which have long formed the basis of all schools of organ music. Is it because these fugue subjects, some of which express nothing while others are often pretty contorted in shape, become sacred and serious simply because they are treated in fugal style, that is to say in the form which tends to repeat them most often and to put them most insistently on view? Is it because this stream of entries of different voices, these imitations in canon, these strips of twisted, tangled phrases chasing each other, fleeing from each other, rolling over each other, this mumbo-jumbo with no trace of true melody where chords follow one another so rapidly that one can scarcely grasp their character, this ceaseless agitation of the whole system, this display of chaos, these abrupt interruptions of one voice by another, all that horrible harmonic horseplay fine for depicting a savage orgy or a demonic dance – is it because these things are transfigured by passing through the pipes of an organ, taking on the tone of gravity, grandeur, calm, supplication, or ecstasy derived from prayer, meditation or even terror, even from Holy Dread? . . . There are some human beings sufficiently abnormal to believe this to be true. At all events the critics I mentioned just now do not argue that fast organ fugues are imbued with religious feeling exactly, but they have never condemned their inappropriateness and absurdity, probably because they know that the tradition is long established, or because the most learned masters (themselves also at the mercy of routine) wrote them in great numbers, or perhaps because those writers who discuss sacred music are generally committed to Christian dogma and would automatically assume that whatever changes the nature of established ideas is dangerous and incompatible with the immutability of the faith. As for myself (to come back to the subject), I am certain that if Erard's invention were applied to the traditional organ as if it were a new stop for making expressive sounds, which an organist might or might not use at his discretion, or if it were a method for swelling or diminishing certain sounds independently of the rest, this would be a real improvement entirely to the benefit of the true religious style.

This is a noble sermon on a text Berlioz returned to many times. In the sphere of sacred music he vigorously upheld the belief that expression and feeling were essential to the vitality of the music, and he equally vigorously opposed what he saw as the main abuses of the genre: fugal settings of words like 'amen' and 'kyrie', the plainness of plainchant, the provision of too few voices for solemnities that ought to be grand, and the inadequacy of instrumental support for voices.[20] His fundamental difference of opinion on these issues with d'Ortigue never interfered with their close friendship and mutual respect.

[20] Among many passages in his writings and letters which develop these ideas the following may be cited: an essay 'Considérations sur la musique religieuse', *Le correspondant*, 21 April 1829, reprinted in J.-G. Prod'homme, *L'enfance du Christ* (Paris, 1898), pp. 287–93, and *Cm*, 1, pp. 13–16; *Memoirs*, chapter 39 (on Palestrina and music at St Peter's); an open letter to Martin d'Angers, *Cg*, 3, p. 351; 'Les puritains de la musique religieuse', in *Les soirées de l'orchestre*, pp. 241–4; part of 'Euphonia', in *ibid.*, pp. 345–6; 'La musique à l'église par M. Joseph d'Ortigue', in *A travers chants*, pp. 273–8.

8

Brass with mouthpiece

THE HORN

Since this instrument has a great many crooks to bring its pitch up or down by however much is required, one cannot specify its range without at the same time indicating which type of horn is being discussed. The fact is that high notes are easier than low notes on low-pitched horns, with the exception of horns in low A, B♭ and C, whose extra long bore makes high notes very difficult. On high-pitched horns low notes are correspondingly easier to play than high notes. Furthermore some horn players who use a wide mouthpiece to specialise in low notes cannot produce top notes, while others who use a narrow mouthpiece to specialise in high notes cannot produce bottom notes. There is thus a particular range for each key the instrument may be in and also two further ranges practised by specialists who play the high part (first horn) or the low part (second horn).

The horn is written on the treble and bass clefs, with the peculiarity hallowed by tradition that the bass clef is regarded as being an octave lower than it really is. This will be seen in Ex. 116.

Ex. 116

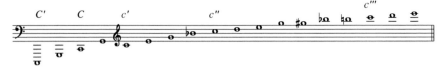

All horns except those in high C are transposing instruments, in other words their written notes do not represent their actual sounds.

There are two kinds of sound quite different in character: 'open' notes, which are almost all produced by the natural resonance of the harmonic divisions of the instrument's tube and which sound without any agency but that of the player's lips and breathing, and 'stopped' notes, which are only obtained by closing the bell (the lower aperture of the horn) to a lesser or greater extent with the hand.

164

Open notes are shown in Ex. 116. The open $g\sharp''$ cannot be sounded as easily as the g'' but it sounds very well if approached from a nearby note such as g'', $f\sharp''$ or a''. It is a little sharp. The low G' is easier in higher keys but in general it is poor and uncertain in all keys.

Table 1 shows the ranges of the different horns and the actual pitch of each.

Table 1

crook	first-horn range			second-horn range		actual sound	
	from	to		from	to	(c)	(c'')
low Bb	c'	e'''	(top 2 notes rare)	C	$g\sharp''$	Bb'	bb
low C	c'	e'''	(top 2 notes rare)	C	$g\sharp''$	C	c'
D	c'	c'''		G'	e''	D	d'
Eb	c'	c'''		G'	e''	Eb	eb'
E	c'	c'''	(top 3 notes rare)	G'	e''	E	e'
F	c'	c'''	(top 3 notes rare)	G'	e''	F	f'
G	G	$g\sharp''$		G'	d''	G	g'
Ab	G	g''		G'	c''	Ab	ab'
A	G	g''	(top note rare)	G'	c''	A	a'
Bb	G	g''	(top note very rare)	C'	c''	Bb	bb'
high C	G	e''		C'	bb'	c	c''

Horns in high C are not transposing instruments when written on the treble clef. This is the worst key to be pitched in.

Berlioz sets out a separate chart for each key, amalgamated here into a single table. In the sentence 'the bass clef is regarded as being an octave lower than it really is' Berlioz in fact wrote 'treble clef', evidently by mistake. He was consistent in using horn clefs in this traditional manner and only rarely – as in *Le cinq mai* (*NBE* 12a: 370–4) – might there be any confusion.

The sentence 'The low G' is easier in higher keys but in general it is poor and uncertain in all keys' is a correction made in 1855 of the earlier reading: 'The low G' is poor and uncertain in all higher keys.' In any case this was a note he never wrote in his own music. His lowest note is C on the bass clef (or c on the treble clef), frequently used. At the top of the range he wrote top c''' three times in the early *Messe solennelle*, twice for horn in low C, once for horn in F (*NBE* 23:

14–15). In his mature music this note is found only once, in *Roméo et Juliette* for horn in D (*NBE* 18: 103). Normally he treats *a″* as the top of the horn's range. A passage in the *Reine Mab* scherzo in *Roméo et Juliette* for the third horn in Ab *sounds* exceptionally high, although its top written note is *g″* (*NBE* 18: 215–16).

Berlioz occasionally transgresses his own recommendation by allowing his first horn (i.e. first or third in modern usage) to play the note *g* when pitched in F, E, Eb or D. Notable cases are the solo horn part in *Le jeune pâtre breton* (*NBE* 13: 26) and the septet in Act IV of *Les Troyens* (*NBE* 2b: 567), where the first horn plays only that note throughout. In *L'île inconnue* the first horn has a low *C* (*NBE* 13: 78), and in Act V of *Les Troyens* all four horns (in D) play low *C* several times for the appearance of the ghosts (*NBE* 2b: 639). Similarly he sometimes allows his second horn (modern second or fourth) to rise to *g″* (horn in D, *Requiem*, *NBE* 9: 95; horn in E, *Benvenuto Cellini* overture, *NBE* 1a: 57, 112) and once to *ab″* (horn in D, *Benvenuto Cellini*, *NBE* 1a: 337).

On the difference between first and second horns Berlioz had more to say in the *Rgm* text:

> One should also take note of what I regard as the vexatious habit still found in many players of dividing into first-horn and second-horn players as if they were different instruments. The former use a narrow mouthpiece to help the production of high notes and find it as easy to play high as it is hard to play low. These are the first horns, not to be relied upon for notes at the very bottom. The others have a wide mouthpiece and find it hard to go high, while low notes are familiar to them. They like low *G*, *C* and *G′* pedals: these are second horns.

In the *Treatise* Berlioz recognised this practice with greater equanimity although he made no mention of the *cor mixte*, the technique of combining both upper and lower registers.

The family of horns is complete; it is found in every key, contrary to common belief. Keys of the chromatic scale which seem to be missing can be obtained by means of a shank which lowers the instrument by a semitone. Thus we have a basic series of horns in low Bb, C, D, Eb, F, G, Ab, high A, high Bb and high C. But by adding an extension in the keys of low Bb and low C you can get low A and low B and by the same means turn D into Db (or C♯), G into Gb (or F♯) and high C into high B (or Cb). One can get this last key by simply pulling out the tuning-slide of the horn in high C.

Of the keys listed here Berlioz never used horns in high Bb, high B or high C. He did call for horns in every other key he mentions, down to low A (in *Chant du neuf Thermidor* and *Sara la baigneuse*). The three keys which need a shank he began to use later than the others: B for the first time in *Le chant des chemins de fer* and *La damnation de Faust* (both in 1846), Db for the first time in *Roméo au tombeau des Capulets*, and Gb for the first time in *La nonne sanglante*.

Stopped notes make a sound that differs markedly not only from that of open notes but also one from another. These differences arise from the degree of closure applied to the bell by the player's hand. Some notes require the bell to be stopped a quarter or a third or a half; for others it has to be closed almost completely. The narrower the aperture left through the bell, the more muffled and the more pinched is the sound – and the more difficult to attack accurately and in tune. There is therefore an important distinction to be made within stopped notes. We do this by means of the sign '$\frac{1}{2}$' against the better notes, those for which the bell has only to be half stopped.

In Ex. 116 we showed a series of open notes. Ex. 117 shows stopped notes (at written pitch). The notes *a*, *b*♭, *d*♭′ and *d*′ are very difficult and muffled; *f*′ is muffled; *a*♭′ is pinched and muffled; *f*♯″ is very muffled; *a*″ is muffled.

Ex. 117

Before proceeding further, and in order to be able to give a table of the complete range of the horn, we must here add that there are some extra open notes less well known than those given above but nevertheless very useful. One of these is *g*♭″, which is always a bit flat and only seems in tune when preceded and followed by *f*″; it can therefore never substitute for *f*♯″. Others are *a*♭, obtained by pinching the lips and forcing up the *g*, and *f*, obtained in the opposite way by relaxing the lips. These last two notes are very valuable, especially the *a*♭, which can sound excellent in any key from D upwards. As for *f*, it is more hazardous and hard to sustain safely in tune. If necessary these low notes can be played without any preparation, so long as they are not preceded by too high a note. It is normally much better to let them follow a *g*, as in Ex. 118a. The transition from *a*♭ to *f* is practicable at a moderate tempo, as in Ex. 118b. Some horn players can also play the *e* below this, a horrible and almost unobtainable note which I urge composers never to use. Some can also play the five additional notes *B*′, *B*♭′, *A*′, *A*♭′ and *F*♯′, which are very rarely in tune, very hard to pitch and should in any case only be tried on horns of the middle range such as horns in D, E and F, and only in a descending progression, as in Ex. 118c.

Ex. 118

At the bottom end of the range Berlioz confined his requirements to the two open notes *g* and pedal *c*, along with the artificial notes *a*♭, *f*♯ and *f*. His fondness for these effects is well demonstrated by the 'Dies iræ' passage in the *Symphonie fantastique* (*NBE* 16: 147) and the Caliban theme in the *Tempête* fantasy in *Lélio* (*NBE* 7: 114–17). These are the only occasions when he wrote the note *f* for the natural horn.

Combining the ranges of both first and second horns and listing natural open, artificial open and stopped notes, Ex. 119 gives the horn's immense chromatic range from bottom to top.

Ex. 119

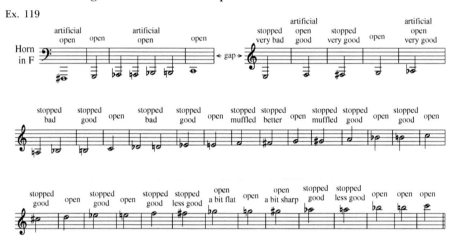

It should be pointed out that rapid passages are harder the lower-pitched the horn, its tube being then of great length and unable therefore to be set in vibration instantaneously. As for the lower register, even on open notes, a succession of notes can only be done at moderate tempo, in almost all keys. This is a general rule in fact, to be observed in the function of all instruments, since low notes result from a lower number of vibrations in a given period. The resonating body must have time to produce the sound. So Ex. 120a would be impracticable and ineffective on a low-pitched horn, and Ex. 120b, which is possible on a horn in F (or higher), would similarly be very bad in the keys of low C or B♭.

Ex. 120

When writing stopped notes, especially in orchestral music, one should mix them as much as possible with open notes and not leap from one stopped note to another, or at least not from a bad stopped note to another equally bad. So it would be absurd to write Ex. 121a, whereas a passage like Ex. 121b has good sonority and can easily be played, since it contains only one bad stopped note (the opening *ab'*). The same passage transposed down would be ridiculous and much too difficult (Exx. 121c and 121d).

Ex. 121

It will be seen from these last three examples (Exx. 121b–d) that the best stopped notes (apart from the four lower notes *f♯*, *b*, *eb'/d♯'*, and *f♯'*) are found above *ab'* in the series already indicated in Ex. 119: *a'*, *b'*, *c♯"/db"*, *d♯"/eb"*, *f"*, *f♯"*, *ab"* and *a"*. That is why the phrase in Ab shown in Ex. 121b though good in one octave is horrible when transposed down. In the lower octave it moves almost entirely on the worst stopped notes such as *bb*, *db'*, *f'* and *ab'*, even though it begins on the open *ab*, an artificial open note which is very dangerous to play since it is played rapidly without preparation.

Earlier composers confined themselves to the use of open notes, in general, which they wrote very clumsily, it must be admitted. Beethoven himself is extremely guarded in his employment of stopped notes except when treating the horn as a solo. Examples of stopped notes in his orchestral music are quite rare, and when he does write them it is almost always for a striking effect. Such examples are the stopped and artificial notes on three horns in the scherzo of the 'Eroica' symphony and the low *f♯* on the second horn in the scherzo of the Seventh.

Ex. 121b is taken from the famous fourth-horn solo in the slow movement of Beethoven's Ninth Symphony, written out in halved note-values.

This system is definitely superior to the opposite method adopted today by most French and Italian composers, which consists of writing for horns in exactly the same way as for bassoons or clarinets without taking any notice of the enormous difference between stopped and open notes or between certain stopped notes and others, without observing how difficult the player finds it to approach a particular note after another which does not lead naturally into it, without considering the awkward intonation, the lack of sound or the harsh, strange quality of notes produced with the bell two-thirds or three-quarters stopped, without – finally – appearing to realise that a profound knowledge of the nature of the instrument, along with taste and common sense, might militate against the kind of notes these novice composers scatter liberally over their scores. Even the poverty of early music is preferable to this ignorant and wasteful nonsense. Unless you are writing stopped notes for a particular effect you should at least avoid those whose tone is too weak and too unlike the rest of the horn's range, such as *d'*, *db'*, *bb*, *a* and *ab*, which should never be used for filling in but only for the special effect of their harsh, muffled, savage sound. For a melodic shape which absolutely demands the inclusion of such a note I would make an exception just for the *ab'*, as for example in Ex. 122.

Ex. 122

In all his music for the natural horn Berlioz follows the precepts outlined here by avoiding the 'bad' notes except when their special sound was required. The note *f'*, for example, is occasionally found where its weak sound is not important (for example in *Sara la baigneuse*, *NBE* 13: 313), but if a loud, full sound is required Berlioz avoided it. A good case is a passage in the overture *Le roi Lear*. Although the melody requires *f'*, Berlioz twice broke the unison by writing *a'* (*NBE* 20: 90, 92). The notes *bb* and *d'* are used only for scenes of horror. The best examples are found in *La nonne sanglante*, where the *Légende de la nonne sanglante* is recounted in A minor against stopped chords on horns pitched respectively in Ab, Eb, Gb and Db. Here Berlioz avoids open notes almost entirely (as in the Méhul example, Ex. 123c) and makes much use of pitches such as *bb*, *b*, *d'*, *d♯'*, *f♯'* and *g♯'*. In *La damnation de Faust* Mephistopheles is greeted with the words 'Oh! qu'il est pâle' with horns on pitches *d'* and *a'*, marked *son bouché*, and some reiterations of the note *d'* are prominent in Mephistopheles's *Évocation* in the same work, again *bouché* (*NBE* 8a: 153, 273). A similar concentration of *bouché* horn chords is found at the end of *Le cinq mai* (*NBE* 12a: 383–4). (For more on this topic see below, under valve horns.)

The note *bb* was once used for an excellent dramatic purpose by Weber in the scene in *Der Freischütz* where Caspar invokes Samiel (Ex. 123a). But the note is so heavily stopped and thus so muffled that it is not heard; it would only be noticed if the whole orchestra were silent while it is played. Similarly the *ab'* called for by Meyerbeer in the nuns' scene in *Robert le diable*, when Robert approaches the tomb to seize the magic branch, would scarcely be audible but for the fact that nearly all the other instruments are silent. Yet this note is much more sonorous than the low *bb* (Ex. 123b). In scenes of silent horror these stopped notes can be very effective in several parts. Méhul, in his opera *Mélidore et Phrosine*, is the only composer to my knowledge to have grasped this idea (Ex. 123c).

Ex. 123

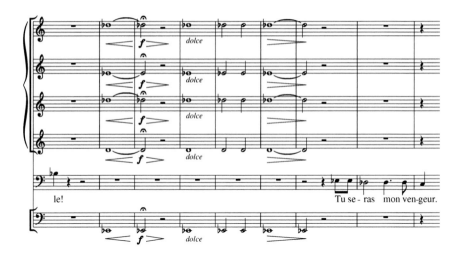

Berlioz did not print the Weber and Meyerbeer excerpts in the *Treatise*, but he did give the Méhul. He had praised the Meyerbeer passage before, in his essay on the instrumentation of *Robert le diable*:

> M. Meyerbeer has given the horns the most distinctive and original role of all; I know no opera in which this fine instrument's wide resources are put to better use. Of the most striking illustrations we will mention the *ab′* ('son bouché') which the composer has given to the unison horns at the moment when Robert, enticed by the nuns, approaches the magic branch. This strange voice had certainly never been heard before at the Opéra, and the odd thing is that Weber, who is said to have played the horn very well, did not use a single effect of this kind in the demonic scenes in his *Freischütz*.
>
> Then, later on, in the magnificent duet for Robert and Isabelle, open notes in the lowest register are explored, such as *G* and *C* on the bass clef. This accompaniment, with constant syncopations on the second horn, is so sharply distinct from the rest of the orchestra that it is at least as striking as the vocal parts. I have heard several people call this piece the 'horn duet'.[1]

Méhul's *Mélidore et Phrosine* was not a success in 1794 and was not revived in Berlioz's lifetime. Berlioz had evidently studied the score at the Conservatoire, as he implies in a later article on Méhul.[2] There Berlioz described these stopped horns as accompanying 'the voice of a dying man with a kind of instrumental death-rattle'.

Major and minor trills are possible on the horn, but only within a small part of its range. The best are on *a′* (minor and major), *bb′* (major), *b′*

[1] *Gm*, 12 July 1835; *Cm*, 2, p. 214.   [2] *Les soirées de l'orchestre*, p. 441.

(minor), *c″* (minor and major), *d″* (minor and major) and *e″* (minor); the major trill on *g′* is less good.

Horns are normally written without any sharps or flats in the key-signature, whatever the key of the horn or of the piece. But if the horn has a solo or concertante part and if it is not in the same key as the orchestra, it is best to mark whatever sharps or flats are needed in the key-signature, always so long as very few are required. Thus the horn in F is a good choice to play a solo when the orchestra is in E♭, firstly because F is one of the instrument's best keys, secondly because this arrangement requires only two flats (B♭ and E♭) in the key-signature, of which one (B♭), being an open note in the middle and upper octaves, will not affect the sonority of this part of its range – which should in any case be the part most often required (Ex. 124a). In a passage like this a horn in E♭ would have been equally suitable, it is true (Ex. 124b). But if the melody keeps needing the fourth and sixth of this key (A♭ and C), the F horn would then be better than the E♭ horn, its two notes *eb″* and *g″* (sounding *ab′* and *c″*) being much better than those on the E♭ horn (*f″* and *a″*) which achieve the same result.

Ex. 124

Berlioz rarely asked the horns to trill. There is an example at the beginning of *Benvenuto Cellini* with a minor trill on *a′* (*NBE* 1a: 121) and some major trills on *c″* and *d″* in *La course à l'abîme* in *La damnation de Faust* (*NBE* 8a: 414).

The only occasion when Berlioz wrote a key-signature in a horn part was in the overture to *Béatrice et Bénédict* (*NBE* 3: 3–42), where the cylinder horns in D have one flat in the signature when the music is in G and two flats when it is in C.

In earlier times the orchestra had only two horns, while today composers find four everywhere they go. With only two, even using stopped notes to modulate away from the main key, the instrument's capabilities are rather restricted. With four, on the other hand, modulation away from the key can easily be done by means of overlapping keys, even when you want to use open notes only. The composer who puts all four horns in the same key nearly always reveals his remarkable clumsiness. It is incomparably better to have two horns in one key and two in another, or better still the first and second in one key, the third in another and the fourth in another; or finally four horns in four different keys, which should be done particularly when a great number of open notes is required. If the orchestra is playing in A♭ for example, the four horns could be in A♭, E (whose E produces G♯, enharmonically the same as A♭), F and C; or alternatively A♭, D♭, E and low B (whose E produces D♯, enharmonically the same as E♭). Depending on the nature of the piece one might choose the four keys in several other ways; the composer has to work out his harmonic needs and devise the choice of horns accordingly. In this way there are very few chords which cannot be obtained with four, three, or at least two open notes (Exx. 125a–b).

Ex. 125

When using horns in several different keys at once, one should give the higher keys to the first horns and the lower keys to the seconds. Another precaution overlooked by many composers is never to make the player change in the same piece from a high key to a very low one, or vice versa. The horn player finds a sudden switch from high A to low Bb, for example, very uncomfortable; with four horns now found in every orchestra there is no need to make such enormous leaps when changing the horn's key.

Berlioz's usual complement of horns is four. Sometimes just a single pair is used in smaller works such as *L'enfance du Christ* and most of *Les nuits d'été*, usually both in the same key. Only two horns are required in the Sylphs' scene and *L'invocation à la nature* in *La damnation de Faust* and in many parts of *Béatrice et Bénédict*. In *Sur les lagunes* and *Absence* (in *Les nuits d'été*) the two horns are in different keys. Three horns are called for in *Sara la baigneuse*, *L'île inconnue* and *La mort d'Ophélie*. There are six horns in up to six parts in the *Symphonie funèbre et triomphale* and twelve horns in up to six parts in the *Requiem* and *L'impériale*.

With four horns an astonishing variety of tunings is called for. Berlioz was guilty of the 'clumsiness' of having all four in the same key in certain early works, namely parts of the *Resurrexit*, the overtures to *Les francs-juges* and *Waverley*, and *Herminie*. When he did this in later works it was for a special purpose, such as the continuous tonic pedal at the end of the *Chant de la fête de Pâques* in *La damnation de Faust*, the raucous and violent entry of four horns in Ab for Mercury's appearance at the end of Act IV of *Les Troyens* (*NBE* 2c: 944), or for the ghosts in Act V of *Les Troyens*, where all four horns play low *C* on D crooks (*NBE* 2b: 639).

When Berlioz has two pairs of horns with each pair in a different key it is not uncommon to find neither pair in the tonic key of the music, and when the first pair is in the tonic there is no regularity in the choice of the second key. For pieces in D major, for example, he might have pairs in D and A, D and C, D and G, D and Bb, D and F, D and B, or G and E. For pieces in Bb he seems to have avoided using horns in Bb; the finale of the *Te deum*, in Bb major/minor, has pairs of horns in F and Db, then Eb and Db. The long finale of Act I of *Les Troyens*, in Bb major, has pairs of horns in D and Eb. If the first pair is in the tonic, the key of the second pair will often be chosen to support an important incidental key of the piece. In the first part of the *Chant de la fête de Pâques* in *La damnation de Faust* the first pair is in F, the tonic, while the second pair is in Ab, the secondary key.

Four horns in three different keys (with either the first or second pair the same) is a common disposition in the early music and is used almost throughout *Benvenuto Cellini*, though not in *La damnation de Faust* and hardly at all in *Les Troyens*. The variety is again very great; the same arrangement of keys is never used twice.

Four horns in four different keys, as advocated here in the *Treatise*, are found in the *Requiem*, *Benvenuto Cellini* and many parts of *Roméo et Juliette*. But after the publication of the *Treatise* this disposition is found on only two occasions, in Act I of *Les Troyens*, one of which is the appearance of Hector's ghost (see under valve horn). Again, the same arrangement of keys is never used twice.

Berlioz always allows sufficient time for the players to change crooks; a passage in the finale of *Roméo et Juliette* (*NBE* 18: 321–3) suggests that he thought about a quarter of a minute was needed. An interesting case is found in *Les Troyens* Act V (*NBE* 2b: 634), where all four horns change to D during Aeneas's Air and play the end of the piece on the new crooks in order to be ready for the unison low *C*s at the appearance of the ghosts immediately following.

The horn is a noble, melancholy instrument, yet the expressiveness of its tone and sonority does not mean there are types of music in which it cannot take part. It blends well in the harmonic ensemble and even the least able composer can, if he wishes, make it prominent or give it an essential but less noticeable role. No composer, in my view, has made such original, poetic and wide-ranging use of it as Weber. In his three masterpieces *Oberon*, *Euryanthe* and *Der Freischütz* he makes it speak a language as admirable as it is original, grasped earlier only by Méhul and Beethoven, and carried forward in its essential purity by Meyerbeer above all. The horn is the orchestral instrument for which Gluck wrote least well; a glance at any of his works will suffice to show his limitations in this field. Yet the three notes imitating Charon's conch in the air 'Caron t'appelle' from *Alceste* must be cited as a stroke of genius. They are on the note *c″* played by two D horns in unison, but the composer had the idea of placing the bells one against the other, making each instrument act as a mute to the other. The colliding sounds thus seem distant and cavernous in the most strange and dramatic way (Ex. 126). Actually I believe Gluck could have got almost the same result by writing *ab″* (stopped) on two horns in G♭, but perhaps in those days when players were not confident of these pitches the composer was wise to use this singular device to make the most open note on the D horn sound dark and distant.

Ex. 126

As David Cairns has pointed out, Berlioz read about Gluck's discovery of the device described here in the entry on Gluck in Michaud's *Biographie universelle* at the age of fifteen.[3] He was still wholly absorbed by it in his 1861 essay on *Alceste*.[4]

[3] Cairns, *Berlioz*, p. 90.   [4] *A travers chants*, pp. 210–11.

Yet no eighteenth-century source for this passage in Act III of *Alceste* suggests that the horns are to be muted in any way.[5]

In the hunting chorus in Act II of *Guillaume Tell* (Ex. 127a) Rossini had the idea of giving four horns in E♭ a diatonic passage in unison. It is highly original. But when one wishes to use all four horns together either on a sustained melody or on a rapid phrase requiring the alternation of open and stopped notes, it is infinitely better to put them in different keys (unless of course the inequality of sound is the main idea). Open notes on some will compensate for the weaker stopped notes on the others, restoring balance and giving the whole scale of the four horns a certain homogeneity. Thus while the C horn has *eb″* (stopped), if the E♭ horn has *c″* (open), the F horn has *bb′* (open) and a horn in low B♭ has *f″* (stopped), the result of these four different timbres is a fourfold *eb′* of very fine sonority (Ex. 127b). It will be seen that the same, more or less, will apply to the other notes.

Ex. 127

A useful technique (of which I know of only one example) is to make three or four horns in different keys take turns in playing a solo melody. Each one thus takes those notes of the phrase which correspond to its

[5] Gluck, *Werke*, 1/7, p. 302.

open notes, with the result that if the sections of the melody are cleverly dovetailed it will sound as if it is being played by a single horn with nearly all the notes open and even (Ex. 128).

Ex. 128

The apogee of Berlioz's writing for the natural horn is found in *Benvenuto Cellini* and *Roméo et Juliette*, where many examples of the careful distribution of open and stopped notes may be found. Strong unison melodies on horns pitched in different keys reveal his command of the technique indicated here. A good example is found at the end of the overture to *Benvenuto Cellini* (*NBE* 1a: 55, 110) and again for the Pope's entry in the fourth tableau (*NBE* 1c: 1114). The intervention of the prince in the opening movement of *Roméo et Juliette* (*NBE* 18: 18–26) is another example.

Berlioz seems to suggest that Ex. 128 is taken from the orchestral or operatic repertory, but it is not from one of his own works nor does he give any identification.

I said just now that the horn is a noble, melancholy instrument despite the jolly hunting fanfares so often associated with it. In fact the jollity of these tunes arises more from the melody itself than from the horn's tone quality. Hunting calls are only jolly when played on a proper hunting-horn, a rather unmusical instrument whose strident blast bears little resemblance to the horn's chaste and shy voice. By forcing air through the bore of the horn in a particular way it can be made to sound like a hunting-horn. This is known by the expression 'cuivrer les sons' – make a brassy sound. This can sometimes have an excellent effect, even on stopped notes. When open notes have to be forced the composer usually asks the player to raise the bell in order to make the sound as coarse as possible. This posture of the instrument is given by the words 'pavillons en l'air'. There is a magnificent example of this device in the final climax of the duet in Méhul's *Euphrosine et Coradin*, 'Gardez-vous de la jalousie!' When Grétry was asked his opinion of this overwhelming duet, still under the spell of the horns' bloodcurdling shriek he replied: 'It's enough to blow the listener's skull right through the roof!'

The instruction to 'cuivrer le son' is not to be confused with the term 'bouché', since the sound has a distinctive brassy rattle and can be produced on both open and stopped notes. A four-horn chord, with two notes stopped and two notes open, bears the direction 'faites cuivrer le son' in the *Course à l'abîme* in *La damnation de Faust* (*NBE* 8a: 412). Other uses of *cuivré* effects are found in the *Tuba mirum* of the *Requiem* (*NBE* 9: 36) and twice in *Benvenuto Cellini*: first, when Balducci explodes with anger in the carnival scene (*NBE* 1b: 646), with all four horns on the written pitch $f\sharp'$ and the instruction 'faites cuivrer très fort ces notes bouchées', and second, in the final scene when the foundrymen discover that the metal is running out (*NBE* 1c: 1146).

The instruction 'pavillons en l'air' is found five times. The first is in the original text of the *Messe solennelle* fanfares (*NBE* 23: 289); the second is at the end of the *Scène héroïque* (where the only source, a copyist's manuscript, has 'pavillons en bas' in error: *NBE* 12a: 191). In the second version of this work (*NBE* 12a: 259) the instruction comes a little earlier, and the addition of a coda at the end which requires hand-stopping suggests that Berlioz had forgotten that the bells were up. The third is a brief noisy passage in the finale of the *Symphonie fantastique* (*NBE* 16: 121–2); the fourth is for the conflagration in *Sardanapale* (*NBE* 6: 217); and the fifth is a passage of two bars in the *Rex tremendæ* of the *Requiem* (*NBE* 9: 59) where two of the four players are required to play stopped notes. This passage also carries the cancellation 'pavillons en bas'. Méhul's instruction in the duet from *Euphrosine et Coradin* cited by Berlioz is 'il faut lever les pavillons', intended for both the horns and the trumpets. This duet caused a sensation when it was first heard in 1790, although Grétry's words were 'L'explosion [. . .] semble ouvrir le crâne des spectateurs avec la voûte du théâtre', not, as Berlioz gives it, 'C'est à ouvrir la voûte du théâtre avec le crâne des auditeurs.'[6] Berlioz repeated

[6] Grétry, *Mémoires ou essais sur la musique* (new edn, Paris, 1829), 2, p. 61.

this tale in his later essay on Méhul, where he recalls hearing the opera in the 1820s.[7]

In the *Treatise* Berlioz does not mention horn mutes, although he called for them, as Beethoven and Weber had, in his early music. An echo effect in *La mort d'Orphée* (1827) is achieved by muting cornets, trumpets, trombones and horns (*NBE* 6: 26–7). In the *Huit scènes de Faust* an effect of distance is obtained by muting horns and trumpets (*NBE* 5: 91, 95). In the last movement of the *Symphonie fantastique* mutes were originally used for an echo effect later achieved by hand-stopping (*NBE* 16: 210), and in *Lélio*, at the end of the *Chœur d'ombres*, the last phrase was originally divided between four horns on open notes, all muted, but was later revised as a solo for one player using cylinders to obtain a *bouché* sound (*NBE* 7: 23, 199).

Berlioz is scornful of 'jolly hunting fanfares', yet he sometimes used the horn for that very purpose – in, for example, the opening of the *Rob Roy* overture (*NBE* 20: 119), the song *Hélène* for four men's voices (*NBE* 12: 280) and *Le chasseur danois* (*NBE* 13: 91). This association of the horn is poetically transformed at the end of the *Reine Mab* scherzo in *Roméo et Juliette*, where the horns have a brilliantly light passage suggestive of the galloping of Mab's tiny team. Transformed in a diabolic direction, the horns summon Mephistopheles and Faust to the *Course à l'abîme*. These two passages, along with the appearance of Hector's ghost in Act I of *Les Troyens*, represent the most prominent use of the horn section in Berlioz's music. For although he describes the instrument as noble and melancholy, there are few extended solos in his music to support that characterisation. It has some melodies in combination with wind or strings, such as at the beginning of *La mort d'Orphée*, where it is coupled with two flutes and the violas (*NBE* 6: 8), or in the *Scène d'amour* and *Roméo au tombeau des Capulets* in *Roméo et Juliette*, where it is always in unison with woodwind or strings. Its most touching solo functions are valedictory, especially at the end of the *Méditation religieuse* (*NBE* 12b: 80) and of the *Chasse royale et orage* in *Les Troyens* (*NBE* 2b: 476). Berlioz's conception of the horn section as a multiple unit contributing to a collective effect is a fine illustration of his modern approach to orchestration wherein the composer's concern is for aural effect, not for the player's sense of playing a part. The only real horn solo in Berlioz's music is the accompaniment to the song *Le jeune paysan breton*, which in its orchestral version as *Le jeune pâtre breton* requires two players, one offstage (*NBE* 13: 24).

THE PISTON OR CYLINDER HORN

On this instrument all notes can be made open by means of a special mechanism which instantaneously changes the horn's key. Individual pistons will thus transform a horn in F into a horn in E or E♭ or D, etc. Consequently the open notes in one key plus the open notes of the other keys produce a complete chromatic scale in open notes. The three pistons have a further

[7] *Les soirées de l'orchestre*, p. 440.

advantage in that they add six semitones below the lowest open note. So if one takes low *C* (bass clef) as the bottom note of the horn's range, pistons will give the following extra notes: *B'*, *Bb'*, *A'*, *Ab'*, *G'* and *F♯'*.

The same applies when pistons are fitted to other brass instruments such as trumpets, cornets, bugles or trombones. The range of the three-piston horn in a central key such as Eb would therefore be from low *F♯'* (bass clef) to top *c'''* (sounding *A'* up to *eb''*) with all chromatic notes in between. The lowest six notes are very rare and difficult to pitch. This system is especially useful for second horns in view of the many gaps it fills between their low open notes up from low *C*, but the tone of the piston horn is a little different from that of the usual horn; it would not do to substitute it on any occasion. In my opinion it should be treated rather as a special instrument whose particular feature is the provision of a good strong, agile bass line though without the force of the tenor trombone's low notes, which its own low notes closely resemble. It is also good at taking a melody, especially if it is set mostly in the middle range.

The best keys to use on the piston horn and the only ones to leave nothing to be desired in the matter of intonation are the intermediate ones, E, F, G and Ab, which are much to be preferred to the rest.

Many composers object to this new instrument because, since it began to appear in orchestras, certain horn players use pistons to play parts written for the ordinary horn; they find it more convenient to use the mechanism to play as open notes those notes which the composer *intended* to be played stopped. This is in fact a dangerous misuse and it is up to conductors to stop it spreading. One should not forget, after all, that in the hands of an able player the piston horn can produce all the stopped notes available on the ordinary horn *and more besides*, since it can play a complete scale without a single open note. This is how: by changing the instrument's key, pistons add the open notes of various other keys to those of the basic key. Clearly it will produce a range of stopped notes in every key also. Thus the horn in F in its natural form has the note *c'* open (producing *f*), and by using pistons the note *d'* open (producing *g*). But if you use the hand in the bell to lower these two notes by a tone the first will become *bb* (producing *eb*) stopped, and the second *c'* (producing *f*), also stopped.

The composer must use the word *bouché* and the figures $\frac{1}{2}$ or $\frac{2}{3}$ (showing how far the bell is to be closed) to indicate those notes which he does not want to be played open. For a scale written as in Ex. 129 the player will apply the pistons needed for a scale of open notes in C major and use the hand to close two thirds of the bell on each note, making a scale of Bb with every note as muffled and stopped as possible. In this way a piston horn can produce a phrase in open notes followed by the same phrase in stopped notes like a far distant echo.

Ex. 129

The cylinder horn differs from the piston horn only in mechanical detail. This difference has advantages in mobility and tone. The cylinder horn's sound scarcely differs from that of the ordinary horn. This instrument is already widely used in Germany and will undoubtedly be adopted everywhere before long.

Although chromatic horns, usually with pistons, had been used in Paris since about 1826, Berlioz showed no interest in them until after his first visit to Germany in 1842–3. He remained convinced that the variety of tone produced by stopped notes was a positive merit of the natural horn and that pistons, with their apparent advantage of equalising tone-quality throughout the instrument, posed a threat to this sophisticated style of playing. Having several horns in different keys seemed to Berlioz to be a better solution since the composer controlled the quality of sound. Pistons, as he well recognised, encouraged the lazy player to play all notes open, even though the composer had (or should have) borne the particular sound of a particular note in mind when scoring the music. Hence his urge to point out that even when equipped with pistons the horn could still produce stopped sounds when required.

He later recalled an incident during rehearsals of *Benvenuto Cellini* in 1838:

> I had occasion to point out to the second horn a mistake in an important passage. I did so in the mildest and politest manner; but the player, Meifred, though an intelligent man, rose in wrath and, losing his head completely, shouted, 'I'm playing what's there. Why do you suspect the orchestra like this?' To which I replied, even more mildly, that it had nothing to do with the orchestra but only with him, and that secondly I suspected nothing, for suspicion implied doubt, and I was quite certain he had made a mistake.[8]

Meifred, one of the leading players of the day, was an ardent champion of the piston horn and was undoubtedly in the habit of playing it in the Opéra orchestra. His dispute with Berlioz almost certainly arose from something in the part which Berlioz would expect to be played stopped, while Meifred would normally play it open by using pistons.

In the *Treatise* this section on the piston horn was the part most radically revised from what Berlioz had written in the *Rgm* chapter on the horn, published on 9 January 1842:

> The piston horn, which makes all notes open by means of its special mechanism, will one day offer great benefits in the field of instrumentation, no doubt. But I am firmly convinced that one should never consider it an improvement on the horn, from which it differs in quality of tone. It must

---

[8] *Memoirs*, 'Travels in Russia, Sequel'.

be treated as a new instrument whose special feature is the provision of a good strong, agile bass line though without the force of the trombone's low notes, which its own low notes closely resemble. The manufacture of the piston horn has not yet been researched sufficiently to get rid of the poor intonation and unstable tone of certain notes, and these imperfections have until now discouraged most composers from using it. They object to it also because, since it began to appear in orchestras, certain horn players are content to use pistons to play parts written for the ordinary horn; they find it more convenient to use pistons to play as open notes those notes which the composer intended to be played stopped. The piston horn can produce stopped notes all the same, but since the very purpose of its mechanism is to open the sound it is evidently better to leave it to its special functions and call for stopped effects just from ordinary horns.

This brought an immediate response from the horn-maker A. Raoux, who sought to convince Berlioz that the piston horn was much more advanced than he thought.[9] Within a few months he had made the acquaintance of Adolphe Sax, newly arrived from Brussels, who won him over to the advantages of new brass mechanisms, and later the same year he set out on his first visit to Germany and there found that chromatic horns were widely established. He observed this in Stuttgart, Dresden and Berlin, while in Leipzig there was still some resistance. In 1843 he wrote: 'Cylinder, or chromatic, horns are the only kind in use in Stuttgart. That able instrument-maker Adolphe Sax, who has now settled in Paris, has conclusively demonstrated the superiority of this system to the piston method. The latter has been virtually abandoned all over Germany, and the cylinder method is becoming generally used for horns, trumpets, bombardons and bass tubas.'[10] His visit to Berlin confirmed his new view of the matter:

> The horns are splendid, and all use cylinders – much to the regret of Meyerbeer, who thinks as I did until recently about the new mechanism. A number of composers object to cylinder horns because, they maintain, their timbre is inferior to that of the natural horn. I have several times experimented by listening to the open notes of the natural horn and of the chromatic or cylinder horn one after the other, and I must confess I could not detect the slightest difference in tone or volume. There is at first sight more substance in another objection that has been raised against the new horns, but it can be easily disposed of. Since this instrument (now perfected, in my opinion) was introduced into orchestras, certain hornists who play natural horn parts on cylinder horns find it less trouble to produce the stopped notes indicated by the composer as open notes. This is certainly a serious abuse, but the fault lies in the player and not in the instrument. Far from it, indeed, for in the hands of a skilful artist the cylinder horn not merely produces all the stopped notes which the natural horn produces but can actually play the entire compass without resorting to a single open note. The conclusion is simply that horn players should know the technique of

[9] *Cg*, 2, p. 713.   [10] *Memoirs*, 'Travels in Germany', I/2.

hand-stopping as if the cylinder mechanism did not exist, and that composers should henceforth indicate the notes that are to be played stopped by some special sign, the player producing as open sounds only those notes which carry no such indication.[11]

So after 1843 Berlioz set about marking his scores more carefully to show which notes had to be stopped. Those scores which he was preparing for publication, such as the *Symphonie fantastique* and *Le cinq mai*, were furnished with directions such as 'bouché avec les cylindres', 'ouvert avec les cylindres', 'avec les cylindres, tous les sons ouverts' and 'faites les notes bouchées avec la main sans employer les cylindres', even though they had been written without cylinder horns in mind. To the score of the *Symphonie funèbre et triomphale* he added the marginal note 'piston horns or ordinary horns' at the last minute. One of the optional alternatives to the trombone as soloist in the slow movement of that work is a piston horn in G, going down to low *e* (*NBE* 19: 107). His new compositions thereafter were written with the availability of chromatic horns in mind, which is why he resorted less often to disposing his horn section in three or four different keys.

He specified both cylinder and piston systems. In *La damnation de Faust*, for example, he requires piston horns for the *Récitatif et chasse* in Part IV (*NBE* 8a: 395). This passage was perhaps the source of an incident at a rehearsal for the first performance of the work in 1846. One of the players objected: 'Sir, you have written a note here which does not exist; it is a sort of sneeze like nothing on earth, an impossible din!' 'That is exactly what I want', Berlioz replied.[12]

Les Troyens presupposes that all four players have piston horns, even though much of the part is written for natural horns. The scene for Hector's ghost in Act II (*NBE* 2a: 211–19) is an admirable demonstration of how Berlioz liked to specify stopped notes to the players of piston horns but did not need to do so to the players of natural horns. *Béatrice et Bénédict* requires the availability of two cylinder horns. In these two operas his main reason for using chromatic horns was to have a more extensive lower range, as can be seen in Aeneas's description of serpents in *Les Troyens* (*NBE* 2a: 126) and in the use of a cylinder horn to provide the bass line in the Trio of *Béatrice et Bénédict* (*NBE* 3: 249–51). He made a special feature of it when orchestrating *Sur les lagunes* in 1856 with the second horn needing cylinders to play its predominantly low-pitched part (*NBE* 13: 49), and his orchestration of Schubert's *Erlkönig* (1861) has two natural horns in G with a third horn playing a piston horn in E♭ to provide the lower notes, some requiring great agility.

He only once specified the fractional stopping of the bell shown in Ex. 129. In *L'enfance du Christ* at the entry of the soothsayers a series of stopped notes on the horn alternates with sinister shuffling phrases in the lower strings. The second horn note, written *g'*, is marked 'son bouché des 2/3 avec les cylindres' for which the player applies the pistons for *a'* and lowers the pitch by stopping the bell (*NBE* 11: 45).

Berlioz had only professional, not personal, relations with the two great French hornists of his day, Louis-François Dauprat (1781–1868) and Pierre-Joseph-Emile

[11] *Ibid.*, I/7.   [12] *NBE*, 8b, p. 459.

Meifred (1791–1867). Dauprat taught at the Conservatoire and Meifred, as we have seen, played in the Opéra orchestra. The hornist whose friendship Berlioz most enjoyed was Eugène Vivier (1821–?), well known for his practical jokes and satirical writing as well as for his fondness for demonstrating chords of three or four notes on the horn. Berlioz retails some of his jokes in *Les grotesques de la musique*. Whether Berlioz had a player's assistance in compiling the horn section of the *Treatise* it is hard to say. His table of stopped notes does not exactly correspond with any of those given in tutors by Duvernoy (1803), Domnich (1808), Fröhlich (1811), Dauprat (1824) or Mengal (1835), yet Berlioz must at least have consulted Dauprat's exhaustive *Méthode*.[13]

THE TRUMPET

The trumpet's range is more or less the same as that of the horn, an octave higher, with all the same natural open notes. It is written on the treble clef, as in Ex. 130. The low *C* is used only on high-pitched trumpets and the top three notes are very rare.

Ex. 130

Some players can produce passable stopped notes on the trumpet by placing the hand in the bell, as on the horn, but the effect of these notes is so poor and their intonation so uncertain that almost all composers have rightly refrained from using them, and still do. An exception to this proscription is the note *f″*, produced simply by using the lips, but it is always sharp and it should only be written as a passing note between *g″* and *e″*, and it must not be sounded without preparation or as a sustained note. The *bb′* in the middle register, on the other hand, is a little flat.

It is wise to avoid the low *c* on trumpets in keys lower than F. The sonority of the note is weak and the tone undistinguished with no scope for any special effect. One can easily give the note to the horn, which is incomparably better in every way. The extreme top three notes *bb″*, *b″* and *c‴* are very risky on trumpets in low Ab, Bb and C, and impracticable in higher keys. Yet one can reach top *c‴*, even in the key of Eb, by approaching it as in Ex. 131 with plenty of force. Most German or English players would tackle a passage like this without hesitation, yet it would seem very risky in France where brass players in general have great difficulty playing high.

Ex. 131

[13] R. Morley-Pegge, *The French Horn* (2nd edn, London, 1973), p. 99. For further discussion of Berlioz's writing for the horn, see Cecil B. Wilson, 'Berlioz's use of brass instruments' (Ph.D. diss., Case Western Reserve University, 1971).

In the basic series of trumpets the keys are B♭, C, D, E♭, E, F, G, and, very rarely, high A♭. By means of the shank (mentioned in connection with the horn) which lowers the instrument a semitone you get trumpets in A, B, D♭/C♯ and G♭/F♯. With a double shank which lowers the trumpet a whole tone you even get a trumpet in low A♭, though this key is the worst of all. The finest tone quality, on the other hand, is that of the trumpet in D♭, an instrument of great brilliance, well in tune and hardly ever used because most composers are unaware of its existence.

From what I have said here about the two extremities of the trumpet's compass it is easy to deduce that the range is not the same for every key. Low-pitched trumpets, like every other instrument of this kind, should avoid the bottom note, and high-pitched trumpets cannot reach the uppermost notes (see Table 2).

Table 2 *Table of ranges in different keys*

low A♭		very poor	✓	✓	✓	✓ ✓	difficult
A		poor	✓	✓	✓	✓ ✓	difficult
B♭		rather poor	✓	✓	✓	✓ ✓	difficult
B		✓	✓	✓	✓	✓ ✓	difficult
C		✓	✓	✓	✓	✓ ✓	very difficult
D♭		✓	✓	✓	✓	✓ ✓	
D	poor	✓	✓	✓	✓	✓ ✓	
E♭	poor	✓	✓	✓	✓	✓	difficult
E	mediocre	✓	✓	✓	✓	✓	difficult
F	✳ ✓	✓	✓	✓	✓	very difficult	
G♭	✳ ✓	✓	✓	✓	difficult		
G	✳ ✓	✓	✓	✓	very difficult		
A♭	✳ ✓	✓	✓	difficult			

✳ This low C, written on the bass clef, sounds excellent in these keys; it can often be put to admirable use.

Trumpets in high A♭ are found virtually only in military bands; their sound is very brilliant but their range is narrower than that of trumpets in G since they cannot be taken above *c″*.

The actual pitch of *c, c′, c″* and top *c‴* for the different trumpets is shown in Table 3.

Table 3

	c	*c′*	*c″*	*c‴*
low A♭	—	*a*♭	*a*♭′	*a*♭″
A	—	*a*	*a′*	*a″*
B♭	—	*b*♭	*b*♭′	*b*♭″
B	—	*b*	*b′*	*b″*
C	—	*c′*	*c″*	*c‴* (non-transposing)
D♭	—	*d*♭′	*d*♭″	—
D	*d*	*d′*	*d″*	—
E♭	*e*♭	*e*♭′	*e*♭″	—
E	*e*	*e′*	*e″*	—
F	*f*	*f′*	*f″*	—
G♭	*g*♭	*g*♭′	*g*♭″	—
G	*g*	*g′*	*g″*	—
A♭	*a*♭	*a*♭′	*a*♭″	—

Adolphe Sax is now making little octave trumpets and tenth trumpets (in C and high E♭) of excellent sonority. They should be adopted in all orchestras and military bands.

Berlioz never himself ventured into the trumpet's outer range, confining himself to the two octaves *g–g″* in all keys. Writing as he normally was for French players, he was evidently constrained by their cautious upper limits. He had heard and admired German trumpeters' ability to play high,[14] but his knowledge of English players was then strictly second-hand. He occasionally wrote notes that he described as 'difficult', e.g. a *g″* for trumpet in E♭ in the *Resurrexit* of the *Messe solennelle* (*NBE* 23: 145) and again with splendid effect at the climax of the *Dies iræ* fanfares in the *Requiem* (*NBE* 9: 35); even sometimes a 'very difficult' note, such as the *g″* for trumpet in F in the *Messe solennelle* (*NBE* 23: 147) and the *d″* for trumpet in G in the second version of the *Scène héroïque* (*NBE* 12a: 204). Another 'very difficult' note is the *f″* for trumpet in E♭ in the *Messe solennelle* (*NBE* 23: 140, 157) and the same note for trumpet in F in the *Francs-juges* overture (*B&H* 4: 78), a note deliberately avoided seventeen bars earlier where it would be more keenly exposed. (Although this part is for chromatic trumpet, Berlioz's strictures about range still hold good.) The low *g*, described as 'rather poor' on a trumpet in B♭, is found in the *Huit scènes de Faust* (*NBE* 5: 91), the fourth movement of the *Symphonie fantastique* and elsewhere, but no such 'poor' and 'difficult' notes are found after the writing of the *Treatise*. The *Messe solennelle*, Berlioz's first surviving orchestral work, even includes an impossible *f♯″* (*NBE* 23: 147) and, in its revised form, an equally unlisted *b′* (*NBE* 12a: 18), both perhaps to be obtained by hand-stopping or perhaps written in error.

[14] *Cg*, 3, p. 74.

The note *f″*, used as a passing note, is found quite frequently throughout his works. The prohibited sustained *f″* is found in the first movement of *Harold en Italie* (*NBE* 17: 61).

Berlioz has more to say on the trumpet's upper range in the section on the cornet, below (pp. 201–2).

He used trumpets pitched in all the main seven keys he lists. Relying on the shank he called for trumpets in low A quite frequently, B (in the *Serment* of *Roméo et Juliette*, *Pandæmonium* in *La damnation de Faust* and the *Tibi omnes* in the *Te deum*) and D♭. Despite his warm commendation of this key for trumpets he did not write for it until the *Judex crederis* in the *Te deum* and on one or two occasions in *Les Troyens*. He never used trumpets in G♭ or either high or low A♭. The high E♭ trumpet made by Sax was evidently a valved instrument (see below); the reference to Sax was a late revision to the proofs in 1843.

The trill is in general almost impracticable on the trumpet and should not be used in orchestral writing, in my view. Nevertheless the three trills *bb′–c″*, *c″–d″* and *d″–e″* do work quite well.

What I said about the method of overlapping horns in different keys applies in exactly the same way to trumpets, with the single comment that the occasion for writing for them in different keys does not often arise. Most of our orchestras offer the composer only two trumpets in the same key, while the cornets, with their full chromatic range and their tone quality not so unlike that of the trumpets as to prevent them blending in the ensemble, complete the harmony. Only in the minor mode is it normally necessary to write for trumpets in two different keys if you want to give them fanfares requiring the third and fifth of the scale. In G♯ minor, for example, to give one trumpet the two notes G♯ and B while the other sounds a third above or a sixth below on the two other notes B and D♯, you have to put one trumpet in E (whose E and G sound G♯ and B) and one trumpet in B (whose C and E sound B and D♯). This is what M. Meyerbeer did in the great scene in Act IV of *Les huguenots* (Ex. 132).

Ex. 132

Berlioz never invited his trumpets to trill.

He did not often follow up his suggestion of pitching two trumpets in different keys, nearly all the cases of this practice being found in *Benvenuto Cellini*, written within a year of the appearance of *Les huguenots*; the *Prélude* in the *Te deum* is another. The only example which might be compared to the Meyerbeer extract is the opening of Act II of *Les Troyens*, where offstage trumpets in G and E (later E♭ and E) blow distorted fanfares with cornets in support, giving the effect of chromatic instruments (*NBE* 2a: 205). A unique example of 'overlapping' trumpets, in the manner of horns, is found at the end of the overture to *Benvenuto Cellini*, where four trumpets in three different keys divide the melody between them, one note at a time (*NBE* 1a: 55, 110).

That overture's unusual (and in concert performance expensive) requirement of four trumpets in addition to two cornets is explained by the fact that the two stage trumpeters needed in the second Tableau of the opera are available to join the regular two orchestral trumpeters. In that scene, incidentally, the trumpets are played by two 'saltimbanques' who, when it is time to recrook the instrument into a different key, are given directions to leave the stage to do so.

There are parts for four natural trumpets in the second version of the *Resurrexit* (from the *Messe solennelle*) and in his arrangement of the *Marseillaise*. *L'impériale* calls for six trumpets in two parts, the *Symphonie funèbre et triomphale* for eight trumpets in four parts, and the *Requiem* for twelve trumpets in six parts.

Despite widespread force of habit, one can get some delightful *piano* effects with trumpets. Gluck was one of the first to demonstrate this, with his long held note on two unison trumpets on the dominant, in the Andante part of the introduction to *Iphigénie en Tauride*. Then Beethoven, notably in the slow movement of the Seventh Symphony, and Weber too have made fine use of it.

Berlioz had already drawn attention to this passage in *Iphigénie en Tauride* in an earlier essay: 'There is here an instrumental effect which no one has ever tried to imitate: a held note, *pianissimo*, on two trumpets in unison on the dominant. Although this instrument is scarcely ever used except in *forte* and *mezzo-forte*, its mordant tone gives this pedal note a special quality and sharply accentuates the interest of the music when it enters.'[15] *Le cinq mai* contains a good example of a *piano* trumpet effect (*NBE* 12a: 388).

To be sure that these soft notes speak clearly they should normally be placed in the middle register and not follow each other in too rapid succession. The five notes *g*, *c′*, *e′*, *g′* and *c″* can be attacked and sustained *pianissimo*. The *bb′* being flat, its faulty intonation can best be corrected by forceful blowing, so it cannot be included in the list of soft notes. The *c″* above it is open to no such risk; it can be sustained and attacked softly, at least in the four lower keys A, B♭, B and C. In the key of D I believe a capable player can still give this *c″* really softly, sustaining the note, but it would be wise to cover the entry with a *forte* in the rest of the orchestra.

The trumpet's tone quality is noble and bright. It is appropriate for suggestions of war, for cries of fury or vengeance, or for hymns of triumph.

[15] *Gm*, 16 November 1834; Condé, p. 189; *Cm*, 1, p. 445.

It lends itself to any expression of vigour, pride or grandeur and to most moods of tragedy. It can even play a part in a joyous piece, provided that the joy has an abandoned quality or a feeling of pomp or grandeur.

Despite the real splendour and distinctiveness of its tone there are few instruments more abused than the trumpet. Before Beethoven and Weber every composer, including Mozart, persisted in confining it either to a wretched filling-in role or to sounding two or three rhythmic formulæ endlessly repeated, as boring and ridiculous as they are in conflict (as often as not) with the character of the pieces they are found in. This appalling commonplace has at last vanished nowadays; a composer of any worth gives his melodic shapes, accompaniment figures and trumpet fanfares such flexibility, variety and independence as the nature of the instrument permits. It has taken almost a century to reach this point.

Despite Berlioz's strictures on eighteenth-century trumpet parts, he was able to do little to enlarge the instrument's versatility, confined as it was in his practice to just ten notes. Its limitations are particularly noticeable in *Le roi Lear* where, with no chromatic trumpets in support, the trumpets in E can contribute only fitfully to a composition in C. And yet he remained faithful to it nearly to the end of his life and retained two natural trumpets in his normal orchestral line-up, usually alongside two chromatic cornets. Whether this was due to his genuine attachment to the instrument or whether he was simply serving the standard Parisian orchestra of his time, in which natural trumpets were to be found throughout his lifetime, is hard to say. He entrusted the upper brass role to valved instruments alone only when he was writing for orchestras outside Paris (*Chant des chemins de fer* and *Béatrice et Bénédict*) or when, as in the Trio in Part III of *La damnation de Faust*, the natural trumpets are absent offstage. Although he accepted the cornet in his orchestra he did not press for the adoption of chromatic trumpets, a conservative attitude that may be attributed, like much else, to his profound admiration for Gluck and Beethoven.

The most distinctive role given to the trumpets in Berlioz's work is in support of traditional fanfares, such as at the beginning of the *Marche hongroise* in *La damnation de Faust* (*NBE* 8a: 56) and at the beginning of the *Marche troyenne* (*NBE* 2a: 169). They only occasionally take a melodic lead, as for example at the end of the *Corsaire* overture (*NBE* 20: 296), and they have no special association with the timpani, as they often have in Mozart and Beethoven. Two special effects not mentioned in the *Treatise* are mutes, called for in *La mort d'Orphée* for an echo effect (*NBE* 6: 26–7) and in the *Huit scènes de Faust* for the distant *Chœur de soldats* (*NBE* 5: 91), and the indication 'pavillons en l'air' in the *Scène héroïque* (*NBE* 12a: 191).

The piston trumpet and cylinder trumpet have the advantage of being able to give every note of the chromatic scale, like the piston horn. There is no loss of quality from these modifications compared with the ordinary trumpet, and intonation is satisfactory. Cylinder trumpets are the better of the two and will soon be in general use.

Keyed trumpets, still in use in some Italian orchestras, cannot be compared with them. The general range of cylinder trumpets and piston trumpets includes every chromatic note from c up to c'''. The lowest notes, from
c to $f\sharp$, are mediocre and only acceptable in higher keys; the top five notes,
from $g\sharp''$ to c''', are rarely used, and only in lower keys. High cylinder trumpets, such as those in F and G, can also descend chromatically to low $F\sharp$,
but these extreme notes are of rather poor quality.

Major and minor trills feasible on the cylinder trumpet are the same as
on the three-piston cornet (see below, p. 200).

The slide trumpet, so called because of its movable slide activated by
the right hand like that of the trombone, has the advantage of perfectly
correct intonation. Its sound is exactly the same as that of the ordinary
trumpet and its range is c and all chromatic notes from $e\flat$ up to $a\flat''$, except
that $e\flat$ and $a\flat$ are impossible in the keys of C, B and below.

Berlioz began writing for the chromatic trumpet almost as soon as it became
available. From 1823 to 1831, according to Kastner,[16] Spontini was sending valved
trumpets and horns to Paris from Berlin. Berlioz had no personal contact with
Spontini at that time, but the new trumpets made their first appearance in
Chélard's *Macbeth* at the Opéra on 29 June 1827,[17] and we may be sure that
Berlioz's assiduous attention to such novelties prompted him to introduce the
instrument into his current compositions. Thus a piston trumpet in D is found
in the score of *Waverley* alongside two natural trumpets, which suggests that the
overture may not have been begun until the summer of 1827.[18] The instrument
at that time had only two pistons and was not fully chromatic. Berlioz evidently
became aware of this shortly after, for the autograph of *Waverley* shows that he
changed all occurrences of the note $g\sharp'$ and of pitches below $e\flat'$. In fact he
need not have done that since unlike on the cornet (see below) the missing
note is $g\sharp$, not $g\sharp'$, the trumpet in D having its fundamental an octave below the
cornet in D.

From then until 1834 Berlioz combined natural and piston trumpets in his
larger orchestral works. Two natural trumpets and one piston trumpet are called
for in the *Francs-juges* overture, the *Symphonie fantastique*, *Rob Roy* and (doubled in
number) the *Marseillaise*. (The brilliant effect of a piston trumpet in E♭ playing the
march theme in the *Marche au supplice* must have been astonishing to an audience
of 1830.) The *Chansons de brigands* and *Sardanapale* call for two piston trumpets
and no natural trumpets. The *Tempête* and *Harold en Italie* have two of each. The
lack of piston trumpets in *Le roi Lear* is rather surprising.

The success of the cornet in the 1830s overshadowed the piston trumpet, with
the result that most of these works were revised and published with parts for two
cornets in place of the one or two piston trumpets. The latter made no further

---

[16] *Manuel général de musique militaire* (Paris, 1848), p. 192. For the history of the valved trumpet, see
Eduard H. Tarr, 'The Romantic trumpet', *Historic Brass Society Journal*, 5 (1993), pp. 213–61.
[17] *Encyclopédie de la musique*, ed. Lavignac and Laurencie (Paris, 1925), Part 2, p. 1608.
[18] See Diana Bickley, 'The trumpet shall sound', *Historic Brass Society Journal*, 6 (1994), pp. 61–83.

appearance in Berlioz's music until the end of his career, when *Béatrice et Bénédict* was composed for two piston or cylinder trumpets and one cornet, an arrangement obviously dictated by the orchestral resources of Baden-Baden.

In Germany Berlioz had observed with admiration that the chromatic trumpet had never been ousted by the cornet. He suggested that his cornet parts should be played on the chromatic trumpet whenever performance in Germany was likely. He deplored resistance to the new chromatic trumpet:

> Opposition has been confined to the argument that the tone of the trumpet loses much of its brilliance with the cylinder mechanism. This is not true, to my ear at least. Even if a more sensitive ear than mine can perceive a difference between the two instruments, it will surely be admitted that the disadvantage resulting from such a difference is not to be compared with the advantage of being able to play up and down the chromatic scale easily and without the smallest unevenness of tone over a range of two and a half octaves. For this reason I can only rejoice that the natural trumpet has been almost completely superseded in Germany today.[19]

When Berlioz mentioned Sax's introduction of high trumpets in C and E♭, he clearly referred to valved, not natural, trumpets. At the time of the *Treatise's* publication Berlioz arranged his choral piece *Chant sacré* for six instruments built by Sax, including the newly invented saxophone, for a concert on 3 February 1844. One of the instruments was a 'petite trompette dixième à cylindres en mi♭ aigu', the high E♭ cylinder trumpet.

Berlioz wrote for piston trumpet (never cylinder trumpet in the early works) in the keys of F, E♭, D and B♭. In *Béatrice et Bénédict* they are required in D, E♭ and E. As with the cornet, Berlioz always felt that an appropriate key must be chosen even though the whole chromatic range was available.

He never wrote for keyed trumpet or slide trumpet. The keyed trumpet was indeed well known in Italy, hence its appearance in the scores of *Guillaume Tell* and *Robert le diable*, although in Paris the part was usually played on piston trumpet.[20] It was also common in central Europe, as the celebrated concertos by Haydn and Hummel testify.

The leading French trumpeter of Berlioz's time was François-Georges-Auguste Dauverné (1800–74), principal trumpeter at the Opéra, professor of trumpet at the Conservatoire and author of a *Méthode de trompette*.[21] His younger brother was also a trumpeter, and the two of them probably played in many of Berlioz's concerts. We know they both played for him in a concert on 1 November 1840 since Berlioz recounts a friendly exchange with them.[22] Dauverné *aîné* played the high cylinder trumpet in Berlioz's concert of 3 February 1844.

---

[19] *Memoirs*, 'Travels in Germany', I/7.
[20] Anthony Baines, *Brass Instruments* (New York, 1981), p. 194.
[21] Philip Bate, in *The Trumpet and Trombone* (2nd edn, London, 1978), p. 275, lists three Dauverné tutors: *Méthode de trompette*, before 1848; *Méthode complète de trompette à cylindres*, before 1848; and *Méthode pour la trompette*, 1857.
[22] *Memoirs*, chapter 51.

THE CORNET

The piston cornet made its dazzling debut in Paris in about 1830 and within ten years established itself in French orchestras. Berlioz's perception of this new instrument changed rapidly and radically at the time he was writing the *Treatise*, so that the *Rgm* text of 1842 and the two editions of the *Treatise* all differ considerably here. He was also trying to bring clarity, not wholly successfully, to the matter of transpositions and the relative pitches of brass instruments. I therefore give the three texts of this section in chronological order. First the *Rgm* article of 23 January 1842:

The cornet is highly fashionable in France today, especially in circles where pure elevated styles are held in low esteem. It has thus become the indispensable solo instrument for *contredanses, galops, airs variés* and other such inferior compositions. Being now accustomed to hearing it in dance orchestras playing tunes of little originality or distinction – not to mention its tone quality with neither the nobility of the horn nor the swagger of the trumpet, one cannot easily adapt the cornet to the elevated melodic style. Yet it can on occasion be well used for such a purpose, provided only that it plays phrases of incontestable dignity at a broad tempo. Such a case is the refrain in the trio in *Robert le diable*, 'Mon fils, mon fils, ma tendresse assidue', which goes well on the cornet (Ex. 133).

Ex. 133

A cheerful melody assigned to the cornet will always run the risk of losing some of its nobility, if it has any, or compounding its triviality if it has none. A phrase which seems quite tolerable when played on violins or woodwind becomes a vile commonplace platitude when thrown into relief by the saucy, swashbuckling, shameless sound of the cornet. This danger disappears if the phrase is such that it can be played at the same time by one or more trombones, whose grand voice covers and ennobles that of the cornet. For harmonic functions it blends very well in the body of brass sound. It can fill out trumpet chords and can project across the orchestra groups of notes, both diatonic and chromatic, which are too rapid to suit either the trombones or the horns.

There are cornets both with two and with three pistons. The latter can produce all the notes of the chromatic scale; the former are less serviceable, lacking both *d'* and *a*b'. These gaps in their scale have inevitably given the advantage to the three-piston cornet which will soon be in general use, no doubt.

Despite its small size this instrument is not nearly as high as people suppose. The shape of its bore is such that high notes sound less easily than on a trumpet. Thus it is easier to play *e″* on a D trumpet than *a″* on an A cornet (both notes sounding *f♯″*). This difference must not be overlooked. There are the same number of cornet crooks as trumpet crooks, which cover a seventh in range from low A up to G; cornet crooks go from D up to high C. These terms 'low A' and 'high C' are incorrect, as habitually used. One should say simply 'A' or 'C', since there is no trumpet in high A and no cornet in low C.

When this is explained, it will be better understood why it is normal practice to write for cornets as for horns and not as for trumpets, that is, a seventh higher than its actual pitch for the D cornet, a fourth higher for the G cornet, etc., etc., exactly as when writing for horns in G and D, while the D trumpet is written a tone lower than its actual pitch and the G trumpet a fifth lower. The cornet has more high-pitch keys than the trumpet; cornets in F, G, A and B♭ are the most useful, with the best sound, and are therefore the most often used. Cornets reach their upper range less easily than trumpets, so since the piston mechanism has filled the immense gap there used to be on this type of instrument between bottom *G*, bottom *c*, low *g* and the second *c'*, the favourite notes of cornets in higher keys have inevitably become just those low notes which trumpets lack. Writing for them requires a number of leger lines below the stave, which are as annoying to the composer as they are to the player, so cornets have come to be written above, not below, their actual pitch, like horns in the equivalent keys. Thus in this system the C cornet is in unison with the high C horn, cornets in B and A are in unison with horns in high B and A; consequently cornets in G, F, E and D are an octave lower than trumpets in those same keys.

I have stressed these differences because they are too often misunderstood by composers, many of whom still have no idea of the true relationship between the pitch of cornets and that of trumpets.

The remark I made earlier about the low range of high-pitched horns and the high range of low-pitched horns applies also to cornets. Although they possess one or two more notes, they should be given a range of only two octaves, from (written pitch) *b* up to *bb″* (cornets in D, Eb, E and F). I should also add that very few players can get high *bb″* on an A cornet, high *a″* on a Bb cornet, or high *g″* on a C cornet, i.e. three ways of getting the pitch *g″*; far less could they get this same *g″* on a D cornet (written high *f‴*).

Although the three-piston cornet possesses all the notes of the chromatic scale, the choice of crook is not a matter of indifference. It is always worth choosing the one which allows the greatest number of natural notes and which requires few accidentals (or none) in the key-signature. When the music is in E, for example, if there is no cornet in E, the best would be the cornet in A, which will then play in G. It would be better too, when the music is in D, to take the cornet in A, playing in F. And so on for the other keys.

Berlioz's explanation of the differences in range and transposition between cornets and trumpets may best be understood by reference to the comparative table (below, p. 201) provided in the first edition of the Treatise. He might also have pointed out that the trumpet has a narrower bore and a lower fundamental than the cornet and can use higher overtones more easily. This is clear from his two tables of open notes, Exx. 130 and 134.

The mention of the two-valve cornet, removed from the *Treatise* itself, is of great importance since, as Cecil B. Wilson pointed out,[23] Berlioz's first music for the piston cornet was for this instrument. The cornet part in *La mort d'Orphée* (1827) was for simple cornet (see below, p. 207) without valves. The first score in which piston cornets were an original part was *Benvenuto Cellini*, composed mostly in 1836. From then until 1840 Berlioz wrote for the two-piston cornet, so that in three major scores – *Benvenuto Cellini*, the *Requiem* and *Roméo et Juliette* – the original cornet parts assiduously avoid the note *g♯′* and all pitches below *eb′*. There are many occasions in these works where a unison is spoilt or a rest provided in order to avoid *d′* or *g♯′*. If these notes are found, they will almost invariably be later additions or revisions for the three-piston cornet. The two puzzling exceptions, which can only be attributed to oversight, are found in *Benvenuto Cellini*: a truant *ab′* in the *Chant des ciseleurs* (*NBE* 1b: 445) and a low *c♯′* in the Act I finale (*NBE* 1b: 699), both of which belong to the original version of the opera.

In the *Symphonie funèbre et triomphale*, composed in 1840, the cornet parts were evidently revised in 1842 for three-piston instruments, but a carefully avoided *ab′* was overlooked and left unrevised in the published version (*NBE* 19: 10).

Technically, of course, the note *eb′* is not available on the two-piston cornet either, but Berlioz must have thought it was since he does not avoid it.

Berlioz's scorn of the cornet and its association with vulgar music derived from its success in Musard's Opéra balls, especially in 1835–6, when Dufresne achieved great celebrity as cornet soloist. Berlioz mocked Musard's arrangements: 'I am

---

[23] Wilson, 'Berlioz's use of brass instruments', p. 75.

told that the *Don Giovanni* quadrille (the "Mozart Quadrille") has just made an appearance duly decked out with bass drum, piccolo, flageolet and cornet.' His adoption of the instrument immediately afterwards in *Benvenuto Cellini* was a very curious and bold step to take. The Opéra orchestra had no players of the instrument and although the Opéra Comique introduced a cornet in Adam's *Le chalet* in 1834 it had not been heard before at the Opéra. The printed scores of both *La juive* and *Les huguenots* specify piston trumpets, not cornets. The trio from *Robert le diable* which Berlioz cites as well suited to the cornet (Ex. 133) was in fact written for a keyed trumpet but probably played at first on a piston trumpet, as Berlioz reported in his article on the opera in 1835.[24] Perhaps by 1842 the solo had been taken over by the cornet.

The explanation for his adoption of the cornet rather than the chromatic trumpet is to be found in the *Memoirs*, in his report of music in Berlin written in 1843: 'In France we still have practically no chromatic or cylinder trumpets. Up till now the incredible popularity of the cornet has stood in their way – quite wrongly, in my view, for the cornet has nothing like the trumpet's nobility and splendour of timbre.' He was impressed by the fact that German orchestras had chromatic trumpets but not cornets, remarking on their excellence in Weimar, Dresden and Berlin, noting that in Stuttgart the old two-piston trumpet was still in use, 'a very unsatisfactory instrument, in sonority and tone quality far behind the cylinder trumpet which has been adopted almost everywhere else. I do not, of course, include Paris. We shall discover it some ten years from now.'[25]

This *Rgm* article on the cornet was much revised for the first edition of the *Treatise*, and the proofs show that the process of revision was arduous. In these proofs the section on the cornet began as follows:

This instrument is a little higher than the horn but not so high as the trumpet; but it is not, as is generally thought, an octave higher than the horn. We give below a comparative table of its compass and range in different keys, along with the range of horns and trumpets. Its usual range is two octaves and a fifth. Its piston mechanism allows it to play all the chromatic notes of its range. Not so long ago the two-piston cornet was common, but since two important notes, d' and $g\sharp'$, were missing on this instrument it has fallen out of use in favour of the three-piston cornet with a complete chromatic scale.

In the 1844 edition itself this paragraph was revised as:

The cornet's usual range is two octaves and two or three notes. Its piston mechanism allows it to play all the chromatic notes of its range down to $f\sharp$. However, this note and the two or three notes above it – g, $g\sharp$ and a – are impracticable except on the higher-pitched cornets. These high cornets can produce the low c, in unison with the trumpet's C, as we shall see shortly. But this note is very risky, poor in quality, and not really very useful.

[24] *Gm*, 12 July 1835; *Cm*, 2, p. 209.   [25] *Memoirs*, 'Travels in Germany', I/7.

The 1844 edition continues:

The cornet exists in D, Eb, E, F, G, Ab, A, Bb and C. By means of the shank which we have mentioned above in connection with horns and trumpets and which lowers the instrument a semitone, one can evidently obtain the keys of Db, Gb and B, but with its ability to modulate by means of the pistons these shanks are not really necessary. Furthermore the lower keys like D, Eb, E and even F are of rather poor quality and are hard to play in tune. The best cornets, and the ones I think should be used almost exclusively, are the cornets in G, and even more those in Ab, A and Bb. The highest of all, the C cornet, is pretty hard to play and its intonation is far from perfect.

The 1843 proofs continue:

Table 4 gives the ranges of the variously pitched cornets. Some players can get some very risky extra notes at the top or the bottom, of which we need take little notice. Like the trumpet it is written on the treble clef.

Table 4

Cornet in	from	(sounding)	up to	(sounding)	
D	bb	(c)	f'''	(g'')	
Eb	a	(c)	e'''	(g'')	
E	a	(c♯)	eb'''	(g'')	
F	g	(c)	d'''	(g'')	
G	f	(c)	c'''	(g'')	
Ab	e	(c)	b''	(g'')	
A	e	(c♯)	bb''	(g'')	
Bb	d	(c)	a''	(g'')	
C	c	(c)	g''	(g'')	(non-transposing)

In the 1844 edition itself this table is given as in Table 5.

The bottom two notes on the D and Eb cornets are muffled, as is the bottom note on the E cornet; the top six notes on the D cornet and the top four notes on the Eb cornet are difficult. Cornets in A, Bb and C have the low *c* in addition (see Ex. 134).

Ex. 134

Table 5

Cornet in	from	(sounding)	up to	(sounding)
D	bb	(c)	g'''	(a'')
Eb	a	(c)	e'''	(g'')
E	a	$(c\sharp)$	eb'''	(g'')
F	g	(c)	d'''	(g'')
G	$f\sharp$	$(c\sharp)$	c'''	(g'')
Ab	$f\sharp$	(d)	b''	(g'')
A	$f\sharp$	$(d\sharp)$	bb''	(g'')
Bb	$f\sharp$	(e)	a''	(g'')
C	$f\sharp$	$(f\sharp)$	g''	(g'')

In the 1855 edition Berlioz no longer recommended the cornet in G as one of the best for general use. He set out the notes given by the natural resonance of the tube as in Ex. 134 and gave a final table of recommended ranges (Table 6).

Table 6

C	poor	✓	✓	✓	✓	✓	✓	✓	d	d								
Bb	very poor	✓	✓	✓	✓	✓	✓	✓	✓	d	d	d						
A	worse		✓	✓	✓	✓	✓	✓	✓	✓	d	d						
Ab				✓	✓	✓	✓	✓	✓	✓	✓	d	d					
G					✓	✓	✓	✓	✓	✓	✓	✓	d					
F						✓	✓	✓	✓	✓	✓	✓	✓	d	d			
E						✓	✓	✓	✓	✓	✓	✓	✓	✓	d	d		
Eb						✓	✓	✓	✓	✓	✓	✓	✓	✓	✓	d		
D							✓	✓	✓	✓	✓	✓	✓	✓	✓	✓		

d = difficult

The actual pitch of c, c', c'' and top c''' for the different cornets is as in Table 7.

Berlioz used cornets in all the nine principal keys he listed. Of the keys that require the shank he used B but not F$\sharp$ or Db. The lower keys are found only in

Table 7

	c	*c'*	*c''*	*c'''*
C	*c*	*c'*	*c''*	—
B♭	*B♭*	*b♭*	*b♭'*	*b♭''*
A	*A*	*a*	*a'*	*a''*
A♭	—	*a♭*	*a♭'*	*a♭''*
G	—	*g*	*g'*	*g''*
F	—	*f*	*f'*	*f''*
E	—	*e*	*e'*	*e''*
E♭	—	*e♭*	*e♭'*	*e♭''*
D	—	*d*	*d'*	*d''*

works written or revised in the period 1836 to 1840. Thus D is required only in an early revision of *Harold en Italie*, E♭ in the printed scores of the *Symphonie fantastique* and *Roméo et Juliette* (both with the recommendation that B♭ instruments be used), E and F only in the original version of *Benvenuto Cellini*, and G and A♭ no later than the *Symphonie funèbre et triomphale*. In all his later music he confined the cornet to the keys of A and B♭ with some occasional use of B and C in *Les Troyens*; the C cornet in the *Aubade* (*NBE* 13: 113) is very unusual. His change of attitude to the cornet clearly coincided with his work on the *Treatise*.

As for the instrument's range, parts for two-piston cornets go no lower than *e♭'*, as we have seen. The three-piston cornet is taken down to *g* and up to *b♭''*, with occasional examples of *b♮''* on the B♭ cornet, described as 'difficult': in *La damnation de Faust* (*NBE* 8a: 367), in the *Tempête* fantasy (1855 version, *NBE* 7: 166) and in *Les Troyens* (*NBE* 2a: 148). A written *c'''* for cornet in E is found in *Benvenuto Cellini* (*NBE* 1c: 1050) and an *e'''* for cornet in D in *Harold en Italie* (*NBE* 17: 237).

Berlioz also substituted cornets for piston trumpets in those early works in which they appeared: not in the overture to *Les francs-juges* (published in parts in 1833) nor in *Waverley* (published in score in 1839), but in the *Symphonie fantastique*, *Lélio* and *Harold en Italie*. The process in each case reveals Berlioz's constant updating of this aspect of his orchestral technique. In the *Symphonie fantastique* the part for one piston trumpet in E♭ in the last two movements was replaced first by two piston trumpets, then by two cornets in E♭. They appeared thus in the printed score with a note to explain that the parts were printed in B♭, the key which Berlioz undoubtedly preferred.[26] Parts for two cornets in G were added to the first movement and an obbligato solo part for one cornet in A survives in the autograph of the second movement, *Un bal* (*NBE* 16: 197). The origin and purpose of this solo is unknown, although it has been associated with the great cornettist Jean-Baptiste Arban (1825–89).[27]

[26] *NBE*, 16, p. xiv; Nicholas Temperley states that cornets played this work as early as December 1833.
[27] David Cairns, 'Berlioz, the cornet, and the Symphonie fantastique', *Berlioz Society Bulletin*, 47 (July 1964), pp. 2–6.

In the 1832 version of *Lélio* there were two piston trumpets in F in the *Chanson de brigands* which were replaced in 1855 by two natural trumpets in E and two cornets in B♭; in the *Tempête* fantasy two cornets in B♭ eventually replaced the two piston trumpets in E♭. In the first movement of *Harold en Italie* the original requirement in 1834 was two natural trumpets and one piston trumpet in D. Later Berlioz replaced the piston trumpet with two two-piston cornets in D. Realising that to obtain the same pitches the cornets would need to be written an octave higher, a number of *all'ottava* signs were inserted. He finally transposed the parts for three-piston cornets in A before the score was published in 1847. The rewriting of this part accounts for a good deal of the heavy working to which the autograph has been subjected. The finale was similarly revised, although Berlioz never revised the part for the three-piston instrument. Both in *Benvenuto Cellini* and in *Roméo et Juliette* the cornet parts were revised and transposed when Berlioz had occasion to revise the scores for publication or later performances.

Both editions continue:

One should observe that the top note in each case (excluding the difficult notes) gives the sounding pitch g''; it has more security and better sonority in the high keys than in the low keys. Thus bb'' on the A cornet, a'' on the B♭ cornet, and g'' on the C cornet are incomparably better and easier to blow than f''' on the D cornet or e''' on the E♭ cornet. Yet all these produce the same pitch g''. This observation applies to all brass instruments, furthermore.

Most major and minor trills are playable and effective from e' up to g'' on the high cornets such as those in A, B♭ and C, with the following exceptions:

$f'-g\flat'$	poor
$f\sharp'-g\sharp'$	dubious
$g\sharp'-a\sharp'$	difficult
$a\sharp'-b'$	poor
$e\flat''-f''$	poor
$e''-f\sharp''$	dubious
$f''-g''$	dubious
$f\sharp''-g\sharp''$	dubious

There are few trills for cornet in Berlioz's scores. They are prominent in the *Aubade* (*NBE* 13: 113) and are also to be found in the *Tempête* fantasy (*NBE* 7: 178).

The 1844 edition continues:

Here now, in Ex. 135, is a comparative table of relationships between pitches of the various keys of horns, cornets and trumpets in France. Black notes show actual pitches.

Ex. 135

It can be seen from this table that the first six keys on the cornet (the lowest) are in unison with the low horns in these keys and an octave lower than trumpets. Observe also that cornets in A, B♭ and C are in unison with the high horns in A, B♭ and C, an octave higher than low horns in A, B♭ and C, and in unison with the lowest trumpets in A, B♭ and C. But this is only true for the method adopted in France of writing cornets an octave higher than trumpets, and that is simply to avoid using the large number of leger lines which would be constantly required when writing for the most commonly used high cornets, whose best notes are in the middle register.

For the cornet's natural notes are in fact the same as those of the trumpet, even though the tone of the two instruments is different. Ex. 136a shows the natural notes of the cornet in G, written in the French manner; Ex. 136b shows the natural notes of the cornet in G, written as they should be and as it is done in Prussia. These are also the natural notes of the trumpet in G.

Ex. 136

(a)

(b)

By giving *g″* (actual pitch) as the cornet's highest note we have shown that it can go a bit higher than the horn and not as high as the trumpet. In fact the horn in high C can only just reach *e″*, with considerable difficulty. Some horn players can produce a top *c‴* on an F horn, sounding *f″*, but only at the end of a phrase, without sustaining, and led into from *g″*, *a″* and *b″*, as in Ex. 137.

Ex. 137

On the other hand trumpets not only produce *g″* (on a C trumpet) without any difficulty but can also manage *e″* (on an F trumpet) and *g″* (on a D trumpet), both sounding *a″*. Players with a strong embouchure can play *e″* (on a G trumpet), sounding *b″*, and *g″* (on an F trumpet), sounding *c‴*, but only in passing and when these notes are carefully prepared. Players who can reach these extreme points of the range are very rare; the composer should not count on them.

To return to the cornet:

In 1855 this section was replaced with the following:

Here now, in Ex. 138, is a comparative table of relationships between pitches of the various keys of horns, trumpets and cornets. The lowest note of a cornet in C, as we have seen, is an octave higher than that of the trumpet in C, just as the lowest note of this trumpet is an octave higher than that of the horn in low C. The horn's natural notes, arising from the resonance of the tube, are therefore duplicated in the same order an octave higher to form the trumpet's natural notes, and these would be duplicated in the same order another octave higher to form the cornet's natural notes if the player's lips had the necessary strength to blow the highest notes, which they haven't.

Ex. 138

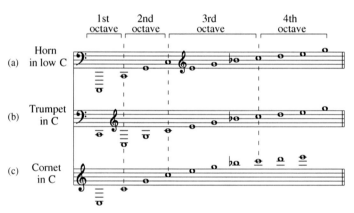

The horn's lowest note, as shown here, does exist, but in low keys it is so unpleasant and of such uncertain pitch that we did not include it in the range of the horn in low C (on p. 165) nor, for even stronger reasons, in the range of the horn in low B♭. When notated in the treble clef the horn in low C sounds an octave below its written pitch, according to the horn's normal practice. On the cornet in C the fourth octave is only practicable in lower keys.

It will be seen from Ex. 138 – and this is most important to remember – that the part of a brass instrument's range where without using valves it can only play the three notes *c′–g′–c″* or *c–g–c′* or *C–G–c* is *always the second octave*, counting from the bottom.

Now the cornet's best notes fall precisely into this second octave. If cornets in A, B♭ and C were treated as high trumpets an octave above A, B♭ and C trumpets, they could have been written that way. But it was right not to do so, but instead to write for cornets in their place on the musical scale, having their lowest note an octave above the trumpet's lowest note and their best notes within or near their second octave (Ex. 139a). If cornets were written in the same way as trumpets, these notes would always have been below the stave and would have necessitated endless leger lines (Ex. 139b). This awkward way of writing for cornets is nevertheless still retained in Prussian military bands. It is as well to be warned about it.

Ex. 139

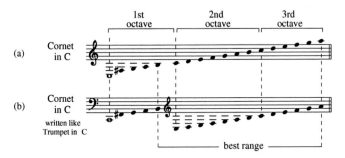

Next one must observe that if the key of C is taken as the point of reference for horns, trumpets and cornets, the cornet's crooks get longer, making the instrument lower. That is why we set out their ranges beginning with the highest, while trumpet and horn crooks (except the three horn crooks in B, B♭ and low A, which are lower than the C) get shorter, making the instrument higher (see Table 8).

Table 8

Cornet keys		Trumpet keys		Horn keys	
C (basic)	↑ descending keys ↓	A♭ (rare)	↑ ascending keys — ↓ descending keys	high C	↑ ascending keys — ↓ descending keys
B		G		high B	
B♭		G♭		high B♭	
A		F		high A	
A♭		E		A♭	
G		E♭		G	
G♭		D		G♭	
F		D♭		F	
E		C (basic)		E	
E♭		B		E♭	
D		B♭		D	
		A (very rare)		D♭	
				C (basic)	
				B	
				B♭	
				A (very rare)	

The relationship between horns, trumpets and cornets and their respective positions in the range of pitches should now be understood.

I should add that since the piston or cylinder trumpet has its best notes in and around its third octave, *which is in unison with the cornet's second octave,* passages written for cornet in A, B or C in the range *f♯–a″* can if necessary be played on trumpets in A, B or C unchanged. This permits the substitution of cylinder trumpets for cornets without any ill effect in those orchestras, such as German ones, which do not have cornets. In actual fact the cornet in A, B♭ or C has a narrower range than the trumpet in A, B♭ or C since it cannot really go above *a″* (sounding pitch, i.e. *c‴* on the A cornet, *b″* on the B♭ cornet, or *a″* on the C cornet). The trumpet, on the other hand, has several more notes at the bottom, poor though they are, and it can also sound that same *a″* more easily than the cornet (i.e. *g″* on a D trumpet, *e″* on an F trumpet). Players with a strong embouchure can play *e″* (on a G trumpet), sounding *b″*, and *g″* (on an F trumpet), sounding *c‴*, but only in passing and when these notes are carefully prepared. Players who can reach these extreme points of the range are very rare; the composer should not count on them.

The fierce determination with which Berlioz expounds these relative pitches between members of the brass family suggests that he himself had been confounded by the problem and been compelled to master it, or at least that he had found both composers and players confusing the different transpositions made by trumpets and cornets. So long as the cornet was regarded as an off-shoot of the horn (which it was) and played by horn players (which was the case in its early days) there was probably little confusion. But for trumpeters, who increasingly took over the playing of cornets, there were obvious pitfalls. As for Berlioz's change of mind about the superiority of Prussian practice, his two visits to Berlin in 1843 and 1847 may have convinced him that the French way was after all the best.

At some point, probably between 1846 and 1855, Berlioz drafted another passage on this knotty problem on the last page of the autograph score of Part I of *La damnation de Faust.*[28] Below tables of the open notes of trumpets in D and low A and cornets in D and A he wrote:

> If it were written like a trumpet in high A there would always be leger lines to write, thus:

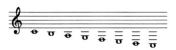

The cornet in C is regarded as the remnant of another family of instruments, and the crooks go down as far as G which is itself of no value. Consequently with the cornet written as it normally is, only notes which seem to be in unison with the corresponding notes on the trumpet, while they are actually in unison, belong to another octave than the trumpet's, thus:

[28] Paris, Bibliothèque nationale, MS 1.190a, p. 104; see *NBE*, 8b, p. 479.

[A diagram follows here, showing the trumpet's third octave to be the same as the cornet's second octave].

As Berlioz no doubt realised, this draft sheds little new light on the problem. The 1855 edition continues:

The trumpet can attack high notes more easily since it has a straight bore, a small mouthpiece and a narrow bell. The cornet, in contrast, with its larger, almost conical bore and wider bell and mouthpiece, can get low notes more easily than high ones, and its tone has accordingly those special characteristics that distinguish it from the trumpet. The difference is attributable to these factors.

Before examining the expressive qualities of the cornet, it may be as well to repeat here what I said earlier, when discussing the piston horn, about the action of the three cylinders or pistons applied to brass instruments in general.

Not only do the three cylinders give the instruments a chromatic scale (above the first octave) filling the gaps between the natural harmonics, they also add six chromatic semitones at the bottom, descending from the two lowest natural notes. Thus from the second-lowest note on the cornet, c', you can get chromatically down to $f\sharp$, and from the lowest note, c, you can get chromatically down to $F\sharp$ (though these notes are poor and impracticable). From the second-lowest note on the trumpet, c, you can get chromatically down to $F\sharp$ (though these notes are detestable), and from the lowest note, C, you can get down chromatically to $F\sharp'$ (these are even more detestable). This low C is already so approximate and hard to blow that any lower notes supplied by the pistons become, clearly, quite impracticable. The same applies to horns.

Both editions then continue with a section derived from the 1842 *Rgm* text:

Although the cornet possesses all the notes of the chromatic scale, the choice of crook is not a matter of indifference. It is always worth choosing the one which allows the greatest number of natural notes (do I need to repeat that the natural notes are those produced from the simple resonance of the instrument's bore without using the pistons, namely the notes set out in Ex. 134?) and which requires few accidentals (or none) in the key-signature. When the music is in E, for example, since the E cornet is one of the less good ones, one should use a cornet in A, which would then be playing in G (Ex. 140a). It is also a good idea to pick the A cornet if the music is in D; it will then be playing in F (Ex. 140b). If the orchestra is in Eb, take the cornet in Bb with one flat in the key-signature, since it will be playing in F; and so on.

Ex. 140

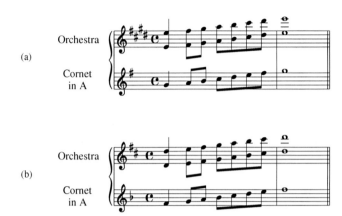

The cornet is highly fashionable in France today...

[etc, as in the 1842 text given above.]

One normally writes two cornet parts, often in two different keys.

The allocation of the two cornets to two different keys is very rare in Berlioz's music. This is found only in the opening movement of *Roméo et Juliette* and in an intermediate version of the entr'acte to the third Tableau of *Benvenuto Cellini*.

It will be seen that Berlioz's regard for the cornet, particularly abusive in the *Rgm* text, was thus softened somewhat in the pages of the *Treatise* itself. From the evidence of his scores we may observe a further amelioration of his attitude. Even if he felt forced to accept the cornet rather than the piston trumpet as the only available chromatic brass instrument in that range, it played an increasingly versatile and important role in his music. Already in *La damnation de Faust* the cornet is given a strain of nobility in Mephistopheles's 'Voici des roses' in Part II, acting as the upper voice to three trombones (*NBE* 8a: 170). The nobility is no doubt ironic, but a similar combination was used, in a more solemn context, for the choral refrain in the *Te ergo quaesumus* in the *Te deum* (*NBE* 10: 93) and for the scene in *Les Troyens* where Priam blesses Andromache's infant son (*NBE* 2a: 120). For the depiction of hollow vulgarity Berlioz invariably turned to the cornet, as in Auerbach's cellar in *La damnation de Faust*, or to convey the falsity of the Trojans' joy at the opening of *Les Troyens*, whose first melodic gesture is a remarkable two-octave rising scale on two unison cornets (*NBE* 2a: 7). He also liked the sound of cornets for orchestral brilliance, as at the end of the *Tempête* fantasy, the end of the first Tableau of *Benvenuto Cellini*, the love duet in the third Tableau of the same opera, and the *Entrée des constructeurs* in *Les Troyens*. But in *Les Troyens* the cornets are used for very much more than special effects; for the first time they are an essential part of the orchestral texture, as constantly engaged as the horns. The prominence of cornets throughout *Les Troyens* is one of the most remarkable features of the scoring of that opera.

This may be attributed to the advocacy and artistry of Arban, the most cele-brated cornettist of the second generation. The first cornet stars, Dufresne and

Forestier, were originally horn players who did not win Berlioz to their cause. But Arban became an admired friend, particularly during the 1850s. A letter of 13 February 1857 recounts a significant episode: 'The other day I was just finishing the instrumental movement with chorus for the *Pantomime* of Andromache [in Act I of *Les Troyens*] when there arrives at my door the cornettist Arban, who has a remarkable feeling for melodic expression. He begins to play the clarinet solo exactly as it should be, and there am I in seventeenth heaven.'[29] Berlioz praised Arban's performances on a number of occasions.

Arban's cornet tutor, the *Grande méthode complète pour cornet à pistons et de saxhorn*, still in use today, was published in 1864, too late to be of use to Berlioz. The earlier tutor by Forestier (*Méthode pour le cornet à pistons*, c. 1835) was available to him when he wrote the *Treatise*.

The 1855 edition ended its cornet chapter here, but the 1844 edition concluded with a passage on the simple cornet drafted in the proofs as follows:

Some military bands used to have 'simple' cornets in C and A♭ (and some still do). The first was in unison with the horn in high C and an octave higher than the horn in low C, the second was in unison with the horn in high A♭ and an octave higher than the trumpet in low A♭. They were probably called cornets because they were regarded as diminutive horns ('petit cor'). They kept this name when the piston mechanism was added.

Simple cornets had almost the same number of notes and the same range (apart from the very top of the range) as trumpets in C, i.e. the main range shown in Ex. 130.

The piston cornet in high D♭ would be very useful. Its top range should go no higher than *e″*. In Prussia you find little cylinder cornets which sound an octave higher than French cornets. Their range is two octaves and a third, in the keys of A and B♭, which are the best. The Prussian cornet in B♭ has a range written from *c* up to *e″* (sounding *bb* up to *d″*).

This appeared in the 1844 edition much revised:

In military bands simple cornets in C, B♭ and A♭ are used with considerable success. They provide a continuation of the trumpet's scale upwards. They are thus an octave higher than horns in high A♭, high B♭ and high C. The simple cornet is a transposing instrument which has just the same notes as the trumpet: *C* (a poor note), *c*, *g*, *c′*, *e′*, *g′*, *bb′*, *c″*, *d″*, *e″*. On the A♭ cornet the last three notes are very difficult, and on the B♭ cornet they are almost impossible. On the C cornet *bb′* and *c″* are very difficult and *d″* and *e″* are impossible. They sound respectively a minor sixth, a seventh and an octave higher than written. The practice of writing cornets an

[29] *Cg*, 5, p. 428.

octave higher than trumpets are written has not been adopted for simple cornets, which are written exactly the same as trumpets in high A♭, high B♭ and high C.

The simple cornet was in essence a German post-horn with circular coils and a number of crooks.[30] Berlioz used it once only, in his first Prix de Rome cantata *La mort d'Orphée* of 1827, where it is in B♭ and C with very few notes to play. Its appearance in this work has been the cause of some confusion, being cited by many writers as the first appearance of the cornet in the romantic orchestra.[31] In fact it is still the eighteenth-century post-horn (best known from Mozart's *Serenade* K. 320) in a late reappearance before its transformation into the piston cornet.

Berlioz was later to be confused about it himself. A feuilleton of February 1834 recounted the annual ceremony for playing the Prix de Rome laureates' cantatas: 'A full orchestra is assembled, with nothing missing: strings, two flutes, two oboes, two clarinets. [...] There are four horns, three trombones, even *piston trumpets*, modern instruments!'[32] Thirty years later, when revising this article for chapter 30 of his *Memoirs*, Berlioz wrote 'piston cornets' instead of 'piston trumpets', forgetting that there were no piston cornets available in 1830 and that his *Sardanapale* did indeed require piston trumpets.

In November 1837 Berlioz was still enthusiastic about the simple cornet. Reporting a concert given by a Viennese orchestra under Johann Strauss the elder he wrote: 'The trumpeters play the piston cornet and the simple cornet, a valuable instrument which we have foolishly neglected in our own orchestras.'[33] His entry on the simple cornet then appeared in the first edition of the *Treatise* but was removed from the second edition of 1855, leaving a conspicuously blank space.

THE TROMBONE

There are four types of trombone, each bearing the name of the human voice to which it most closely approximates in range and tone. The soprano trombone, the smallest and highest of all, is found in Germany, but we have never come across it in France. It has hardly ever been used in the works of the great masters, which is no reason of course why it should not be, sooner or later, and even the highest piston trumpet may not be a satisfactory substitute. Gluck, who wrote for the soprano trombone under the name 'cornetto' in the Italian version of *Orfeo*, is the only one to do so. He has it doubling the chorus sopranos while the alto, tenor and bass trombones double the other voices.

---

[30] For an illustration see *The New Grove Dictionary of Music and Musicians*, ed. Stanley Sadie (20 vols., London, 1980), 4, p. 786.

[31] The error derives from Jacques Barzun, *Berlioz and the Romantic Century* (2 vols., Boston, 1950), 1, p. 75, and has been repeated in David Whitwell, *A New History of Wind Music* (Evanston, 1972), p. 42; Edward P. Sandor, 'The development and use of the chromatic trumpet in the nineteenth-century orchestra', *NACWPI Journal*, 32/4 (1985), p. 4; and Cairns, *Berlioz, The Making of an Artist*, p. 206.

[32] *Cm*, 1, p. 156.   [33] *Jd*, 10 November 1837; *Cm*, 3, p. 329; Condé, p. 123.

These last three trombones are the only ones in general use. Still it must be said that the alto trombone is not found in every French orchestra and that the bass trombone is almost unknown in France. It is almost always confused with the third tenor trombone, which plays the lowest part and which is thus quite wrongly named 'bass trombone', a very different instrument.

Trombones have slides, with a double tube that can be lengthened or shortened at will by a simple movement of the player's arm. Varying the length of the tube will clearly change the key of the instrument – which is in fact what happens. Trombones hence possess all the notes that result from the natural resonance of the tube, like other brass instruments, but *in every position*. This gives them a complete chromatic scale except for a gap near the bottom, as we shall see.

In *Orfeo* (1762) Gluck was indeed writing for the cornetto, an instrument which had served as partner to trombones in Italy and Germany for nearly two hundred years. The soprano trombone, though rarer, had served the same functions since the late seventeenth century. It seems unlikely that the soprano trombone had ever played this part in Gluck's opera, although it is not impossible. It was pitched an octave higher than the tenor trombone.

The alto trombone is written on the alto clef and has a chromatic range of over two and a half octaves from *A* up to *g♭"*. From *A* to *d* is of poor quality, and top *g♭"* is very difficult. Its tone is a bit shrill compared to that of the lower members of the trombone family. Its low notes are rather poor, and the fact that these very notes are excellent on the tenor trombone, which is never far from the alto trombone in any orchestra, is a good reason for avoiding them. On the other hand the top notes, *b'*, *c"*, *d"*, *e"* and *f"*, can be very useful; it is a matter for regret therefore that the alto trombone is now to be found in very few of our French orchestras. With its slide in closed position the notes which may be obtained with the lips alone are shown in Ex. 141a, the same series as that produced by the natural resonance of the tube on horns, trumpets, cornets and all other brass instruments in E♭. Hence the name 'little' or 'alto' trombone in E♭, as players call it, though this need not be specified in scores since it sounds at its written pitch and is not one of the transposing instruments for which alone (as we have said earlier) these various designations of key are always required.

Berlioz wrote for the alto trombone in his early music with the upper trombone part notated on the alto clef, at least until the composition of *Harold en Italie*. Thereafter, beginning with *Le cinq mai*, composed in 1835, he wrote his three trombones on tenor and bass clefs and presumed that all the players would play tenor trombones. This is specified in the *Requiem* and implied elsewhere. The range of his alto trombone parts reaches up to eb'' in the *Messe solennelle* (*NBE* 23: 172) and in the *Marche au supplice* (*NBE* 16: 106). In an early document listing the instruments for the *Symphonie fantastique* he wrote: 'The alto trombone part must not be played on a big trombone, as is often done in France: I demand a true alto trombone.'[34] The alto trombone was also intended in the *Messe solennelle*, the *Scène héroïque*, *La mort d'Orphée*, the *Waverley* and *Roi Lear* overtures, *Cléopâtre* and the 1832 version of *Lélio*.

The alto trombone part in *Cléopâtre* is puzzling, since it is notated on the tenor clef. (Perhaps this defiance of convention was a further cause of the Prix de Rome judges' displeasure in 1829.) The tenor clef and tenor instrument were adopted after 1834, even though some later works allow or imply the alto instrument. The printed parts (but not the score) of *Roméo et Juliette* take the top trombone up to d'' in the *Fête chez Capulet* (*NBE* 18: 101–3). The top trombone part in the *Symphonie funèbre et triomphale* is for 'alto or tenor' trombone and reaches up to c'' (*NBE* 19: 6). Since the alto trombone survived in general use longer in Germany than in France, Berlioz's first trombone parts were sometimes adapted for alto trombone on tour, as was the case with *La damnation de Faust*.[35] The top trombone part in the *Te deum* was also evidently first written with an alto trombone in mind,[36] which strongly supports the notion that parts of that work originated in one of the grandiose projects of the early 1830s. Even in its final form the part goes up to c'' on several occasions (*NBE* 10: 126, 136–7).

In the *Rgm* text Berlioz's observation that the alto trombone had almost disappeared from French orchestras made a point of excepting the orchestra of the Opéra Comique. The published registers of that orchestra list one player of the alto trombone, one who played alto or tenor, and two who played tenor or bass.[37] In 1843 Berlioz described the tone of the alto trombone as 'thin; its high notes are poor; I would vote to exclude it from theatre orchestras'.[38]

The tenor trombone is incontestably the best of all the trombones. Its sound is strong and full, it can play passages too rapid for a bass trombone, and its tone is good throughout its range. It is normally written on the tenor clef, but since in some orchestras the three trombone parts are given three different names but are played on three tenor trombones, they are now often written one on the alto clef, one on the tenor clef and one on the bass clef. With its slide in closed position the notes which may be obtained as the natural series are shown in Ex. 141b, being produced by the resonance of the tube by all brass instruments in Bb, that is, by those tubes which when vibrating as a single tube give low Bb' as their first note. This is why it is called the 'Bb trombone'. It is thus a fourth lower than the alto trombone and its range is from E up to db'' with all chromatic intervals. Top db'' is very difficult. Low Eb is unavailable on the tenor trombone, a common cause of error even in the most skilfully written scores. One of today's composers,

[34] *NBE*, 16, pp. xiv, 185.   [35] *NBE*, 8b, p. 459.   [36] *NBE*, 10, p. x.
[37] Adam Carse, *The Orchestra from Beethoven to Berlioz* (Cambridge, 1948), p. 493.
[38] *Memoirs*, 'Travels in Germany', I/7.

whose skill in the art of instrumentation is one of his most eminent and
undisputed qualities, begins one of his operas with several low E♭s on the
third tenor trombone. In practice the ophicleide plays it with the trombone
doubling an octave higher, and the composer has perhaps never noticed
that his low E♭ is not heard on the instrument for which he wrote it.

Unlike the obsolescent alto and bass trombones, the tenor instrument remained
a permanent member of Berlioz's orchestra, unaffected by change. In his mature
orchestral scores the group of three tenor trombones is standard. He learned to
refine its upper range. In the 1842 *Rgm* text he wrote: 'It goes up to *bb'*, even to
bᵇ', *c"* and *d"*, depending on the player and provided he is not required to play
low notes beforehand, a bad preparation for the lips before playing high. It is
prudent not to write above *bb'* in orchestral music.' In the 1844 edition of the
Treatise he called the notes *c"* and *db"* 'difficult', revising that in 1855 to mention
db" only. In general he treats *bb'* as the upper limit, allowing a number of *bᵇ*'s
in the solo trombone part in the second movement of the *Symphonie funèbre et
triomphale*. The high *c"* for the tutti trombones in the first movement of that work
(*NBE* 19: 6) and in the *Judex crederis* in the *Te deum* (*NBE* 10: 126) may be, as we
have seen, residual parts for alto trombone, even though the 1855 edition of the
Treatise recognised that tenor trombones could play *c"* without difficulty.

The opera which begins with low E♭ for tenor trombone has defied identification.

A notable case where Berlioz had to write the note *G* for the tenor trombone
when he might have preferred to write E♭ is found in the second version of the
overture to *Benvenuto Cellini* (*NBE* 1a: 107). He similarly substituted *F* for an
unreachable *D* in *L'enfance du Christ* (*NBE* 11: 37).

The bass trombone is rare only because of the fatigue experienced by
even the most robust players. It is the largest and therefore the lowest of all.
It must be given quite long gaps for the player to rest in and only be used
in a discreet and well justified manner. With its slide closed it produces the
notes shown in Ex. 141c. It is known as the 'large trombone' or 'trombone
in E♭'. It is thus an octave lower than the alto trombone and a fifth lower
than the tenor trombone. It is written on the bass clef. Its range is from *A'*
up to *gb'* with all the chromatic intervals; top *f'* and *gb'* are difficult.

Ex. 141

The bass trombone's sound is majestic, formidable and awe-inspiring. It takes charge of the bottom line of the whole brass section. In Paris, however, we have the misfortune to lack the instrument altogether; it is not taught at the Conservatoire and no trombonist has yet taken it upon himself to become a practised exponent of it. Consequently most modern German scores and even some earlier French and Italian works have to be adapted to some extent when they are played in Paris, being written for orchestras which possess – or used to possess – this instrument. Thus in Weber's *Der Freischütz* there are some low *D*s in the accompaniment of the Huntsmen's Chorus, and later on some low *E*♭s for the Hermit's entrance. These notes are inevitably heard an octave higher, since the Opéra's three players all play tenor trombones, on which the notes are unobtainable. It is the same with the sustained low *C*s in the chorus 'Pleure ô patrie, ô Thessalie!' in Gluck's *Alceste*. But here the effect of these bottom *C*s is extremely important, so to transpose them is a deplorable alteration.

The bass trombone cannot join in at tempos as fast as the other instruments of this family can. The length and width of its bore require a little longer to begin vibrating, and its slide clearly does not permit much agility, being activated by a handle which extends the length of the arm for certain positions. So German players who use the bass trombone cannot play a host of passages in our modern French scores which our trombonists play (somehow or other) on the tenor trombone. Despite the ability of some of our players the faulty performance of these passages proves in fact that they are too rapid even for the tenor trombone and that trombones in general are really not appropriate for such figurations. At the very least it proves that one must always use the instrument indicated by the composer (assuming that composers are guilty of only slight extravagance in their demands), and not something different. Unfortunately many composers continue to write 'alto trombone', 'tenor trombone' and 'bass trombone' instead of calling them first, second and third tenor trombones, although they know full well that most of our orchestras have only tenor trombones. So in order to be able to perform their operas abroad as they are done in Paris one would have to disregard the printed indications and use the instruments that are used in Paris. But as a matter of principle, how can such laxity in interpreting a composer's wishes be allowed? Does it not open the door to all kinds of infidelity and abuse? And is it not right that composers should suffer a little for marking their scores so negligently, rather than that those who compose with care and a profound knowledge of the resources of instruments should be made to risk having their works mutilated?

Ex. 141, as given in the *Treatise*, corrected the list of open notes that Berlioz put forward in the *Rgm* text, where the first, sixth and last notes in each list were omitted.

Berlioz's text on the bass trombone is a clear warning against confusion and misunderstanding. Although the third trombone in the group was regularly referred to as the 'bass' trombone, in France the instrument was always a tenor trombone. Berlioz encountered the true bass trombone for the first time in 1837 when Johann Strauss the elder brought his Viennese orchestra to Paris. He observed that its low notes were 'full, rich and powerful in effect'.[39] He called for a true bass trombone only once, in the *Symphonie funèbre et triomphale*, where he calls it 'grand trombone basse'. It is written in C although the Eb instrument is implied. It is much exploited for low notes such as *C* and *Db*, and in keeping with his cautionary remarks he gives the part rests and gaps to allow for its greater demands on the player's lungs. Berlioz marked it 'non obligé' in the score and may never have had a player available to perform the part in Paris.

When he visited Berlin in 1843 he found two bass trombones in the opera orchestra there, the only place in Germany he encountered them, and remarked that there were none in Paris: 'Parisian musicians refuse to play an instrument that is so tiring to the chest. Prussian lungs are evidently more robust than ours.' Of the Berlin players he reported:

> Their combined volume of tone is so great as to obliterate the alto and tenor trombones playing the two upper parts. The aggressive tone of one bass trombone would be enough to upset the balance of the three trombone parts as written by composers nowadays. But there being no ophicleide at the Berlin Opera, [...] they give the part to a second bass trombone. The effect of having two of these formidable instruments one above the other (the ophicleide part being frequently written an octave below the third trombone) is disastrous. You hear nothing but the bottom line; even the trumpets are all but drowned. When I came to give my concerts I found that the bass trombone was much too prominent – although in the symphonies I was using only one – and had to ask the player to sit so that the bell of the instrument was facing into his stand, which acted as a sort of mute, while the alto and tenor trombonists stood up to play with their bells pointing over the top of their stands. Only in this way could all three parts be heard.[40]

Problems with the low trombone notes in *Der Freischütz* were fresh in Berlioz's mind from the Opéra's revival of that work in 1841. The low *C*s in *Alceste* appear in the 1776 printed score but not in Gluck's autograph, which shows them an octave higher.[41]

All trombones have the same compass of two octaves and a sixth measured from their various bottom notes, as we have seen. But that is not

[39] *Rgm*, 5 November 1837; *Cm*, 3, p. 328; Condé, p. 123.   [40] *Memoirs*, 'Travels in Germany', I/7.
[41] Gluck, *Werke*, I/7, pp. 259, 445.

all. In addition to this vast range they also possess three notes at the very bottom as well as the fundamental note of the natural resonance of the tube. These notes are enormous and magnificent on the tenor trombone, mediocre in sound on the alto trombone, and awe-inspiring on the bass trombone – when they can be produced. They are called 'pedals', probably because of the similarity of their tone to that of the organ's low notes bearing the same name. It is quite hard to write for them well and they are unknown even to many trombonists.

These notes are shown in Ex. 142. Ex. 142a gives them for the alto trombone, Ex. 142b for the tenor trombone, and Ex. 142c would be those for the bass trombone if players were strong enough to produce them. Even if we accept that the large bass trombone has only the first of these pedal notes (Eb'), it will still be invaluable for certain effects not otherwise obtainable, since no other orchestral instrument except the bass tuba and the contrabassoon can get so extraordinarily low. On all trombones these notes are isolated from the rest by a gap of an augmented fourth between the fundamental and the last note (going downwards) produced by the slide.

Ex. 142

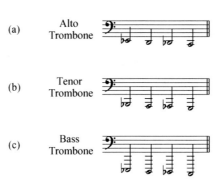

In the 1855 edition the following was added, down to the table:

On a B♭ trombone the gap lies between Bb' and $E\natural$. Because of this gap it is sometimes essential to specify the key of the trombone you are using; the gap moves about depending on the length of the tube and the key of the instrument. So one or more pedals (or all of them) in one key can be missing from a trombone in another key.

For example, if a composer writes the Bb', A', Ab', G' without taking care to indicate that he requires a trombone in B♭, he might find that the orchestra playing his work has a genuine bass trombone in E♭, which lacks the low Ab' and G', or a bass trombone in F (these instruments are common in Germany), which lacks the four notes Bb', A', Ab' and G', or even a bass trombone in G (sometimes found in England), which similarly lacks Bb', A' and Ab'. This can best be illustrated by means of the following table:

Table 9

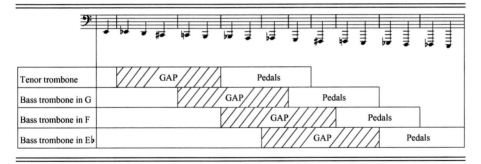

The bass trombone in G has one of the tenor's pedals (G')
The bass trombone in F has none of the tenor's pedals
The bass trombone in E♭ has two of the tenor's pedals ($B♭'$ and A')

    The general ranges are as follows:

alto trombone:	C to $E♭$ pedals, of poor quality
	A to $g♭''$ chromatic (A to d are of poor quality)
tenor trombone:	G' to $B♭'$ pedals (G' is very difficult)
	E to $d♭''$ chromatic
bass trombone:	C' to $E♭'$ pedals (C, $D♭'$ and D' are almost impossible,
	$E♭'$ is very difficult)
	A' to $g♭'$ chromatic

If the alto trombone's pedals were not of such poor quality one could use them in orchestras which have no bass trombone to fill the gap between E on the tenor trombone and its first pedal $B♭'$. Unfortunately they are so thin and feeble that they cannot be relied on to stand in for the tenor trombone's fine low notes. This can only be done by the bass trombone, with its powerful low range from $E♭$ down to B'.

    The ingenious instrument-maker Sax (of Paris) has happily resolved this difficulty by means of a single piston fitted to the body of the tenor trombone. The player activates this piston with his left thumb, leaving his right arm free to manipulate the slide. By filling the gap it now gives the B♭ tenor trombone an immense range from top c'' down to G', the notes $E♭$ down to B' being obtained with the thumb-piston and the notes $B♭'$ down to G' being pedals. Every orchestra ought to have at least one of these fine instruments.

    This paragraph, added in 1855, records Sax's production of the trombone known either as 'tenor-bass' or 'B♭-F' trombone still widely used today. It was not in fact Sax's invention, being usually credited to C. F. Sattler of Leipzig in 1839.[42] In practice the note $B\natural'$ was still unavailable since the valve reduced the slide's seven positions to six.

The vibration of pedal notes is slow, needing a lot of air. To make them sound well therefore, they must be given quite long note-values and must follow one another slowly with rests in between to let the player breathe. Care must be taken to ensure that the piece where they appear is written consistently low enough to let the trombonist's lips get used to very low pitches. On the tenor trombone, for example, the best way to write pedals is to leap to the first one, Bb', down a fifth or an octave from the F or Bb above. Then, leaving space for breathing, descend chromatically to A' and $G\sharp'$ (the $G\natural'$ is harder, extremely rough and very hazardous to produce). At least this is the way the composer has introduced these three notes in a modern Requiem Mass. And although at the first rehearsal five or six out of the eight trombonists engaged to play them exclaimed that they were not possible, the eight Bbs, eight As and eight $G\sharp$s sounded nonetheless very full and in tune, performed by several players who had never even tried to produce them before and therefore did not believe they existed.

The sound of the three pedal notes seemed even better than that of the notes $F\sharp$ and $F\natural$ which are higher and more frequently heard.

In the work I have just mentioned this effect is set beneath flutes in three-part harmony, with no voices and no other instruments. The sound of flutes separated by an immense interval from the trombones thus seems like an extremely high harmonic resonance of the pedals, whose slow pace and deep voice are meant to intensify the solemn effect of the silences between the chorus's utterances in the verse 'Hostias et preces tibi laudis offerimus' (Ex. 143).

Ex. 143

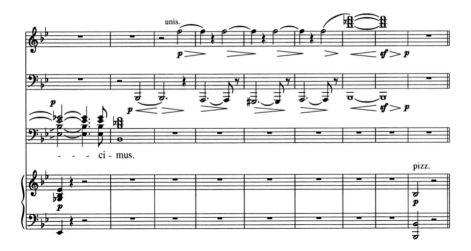

Berlioz's reticence in identifying the work (his own *Requiem*) was designed for the *Rgm* serialisation, which included few identifications and no musical examples. In the *Treatise* the passage (bars 33 to the end of the *Hostias, NBE* 9: 114) is printed in full score and identified as his. In the published score of the *Requiem* he had inserted the footnote: 'These low notes for tenor trombone are little known even by players, but they exist and can sound quite easily when they are introduced in this way.' The pedals are preceded by $F\sharp$ and $F\natural$ with long gaps in between. Elsewhere in the score of the *Requiem* Berlioz noted: 'All the tenor trombones used in this work must be in B♭' (*NBE* 9: 28), a precaution to ensure that the pedal notes will be available.

Of this passage in the *Requiem* Cecil Forsyth, who had never heard it, wrote: 'It probably sounds very nasty.' To which Gordon Jacob responded: 'The present writer has heard the passage. It does!'[43] Their unease may well be explained by the strong overtones that trombone pedals generate. The major third is particularly audible (d' from a pedal $B\flat'$), so that only the root-position major chords are free of discordant overtones. The B♭ minor chord that ends Ex. 143 produces a particularly jarring effect at its *sforzando* apex from the collision of major and minor.[44]

I have used tenor trombone pedals on another occasion, for a quite different purpose. I needed to devise low harmonies of exceptional savagery in an unusual sonority. I believe I achieved this by writing a perfect fifth $B\flat'$–F on two tenor trombones, and later on by this diminished seventh between an ophicleide and a tenor trombone's pedal A' (Ex. 144).

[43] Cecil Forsyth, *Orchestration* (2nd edn, London, 1935), p. 136; Gordon Jacob, *Orchestral Technique* (2nd edn, London, 1940), p. 61.
[44] Hugh Macdonald, 'Berlioz's orchestration: human or divine?', *Musical Times*, 110 (1969), p. 256.

Ex. 144

This is from the *Marche au supplice* in the *Symphonie fantastique* (*NBE* 16: 99) and the open fifth *B♭–F* is found a dozen bars later. These pedals are not in the autograph and were added later, probably after 1837. Berlioz may have derived the idea of using pedal notes from Hérold's *Zampa* (1831), whose first act finale has ten bars of held pedal *B♭'* for three tenor trombones in unison (although if the Opéra Comique still used alto trombones, there would not have been three instruments to play it). His first use of trombone pedals may have been the scene in the second tableau of *Benvenuto Cellini* after the death of Pompeo (*NBE* 1b: 674), probably composed in 1836. Here Berlioz gives the pedal *B♭'* to the first trombone but suggests that it be played by whichever player can do it best. Later occurrences of trombone pedals in his music are found in the *Marche marocaine*, the *Hamlet* March, the *Course à l'abîme* in *La damnation de Faust* (for the depiction of 'a hideous monster'), in the first movement and the *Judex crederis* of the *Te deum*, and on several occasions in *Les Troyens*, most notably to illustrate the serpents that devoured Laocoon (*NBE* 2a: 125). At the end of Dido's farewell in Act V Berlioz originally wrote, and then removed, some pedal *A♭*s for the third trombone (*NBE* 2b: 712).

Only in *La damnation de Faust* and the *Te deum* did he write the lowest pedal, *G'*, and he wrote pedals only for the tenor trombone.

A further idiosyncrasy of which most composers are unaware, yet which is very important to know about, is the difficulty, sometimes impossibility, for trombones to play the notes of Ex. 145 in rapid succession. The shift from one note to the next requires an enormous change in the position of the slide with a considerable stretch of the player's arm, so it can only be done at a very moderate tempo. When a well-known composer wrote the rapid succession *B–A♯–B*, repeated many times, the trombonists of the Théâtre Italien orchestra adopted the principle of the Russian horn, with one player for each note. One played *B*, the other played *A♯*, to the great amusement of their colleagues who particularly enjoyed the second trombone's attempts to get the *A♯* on the off-beat.

Ex. 145

For the same reason it is also very difficult to play Ex. 146a at all fast on the tenor trombone. It is better to write it the other way up, as in Ex. 146b, which requires no change of position.

Ex. 146

(a)

(b)

A striking example of Berlioz's avoidance of the problem illustrated in Ex. 145 is found in the chorus 'Peuple ouvrier' in *Benvenuto Cellini* (*NBE* 1d: 1059–60). Another example is prominent in the *Rex tremendæ* of the *Requiem* (*NBE* 9: 64), where a scale including $A\sharp$–B–$c\sharp$ was changed in the autograph to $A\sharp$–$f\sharp$–$c\sharp$. On the other hand he expects all three trombones to play $B\natural$–$B\flat$ legato in the finale of *Roméo et Juliette* (*NBE* 18: 292).

The Russian horn bands were evolved by Maresch, a Bohemian horn player at the court of St Petersburg in the 1750s. He set up a group of one-note horns which together provided a diatonic scale of several octaves, each of thirty-two men sounding his note when his turn came. These bands were imitated in Germany and lasted until the 1830s.[45]

Trills are practicable on the trombone, but only on the notes of the top octave. They should be avoided on the bass trombone, in my view, because of their extreme difficulty. In the hands of a good player the alto trombone can trill on all notes between c' and $e\flat'$ and the tenor trombone on all notes between $b\flat$ and $b\flat'$. These are trills of a major second, the minor second being impossible.

Berlioz is describing the lip trill, whose effect is somewhat different from a true trill. The lowest note on which a tenor trombone can offer a major second lip trill is d' (in seventh position). Below that the interval is a minor third. He never wrote a trombone trill himself.

I regard the trombone as the true leader of the race of wind instruments which I have described as 'epic'. It possesses nobility and grandeur to a high degree and it has all the solemnity of high musical poetry, ranging from a calm, imposing, devotional aura to the wild clamours of an orgy. It is up to the composer to make it chant like a chorus of priests, or utter threats, then muffled groans, then a subdued funeral knell, then a resounding hymn of glory, then a piercing shriek, then a mighty fanfare for the waking of the dead or the death of the living.

---

[45] Baines, *Brass Instruments*, p. 177. For an illustration of the horn bands see Baines, *European and American Musical Instruments* (London, 1983), plates 699, 700.

Yet some thirty years ago they found a way of cheapening it by reducing it to the servile, pointless, grotesque task of doubling the bass line. Fortunately this practice has been more or less abandoned today. But one can find hosts of otherwise excellent scores with the basses doubled at the unison almost continually by a single trombone. I know no style of instrumentation more disagreeable or vulgar than this. The trombone's sound is so individual that one should never use it except for special effects; its task is therefore not to reinforce the double basses, whose tone it does not match in the least. Also one must realise that a single trombone in an orchestra always seems rather out of place. The instrument needs harmony, or at least unison support from other members of its family, if its range of possibilities is to be completely evident. Beethoven sometimes used them in pairs, like trumpets, but the established practice of writing for them in threes seems preferable to me.

Examples of the orchestration Berlioz deplores, with a single trombone doubling the bass line, may be found in Rossini (the overture to *La gazza ladra*, for example) and in Chopin's piano concertos and Paganini's violin concertos. There is one curious example of it in Berlioz's own music, in the closing finale of *Benvenuto Cellini* (*NBE* 1c: 1141–4, 1838 version) where the third trombone and double basses share the bass line. This was probably necessary because both the bassoons and the cellos are given a countermelody and the double basses on their own might be too weak.

Berlioz never called for fewer than three trombones. Beethoven used just two trombones in the Pastoral Symphony, *Fidelio* and elsewhere. The extra trombones in the *Requiem* are divided into four teams of players playing in two parts, sixteen players in all (Berlioz originally planned to have twenty). In another grandiose work, *L'impériale*, he required eight players in two parts, four on each part. A footnote suggests that if the piece were played by a normal group of three trombones, the third should double the ophicleide part. He proposed an extra group of three ripieno trombones to reinforce the first three in the *Tempête* fantasy in *Lélio* but later withdrew them (*NBE* 7: 202). The *Te deum* is scored for six trombones in three parts, and *Les Troyens* requires an offstage group of three trombones as well as the three in the orchestra. For the last sixty bars of the *Marche hongroise* in *La damnation de Faust* Berlioz required a fourth trombone to reinforce the first player (*NBE* 8a: 69). The single trombone by which Mozart depicted the Last Judgment in his *Requiem* struck Berlioz as inadequate: 'Why just one trombone to sound the terrible blast that should echo round the world and raise the dead from the grave? Why keep the other two trombones silent when not three, not thirty, not three hundred would be enough?'[46]

It is hard to be precise about the rapidity with which trombones can manage figurations, but one can perhaps say this: with four beats in a bar and a tempo of Allegro moderato, for example, a passage in simple quavers

---

[46] *Le rénovateur*, 30 March 1834, echoed in similar terms in *Gm*, 7 September 1834; *Cm*, 1, pp. 204, 376.

(eight notes to a bar) is feasible on the bass trombone, as in Ex. 147a. The other trombones, tenor and alto, being rather more agile, can play passages in triplet quavers (twelve notes to a bar) without too much difficulty, as in Ex. 147b. But these are the natural limits of their agility; to go beyond that is to fall into a mire of confusion, if not to attempt the impossible.

Ex. 147

Ex. 147b is taken from the finale of the *Symphonie funèbre et triomphale* (*NBE* 19: 62); this is played by tenor trombones while the bass trombone has a simplified line.

The tone quality of trombones varies with the degree of force with which the sound is produced. At *fortissimo* it is menacing and awe-inspiring, especially if the three trombones are in unison, or at least if two are in unison and the third an octave below the other two. Of such a kind is the thunderous D minor scale by which Gluck depicted the chorus of furies in Act II of *Iphigénie en Tauride*. Of such a kind, and even more sublime, is the colossal voice of three unison trombones replying as if with the enraged voice of the gods of Hades to Alceste's entreaty 'Ombre! larve! compagne di morte!' in that prodigious aria whose main idea Gluck allowed the French translator to spoil, but which has nonetheless settled in everyone's memory with its awkward opening line 'Divinités du Styx! ministres de la mort!' (Ex. 148). Observe, moreover, towards the end of the first section of the piece, when the trombones divided into three parts imitate the rhythm of the vocal line at the phrase 'Je n'invoquerai point votre pitié cruelle!', how from the very fact of the parts being divided the trombone tone for a moment becomes somehow ironic, harsh and horribly exultant, quite different from the grandiose fury of the preceding unisons.

Ex. 148

Of the Air 'Divinités du Styx!' Berlioz included in the *Treatise* a much longer extract, eighty-eight bars in all. In the lengthy study of Gluck's *Alceste* which he wrote in 1861 he devoted considerable attention to this air and to the French text that replaced the original Italian words.[47]

At plain *forte*, when they are in three-part harmony, especially in the middle of the range, trombones can express heroic pomp, majesty and pride which a mere vulgar melody would prosaically water down and ruin. At such times they have the expressive force of trumpets enormously enlarged; they no longer threaten, they proclaim; instead of bellowing, they sing. One should simply observe that the bass trombone is always inclined to drown the other two on such occasions, especially if the first is an alto trombone.

Berlioz here inserted, without comment, the beginning of the finale of his *Symphonie funèbre et triomphale*.

At *mezzo-forte* in the middle register, in unison or in harmony at a slow tempo, trombones assume a religious character. In the choruses for the priests of Isis in *Die Zauberflöte* Mozart devised some admirable ways of giving trombones a pontifical voice. A *pianissimo* on trombones in the minor key is sombre and gloomy, I might even say horrifying. Especially if the chords are short and interspersed with rests one can imagine strange monsters in the darkness breathing roars of rage barely held in check. Nowhere, in my opinion, is this special trombone quality more dramatic than in the incomparable funeral march in Spontini's *La vestale*, 'Périsse la Vestale impie!' (Ex. 149), and in the immortal duet in Act II of Beethoven's *Fidelio* sung by Leonora and the gaoler as they dig the grave of the condemned prisoner.

Ex. 149

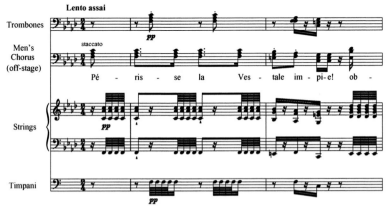

---

[47] *A travers chants*, pp. 190–4.

As a further illustration of the trombones' *mezzo-forte* Berlioz added in the *Rgm* text: 'An example could have been shown to Mozart here by Gluck, in the chorus of priests of Diana in Act III of *Iphigénie en Aulide*, "Pour prix du sang que nous allons répandre".' He removed this suggestion from the *Treatise* on realising that there are no trombones in *Iphigénie en Aulide* and that the work had been 'trombonisé' by other hands.[48]

In the *Rgm* he had an additional illustration of the trombones' *pianissimo*, the descending scales of the air 'Caron t'appelle' in Act III of Gluck's *Alceste*, but this too he removed from the *Treatise*. He had again no doubt been deceived by a corrupt version of the score: the single alto trombone in that air has only one descending scale, in an orchestral tutti.[49]

The caution about not allowing the bass trombone to drown the others was added to the proofs of the *Treatise* after Berlioz's experience in Berlin (see above, p. 213).

[48] *Ibid.*, p. 239.   [49] Gluck, *Werke*, I/7, p. 303.

The practice today adopted by some composers of forming a four-part unit of three trombones and ophicleide, putting the latter on the true bass line, is perhaps not beyond reproach. The trombone's penetrating, lordly tone is not at all the same as that of the ophicleide; it is much better simply to double the bottom part with the latter, or at least give the trombones a correct bass as if their three parts were to be heard on their own.

A good example of Berlioz scoring for three trombones and ophicleide as a four-part unit is the entry of the Pope in Tableau Three of *Benvenuto Cellini* (*NBE* 1c: 853), supported by bassoons in four parts and cellos in four parts. In general, though, he puts the third trombone on the bass line with or without the ophicleide.

Gluck, Beethoven, Mozart, Weber, Spontini and a few others have fully understood the importance of the trombone. These composers have shown exceptional intelligence in using this noble instrument to paint human passion or reproduce the sounds of nature. They have thus preserved its power, its dignity and its poetry. But to force it, as most composers now do, to yell brutal phrases in a Credo more worthy of a tavern than a holy shrine, or to resound as if for the entry of Alexander into Babylon when it is just for a dancer's pirouette, or to plonk tonic and dominant chords under a little tune that needs only a guitar to accompany it, or to match its Olympian voice with a wretched vaudeville melody or with a contredanse's idiotic thump, or to make way for the triumphal arrival of an oboe or a flute in a concerto tutti – this is to impoverish and degrade its magnificent individuality. It makes a slave and a clown out of a hero, it tarnishes the orchestra, it undermines and nullifies all proper progress in instrumental music, it destroys the past, present and future of art, it is a gratuitous act of vandalism demonstrating a lack of feeling for expression bordering on idiocy.

When the *Rgm* articles were written, Berlioz's disgust at the abuses of the trombone had recently been aired in a review of Montfort's opéra-comique *La jeunesse de Charles-Quint*:

The craze for the bass drum began to recede a few months ago, but the trombone craze is on the rise. Just when we were learning to admire the magnificent orchestration of *Der Freischütz*, where Weber uses the trombones only three or four times and with remarkable reserve, those hounds started barking, howling and bellowing at the Opéra Comique in the middle of a love duet or a comic ensemble.[50]

The review also rebukes a Mass by Dietsch for using trombones

[50] *Jd*, 14 December 1841.

to reinforce the orchestra without any regard for their tone, which disqual-ifies them from the appropriate style of so many pieces. Let them mutter a solemn prayer in the *Kyrie* or blaze away with fanfares in the *Iterum ven-turus*, but [...] So this is where the art of instrumentation now stands! If the trombones shriek like demons at the Opéra, you would think you were hearing the chorus of furies in *Iphigénie en Tauride* or the entrance of the Commendatore in *Don Giovanni* or the nuns' orgy in *Robert le diable*, would you not? But no, it is M. Petipa or M. Mabille stepping on stage to dance a...pas de deux. [...] At the Opéra Comique an old chap is upset at los-ing his snuffbox – three trombones! He rejoices when he finds it – three trombones! A blind man drinks a glass of cheap wine – three trombones! A stable lad tightens some layabout's belt – three trombones! Every time! [...] It is the present leader of the so-called School of Melody whom we have to blame for this horrible instrumental abuse, while Beethoven and Weber, the leaders of the rival school regarded as a School of Violence and Noise, were alone in upholding the principle of moderation and the intelligent use of instruments.

The 'leader of the so-called School of Melody' is of course Rossini.

Berlioz's own writing for the trombone bears out his faith in its nobility, grandeur and power. From the broad statement in the introduction of the *Francs-juges* overture (of which Berlioz said 'Voilà le *monstrum, horrendum, ingens*'[51]) to the many-hued trombone entries in *Les Troyens* his regard for the instrument was based firmly on Gluck's bold development of it as an operatic voice. There are many cases where the trombones are brilliantly displayed, as in the *Carnaval romain* and *Corsaire* overtures; sometimes that brilliance has a feverish edge, as in the *Songe d'une nuit de sabbat* in the *Symphonie fantastique* or in the *Orgie de brigands* in *Harold en Italie*; sometimes it is lugubrious and sinister, as in the *Chœur d'ombres* in *Lélio*. In *Benvenuto Cellini* the trombones are relatively restrained: in the orig-inal version they had very little to play in the overture and nothing at all in the first Tableau. There is a striking advance in *Roméo et Juliette*, where the trombone writing is remarkably sophisticated, even more so in *La damnation de Faust*. The peak is undoubtedly *Les Troyens*, whose trombone parts illustrate the full range of characters of which the instrument was capable; like the cornets, the trombones are kept busy throughout.

Certain fine passages for trombones may perhaps be singled out. The *Interven-tion du Prince* at the beginning of *Roméo et Juliette* is the voice of authority, grandly delivered. In *La damnation de Faust* the trombones are Mephistopheles's constant escort, with a darting flash for his sudden appearances (often with a cymbal clash) and a solemn mock-religious tone in his air 'Voici des roses' at the opening of the scene by the banks of the Elbe. Herod's dark premonitions in the first part of *L'enfance du Christ* are given a certain nobility by the timbre of trombones in sup-port, and Narbal, in Act IV of *Les Troyens*, expresses dignified alarm over sonorous trombone harmony.

---

[51] Letter to Ferrand of 28 June 1828 printed with many omissions, including this phrase, in *Cg*, 1, pp. 197–202.

Two treatments are very characteristic of Berlioz's writing for trombones. A unison conjunct line for three trombones, *piano*, is effectively used on many occasions in *Benvenuto Cellini*, *Roméo et Juliette* and elsewhere; an outstanding example is the brief scene 'Errante sur les mers' when Dido welcomes the Trojans to Carthage (*NBE* 2b: 384). A succession of short *piano* chords for the three trombones, often on the off-beat, is another recurrent device. The passage here in the *Treatise* evoking 'strange monsters in the darkness' is strikingly prophetic of Cassandra's air in Act I of *Les Troyens*, 'Non, je ne verrai pas' (*NBE* 2a: 161), where throbbing off-beat *pianissimo* trombone chords in Eb minor reinforce Cassandra's horrified alarm at the Trojans' heedless folly.

Trombones did not use mutes in Berlioz's time and he does not mention them. Yet they are directed to mute in *La mort d'Orphée* (*NBE* 6: 26), an obscure instruction, since the whole group of brass (cornets, trumpets, horns and trombones) is covered by the single entry 'mettez la sourdine' in the surviving copyist's manuscript, followed shortly after by 'sans sourdines'.

In the second movement of the *Symphonie funèbre et triomphale*, the *Oraison funèbre*, the trombone is given one of Berlioz's rare instrumental solos. This was a transcription of an air from the opera *Les francs-juges* which suits the trombone's declamatory style very well. A footnote in the score suggests that if there is no one capable of playing it well on the tenor trombone, it should be played on an alto valve trombone in F or on a piston horn in G or on a bass clarinet (*NBE* 19: xi).

This solo was played at the first performances by Antoine-Guillaume Dieppo (1808–?), the leading trombonist of his day in France, whom Berlioz admired. When he conducted it in Dresden in February 1843 he sent a message to Dieppo to say that he had not found his equal and that German trombonists had given him chest-ache, not to mention ear-ache.[52] This was true of Mannheim, where he had to abandon the finale of *Harold en Italie* because the trombones were not up to it,[53] but was not true of Stuttgart, since Schrade, the first trombone there who had previously worked in Paris, was in Berlioz's words 'a most gifted player, a complete master of his instrument who makes light of the most formidable difficulties and produces a magnificent tone from the tenor trombone'. Like Vivier on the horn, Schrade could produce four-note chords on the trombone. In 1851 Berlioz praised Nabich, a trombonist from Weimar, who could 'do anything on it'.[54]

Dieppo, who published a *Méthode complète pour le trombone* in about 1840, played on a narrow-bore instrument which was standard in France throughout the nineteenth century and which has an entirely different sound from the huge trombone in general orchestral use today, being lighter in timbre and more transparent. Perhaps no section of Berlioz's orchestra has changed so markedly in modern times as the trombones, as performances on period instruments now serve to remind us.

In his first large work, the *Messe solennelle* of 1824, Berlioz calls for a 'buccin', an instrument of the trombone family which he does not mention in the *Treatise*. Developed in the early years of the century by French and Belgian makers, the buccin had a bell which instead of lying parallel with the other joints as in an

---

[52] *Cg*, 3, p. 74.   [53] *Memoirs*, 'Travels in Germany', I/3.   [54] *Ibid.*, 1/2; *Jd*, 13 April 1851.

ordinary trombone, curved upwards and terminated in a painted dragon's head.[55] It had no connection with the 'buccina', the circular instrument developed after the Revolution on the model of Roman military instruments.

THE ALTO VALVE TROMBONE

This alto trombone is found in both E♭ and F. It is essential to specify which of these two keys one is writing for, since this trombone is customarily treated as a transposing instrument. It has no slide. It is really no more than a cornet in E♭ or F with a little stronger sound than a true cornet.

The range of the alto valve trombone is the same as that of the ordinary alto trombone. It is written on the treble clef, transposed like a cornet. The alto valve trombone in F has a range from $f\sharp$ (sounding B) chromatically up to $d\flat'''$ (sounding $g\flat''$). The bottom fourth of this range, from written b downwards, has poor tone quality; the top two notes are difficult to play. The alto valve trombone in E♭ has a range from $f\sharp$ (sounding A) chromatically up to $e\flat'''$ (sounding $g\flat''$). The bottom augmented fourth of this range, from written c' downwards, has very poor tone quality.

Since the valve trombone has no slide mechanism, it cannot produce the low notes known as pedals and found on other trombones.

Trills which the slide trombonist can play using the lips are practicable on the valve trombone. Some trills can also be done with the valves, but it should be said that only minor trills are effective; they are the only ones which can be played rapidly. The best are semitone trills on the following notes (written pitches): $f\sharp'$, b', c'', $d\sharp''$, e'', $f\sharp''$, g'', a'', b'', c'''.

The fitting of valves to the trombone gives it great agility, but at the cost of some accuracy of intonation. The movable slide which responds instantly to the slightest adjustment clearly makes the ordinary trombone the most in tune of all wind instruments, if the player has a sensitive ear. The valve trombone, with no slide, on the other hand belongs to that class of instruments with fixed intonation which can be modified by the lips only slightly. Melodic solos are frequently written for the alto valve trombone. If well phrased, a melody can have considerable charm on this instrument. But it is a mistake to believe it would have any less charm on the slide trombone in the hands of a true virtuoso; M. Dieppo has made that triumphantly plain on many occasions. Furthermore, I repeat, except for playing rapid passages the advantage of more secure intonation must be taken into account and carry considerable weight in a composer's choice.

In Germany there are some tenor valve trombones which go down to low $B\flat'$; despite this advantage slide trombones will always be preferable, in my view.

[55] *Grove's Dictionary of Music and Musicians* (5th edn, 9 vols., London, 1954), 1, p. 991. The buccin is illustrated in Baines, *European and American Musical Instruments*, plate 755.

Berlioz's heading is 'alto piston or cylinder trombone', although he does not distinguish between the two types in his text.

The valve trombone was invented in Prague or Vienna in the late 1820s. Berlioz encountered it before he went to Germany, since the penultimate paragraph of this text appeared in the *Rgm*. The final paragraph was added in 1843, no doubt referring to the instrument he heard in Mannheim, a valve trombone made for Vincenz Lachner which played 'low *C* and low *B*'.[56] Despite Berlioz's specific mention of *tenor* trombones, this was probably pitched in F like a bass trombone. The proofs of the *Treatise* mentioned the low *C*, but in the first edition this was changed to *Bb′*, suggesting a bass valve trombone in Eb.

He wrote for the valve trombone on two occasions. The tenor trombone solo in the second movement of the *Symphonie funèbre et triomphale* was issued in the printed parts with three alternative arrangements including one for alto valve trombone in F, written on the treble clef (*NBE* 19: 106). When Berlioz conducted the *Symphonie funèbre et triomphale* in London in 1848 the solo was played on an alto trombone by Koenig. At the end of the *Marche hongroise* in *La damnation de Faust* Berlioz brings in a tenor valve trombone in unison with the orchestra's normal first tenor trombone to reinforce the line for the last sixty bars of the piece (*NBE* 8a: 69).

THE BUGLE OR CLARION

We will conclude our study of wind instruments with a few words on the bugle family.

The simple bugle, or clarion, is written on the treble clef like the trumpet. It has a total of eight notes: *c*, *c′*, *g′*, *c″*, *e″*, *g″*, *bb″* and *c‴*. In fact the last of these, high *c‴*, is really only possible on the lowest clarion, and the bottom note, *c*, has very poor tone. Clarions are found in Bb, C and Eb, and occasionally in other keys. The fanfares they are given to play, always confined to the three notes of the perfect triad, are inevitably monotonous to the point of inanity. The tone of the instrument is rather uncouth. It generally lacks nobility and is difficult to play in tune. Since it can play no diatonic sequences trills are obviously out of the question.

I regard the clarion as occupying no higher place in the hierarchy of brass than that of the fife in the woodwind family. Both can do little more than lead conscripts out to the parade ground, although in my view such music should never be heard by our soldiers, young or old. There is no need to habituate them to such debased things. Since the clarion's sound is very loud it is not impossible that a use might be found for it in the orchestra in order to increase the violence of some terrifying cry for trombones, trumpets and horns in unison. That is probably all one could expect it to do.

---

[56] *Memoirs*, 'Travels in Germany', I/3.

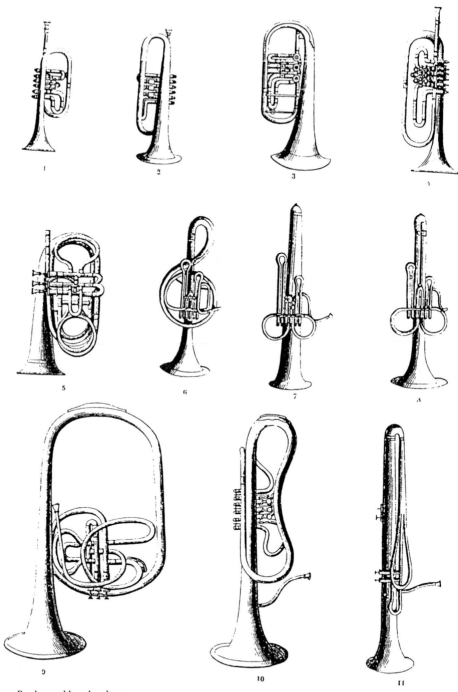

3   Bugles and bombardons.

The bugle, a much shorter instrument than the trumpet, has only the notes of the latter's first three octaves, written C, c, g, c', e', g', bb' and c''. Because of the length of its tube these notes sound an octave higher. That is why it is written c, c', g', c'', e'', g'', bb'' and c'''. Thus the bugle or clarion in C is not a transposing instrument, whereas bugles in Bb and Eb are written transposed, like trumpets in Bb and Eb. The Bb bugle sounds a tone lower than its written pitch, the Eb bugle a minor third higher.

In the *Rgm* the first sentence of this chapter read: 'We will conclude our study of wind instruments with a few words on the horrible bugle family', and we also find there the comment: 'I have often wondered whether the word "bugle" come from "beugler", to bawl or bellow, or if "beugler" comes from "bugle". The truth is that of all instruments, both high and low, I know none with a voice as dreadful as this, none so easily played out of tune, none with such an ignoble sound.' The etymologies of 'bugle' and 'beugler' are indeed connected, being derived from the Latin word 'buculus', a young bullock, although the French name 'bugle' was adopted for the instrument from English.

In his list of the bugle's eight notes, the first (c) and penultimate (bb'') were late additions in 1843, and his comment that the lowest note has very poor tone was added in 1855.

Berlioz is again anxious to deflect any confusion about transposition but is less than perfectly clear in his explanation. The bugle is, in short, an octave higher than the trumpet, being half its length. The bugle found no place in Berlioz's scores, nor, it seems, in any orchestral music of his time.

THE KEYED BUGLE

In cavalry bands and also in certain Italian orchestras there are bugles with seven keys which possess a chromatic range of over two octaves, from b up to top c'''. The top four notes, from a'', are rare. A low c can also be obtained. The keyed bugle can trill on every note of its compass except the semitone trill on f''. It is not without agility, in fact many players perform on it remarkably well, but its tone is no different to that of the clarion or simple bugle.

The mention of the low c was a late addition in 1843. In the *Rgm* this entry concluded: 'Despite the affection in which it is held by some composers it cannot be compared in tone quality or intonation with the cornet, which is generally more popular today.'

The keyed bugle was invented in 1810 by the Irish bandmaster Joseph Halliday, adapting the principles of the keyed trumpet. It quickly became popular both in England and on the continent and it led to the development of its larger cousins the ophicleide family. Originally equipped with five keys it was made with anything up to twelve keys. It played no part in Berlioz's music and appeared only rarely in the orchestra. Examples which Berlioz might have known are Rossini's *Semiramide* (1823) and Kreutzer's *Ipsiboé* (1824).[57]

THE PISTON OR CYLINDER BUGLE

This has a greater range at the bottom than the preceding instrument. This is a feeble advantage, since its low notes have horrible tone. They are only easy to produce on the little E♭ bugle, whose range is from (written) *F♯* chromatically up to *c* and from *f♯* chromatically up to *c'''*. The top four notes, from *a'''*, are rare. This instrument is of much greater worth than the keyed bugle. It can be effective taking melodies at a broad, or at any rate moderate, tempo. In lively or bright passages its tone suffers from the same defect that we have already observed in the cornet: it lacks character. Even so this can be successfully overcome by a skilful player. All major and minor trills on the piston bugle are good above *e'* except the whole-tone trill on *g♯'*, which is very difficult.

The application of valves to the bugle provided additional tubing which extended its lower range, whereas the keys applied to the keyed version of the instrument raised the pitch when opened. The valve bugle is better known by its German name 'flugelhorn'. It was developed in Germany and probably not known in France until the period at which Berlioz was writing; it is not mentioned in the *Rgm* text in 1842. Kastner spoke of it as a 'miraculous transformation of the keyed bugle',[58] and it influenced Sax's development of the saxhorn. Berlioz wrote for two of these instruments in his lost version of the *Chant sacré* arranged for Sax instruments in 1844. One was the little E♭ cylinder bugle, the other was a larger cylinder bugle in B♭. But it had no place in orchestral music until the twentieth century. Its real popularity in the nineteenth century was reserved for brass and military bands.

Berlioz does not mention that the E♭ valve bugle sounds a minor third higher than its written pitch, nor does he record that the instrument was more often constructed in B♭ than in E♭.

THE BASS OPHICLEIDE

Ophicleides are alto and bass bugles. The bass ophicleide is extremely useful for holding the bottom part in the wind section, and is the instrument

[57] Ralph T. Dudgeon, *The Keyed Bugle* (Metuchen and London, 1993). The Garland score of *Semiramide* gives 'trombe a chiavi', which may have been a keyed trumpet rather than a keyed bugle.
[58] Georges Kastner, *Cours d'instrumentation: supplément* (Paris, 1844).

4   The ophicleide.

most commonly found for this purpose. It is written on the bass clef and
its range is three octaves and one note from B' chromatically up to c''.
In the hands of an able player major and minor trills are possible from
c up to a', as M. Caussinus has demonstrated in his excellent *Méthode*,
published recently, although both the trills on $g\sharp'$ are very difficult. Low
$F\sharp$ used to be possible only by using the lips and even then was not very
good; the note was basically insecure and out of tune. M. Caussinus has
added a key to the instrument which makes this note as good as the
rest.

   Quite rapid figures, both diatonic and chromatic, are practicable in the
upper two octaves of the ophicleide but exceedingly difficult in the bottom
octave where in any case they make a dreadful sound. Ex. 150a is good,

while Ex. 150b is bad. Tongued passages are much more awkward at a fast tempo, in fact they are almost impossible.

Ex. 150

There are bass ophicleides in two keys, C and B♭, and they are even made in A♭ now. The latter would be very useful because of the extreme depth of their bottom notes in unison with three-string double basses. The B♭ ophicleide however is eminently serviceable in this respect. Both B♭ and A♭ ophicleides are written at transposed pitch like all transposing instruments. On the B♭ ophicleide written *B* sounds *A*, and so on; on the A♭ ophicleide written *B* sounds *G*, and so on. The low *G'*, bottom note of the A♭ ophicleide, is in unison with the double basses' written *G*. It is a pity that the A♭ ophicleide is so rarely found.

The tone of the low notes is rough, but they can work wonders beneath a body of brass instruments in certain circumstances. The very top notes have a wild character for which no proper use seems yet to have been found. The middle range too strongly recalls the sound of cathedral serpents or herdsmen's horns, especially in the hands of a mediocre player. The ophicleide should only occasionally be allowed to sound on its own. There is nothing more clumsy, nothing, I should say, more monstrous or more at odds with the rest of the orchestra than those quite rapid passages written as solos for the ophicleide's middle range in certain modern operas. They are like an escaped bull running loose in the salon.

The *Rgm* text has, in addition: 'The ophicleide is still today inadequately studied. Good players are rare. Most players leave much to be desired as far as intonation and steadiness are concerned. But M. Caussinus, the true master of this instrument, was recently chosen to teach at the military Gymnase Musical, so we may hope to see a noticeable improvement in a few years' time in this branch of performance. But why is there no ophicleide class at the Conservatoire?'

He echoed this lament in 1848: '[At the Conservatoire] we have no class in the ophicleide, with the result that of the 100 or 150 persons in Paris at present blowing this exacting instrument, hardly three are fit to be in a good orchestra, and only one, M. Caussinus, is a really first-rate player.'[59]

The ophicleide was a bass version of the keyed bugle, devised by the French maker Halary (Jean-Hilaire Asté) in 1817 and patented in 1821. It was Berlioz's

---

[59] *Memoirs*, 'Travels in Germany', II/5.

standard bass brass instrument throughout his career, never abandoned even though he allowed and encouraged the tuba as an alternative in his later works. He usually called for one ophicleide in C beneath a group of three trombones, but a second bass instrument is frequently found. In the *Resurrexit* in the *Messe solennelle* it is paired with a serpent, and in the finale of the *Symphonie fantastique* there is again a serpent in support. The serpent's part was later given to a second ophicleide in Bb. A second ophicleide part in Bb was also a late addition to the first ophicleide in C in the overture to *Les francs-juges*.

There are two ophicleide parts in the *Marseillaise* arrangement (in unspecified keys). The *Requiem* requires four ophicleides in the fourth extra band. In some movements two are in C and two are in Bb, but in the *Sanctus* all four are in C. Since the C and Bb ophicleides are two different instruments (like clarinets in different keys), not single instruments with alternative crooks (like trumpets), the *Requiem* properly requires four players with six instruments.

The *Symphonie funèbre et triomphale* calls for three ophicleides in C and three in Bb. In *La damnation de Faust* Berlioz seems to have been in two minds as to whether the ophicleide's partner is a tuba or another ophicleide,[60] and in the *Te deum* it is partnered by a tuba.

A Bb ophicleide is called for only as a reinforcement to a C ophicleide, never on its own, its main value being the extra low notes down to A'. Berlioz never wrote for the Ab ophicleide, a member of the family not mentioned in any records, including Caussinus's *Méthode*, but it is listed in the first draft of Berlioz's festival orchestra in 1842 (see p. 329 below).

In the *Rgm* text he counselled against taking the ophicleide above g' or a', and he exceeded that range only once, at the end of the *Symphonie fantastique* (*NBE* 16: 160), where a bb' is reached. This passage is a late addition to the score. Berlioz seems never to have avoided the insecure $F\sharp/G\flat$, which is prominently heard in the *Symphonie fantastique* (*NBE* 16: 104) and on many later occasions. At the bottom of the range he normally observed his stated limit of B'. But he also wrote the note Bb' (sounding Ab') for Bb ophicleide several times in the *Francs-juges* overture, which may be an oversight. Some instruments did have an extra Bb' key,[61] but Berlioz does not mention this in the *Treatise*.

In confining rapid figures to the upper two octaves of the ophicleide's range, Berlioz wrote 'upper three octaves', not two, presumably in error.

The ophicleide is sometimes required when there are no trombones, as it is in Mendelssohn's overture to *A Midsummer Night's Dream*. Examples include the *Prière* in the *Scène héroïque*, the *Chanson de Méphistophélès* in the *Huit scènes de Faust*, and the *Offertoire* in the *Requiem*. The four-part harmony of three trombones and ophicleide for the entry of the Pope in *Benvenuto Cellini* has already been mentioned; in general the ophicleide is not treated as a fourth trombone, rather as an independent voice that sometimes doubles the bass line along with the third trombone.

The ophicleide was more firmly established in France and England than in Germany, although Berlioz was greatly impressed by Johann Strauss's Viennese ophicleidist in 1837:

---

[60] *NBE*, 8b, pp. 459–60.   [61] Clifford Bevan, *The Tuba Family* (London, 1878), p. 62.

This artist deserves special mention. He gets from the large ophicleide as much sound as three ordinary ophicleides, and either because he uses a much narrower mouthpiece than our players do, or a more scientific method, or stronger lips, these deafening notes have excellent intonation, normally so rare that being out of tune seemed to be inherent in the nature of the instrument.[62]

Yet on his German tours Berlioz was disappointed by the weakness or complete absence of ophicleides. In Leipzig, for example, 'the ophicleide, or rather the abject brass object masquerading under that name, bore no resemblance to the French variety, having practically no tone'.[63] It also turned out to be pitched in B. A fourth trombone was called in to replace it.

His visit to Germany in 1842–3 convinced him of the superiority of the tuba over the ophicleide:

This instrument [the tuba], which is no more than a giant trumpet with cylinders, has always struck me as superior to the ophicleide, for the following reason. Like the keyed bugle (the brass instrument with the worst intonation) the ophicleide has enormous holes in its bore which are closed by keys made of material quite different from that of the instrument itself. Thick leather is used to cover the aperture beneath the key and this naturally has the effect of a mute. In addition the instrument's bore is constantly subject to changes depending on the number of keys left open, and this makes the sound very uneven. The quite large area beneath each opening deprives the interior surface of smoothness and regularity, causing further intonation problems. That is why there are so very few musicians who play this instrument in tune; there are scarcely three in Paris, the best of whom is M. Caussinus, professor at the Gymnase Musical.[64]

As for its character, Berlioz clearly denied the ophicleide any of the nobility and grandeur possessed by the trombone. He gives negative advice, namely to ensure that its roughness is not exposed, but he does not admit that its bestial character served him well on several occasions. In the finale of the *Symphonie fantastique* its purpose in hammering out the *Dies irae* together with a serpent and four bassoons is clearly to parody ecclesiastical chant and in particular the custom of using these instruments in French parish churches (see below, p. 242). The ophicleide's role as a grotesque was again exploited in the second Tableau of *Benvenuto Cellini*, when the *Cavatine de Pierrot* is a virtuoso ophicleide solo, parodying with its thumping bass drum accompaniment the worst kind of musical showmanship of the 1830s. In the opera this music represents the acme of bad taste, for Balducci is ridiculed by being seen to applaud it extravagantly. At the same time this is perhaps the finest ophicleide solo in the classical repertoire.

In the second part of *La damnation de Faust* the ophicleide is a boisterous leader in the *Chœur de buveurs*, carrying the melody in octaves with the cornet (*NBE* 8a: 119) and showing off its vulgar virtuosity. This continues into the Amen chorus,

[62] *Jd*, 10 November 1837; *Cm*, 3, pp. 329–30; Condé, p. 123.   [63] *Memoirs*, 'Travels in Germany', I/4.
[64] *Jd*, 1 April 1845.

with the two ophicleides taking the lower two fugal voices. The effect is deliberately tasteless.

Berlioz praised Caussinus as the leading French player of his day but had no close relations with him. The method Berlioz refers to is the *Méthode complète d'ophicléide*, published in about 1843 in collaboration with F. Berr. Caussinus also published a *Solfège-méthode pour ophicléide-basse* (Paris, n.d.). The late elaboration of the first ophicleide part in the *Symphonie fantastique* was made possible no doubt by Caussinus's demonstration of the upper range and was perhaps even written for him to play. A similar elaboration is found in the *Chant des ciseleurs* in *Benvenuto Cellini*, where brilliant flourishes for a cornet and ophicleide in octaves embellish the final refrain (*NBE* 1b: 446–7). These were also a late addition to the score, perhaps written for a London player in 1853.

THE ALTO OPHICLEIDE

There are alto ophicleides in F and E♭; their compass is the same as that of the bass ophicleide. Both are written on the treble clef like horns, and, as in the case of horns, this clef sounds an octave lower than the written note. Thus c'' on the treble clef corresponds to c' on the bass clef, which is in fact the same as c' on the treble clef. As a result of the transpositions required by their keys, the actual sounds derived from their written compass is as follows: the alto ophicleide in F has a range from B (sounding E) chromatically up to c''' (sounding f''). Notes down from d (sounding G) are of rather poor quality, and the top two notes, b'' and c''' (sounding e'' and f'') are difficult. The alto ophicleide in E♭ has a range from B (sounding D) chromatically up to c''' (sounding $e♭''$). Notes down from e (sounding G) are of rather poor quality, and the top note c''' (sounding $e♭''$) is difficult.

They are used in certain military bands to fill out the harmony and sometimes play melodies. But their tone is normally unpleasant and vulgar and their intonation is poor. This accounts for the almost complete disappearance of these instruments nowadays.

The alto ophicleide (which might be considered an alto keyed bugle constructed on the vertical plan like the bass ophicleide) had a short career entirely confined to military bands and was supplanted in the 1830s and 1840s by valved instruments. Berlioz never wrote for it.

THE CONTRABASS OPHICLEIDE

The contrabass, or 'monster', ophicleides are very little known. They could be useful in very large orchestras, but no one in Paris has yet taken them up. They require a discharge of air enough to fatigue the lungs of the heaviest men. They are in F and E♭, a fifth below bass ophicleides in C and B♭ and an octave below alto ophicleides in F and E♭. They should not be taken above written f'. The monster ophicleide in F has a range from B' (sounding E') up to f' (sounding $b♭$); in E♭ it has a range from B' (sounding D') up to f' (sounding $a♭$). The bottom notes are rare on the F instrument and very difficult to sustain on the E♭ instrument. It need hardly be said that trills and rapid passages are incompatible with the nature of such instruments.

After completion of the *Requiem* in 1837 but before it went to the engraver in February 1838, perhaps for the first performance in December 1837 (if he could find someone to play it), Berlioz added a part for contrabass ophicleide in F to the first of the four additional brass orchestras.[65] It requires a range from $G♭'$ to $a♭$. Originally headed 'ophicleide in low F' this part was then revised to 'monster ophicleide' and finally 'bombardon, monster ophicleide with pistons'; the music was transposed into C. The first edition of the *Requiem* gives it as 'monster ophicleide with pistons', playing in C.

The 'monster ophicleide' was in fact not an ophicleide at all, since it had pistons, not keys. Kastner's *Traité général* of 1836 illustrated a valved instrument played with the bell facing forward.[66] He mentioned that it was known in Germany as 'bombardon', hence Berlioz's double nomenclature. If Berlioz originally intended a contrabass ophicleide (which was manufactured in limited quantities at the time), he soon changed this to a form of valved instrument which was then in a state of flux and which the *Treatise* then goes on to expound.

THE BOMBARDON IN F

This is a bass instrument with five cylinder valves and no keys, whose tone is a little different from that of the ophicleide. The bombardon in F has a range from F' chromatically up to d'. It has some additional notes both at the bottom and at the top, but they are awkward to produce and are best avoided.

The instrument is very loud and can only play passages at a moderate tempo. Figurations and trills are impossible. It has a good effect in large orchestras with strong wind sections. The natural notes produced by the bore are the chord of F, which is why it is called a 'bombardon in F', yet it is customary in Germany to treat it as a non-transposing instrument like the trombone and to write for it at sounding pitch.

The *Requiem* is the only Berlioz work to use a bombardon (see above, under contrabass ophicleide). In the passage from the *Dies iræ* printed in the *Treatise* the part is for two bombardons. The Paris maker Guichard had designed valved

---

[65] *NBE*, 9, p. 151.
[66] An illustration from an English catalogue of c. 1849 is shown in Baines, *Brass Instruments*, p. 256.

ophicleides from 1832 and such instruments were common from Belgium to Austria, similar to ophicleides in shape but bearing from three to six valves. The *Treatise* mentions three valves in the 1844 edition and five in the 1855 edition. These gave the instrument additional lower notes and also corrected the faulty intonation that always affects bass instruments with valves. These instruments were the direct progenitors of the tuba.

The *Rgm* entry reads: 'The bombardon is a contrabass ophicleide in F with three pistons. Its bottom range is often misunderstood, being thought lower than it really is. The bombardon only goes down to (written) $F\sharp$, sounding B', in unison with the C ophicleide's lowest note. Now when the B♭ ophicleide plays this same B' it gets an A', so it reaches a whole tone lower than the bombardon, whose $F\sharp$ only gives B'. It can only play notes in very slow succession; passagework is absolutely forbidden.' The *Treatise*'s entries on the bombardon and the tuba were written out in autograph in the 1843 proofs.

Although the bombardon was more or less obsolete in 1855, the second edition of the *Treatise* added the key 'in F' to this chapter heading and the words 'in Germany' to the final sentence, as if to imply that in France the F bombardon might have been treated as a transposing instrument.

In Weimar in 1843 Berlioz had a bombardon in his orchestra to replace the ophicleide.[67]

THE BASS TUBA

This is a kind of bombardon with a mechanism perfected by M. Wieprecht, director of military bands to the King of Prussia. The bass tuba is today very common in the north of Germany, especially in Berlin, and has an immense advantage over all other low-pitched wind. Its tone is incomparably more distinguished than that of ophicleides, bombardons and serpents, and has something of the vibrant quality of the trombone. It is less agile than an ophicleide but its sound is louder and its range at the bottom is the *lowest in the orchestra*. As in the case of the bombardon its bore gives the notes of the chord of F. But now Adolphe Sax is making bass tubas in E♭. Despite this difference, they are all regarded as non-transposing instruments. The bass tuba has five valves and its range is four octaves. The E♭ bass tuba goes from A'' chromatically up to ab. In France this compass would be written a minor third lower.

It can produce a few more notes at the top and even at the bottom too, by using the valve mechanism. Those at the top are very risky and those at the bottom are very indistinct. The C', Bb'' and A'' are not really identifiable unless they are doubled an octave higher by another bass tuba. Both notes benefit in resonance when this is done.

---

[67] *Memoirs*, 'Travels in Germany', I/3.

It will be readily understood that this instrument is no better at trills or rapid passages than the bombardon. It can *sing* a certain type of broad melody. It is hard to imagine the effect a section of bass tubas can have in a large wind band; it resembles both the trombone and the organ at the same time.

The words 'in Germany' (when pointing out that the tuba was a non-transposing instrument there) were added in the 1855 edition. The following sentences were also added: 'This instrument has been known for some years in France, where it is written for as a transposing instrument like horns and trumpets. In France the compass of the tuba would be written a third lower.'

Already familiar with the bombardon, Berlioz encountered the tuba for the first time in Dresden, Brunswick and Berlin in 1843. He and Wieprecht developed great mutual admiration during Berlioz's month in Berlin in April 1843, where he heard, among other things, a section of twelve tubas playing in an arrangement of the *Francs-juges* overture under Wieprecht's direction. His account of Berlin's music includes a section on the tuba very similar to that in the *Treatise*.[68] Both were written in 1843, the latter handwritten into the proofs of the *Treatise*. The *Memoirs* passage mentions that the tuba had five cylinder valves. Three of these provided the chromatic diminished fourth below E♭′, and the remaining two, whose main purpose was to rectify the uneven intonation of the first three, could also be used to take the instrument lower still. If the *Francs-juges* overture had not been published some years previously, one might have guessed that the broad melody in the slow introduction (*B&H* 4: 41), with its heavy bass octaves, might have been written especially for tubas in two octaves as he describes them.

In that work, as in many others, Berlioz added the option of tubas in place of ophicleides after his return to Paris in 1843. In his own set of engraved parts[69] he wrote 'ou tuba' on each ophicleide part. In the second edition of the *Symphonie fantastique* the words 'ou tuba' were added to the second ophicleide part (which had originally been a serpent part), though not to the first ophicleide part. The entry in full is: 'Ophicleide in B♭ or tuba in E♭ transposing the part down a fourth' in recognition of the French practice of treating tubas as transposing instruments. In the second edition of the *Requiem* (1853) the bombardons were replaced by tubas (written in C). In the engraved parts (not the score) of *Roméo et Juliette*, published in 1847, one part is headed 'Ophycléide ou Tuba'. The tuba is allowed as an alternative to the ophicleide in the *Hamlet* march, the *Corsaire* overture and *Les Troyens*. Berlioz was happy with either, expecting ophicleides to be used in France and tubas in Germany. The *Marche hongroise*, written for Budapest in 1846, was scored for tuba doubling the third trombone. Incorporated in *La damnation de Faust*, the march acquired new parts for both ophicleide and tuba. One of each instrument was Berlioz's eventual choice in this work, the ophicleide playing above the tuba when they are on separate lines. A similar partnership was used in the *Te deum*. In *L'impériale* three ophicleides and two tubas play in unison.

---

[68] *Ibid.*, I/9.   [69] Now the property of the Orchestre de Paris.

In the *Memoirs*, in a passage written in 1848, Berlioz deplored the lack of tuba teaching at the Paris Conservatoire:

> We have no class in the bass tuba, a powerful valved instrument differing from the ophicleide in timbre, mechanism and range, its position in the trumpet family being exactly equivalent to that of the double bass in the violin family. Most modern scores include a part for either ophicleide or bass tuba, sometimes for both.[70]

Berlioz recognised that the tuba was superior to the ophicleide:

> The sound of Sax's tuba is not only steadier than that of the ophicleide but stronger and of better quality. Its brassy resonance harmonises completely with the trombones and lacks the dull sound made by even the best ophicleide players. In a word it is to the trumpet what the double bass is to the violin. There should at least be kept a few ophicleides for playing certain passages which require more agility than the tuba can provide.[71]

Despite this unequivocal approval of the tuba, Berlioz wrote scarcely any music especially for it, whereas his ophicleide parts are often deliberately and diversely characteristic. The combination of ophicleide with narrow-bore trombones brings us much closer to Berlioz's sound-world than a tuba with wide-bore trombones, and a greater urgency in the revival of the ophicleide as a period instrument can only be encouraged.

[70] *Memoirs*, 'Travels in Germany', II/5.   [71] *Jd*, 1 April 1845.

9

Woodwind with mouthpiece

THE SERPENT

This is an instrument with a mouthpiece made of wood covered with leather with the same range as the bass ophicleide but a little less agility, accuracy of intonation, or resonance. It has three notes, d, a and d', much louder than the rest, and this causes some appalling unevenness of tone which players must do their best to correct. The serpent is in B♭. The range of the serpent is from B' (sounding A') chromatically up to c'' (sounding bb').

The fundamentally barbarous sound of this instrument would have been much more at home in the bloodthirsty rituals of the Druids than in those of the Catholic church, where it is always in evidence, a monstrous monument to the stupidity, tastelessness and lack of feeling which have guided the functions of music at divine service in our churches since time immemorial. An exception must be made for the occasions when the serpent is used to double the awesome *Dies iræ* plainchant at Requiem mass. Its cold, horrible bawling is doubtless appropriate there. It even seems to assume a kind of poetic misery as accompaniment to those words embodying all the horror of death and the vengeance of a jealous God. This implies too that it would be well suited to secular music concerned with the expression of such ideas – but only for that. Besides, it blends poorly with other orchestral and vocal timbres. As the bass line to a wind section the bass tuba and even the ophicleide are much to be preferred.

The serpent was still found in French orchestras and military bands in the 1820s, although rapidly giving way to the ophicleide, whose brass tube and more rational organisation of keys were clearly an improvement on the leaky and uneven serpent. Berlioz does not comment on the instrument's shape, which was no longer always serpentine. The 'serpent Forveille', for example, was shaped more like an ophicleide and made half of wood and half of brass. The serpent's role in French churches was well established and continued throughout the nineteenth century. In 1862, reviewing d'Ortigue's book *La musique à l'église*, Berlioz echoed his own words from the *Treatise*: 'He puts the blame on the performance of plainchant,

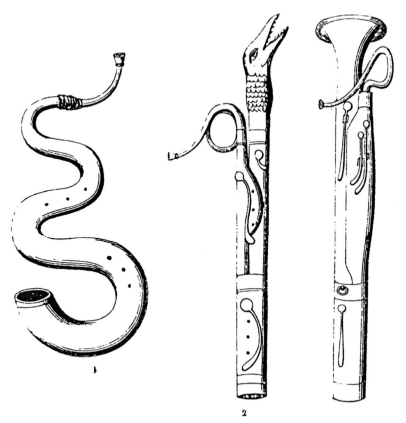

5   Three types of serpent.

always sung or rather bellowed in our churches by bull-like voices accompanied by a serpent or an ophicleide. He is quite right. Hearing those horrible notes delivered in menacing tones one might think the Druids were preparing a human sacrifice. Terrible though it may be, I have to admit that every piece of plainchant I have ever heard has been performed like this.'[1]

In the *Rgm* text, Berlioz gave only two notes 'much louder than the rest': *d* and *g*, not the three notes *d*, *a* and *d'*. Although he gives the serpent's key as B♭, it was widely regarded, at least outside France, as being in C, and he himself wrote for it in C in both of his works in which it appears. The *Messe solennelle* of 1824 has a part for a serpent in three of its movements, in two of them partnered by a buccin. The church of St-Roch, for which it was written, had a serpent player to support its choir.[2]

A serpent was also required in the last movement of the *Symphonie fantastique* in its first version, this time for purposes of parody. The sound of a serpent intoning the *Dies iræ* would have reminded a French audience of the 'cold, horrible bawling' familiar in provincial churches. Its part was confined almost exclusively to the

[1]   *A travers chants*, p. 277.
[2]   *La musique à Paris en 1830–1831*, ed. François Lesure (Paris, 1983), p. 263.

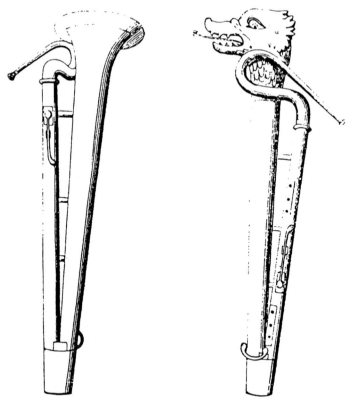

6   Two types of Russian bassoon.

plainchant melody, and it was replaced in the printed score by a second ophicleide. An early autograph list of directions for the symphony reports: 'If the church serpent plays out of tune, as most of them do, an ophicleide will be more suitable.'[3]

Berlioz found serpents in the Dresden orchestra in 1843.[4]

THE RUSSIAN BASSOON

This is a bass instrument of the serpent type with a tone that has no very distinct character, and with notes that are insecure and therefore out of tune. It could be withdrawn from the family of wind instruments, in my view, without the least damage to art. Its normal range is from D chromatically up to ab'. Some instruments go down to C and up as high as d'', but these are exceptions which may be disregarded for all practical purposes. The best notes on the Russian bassoon are the Ds and Ebs. Its trills make a quite dreadful noise. There are Russian bassoons found in military bands, but

---

[3] *NBE*, 16, pp. xv, 185.
[4] *Memoirs*, 'Travels in Germany', I/5.

it is to be hoped that they will play no further part in them when the bass tuba is better known.

The Russian bassoon was simply a serpent in upright configuration like a bassoon, made of wood. Its bore was a little narrower than the old serpent and it produced notes of brighter quality. Many of these instruments were decorated with dragon's heads at the bell. It was in fact neither Russian nor a bassoon. Berlioz never wrote for it.

10

Voices

Voices fall into two main natural categories: male (low) voices and female (high) voices. The latter group includes not only women's voices but also the voices of children of either sex and the voices of castrati. Both groups are further subdivided into two kinds generally regarded in theory as having equal ranges but distinct simply in tessitura. According to established principles in all Italian and German conservatoires the lower male voice, the bass, goes from low F up to d' or $e\flat'$, while the higher male voice, the tenor, pitched a fifth higher than the bass, goes from c up to a' or $b\flat'$. The bass uses the bass clef, the tenor the tenor clef. Then women's and children's voices correspond exactly to the two male voices an octave higher, dividing into contralto and soprano, the former corresponding to bass, the latter to tenor. So the contralto can go from f up to $e\flat''$ (almost two octaves) like the bass, and the soprano can go from c' up to high $b\flat''$ like the tenor. The soprano is written on the soprano clef (first line c'), the contralto on the alto clef.

This well-spaced arrangement of the four most distinctive human voices has doubtless much to commend it. But unfortunately it must be recognised as inadequate and risky in certain respects, since it eliminates a great number of precious voices if it is strictly applied in writing for chorus. For nature works differently in different climates, and if it is true that in Italy she has produced many contraltos, one has to admit that in France she has been very mean with them. Tenors who sail up to a' and $b\flat'$ are common in France and Italy but rarer in Germany, where, in contrast, they produce stronger bass notes than anywhere else. In my view therefore it is decidedly unwise to write for chorus in four real parts of equal importance according to the classical division of the voices into soprano, contralto, tenor and bass. In Paris, in a chorus divided in this way, the contraltos would certainly be so weak compared with the other voices, especially in a large body of singers, that nearly everything the composer asks them to do would be obliterated. In Germany, equally certainly, and even in Italy and France, if one writes for tenors within the limits customarily assigned to the voice, i.e. a fifth above the basses, a good number of singers will stop short at passages where the composer takes them up to high *a'* or *bb'* or will make nasty forced, falsetto noises. The reverse applies to basses. Several singers will fade out below *c* or *B*, so there is no point in writing *G*s or *F*s for them.

Since nature produces sopranos, tenors and basses everywhere, I believe it is infinitely more sensible, more musical in fact, to write for a chorus in six parts, if every voice is to be used: first and second sopranos, first and second tenors, baritones and basses (or first and second basses); or in three parts, taking care to divide the voices at the extremities of their respective ranges and giving the first basses notes a third, fifth or octave higher than the second basses' low notes, and giving the second tenors and second sopranos lower notes when the first tenors or first sopranos go too high. It is less important to separate first sopranos from seconds when the line goes very low than in the opposite situation. High voices do lose their strength and their special tone, it is true, when required to produce notes which belong properly to contraltos or second sopranos, but at least they are not then constrained to make an unpleasant sound, as second sopranos do when forced up too high.

The same applies to the other voices. The second sopranos, second tenors and first basses are usually pitched a third or a fourth below (or in the case of basses, above) the main voice of that designation and possess a range almost equal to that of their partners. But this is more true of the second sopranos than of the second tenors or first basses. If the second soprano is allotted a range of an octave and a sixth from *b* up to *g″*, every note will sound easily and well. The same does not apply to the second tenor, if he is allotted an equal range. His low *d*, *c* and *B* will make almost no sound, and unless some formal design or some special effect is desired it is better to avoid these low notes, especially since it is perfectly simple to give them to the first or second basses who can manage them easily. The opposite applies to the first basses or baritones; taking them to be a third higher than the seconds and writing for them from *A* up to *g'*, low *A* will be heavy and dull and high *g'* will be very strained, to say the least; this latter note really belongs only to the first and second tenors. It follows that the voices with the narrowest range are the second tenors, since they do not go as high as the firsts and go barely any lower than they do, and the first basses, since they do not go as low as the seconds and go barely any higher than they do. In a six-part chorus such as I recommend, true contralto voices (and there will always be one or two in any chorus) must sing the second soprano part, which is why I feel it is a good idea to subdivide the part again when it goes above *f″* to save the contraltos from yelling notes that are too high for them.

Table 10 shows the most resonant range of the seven different voices found in most large choruses (I shall omit notes at the extreme top and bottom which some individuals possess but which should only be written in exceptional circumstances):

Table 10

voice	lowest note	highest note	clef
Soprano I	c'	$b\flat''$	soprano
Soprano II	b	g''	soprano
Contralto	f	$e\flat''$	alto
Tenor I	c	$b\flat'$	tenor
Tenor II	c	g'	tenor
Bass I or baritone	$B\flat$	f'	bass
Bass II	F	$e\flat'$	bass

The distribution of choral voices that Berlioz advocates here is found in all his music before *L'enfance du Christ*. Such works as the *Requiem* and the *Te deum* call for a six-part chorus (Sopranos I–II, Tenors I–II, Basses I–II), allocated in the case of the *Te deum* as two three-part choruses. In some works (such as the *Tempête* fantasy and the *Sanctus* in the *Requiem*) contraltos are required as a third female voice, but if there are only two female voice parts the contraltos are always supported by second sopranos. In the first finale of *Benvenuto Cellini*, where a crowd of enraged women invade the stage, Berlioz suggested that some tenors dress as women and mingle with the contraltos in support (*NBE* 1a: 311).

L'adieu des bergers (of 1850) is the first work to present the four-voice distribution familiar from German and English music, with sopranos and contraltos each on their own line (there is a curious anticipation of this in the humorous 'Chœur de 402 voix en langue celtique inconnue' of 1843[1]). The first work to recognise the potential of contraltos as a low voice is the arrangement of *La mort d'Ophélie* for fifteen sopranos, fifteen contraltos and orchestra, made in London in 1848 with a London chorus in mind. Berlioz had certainly discovered this voice listening to English choruses, perhaps when he heard Mendelssohn's *Elijah* a few months earlier. The contraltos in *La mort d'Ophélie* are repeatedly taken down to $a\flat$, and in *L'enfance du Christ* they go as low as $f\sharp$. In *Les Troyens* and *Béatrice et Bénédict*, the contraltos sometimes have their own line and sometimes share with the second sopranos.

Berlioz attributed the six-part division of voices to Le Sueur,[2] although it was used by Cherubini and other choral composers of the early nineteenth century in France. It was derived from the five-part choral division which had been customary in France since Lully's time. The *grands motets* of Lalande, for example, require the five voices 'dessus', 'haute-contre', 'taille', 'basse-taille' and 'basse-contre'. With the exception of 'basse-contre', these older terms survive in Berlioz's early works such as the *Messe solennelle*, but were superseded by soprano (for 'dessus'), first and second tenors (for 'haute-contre' and 'taille'), and first bass (for 'basse-taille'). The term 'dessus' was retained as late as *Benvenuto Cellini*. (On the 'haute-contre', see below, p. 253.)

In general Berlioz respects the range he assigns to each voice, as for example when he refuses to take the second sopranos below b in the *Requiem* even though

[1] Holoman, *Catalogue*, p. 252.   [2] *Rgm*, 15 October 1837; *Cm*, 3, p. 307; Condé, p. 160.

the melody goes down to *g* (*NBE* 9: 76). In *Les Troyens* (*NBE* 2a: 136) there is a low *a* for the sopranos. He does not ask the sopranos to sing top *b″* in the final refrain of *Benvenuto Cellini*, but gives them *g″* instead. At other times he is not so rigid. He occasionally asks the second basses to go lower than *F* (see below, p. 252); there is a low *B* for second tenors in *Benvenuto Cellini* (*NBE* 1a: 142), and a low *B♭* for tenors in *L'impériale* (*NBE* 12b: 165), even though the same note is avoided in the previous bar.

A female chorus in three parts is marvellous for sacred or tender pieces. This is divided into the three voices I have just described: first soprano, second soprano, and contralto (or third soprano). Sometimes a tenor part acts as the bass line to these three female voices; Weber did it effectively in his Chorus of Spirits in *Oberon* (Ex. 151a), but it can succeed only when the mood is soft and calm since such a choir has little force. Choirs made up solely of men's voices, on the other hand, have a great deal of vigour, the more so the lower and the less divided the voices. Dividing basses into firsts and seconds (to avoid high notes) is less necessary in fierce energetic music in which exceptional strained notes like *f′* and *f♯′* come off better by virtue of their special character than the tenors' more natural sound at the same pitch. Furthermore these notes must be introduced and approached carefully, avoiding a sudden leap from the middle or the bottom to the topmost register. In the tremendous Scythians' Chorus in Act I of *Iphigénie en Tauride* Gluck has all the basses in unison with the tenors singing high *f♯′* on the words 'Ils nous amènent des victimes', but the *f♯′* is preceded by two notes on *d′*, so one can easily slide the voice by slurring the *d′* to the *f♯′* on the syllable 'nous' (Ex. 151b). The sudden unison of tenors and basses in this passage gives the phrase such volume and impact that it never fails to thrill. This is just another example of the genius to be found on nearly every page of the scores of that giant of dramatic music.

Ex. 151

The choral distribution Berlioz admired in the Chorus of Spirits in *Oberon* is found in his *Tempête* fantasy in *Lélio*, where Ariel's Chorus of Airy Spirits consists of sopranos I–II, contraltos, and tenors I–II. Ex. 151b shows only the voice parts of this passage.

Quite apart from the expressive purpose which seems to be the main issue here, mere convenience of vocal instrumentation can often lead to unisons of this kind in choral music. If the direction of a melody takes, say, the first tenors up to high *b'*, a dangerous note to be treated with caution, one may then bring in the second sopranos and contraltos, for this phrase only, to sing in unison with the tenors. It presents no difficulty and they will blend with them, reinforcing their sound (Ex. 152).

Ex. 152

Berlioz does not identify this excerpt (voice parts only) from his own *Requiem* (*NBE* 9: 69) and does not comment on the technique of dropping the second tenors down an octave when the part goes too high. There are many examples of this in his choral music, sometimes producing an unhappy effect like that of 'drones' in church congregations. The basses are treated in this way in the *Hymne à la France* (*NBE* 12b: 142–3).

When the tenors, on the other hand, are compelled to go too low by the demands of a melodic line, the first basses are there to help out and support them without too sharp a tonal difference spoiling their vocal character. It would not be the same having the tenors, let alone the basses, serve as auxiliaries to contraltos and second sopranos. The female voice would be almost obliterated, and the character of vocal sound would change so abruptly the moment the male voices enter that the continuity of the vocal line would be broken. This kind of superimposition of one voice coming to the aid of another therefore is not indiscriminately successful for all voices if one wishes to sustain the quality of the voice that starts and develops a phrase. This, as I say, is because if the contraltos in their middle range are covered when they give unison support to high tenors, tenors in *their* middle range will cover and almost submerge low second sopranos if they suddenly join them in unison.

In the event of wanting simply to add the range of one voice to that of another, in a descending melodic progression for example, one must not let a body of low voices suddenly take over from the full body of high ones, or the seam will be too obvious. It is better first to drop the upper half of the high voices and replace them with the upper half of the lower voices, saving the dovetailing of the other two halves for later. Thus supposing you have a huge descending scale from high *g″* for the first and second sopranos together, as soon as the scale reaches *e′* a tenth below, stop the first sopranos and bring in the first tenors on the *d′*, a tone below the first sopranos' last *e′*. The second sopranos carry on down in unison with the first tenors and stop at their low *b*, after which the second tenors must enter on *a* in unison with the firsts. The first tenors will stop at *f* to be replaced by the first basses, and the link-up of the second tenors with the second basses will be on the *d* or *c* below, then the basses continue on down to *G* together. The result for the listener will be as in Ex. 153, a descending scale of three octaves in which the handover from one voice to another will be barely noticeable.

Ex. 153

From these remarks it will be clear that the composer must choose his vocal registers in the light of the character of the piece he is writing. In a soft sustained Andante he must use only middle registers, since they alone have the appropriate tone quality and they alone can maintain a *pianissimo* smoothly, in tune, and without strain. This is what Mozart did in his heavenly prayer *Ave verum corpus*.

There are some fine effects to be had from the second basses' extreme low notes, such as the *E*♭ and even the *D* below the stave, which many singers can produce quite easily when they have time to place them carefully, that is, when these notes are preceded by a beat's rest for taking a breath and are set to a resonant syllable. Noisy, majestic or violent choral pieces should be written rather higher, on the other hand, but without giving the singers too many words to pronounce at speed. The exhaustion caused by this kind of writing quickly leads to a bad performance; a string of high notes carrying a lot of inarticulate syllables is not a pleasant experience for the listener.

Although the second basses' lower limit is given as *F* in Table 10, Berlioz here allows some exceptional low notes. He takes the second basses down to *E* in *Sara la baigneuse* (*NBE* 12a: 329–30) and down to *E*♭ in the *Requiem* (*NBE* 9: 48). There is a low *D* for the bass soloist in the *Huit scènes de Faust* (*NBE* 5: 59). In 1843 Berlioz heard and admired the German bass Reichel, who could sing low *B′*,[3] and in the Imperial Chapel in St Petersburg in 1847 he heard voices that could reach low *A′* (see below, p. 254).

We have not yet mentioned the very high notes produced by the 'head' voice, or 'falsetto'. In tenors these notes have a fine quality and they greatly increase the range; some can go up to high *e*♭″ or *f*″ in a head voice without difficulty. Much good use could be made of them in choral music if choral singers knew more about the art of singing. In basses and baritones the head voice is only tolerable in a very light style, such as in our French opéras-comiques. Those high female-sounding notes, so unlike the natural notes of low voices called 'chest' notes, are really rather disturbing in anything other than farce. No one has ever tried them in choral music nor in any vocal music of any nobility. The point where the chest voice ends and the head voice begins cannot be fixed exactly. Good tenors can anyway sing certain high notes like *a′*, *b′* and even *c″*, *forte*, either in a head voice or in a chest voice. Yet for the majority high *b*♭′ should, I think, be set as the limit of the first tenor's chest voice. Here is further proof that this voice cannot be strictly regarded as lying a fifth above the bass voice, as conservatoire teaching supposes. For out of twenty basses chosen at random at least ten will be able to sing a high *f*♯′ in a chest voice, if suitably approached, while

[3] *Cg*, 3, p. 85; *Memoirs*, 'Travels in Germany', I/10.

out of the same number of tenors there will not be a single one who can sing a tolerable high $c\sharp''$ in a chest voice.

Earlier composers of the French school never used the head voice in opera but wrote for a voice called 'haute-contre', which foreigners often mistake for the low female voice, being led astray by the natural interpretation of the Italian word 'contralto'. This term in fact indicated a man's voice trained to sing the five top notes of the first tenor's range, up to b', in a chest voice. Pitch was then a tone lower than present-day pitch, it is generally thought, although the evidence for this is not irrefutable in my view, and some doubt persists. Today if a high b' is encountered in choral music most tenors will sing it in a head voice, but very high tenors ('hautes-contre') still unhesitatingly go for it in a chest voice.

Children's voices are admirably effective in large choruses. A boy soprano in fact has a certain incisive, crystalline quality missing from women's voices. In a soft, smooth, calm piece, however, the latter will always be preferable, being fuller in tone and less penetrating. As for castrati, to judge from those I heard in Rome, there seems little cause to regret that they have now almost entirely disappeared.

Berlioz wrote for the haute-contre in his early choral music: in the *Messe solennelle*, the *Scène héroïque* and *Les francs-juges*. It is notated on the alto clef. Despite suggestions by Castil-Blaze and Choron that the haute-contre was a falsetto voice like the English countertenor, Berlioz was right to insist that the true haute-contre sang in the tenor's chest voice. By Berlioz's time the haute-contre had become very rare, as Momigny pointed out in his *Encyclopédie méthodique* of 1818.[4] There is a curious remnant of the haute-contre in the 'petit chœur' which sings the choral recitatives in *Roméo et Juliette*: the choir is divided into contraltos, tenors and basses, echoing the traditional three-part division of the male chorus. The contraltos here sing higher than the haute-contre range and enjoy quasi-solo status (the contralto soloist sings with them).

Children's choruses are found in four Berlioz works. The *Prière du matin* is a strophic song with piano accompaniment for children's choir in two parts; the lower part is pitched very low, going down to a. In *La damnation de Faust* a children's chorus in two parts, described as 'very numerous' in the score and as 'an army' of voices in a letter to Joachim of 16 October 1853,[5] joins the sopranos of the main chorus in the final pages. In the *Te deum* there is a separate part for a third chorus composed of 600 children's voices in unison. Both of these large children's choruses were added to already complete compositions in 1853, probably as a result of the experience of hearing 6500 children singing in St Paul's Cathedral in June 1851, an experience vividly described in *Les soirées de l'orchestre*. There are children among the 'several hundred' extra voices that are called for in Act III of *Les Troyens*.

[4] Neal Zaslaw, 'The enigma of the haute-contre', *Musical Times*, 115 (1974), pp. 939–41.
[5] Collection of Albi Rosenthal, Oxford.

Berlioz never wrote for castrati, of course, but he heard them in Italy. He reports attending High Mass in St Peter's on 1 May 1832:

> To crown all, the solos were dispatched in a soprano voice by a vigorous-looking gentleman with a florid complexion and enormous black side-whiskers. 'Good God,' I exclaimed to my neighbour, who was choking with suppressed laughter, 'is everything miraculous in this favoured country? Have you ever seen a bearded castrato before?'
>
> 'Castrato!' An Italian lady in front of us had overheard our comments, and shot round indignantly. '*D'avvero non è castrato!*'
>
> 'You know him, madam?'
>
> '*Per Bacco! non burlate. Imparate, pezzi d'asino, che quel virtuoso meraviglioso è il marito mio.*' ('Good God! Don't be funny, you great idiots. That splendid singer's my husband.')[6]

In northern Germany and Russia there are basses so low that composers unhesitatingly give them low *D* or low *C* below the stave, to be sustained without preparation. These precious voices, called 'basses-contre', contribute powerfully to the prodigious impact of the Imperial Chapel at St Petersburg, the finest choir in the world in the opinion of those who have heard it. The basse-contre only goes up as high as *b* or *c'*.

Three years after publication of the *Treatise* Berlioz was able to hear the St Petersburg Imperial Chapel for himself:

> The choir of the Tsar's Imperial Chapel, consisting of eighty singers, men and boys, perform pieces in four, six or eight real parts, sometimes at quite a lively pace with all the complexities of fugal writing, sometimes in a calm, seraphic mood at an extremely slow pace, requiring a rare degree of vocal control and sustaining ability. They seem better than anything else of their kind in Europe. They have low voices of a type unknown in our country which go down to low *A'*. To compare the choral singing at the Sistine Chapel in Rome with what these marvellous singers can do is like comparing some wretched little band of fiddlers in some Italian opera house with the Paris Conservatoire orchestra.[7]

Writing for the basses' low notes requires care not to give them too rapid a sequence of notes with too many words. On the other hand choral vocalisation at the bottom end of the range is detestable. It is only fair to add that the middle of the range is not much better and that despite the example of most great composers those ridiculous roulades on the words 'Kyrie eleison' or 'Amen' – enough to turn vocal fugues in church music into an indecent ghastly farce – will in future be banished, it is to be hoped, from all sacred composition worthy of its purpose. On the other hand slow, soft vocalisation for the sopranos alone, to accompany a melody

---

[6] *Memoirs*, chapter 39.   [7] *Les soirées de l'orchestre*, pp. 305–6.

on the other voices beneath, has a pious and angelic quality. Don't forget occasional rests to permit the singers to breathe, as in Ex. 154.

Ex. 154

Berlioz's detestation of choral fugues is a recurrent *cri de cœur* in all his writings. Across the manuscript of the *Quoniam* in his *Messe solennelle* Berlioz wrote 'This execrable fugue must be rewritten.' He then added: 'I swear I will never write a fugue again except in an opera where the situation demands a piece of this type, a chorus of drunks for example, or a battle fought by incarnate devils.'[8] This attitude took musical form in the 'Amen' chorus of drunks in *La damnation de Faust*. Ex. 154 is not drawn from one of Berlioz's works but seems to have been composed for the *Treatise*.

The methods of voice production in male voices known as mixed ('mixte') and covered ('sombre') are extremely valuable and can give considerable character to solo and choral singing. The mixed voice takes its quality from both chest and head voices at once, but like the latter it cannot be assigned a range limit at the top or the bottom. Some voices can produce very high mixed notes, others can do it only lower down. As for the covered voice, whose quality is revealed by its name, its effect depends not only on the method of voice production but also on dynamics and on the feeling the singer puts into it. A chorus at a steady tempo which should be sung *sotto voce* can be performed very easily in a covered voice provided the singers understand expression and have some experience of singing. As a contrast with the rough, brilliant sound of loud, high singing this expressive vocal device is always extremely effective. A magnificent example is the chorus from Gluck's *Armide* 'Suis l'amour puisque tu le veux' with its first two verses in a covered voice giving a terrific impact to the close, sung *fortissimo* in a full voice at the return of the phrase 'Suis l'amour'. There could be no better way to illustrate subdued menace and a sudden explosion of rage. This is certainly how the Spirits of Hatred and Fury should sing it.

It will be clear that our study of voices has been concerned up to now with choral groups. The art of writing for individual voices is in fact conditioned by a thousand different factors which are hard to define but which must always be borne in mind; they vary with the individual singer. One can say

[8] *NBE*, 23, p. x.

how to write for Rubini or Duprez or Haitzinger – three tenors – but there is no way of showing how to compose a tenor role that would suit all three equally well.

The solo tenor is the hardest of all voices to write for because of its three registers – chest notes, mixed notes and head notes – the range and difficulty of which differ, as I have said, from one singer to another. One great artist uses the head voice a lot and can give even his mixed voice great vibration and force; he can easily manage high, sustained phrases at any dynamic or any tempo, he loves to sing vowels like *é* and *i*. Another on the other hand, will have dreadful head notes and will prefer to sing in vibrant chest notes all the time; he will excel in passionate music, but he will always require the tempo to be rather steady to allow his voice to sound at its naturally slow pace. He will prefer open sounds and sonorous vowels, like *a*, and dread having to hold high notes. Several bars on a held high *g'* will pain and alarm him. The first of these can attack a high loud note crisply, thanks to the flexibility of his mixed voice, while the second has to lead in to it gradually in order to give it full force because he is using the chest voice; he uses the mixed voice and head voice only for half-shades or tender moods. Another kind of tenor, formerly known in France as the 'haute-contre', has no fear of high notes and can strike them in a chest voice without any preparation or uncertainty.

Rubini, Duprez and Haitzinger were, with Nourrit, the leading tenors heard in Paris in the dozen years before the time of writing. Rubini was the principal tenor at the Théâtre Italien from 1825, culminating in Bellini's *I puritani* in 1835, with its famous high *f ''*. He may be the kind of tenor Berlioz had in mind as his first example who 'uses the head voice a lot'. In *La nonne sanglante* Berlioz took his tenor up to *d♯''*. Duprez, on the other hand, was famous for his chest voice and the celebrated *ut de poitrine* which he introduced in the role of Arnold in *Guillaume Tell* in 1837, a sound which Rossini likened to the 'squawk of a capon having its throat cut'. From that year on he was the leading tenor at the Opéra. Berlioz had met him in Italy and had to contend with his imperfect commitment to the role of Benvenuto Cellini in 1838. Duprez is clearly the model for the second type of tenor described here, who 'prefers to sing in a chest voice all the time'. 'Several bars on a held high *g'* will pain and alarm him' is precisely the complaint that Berlioz made about his singing of the air 'Sur les monts' in *Benvenuto Cellini*. Berlioz unquestionably conceived the role of Cellini for a lighter and more agile type of voice than Duprez's. Haitzinger was an Austrian tenor well known for his interpretation of the role of Florestan in *Fidelio*. Berlioz heard him in Paris in 1829 and called him an 'incredible singer'.[9] The following year Berlioz briefly entertained the hope that he would sing in a production of *Les francs-juges* in Karlsruhe.

Berlioz's further ruminations on the *ut de poitrine* deserve to be quoted here:

> Tenors, with their different techniques of mixed, head and chest voices, are infinitely varied. One tenor has only three or four head notes, another has

[9] *Cg*, 1, pp. 324, 328.

many more; Rubini has six. Most can only get up to *a'* with the chest voice. Nourrit has a *b'*, Duprez gets to *c"*, Haitzinger used to have a *c♯"*. Some have head notes of exquisite purity and use them more than chest notes thanks to a mixed voice which allows them to slur middle-register notes to high notes without difficulty and without a break in the voice. Nourrit can do this; others, including Duprez, although they have excellent head notes, prefer to use the chest voice firstly because of its great beauty, also because, with their limited mixed voice, the shift from one voice to the other can only be made with great care.

One tenor likes high notes on open vowels like *a* and *o*; another has an extensive range in the chest voice. Another asks the composer to put *is* or nasal diphthongs on high notes, which he can do best with the head voice. In general, singers with a high range in the chest voice have few good notes at the bottom. Haitzinger could barely manage an *f* and Weber changed many passages in *Der Freischütz* for him. Nourrit, similarly, changed a number of notes in the recitatives for Licinius in *La vestale* which were too low for him. [...]

Seeing tenors trying to squeeze a high chest *b'* or *c"* from their ravaged throats makes you fear for an accident. The voice cracks and any moment you expect to see a nerve or a blood vessel burst in his throat and the poor singer collapse in suffocation on the stage.

It's pleasant to hear an exceptionally violent noise; the public should enjoy seeing a man dislocate his vocal organs with the chance of producing such a rough, raw sound one time in every six. That's the way the public is. '*L'ut de poitrine!* The chest high C! Gueymard has apparently found his again! Let's go and hear him!' Those people see chest Cs everywhere. In the duet in Act II of *Guillaume Tell* there are only *a*s. 'Chest high C!' In the trio, *b*s. 'Chest high C!' The actual high *c"* in the last air is for them just a higher high C than the others. It's priceless to listen to these amateur *poitrinaires* and to see their intensity and earnestness. For them all interest in the revival of *Guillaume Tell* rests in this diamond top C, this unattainable top C. The libretto, the score, the chorus, the orchestra, the singers are nothing more than the regrettably necessary frame for the pyramidal top C. Poor things! Benighted fools![10]

The first soprano voice is a little easier to write for than the first tenor; head notes are really no different from the rest of the voice. Yet one must still know the singer for whom one is writing because of the unevenness of some sopranos: some are dull and lacklustre in the middle range, or at the bottom, forcing the composer to choose the register of the principal notes of his melody with care. The voices of mezzo-sopranos (second sopranos) and contraltos are usually more homogeneous and more even, and so much easier to write for. In the case of both voices, however, one must avoid putting too many words on high-pitched phrases, since the articulation of syllables becomes difficult up there and sometimes impossible.

[10] *Jd*, 17 May 1837; Condé, pp. 260–1.

The most convenient voice is the bass, because of its simplicity. Since head notes are excluded from its repertory, there is no need to worry about tonal changes, and the choice of syllables is thus less important. Every singer calling himself a true bass should be able to sing any sensibly written music from low *G* up to *eb′*. Some voices can go much lower, like Levasseur, who can sing low *Eb* or even *D*. Others, like Alizard, can go up to high *f♯′* or even *g′* without sacrificing purity of tone. But these are exceptions. At the other extreme, voices that go no higher than *eb′* and which are inaudible below *c* are incomplete, partial voices which serve no useful purpose however strong or agreeable they may be. Baritones are often in this category; with their narrow range, almost always within an octave from *eb* to *eb′*, they force a tiresome monotony upon the composer.

Levasseur, the leading bass at the Opéra in the 1830s, sang in all the important productions there, though not in *Benvenuto Cellini*. He sang only once for Berlioz, at the opening concert of the Société Philharmonique in February 1850. Alizard on the other hand sang for Berlioz on many occasions. He covered two of the roles in *Benvenuto Cellini* and was the first Père Laurence in *Roméo et Juliette*. He also sang *Le cinq mai* on several occasions. Berlioz later admired the range of over two octaves from *Ab* upwards possessed by the great Bohemian bass Pischek[11] and the even wider range, from low *E* up to *g′*, of the Austrian bass Staudigl.[12]

The success or failure of vocal performance, whether in a chorus or solo, depends not only on the skill with which vocal registers are selected and breathing spaces arranged and on the words the singer has to sing, but also, most importantly, on the way in which the composer treats the accompaniment. It can sometimes crush the voice with an orchestral clamour which would sound well before or after the vocal phrase but not just while the singers are trying to make themselves heard. Or it can sometimes, without making any special demands on the orchestra, highlight a solo instrument, which then performs figurations or complicated patterns during the solo without any clear reason. This distracts the audience's attention from its proper object and annoys, embarrasses and distresses the singer instead of aiding and supporting him. But accompaniments do not have to be so simple as to exclude figurations with expressive articulation and of genuine musical interest, especially when they are interspersed with short rests to give the vocal movement a little rhythmic flexibility and to free the pulse from metronomic regularity. As an example of this, the sighing figure in the cellos in that moving air in the last act of Rossini's *Guillaume Tell*, 'Sois immobile' (Ex. 155), is wonderfully touching and effective, no matter what many great artists may say. It complicates the idea of the piece, no doubt,

[11] *Memoirs*, 'Travels in Germany', II/2.   [12] *Ibid.*, II/1.

but without interfering with the voice. Indeed it enhances its poignancy and sublime expressiveness.

Ex. 155

In his 1834 essay on *Guillaume Tell* Berlioz had a little more to say on this piece:

How admirably the cellos' accompaniment weeps behind the voice of this father whose heart is breaking as he embraces his son! The orchestra, almost silent, is heard only in pizzicato chords, each group followed by half a bar's rest. The bassoons, *pianissimo*, sustain long plaintive notes. How filled all this is with emotion and anguish, how expressive of the great deeds which are about to be accomplished![13]

[13] *Gm*, 2 November 1834; *Cm*, 1, p. 432.

A solo orchestral instrument can shape a phrase to match the vocal melody and make a kind of duet, and this can be extremely effective. The horn solo in Act II of Spontini's *La vestale* murmurs in duet with Julia in her passionately sad air 'Toi que j'implore' (Ex. 156a) and gives much more intensity to the voice. The mysterious, veiled and rather agonising sound of the F horn was never more cleverly or more dramatically used. There is the same effect in Rachel's cavatina, accompanied by a cor anglais solo, in Act II of Halévy's *La juive* (Ex. 156b). In this scene the instrument's soft, affecting voice blends perfectly with the young girl's pleas.

Ex. 156

(b)

Berlioz's extract from the Spontini prints the F horn part at actual pitch on the 'mezzo-soprano' clef (second line c') with a key-signature of three flats. This is how the opera's full score was published, but the notation and the choice of horn in F for a movement in E♭ is very curious. Berlioz did not print the Halévy extract in the *Treatise*.

As for solo instruments performing figures, arpeggios and variations during a vocal solo, they are so disquieting for singers, as I said before, and even for listeners, that extreme skill and some appropriate purpose are needed to make them tolerable. I confess I have always found them unbearable, with the single exception of the viola solo in Ännchen's ballad in Act III of *Der Freischütz*. And despite the example of Mozart and Gluck, along with most earlier composers and some present-day ones, it is seldom a good idea to double the voice part at the octave or in unison with an instrument, especially in an Andante. It is almost always pointless, since the voice is sufficient to state the melody, and is seldom agreeable, since the inflexions of the vocal line, as well as its expressive detail and delicate phrasing, are generally weighed down by this other melodic line alongside. And it is wearisome for the singer, who will perform a fine melody all the better if he performs it absolutely alone (if he is any good).

The pieces in which Berlioz himself used an orchestral instrument to support a solo voice are free of the abuses which he describes. Two scenes in *La damnation de*

Faust (both adapted from the *Huit scènes de Faust*) require such obbligato support. Marguerite's *Chanson gothique*, 'Le roi de Thulé', has a viola solo, and her *Romance* in Part IV, 'D'amour l'ardente flamme', features a cor anglais. In both cases the instrument dialogues with the voice and joins only discreetly with it.

In choruses or large ensembles a kind of vocal orchestration is sometimes possible. Part of the chorus adopts an instrumental style behind the melody with the accompaniment outlined and articulated in various ways. The result is almost always delightful. An example of this device is found in the chorus in the Act III ballet of *Guillaume Tell*, 'Toi que l'oiseau ne suivrait pas' (Ex. 157).

Ex. 157

This is the moment to tell composers that in choruses with instrumental accompaniment the vocal harmony must be correct, as if the voices were on their own. The orchestra's different tone-qualities are too unlike those of voices to act as their harmonic bass. Without it certain chordal progressions are incorrect. For example Gluck, who often used progressions of thirds and sixths in three parts, did this in the chorus of priestesses in *Iphigénie*

en Tauride, where the sopranos are in only two parts. In such harmonic
progressions as this the second voice is a fourth below the first voice, and the
effect of the chain of fourths is tolerable only because of the bass line a third
below the lower part and a sixth below the upper part. Now in this chorus
by Gluck the women's voices singing the upper two parts are in parallel
fourths and the lower note required to complete the harmony satisfactorily
is entrusted to the instrumental basses, whose sound is quintessentially
different from that of the sopranos. It is too far from them in range and
location, too. So instead of singing consonant chords the voices are isolated
on the stage, a long way from the orchestra, singing a series of dissonant-
sounding fourths which are certainly very harsh in the apparent absence
of their sixth (Ex. 158a).

If the harshness of these progressions has a dramatic effect in the first act
chorus of this opera, 'O songe affreux', this is not true when the priestesses
of Diana enter in Act IV to sing the chorus 'Chaste fille de Latone', so
archaic in colour yet so beautiful (Ex. 158b). Harmonic purity was surely
essential here. But the consecutive fourths in the voice parts are an error
on Gluck's part, an error which would vanish if there were a third vocal
part beneath the second, an octave above the orchestral bass.

Ex. 158

Berlioz's criticism, verging on the territory of harmony rather than orchestration, may seem harsh, but the sound of these unsupported fourths obviously irked him and he took care not to write them in his own music for two female voice parts (the choral version of *La mort d'Ophélie*, for example, and the *Prière du matin*). He had made no such criticism when he wrote a longer critical essay on *Iphigénie en Tauride* in 1834.

A male-voice chorus in unison, an idea favoured in modern Italian opera, can sometimes have good results. But it has been singularly abused, one must admit. If a number of composers persist in doing it, it is simply because it suits their laziness and is more within the scope of certain opera choruses who cannot manage music in several parts.

Double choruses, on the other hand, are wonderfully rich and grand. These are certainly not abused nowadays. They take too long for our hasty musicians to write and to learn, whether composers or performers. In fact the early composers who wrote them usually wrote just for two four-part choirs in dialogue; choruses in eight real parts are very rare. There are pieces for three choruses. When the idea they are meant to express is worth such magnificent clothing these vocal masses divided into twelve, or at least nine, real parts make an impact one can never forget. Such things mark off music for big ensembles as the most powerful of the arts.

Berlioz might have had in mind the scene at the end of Act II of *Guillaume Tell* where the three cantons respond to Tell's call and arrive individually on stage, joining in a magnificent twelve-part chorus. Double choruses were common enough in opera at the time. Berlioz's own double chorus for soldiers and students at the end of Part II of *La damnation de Faust* is a *tour de force* of musical ingenuity, based on the operatic principle of two opposing groups singing simultaneously on stage.

11

Pitched percussion

There are two kinds of percussion: the first kind comprises instruments of fixed and musically recognisable pitch; the second comprises those whose less musical sounds can only be classed as noises designed for special effect or for rhythmic colour. Timpani, bells, glockenspiel, keyboard harmonica and the little antique cymbals have fixed pitch. The bass drum, tenor drum, side drum, tambourine, ordinary cymbals, tamtam, triangle and Turkish crescent are in the other category and just make noises of different types.

THE TIMPANI

Of all percussion instruments I regard the timpani as the most precious, or at least the one most widely in use, exploited by modern composers for the widest range of picturesque and dramatic effects. Early composers scarcely used them except to strike the tonic and dominant in a rather vulgar rhythm in pieces which strove for brilliance or for a warlike effect. They were thus almost always paired with trumpets.

In most orchestras there are still no more than two timpani, with the larger one assigned to the lower note. They are customarily given the tonic and dominant notes of the key in which the piece is written. Not many years ago composers used invariably to write G and c on the bass clef for the timpani, with a simple indication at the beginning of the actual pitches these notes should represent. So they wrote 'timpani in D', after which G and c meant A and d: or 'timpani in G', when G and c would mean d and G. These two examples are enough to show the drawbacks of such a method.

The range of the timpani is one octave from F to f. By means of screws holding down the rim (called 'chevalet') of each drum, which raise or lower the tension of the skin, one can tune the lower drum to any chromatic note between F and c and the upper drum to any chromatic note between Bb and f. Now if the timpani are to sound just the tonic

265

and dominant, it is obvious that the dominant will not be in the same position relative to the tonic in each key. The timpani will have to be tuned sometimes a fifth apart, sometimes a fourth. In the key of C they will be a fourth apart, *G* and *c*, with the dominant on low *G*, since there is no high *g* (though it could be obtained). The same applies to Db, D, Eb and E. But in Bb the composer is free to tune his timpani either a fifth or a fourth apart, with the tonic either above or below, since there are two Fs available. The fourth tuning, *F* and *Bb*, will be muffled, since the skin of each drum will be very loose; the low *F*, especially, is limp and poor-sounding; the tuning as a fifth, *Bb* and *f*, is resonant for the opposite reason. Timpani in F can likewise be tuned in two ways, in fifths (*F* and *c*) or fourths (*c* and *f*). In the keys of G, Ab and A, on the other hand, the tuning has to be in fifths, since there is no low *D, Eb* or *E*. In fact there is no need to specify the fifth tuning in this case, since the timpanist is compelled to adopt it. But is it not ridiculous to write a figure in fourths when the player has to sound fifths? What seems to the eye to be the lower note is the one the ear hears as the upper note, and vice versa. Ex. 159a, on timpani in Ab, will sound as in Ex. 159b.

Ex. 159

The main reason for this bizarre custom of treating timpani as a transposing instrument was doubtless the notion subscribed to by every composer that timpani should sound only the tonic and the dominant. When they realised how useful it was sometimes to give them a different note, they were obliged to write the notes at actual pitch. In fact timpani are now tuned in every possible manner: in minor or major thirds, in seconds, fourths (perfect or augmented), fifths, sixths, sevenths or octaves. Beethoven derived some charming effects by tuning to the octave *F* and *f* in the Eighth and Ninth Symphonies.

The practice of designating the key rather than the pitches of the timpani is found in Berlioz's early music, although he never used transposing notation. The timpani are given keys only in the *Messe solennelle, La mort d'Orphée* and in the autograph of *Le roi Lear*. He departed from the standard practice of tuning timpani in fourths or fifths in the *Francs-juges* overture, and in *Herminie* and *Cléopâtre*, in all of which the timpani are required to retune to non-standard intervals in the course of the music.

When writing for a single pair of timpani, Berlioz ultimately found occasion to call for every possible interval within the octave. He requires the octave *F–f* tuning in the *Huit scènes de Faust* (and in the equivalent passage in *La damnation de Faust*) and in the chorus 'A l'atelier' in the last tableau of *Benvenuto Cellini*. For the Weimar version of the opera this chorus was transposed down from F minor to E minor, requiring the low tuning *E–e* unknown elsewhere in Berlioz's music. The upper limit *f* is exceeded in the *Chant des chemins de fer* and in the *Pandæmonium* scene in *La damnation de Faust*, in both of which a high *f*♯ is required. Both works were composed in 1846.[1]

For many years composers complained about the absurd restriction which prevented them using this instrument in chords in which neither of the two notes featured – for lack of a third timpani note. No one wondered whether a single timpanist might not play three timpani. Finally, one fine day when the timpanist at the Paris Opéra showed that it was simple, this bold innovation was tried, and ever since then composers who write for the Opéra have three timpani notes at their disposal. It had taken seventy years to happen! It would be even better, clearly, to have two pairs of timpani with two timpanists. This is what is required in a number of modern symphonies. But progress is slower in the theatre, and it will need at least another twenty-five years to get that far.

Although three timpani had been used before by Salieri, Weber and others, the third drum was evidently not introduced at the Paris Opéra until 1828, when Auber's *La muette de Portici* was heard. The resident timpanist was then Moker. In 1830 he was replaced by Poussard, whom Berlioz praised twice in the *Memoirs* and to whom Kastner dedicated his *Méthode de timbales* in 1845. Soon after Poussard's arrival at the Opéra a fourth drum was conspicuously used in Act IV of *Robert le diable* by Meyerbeer, himself a timpanist, although Berlioz did not comment on this in his essay on that opera's instrumentation, and the Opéra's normal complement of drums remained three. This accounts for the self-imposed limit of three drums found in the scores of *Benvenuto Cellini*, *La nonne sanglante* and *Les Troyens*, all three composed with the Opéra in mind.

One may employ as many drummers in an orchestra as there are drums so as to produce at will rolls, rhythms and simple chords in two, three or four parts, depending on how many there are. With four players and two pairs of drums, one tuned to *A* and *e*♭, for example, and the other on *c* and *f*, one can get chords in two, three and four parts, as in Ex. 160a. Furthermore there are enharmonics of Ex. 160a which can offer chords in D♭ minor (Ex. 160b) or C♯ minor (Ex. 160c), with the advantage of having at least one note belonging to almost every chord not too far distant from the main key.

[1] Berlioz's use of percussion is treated in depth in Peter H. Tanner, 'Timpani and percussion writing in the works of Hector Berlioz' (PhD diss., Catholic University of America, 1969), and in Nancy Benvenga, 'The use of the percussion in the symphonies of Berlioz', unpublished typescript (Boston, 1969). See also James Blades, *Percussion Instruments and their History* (London, 1970).

Ex. 160

So when I wanted a number of chords in three, four and five parts (variously doubled) and the striking effect of very rapid rolls I used eight pairs of timpani (tuned in different ways) and ten timpanists in my *Requiem.*

This famous disposition of sixteen timpani tuned as eight separate pairs played by ten timpanists was the largest array of timpani in his work, indeed in all the orchestral repertory. Berlioz's original plan was to have sixteen pairs with sixteen players.[2] The tunings are arranged so that all thirteen chromatic pitches between *F* and *f* are available, and the three remaining drums reinforce the triad of E♭ major. It is generally assumed that Berlioz derived the idea from Reicha's *Die Harmonie der Sphären* (included in that composer's *Traité de haute composition musicale*, 1826), which calls for four pairs of timpani tuned to eight pitches.

In large ceremonial works Berlioz called for three pairs of timpani (*Marseillaise* and *L'impériale*), and a line-up of two pairs is common in non-operatic works (*Symphonie fantastique, Roméo et Juliette* and *La damnation de Faust,* for example) and some larger choral pieces (such as *Hymne à la France*). The two pairs may require two, three or four players at any one time. In the *Huit scènes de Faust,* the first Berlioz work to introduce two pairs, both pairs are tuned to the same pitches, but in the *Scène aux champs* in the *Symphonie fantastique* he explored both the harmonic and the expressive effects of four different pitches.

We stated just now that the timpani have a range of only one octave. The problem of obtaining a hide large enough to cover any bowl bigger than that of the large lower drum is perhaps the reason why notes below

F cannot be reached. But the same does not apply to high-pitched drums. By reducing the size of the metal bowl it would plainly be easy to get high *g*, *a* and *b♭*. These little timpani could often be most effective.

It used to be very rare for timpanists to be required to retune their instruments in the middle of a piece. Today composers do not scruple to call for a great number of tuning changes with very little time to do it. This practice, so troublesome and difficult for the player, could be generally dispensed with if every orchestra had two pairs of timpani and two timpanists. However, if one does require it, one must be careful to give the timpanist a number of bars' rest in proportion to the complexity of the change required, so that he has time to do it properly. One must also indicate a new tuning as close as possible to the old one. For example, if the timpani are tuned to *A* and *e* and you wish to go into the key of B♭, it would be appallingly clumsy to call for a new tuning of *F* and *B♭* (a fourth apart), requiring the bottom drum to be lowered by a third and the upper drum to be lowered by an augmented fourth, when the fifth tuning *B♭* and *f* requires merely a semitone rise for both drums. Imagine how difficult it is for the timpanist to get a new tuning exactly right when he has to turn the keys or the screws on the rim during a piece full of modulations which might be sounding the key of B major while he is trying to find the key of C or F. This shows that quite apart from the special ability the timpanist must possess in handling the sticks he must also be an excellent musician with an extremely fine ear. That's why good timpanists are so scarce.

Berlioz first called for a retuning of timpani in the *Scène héroïque*, and in the works of 1826–9, especially *Herminie* and *Cléopâtre*, the timpanist is constantly retuning his drums. In *Cléopâtre* he has to traverse the wide intervals (and back) which Berlioz here warns against. In the overture to *Les francs-juges* (*B&H* 4: 48) and in the finale of *Harold en Italie* (*NBE* 17: 132) he retunes a drum for a single drumstroke. But he later preferred to use more drums rather than keep retuning a single pair.

In an essay on open-air music written in 1835, Berlioz discussed timpani tuning, and even mentioned mechanically tuned drums, not mentioned in the *Treatise:*

> In the theatre lazy timpanists often fail to retune and just play a piece in F on timpani tuned in E flat without anyone noticing. While we are on the subject of timpani tuning, I should mention an important discovery for which composers are indebted to M. Brod. This artist, whose fine talent on the oboe is so justly famous, is also an ingenious mechanic. He has tried to meet the constant need for ease and accuracy in timpani tuning, and he has achieved this by placing rings inside the metal bowl which are moved up and down against the underneath of the drumhead by means of a pedal. There are six or seven of these concentric rings. The smallest, in the middle, reduces the diameter of the head by nearly a half.[3]

[3] *Jd*, 21 July 1835; *Cm*, 2, pp. 229–30.

Pedal timpani had been the subject of experiment since 1812,[4] but they made no further impression on Berlioz or his music.

There are three kinds of sticks, the use of which makes so much difference to the timpani's sound that it is worse than negligent for composers not to specify in the score the kind of sticks they want. Wooden-headed sticks ('baguettes à tête de bois') make a hard, dry sound not really suitable for anything except to strike a violent blow or to accompany a big orchestral cacophony. Sticks with wooden heads covered with leather ('baguettes à tête de bois recouverte en peau') are less hard; they make a less ringing sound than the first kind, but still quite dry. These sticks are the only ones used in a great many orchestras, which is very irksome. Sponge-headed sticks ('baguettes à tête d'éponge') are the best, and they should be the most often used, being more musical and less noisy. They give the timpani a dark velvety tone quality which makes the sound very precise and the tuning more clearly audible as a result. They suit a great range of dynamics, loud or soft, where the other kinds of sticks would produce a detestable, or at least inadequate, effect.

Whenever a mysterious, darkly menacing sound is needed, even when the music is loud, sponge-headed sticks should be used. The elasticity of the sponge, moreover, helps the stick to bounce, so the player has only to stroke the drumskin to get fine, soft, very rapid rolls, *pianissimo*. In his Fourth and Fifth Symphonies Beethoven made marvellous use of *pianissimo* timpani; these admirable passages (towards the end of the slow movement of the Fourth Symphony and the link from the scherzo to the finale of the Fifth) have much to lose if they are played with sticks without sponge heads, even though the composer gave no special instructions here.

Both of these Beethoven passages are famous for their prominent use of the timpani. Berlioz evidently assumed that the second kind of stick (with wooden heads covered in leather) would be used in default of any other instruction.[5] An instruction to use this kind of stick is thus rare, in fact it is found only at the opening of Part III of *La damnation de Faust* (*NBE* 8a: 250) where one pair of timpanists is instructed to use sponge-headed sticks and the second pair are to use wooden sticks covered in leather. Directions to use either wooden or sponge-headed sticks, on the other hand, are common, from the *Francs-juges* overture (where both sticks are specified) to the end of his career. Sponge-headed sticks are usually specified when the timpani part is especially expressive or exposed.[6] Berlioz's insistence on using the correct sticks is emphasised by a letter to Lecourt in Marseilles written just as the *Treatise* was about to appear ('Advise the two timpanists not to use

---

[4] James Blades, *Percussion Instruments and their History* (London, 1970), pp. 277–8.
[5] *NBE*, 16, p. 221.
[6] Nancy Benvenga, 'Berlioz and sponge timpani sticks', *Berlioz Society Bulletin*, 100 (Summer 1978), p. 5.

wooden sticks which would make a horrible effect, but sponge-headed sticks; they should have some'[7]) and by his account of a typical rehearsal in Germany during his tours:

> 'You're playing with wooden sticks when you should be using sponge-headed ones. It's the difference between black and white.'
> 'We don't know them,' the kapellmeister interposes. 'What do you mean by sponge-headed sticks? We only know one kind.'
> 'I suspected as much, so I brought some with me from Paris.'[8]

Elsewhere Berlioz reported that the Germans were far behind the French in the use of different sticks.[9]

The indications 'voilées' and 'couvertes' are often found in timpani parts, especially in the music of earlier composers. It means that the skin of the instrument should be covered with a piece of cloth whose purpose is to dampen its sound and make it extremely lugubrious. Sponge-headed sticks are again preferable to the other kinds on such occasions.

It is sometimes good to show which notes the timpanist is to strike with both sticks at once and where a single stick is to be used, as in Ex. 161. The rhythm and the placing of accents are the determining factors.

Ex. 161

Timpani are not very low-pitched; they sound at their written pitch, which is on the bass clef in unison with the corresponding notes on the cello, not an octave lower, as some musicians have supposed.

Berlioz required the timpani to be muted only in his early works. The instructions 'voilées', 'couvertes' and 'découvertes' are found in scores composed between 1824 and 1829; in *Les francs-juges* (Act III Scene iv) the timpani are to be 'covered with a thick cloth'. 'Sourdines' are required in the 1831 version of the *Resurrexit* (*NBE* 12a: 15), and the opening five timpani entries in *Rob Roy* are marked 'con sordini'. But Berlioz soon decided that this effect was better produced by modifying the sticks rather than the drumheads. The entries 'sourdines' and 'sans sourdines' in the autograph of *Waverley* were replaced by 'baguettes d'éponge' and 'baguettes de bois', and similar revisions were made in the *Symphonie fantastique* at an early stage.[10]

Ex. 161 is taken from the opening of the *Marche au supplice* in the *Symphonie fantastique* (*NBE* 16: 91). The full instruction is: 'The first quaver of each beat must be struck with both sticks and the five other quavers with the right-hand stick only', a difficult technique which few timpanists attempt. A passage where

[7] *Cg*, 3, p. 140.   [8] *Memoirs*, 'Travels in Germany', I/3.   [9] *Ibid.*, I/7.   [10] *NBE*, 16, pp. 178–9.

one player strikes two drums simultaneously and repeatedly is found in the last movement of the *Symphonie fantastique* (*NBE* 16: 120).

The *Treatise* offers no advice on the matters of pitch-selection and on the playing of non-harmonic notes. The older style of timpani tuning, on the tonic and dominant of the key of the piece, presupposed that the timpani note would normally be the root of the chord. With the introduction of tunings other than a fourth and fifth apart it became more common for the timpani to strike notes other than the root or even the bass note at any given moment, especially in Beethoven. Berlioz tried a number of tunings that did not necessarily include the tonic, as for example in *Zaïde*, where the pitches are set at *A* and *c* for a piece in F major.

Berlioz is normally careful to give the timpani only notes which belong to the prevailing harmony. The only work to require non-harmonic timpani notes in any quantity is the overture to *Benvenuto Cellini* (see *NBE* 1a: 49–52, 105–7). There is a *fortissimo* G against B major harmony in the band version of the *Scène héroïque* (*NBE* 12a: 208). In 1858 Berlioz removed a dissonant *piano d♮* (against B major harmony) from the finale of *Roméo et Juliette* (*NBE* 18: 334, 439). Normally, unlike for example Wagner and Bizet, Berlioz would rather have the timpani silent than contribute a dissonant note to the harmony. The effect of four or more timpani playing together, however, he sometimes treated more as an effect than as harmony. This is the case at the end of the *Scène aux champs* in the *Symphonie fantastique*, where A♭, B♭, C and *f* are heard together in a roll. The most striking case is found at the end of the *Dies iræ* in the *Requiem*, where ten timpani are heard simultaneously on seven different pitches to lend weight to the final *fortissimo* of the movement (*NBE* 9: 47).

Berlioz's imaginative treatment of the timpani extends further than the use of multiple drums and a concern for correct sticks. Peter H. Tanner asserted that Berlioz's timpani always serve a tonal, not a rhythmic, purpose,[11] but while that is true for such passages as the opening chorus of *Les Troyens* (*NBE* 2a: 14–15) where the timpani provide the essential bass line, it is not so in the slow introduction to the *Waverley* overture (*NBE* 20: 7–11) nor in an effective passage in the *Benvenuto Cellini* overture (*NBE* 1a: 42–3, 99–101) nor in *Roméo seul* (*NBE* 18: 67). A superb example of the rhythmic independence of the timpani is found in the *Francs-juges* overture (*B&H* 4: 57–8), where the timpani play in triple rhythm against the continuing duple pulse of the rest of the orchestra.

The timpani often serve a programmatic function, most obviously in the *Symphonie fantastique*, where they evoke the distant rumble of thunder in the *Scène aux champs* (*NBE* 16: 89–90). Of this passage a footnote to the symphony's programme as issued in 1836–8 has an important comment: 'When the composer attempted to render the rumble of distant thunder in the midst of the calm of nature, it was not for the childish pleasure of imitating that majestic sound but on the contrary to make the *silence* more deeply felt and thus to reinforce the feeling of anxious sorrow and painful loneliness which he wished to convey to his audience at the end of this movement.'[12]

---

[11] Tanner, 'Timpani and percussion writing in the works of Hector Berlioz', p. 55.
[12] *NBE*, 16, p. 170.

There are imitative effects in *Le roi Lear* overture, where they represent the entry of the king in council (*NBE* 20: 60–4),[13] and in *L'enfance du Christ*, where they suggest the sound of Joseph knocking at a wayside door (*NBE* 11: 135). Forceful timpani strokes represent the neighbours' knocking that terrifies Marguerite in *La damnation de Faust* (*NBE* 8a: 350). In the orchestration of *Der Erlkönig* timpani supply the galloping effect suggested in Schubert's piano part (*B&H* 18: 41–2). In *La captive* they provide a Spanish bolero rhythm (*NBE* 13: 18). The timpani have an unusual role in the orchestral version of *Hélène* (*NBE* 12a: 281) where, with the strings, they support the voices while oboe and horns are confined to the refrain between verses.

Timpanists are not exempt from playing other percussion instruments when required. In the finale of the *Symphonie fantastique* the third and fourth players are instructed to play the bass drum (*NBE* 16: 114–15), and in the *Tempête* fantasy in *Lélio* the second timpanist is presumed to move to the cymbals midway through the movement (*NBE* 7: xvi).

The teaching of timpani and percussion was one of those areas which Berlioz felt was neglected at the Paris Conservatoire, as the *Memoirs* remind us:

Is there any orchestra in Europe, large or small, which does not possess a timpanist? They all have a functionary of that name; but how many are true timpanists, thorough-going musicians, accustomed to every complexity of rhythm, masters of the technique of the instrument – which is less easy than is commonly believed – and gifted with a keen ear sufficiently trained to enable them to tune and change key accurately, and to do so during a performance, with all the noise of the orchestra going on around them? I must positively state that, apart from the timpanist at the Opéra, M. Poussard, I know of only three in the whole of Europe – and I have had the opportunity of scrutinizing a few orchestras in the last nine or ten years. Most of the timpanists I met did not even know how to hold their sticks and were consequently helpless when it came to executing a true tremolo or roll. A timpanist who cannot manage a quick roll in every degree of loud and soft is a man of straw.

All conservatoires ought therefore to have a percussion class in which students can acquire a thorough proficiency in timpani, tambourine and side-drum at the hands of first-rate musicians. The old convention, now no longer tolerable and already abandoned by Beethoven and one or two others, whereby the percussion was neglected or treated in a crude and unimaginative way, undoubtedly helped to perpetuate its low status. Since composers till recently used it merely as a source of noise (more or less superfluous or actively disagreeable) or as a means of mechanically emphasising the strong beats of the bar, it was assumed that this modest mission was all that it could or was meant to fulfil in the orchestra, and consequently that there was no need to go into the technique of the thing with any great care or to be a real musician in order to play it. In fact it takes a very capable musician to play even some of the cymbal and bass drum parts in modern scores.[14]

---

[13] *Cg*, 5, p. 601.   [14] *Memoirs*, 'Travels in Germany', II/5.

It was customary for composers to take on the timpanist's duties in performances of their own works. Hérold, Meyerbeer and Adam, for example, were all timpanists at one time or another and Berlioz may well have done the same. Heine recalled the performance of the *Symphonie fantastique* and *Lélio* in December 1832, in which Berlioz was seated at the timpani while Harriet Smithson was in her box: 'Every time he caught her eye he struck the drum with a kind of spasm of fury. [. . .] When I heard the symphony again last winter [1836], he was there as before, at the back of the orchestra near the drums, and the large Englishwoman [Harriet] was in the stage box. Their glances met; but this time he did not strike the drums so furiously.'[15] Whether there is any truth in this account (in 1836 Berlioz was the conductor, not the timpanist, in his concerts) and how often Berlioz played the timpani in his early years it is hard to say.

BELLS

Bells were brought into the orchestra more for dramatic than for musical reasons. The sound of deep bells is only appropriate for solemn or tragic scenes. High bells, on the other hand, give a more serene impression; they have a rather rustic, naive quality especially suitable for religious scenes in a country setting. That is why Rossini used a little bell on high *g′* to accompany the graceful chorus in Act II of *Guillaume Tell*, with its refrain 'Voici la nuit', while Meyerbeer has used a bell on low *f* to give the signal for the massacre of the Huguenots in Act IV of the opera of that name. He was careful to place this *f* a diminished fifth above the *B♮* on the bassoons; with the aid of low notes on two clarinets (in A and B♭) it creates the sinister effect of terror and horror permeating this immortal scene.

The published score of *Guillaume Tell* gives the pitch of the bell as *G*, two octaves lower than Berlioz's version.

Bells had been used in opera as offstage effects since the eighteenth century, but the orchestral use of notated and pitched bells goes back to Grétry's *Cécile et Ermancé* (1792), which has a bell sounding *d′*, and Candeille's *La patrie reconnaissante* (1793), which made use of the two big bells in *C* and *G* which the Opéra then possessed.[16] It is possible that Berlioz knew about these bells in *C* and *G* when he wrote parts for them in the finale of the *Symphonie fantastique*, but whether or not he was able to use them is a mystery. It is not certain that he was ever able to procure bells for any of the performances he gave of this finale. He provided an alternative part for piano and printed it as a piano part in the full score. A sheet

[15] Heinrich Heine, *Über die französische Bühne: zehnter Brief* (1837), quoted in David Cairns, *The Memoirs of Hector Berlioz* (London, 1990), pp. 476–7.

[16] Constant Pierre, *Les hymnes et chansons de la Révolution* (Paris, 1904), p. 193, quoted in David Charlton, 'Orchestration and orchestral practice in Paris, 1789–1810' (Ph.D. diss., Cambridge, 1973), pp. 250–1.

of directions gave the following exhortation: 'If two bells deep enough to sound one of the three Cs and one of the three Gs which are written cannot be found, it is better to use pianos. They will then perform the bells' part in double octaves as it is written.'[17] He allowed the bells to be set at any of three pairs of pitches: *c'* and *g*, *c* and *G*, or *C* and *G'*. The bells are to be offstage.

A higher bell pitched on *a'* (on the treble clef) appears in the fragments of *Les francs-juges*, with an 'echo', presumably another bell, on the same note.

He called for a different kind of bell in *La damnation de Faust* (*NBE* 8a: 411), when a death-knell for Marguerite is heard. Berlioz allowed any of four pitches to be sounded, written as a chord *c–d–f♯–a*. The printed parts of 1854 allow a tamtam as a substitute.

It should be noted that in the *Marche de pèlerins* in *Harold en Italie* Berlioz created a bell effect not with a bell but with a harp, flute and oboe playing the octave *b♭–b''*.

The acoustic properties of bells were of particular interest to him. In 1838 he wrote to the engineer and inventor F.-C. Busset: 'I have the honour to reply that I have often had occasion to observe that a bell's resonance is in the minor. This struck me for the first time when listening to the cathedral bell in Florence, and all my observations since then, both in France and in Italy, confirm this. I have found only a single exception, but the bell in question was a long way from where I was and a strict analysis of its harmonics was difficult if not impossible.'[18]

A later experience is recounted in the *Memoirs*. On a visit to Mannheim in 1843, Berlioz's hotel adjoined a clock whose chime had a resonance of a minor third. He later added a footnote to his account:

> In Germany I was able to make many observations as to the different reso-
> nances of bells, and it is clear to me that once again nature makes mock of the
> experts. Some theoreticians maintain that all resonating bodies without ex-
> ception have a resonance of a major third. A mathematician has lately come
> forward declaring that, on the contrary, all bells produce a minor third.
> The fact is, they create all sorts of intervals. Some produce a minor third,
> others a fourth. One of the bells at Weimar sounds a minor seventh and an
> octave in succession (fundamental F, resonance octave F and seventh E♭).
> There are those that even produce an augmented fourth. Clearly the har-
> monic resonance of a bell depends on the shape created by the bell-founder,
> on the varying degrees of thickness at certain points in the curve of the metal,
> and on the chance irregularities of casting.[19]

At the Great Exhibition in London in 1851 Berlioz remarked upon the great Irish bell set in the east gallery of the Crystal Palace, which 'obstinately struck one, two, three, four, five, six, seven, eight, full of pride at not in the least resembling its sister in the church in Albany Street, which has a resonance of a *major third*'.[20]

[17] *NBE*, 16, pp. 115, 185.   [18] *Cg*, 2, p. 267 (misdated 1835–6).
[19] *Memoirs*, 'Travels in Germany', I/3.
[20] *Les soirées de l'orchestre*, pp. 304–5. As he was staying that year in Cavendish Square, Berlioz's walks in Regent's Park had doubtless taken him past Holy Trinity Church, Albany Street.

JEU DE TIMBRES

Very striking effects can be obtained, especially in military bands, from a string of little bells like clock chimes, fixed one above the other on a metal bar. About eight or ten in number, they are arranged diatonically in order of size; the highest note is naturally at the top of the pyramid and the lowest at the bottom. When struck with a little hammer this kind of carillon can play melodies of modest speed and narrow compass. It comes in different sizes. The highest are the best.

This instrument, sometimes known in English as a bell-lyra or bell-tree, is related to the lyra-glockenspiel, in which the sounding metal objects are bars rather than bells, arranged on a vertical pyramid frame. When Berlioz reported on the concerts given by Johann Strauss's orchestra in Paris in 1837, it was evidently a jeu de timbres he referred to: 'Some of the violinists also play the "glockenspiel" (a series of little steel bells of different sizes fixed to a metal stem).'[21] We here encounter the confusion attached to the terms 'glockenspiel' and 'harmonica' in Berlioz's usage. Even if Strauss called the instrument a glockenspiel, Berlioz normally used that term for a keyboard instrument, as described in the next section.

In the *Rgm* text Berlioz mentioned the use of jeux de timbres in ballet. It was in fact little used outside military bands, a rare case being the score of Adam's *Si j'étais roi* (1852; see also below, under 'Triangle').

THE GLOCKENSPIEL

In his opera *Die Zauberflöte* Mozart wrote an important part for a keyboard instrument he calls a 'glockenspiel', evidently made of a large number of tiny bells arranged so as to be playable from a keyboard. He gave it a chromatic range from *d* up to *d'''* and wrote for it on two staves with treble and bass clefs like a piano. When the Paris Opéra put on the unrecognisable farrago known as *Les mystères d'Isis*, in which part of the music of *Die Zauberflöte* appears in various degrees of distortion, they had a little keyboard made for the glockenspiel piece with hammers striking steel bars instead of bells. It sounds an octave higher than written; its tone is soft, mysterious and extremely refined. It can manage tempos of any speed and makes an incomparably better sound than little bells.

Mozart's requirement is an 'istromento d'acciaio', a 'steel instrument', although in a letter to his wife of October 1791 he called it 'Glocken Spiel' and 'Glöckchenspiel'.[22] As in the case of Handel's 'carillon', it is not known whether

---

[21] *Jd*, 10 November 1837; *Cm*, 3, p. 329; Condé, p. 123.
[22] Mozart, *Briefe und Aufzeichnungen*, ed. W. A. Bauer and O. E. Deutsch (Kassel, 1962–75), 4, p. 157.

the instrument was made of bells or of bars (the term 'glockenspiel' implies bells). Mozart writes for it entirely in the key of G, without any chromatic notes. *Les mystères d'Isis*, with a new libretto by E. Morel de Chédeville and a score which drew on *Die Zauberflöte* and other Mozart operas, was frequently played at the Opéra between 1801 and 1827. Berlioz was appalled at its lack of taste and respect.[23]

The keyboard glockenspiel, as used in *Les mystères d'Isis* at the Opéra, is evidently the instrument Berlioz calls for in two of his early scores under the name 'harmonica-glockenspiel'. In the *Concert de sylphes* in the *Huit scènes de Faust*, composed in 1828 (*NBE* 5: 26), it has an important part with a range from d' to $f\sharp'''$ and chords in both hands requiring a keyboard. Two days before the performance of this movement at the Conservatoire on 1 November 1829 Berlioz wrote to Ferrand: 'I am just going to the Opéra to fetch the harmonica; they brought one this morning which was too flat and we could not use it.'[24] In the *Tempête* fantasy (1830) there was originally a part for the harmonica-glockenspiel (*NBE* 7: 192, 200). Its range is from c' up to $e\flat'''$. It was marked as optional and later taken out, probably within a year or two of its first performance. Since this performance, on 7 November 1830, took place at the Opéra, it is likely that the Opéra's keyboard glockenspiel was again used. It should be noted that this instrument sounds an octave higher than its written pitch.

Between these two works a different kind of harmonica is found. The fragmentary score of *Sardanapale* (1830) has parts for 'first and second harmonica', each on a treble clef, each playing one note at a time (*NBE* 6: 218–19). This is clearly not a keyboard instrument, and must have been more like the modern glockenspiel, played manually with hammers. The bars must have been made of steel, since it has to be heard against an orchestral tutti.

In the years 1829–30 Balzac twice derided the sound of the harmonica: under the date 5 December 1829 he introduced a character whose voice was 'as irritating as the sound of a harmonica', and two months later he described the voice of a soprano singing in church, which 'acted on his nerves as if they had been attacked by the over-rich, overactive notes of a harmonica'.[25]

The harmonica-glockenspiel disappeared from both the *Concert de sylphes* and the *Tempête* when these movements were adapted for *La damnation de Faust* and *Lélio* respectively, and *Sardanapale* was withdrawn. It should be noted that both 'glockenspiel' and 'steel-bar keyboard' are listed in chapter 4 of this *Treatise* (p. 99) as orchestral instruments. The keyboard harmonica with bars made of glass rather than metal, as described in the next section, evidently made a quite different sound.

In 1838 Berlioz reported on a 'piano sans cordes' made by the manufacturer Pape; this had metal strips instead of strings and made a very delicate sound.[26] This instrument must have resembled the keyboard glockenspiel in mechanism and timbre.

[23] *Memoirs*, chapter 16.   [24] *Cg*, 1, p. 278.
[25] Balzac, *Physiologie de mariage*, ed. Calmann Lévy (Paris, 1893), p. 5; *Une double famille* (Paris, 1892), p. 274.
[26] *Jd*, 6 July 1838; *Cm*, 3, p. 494.

THE KEYBOARD HARMONICA

This is an instrument of the same type as the glockenspiel, except that the hammers strike plates of glass. Its tone is incomparably delicate and voluptuous and can often be used for the most poetic effects. Like the steel-bar keyboard which I have just described its tone is extremely soft, which must be borne in mind when using it with other orchestral instruments. Even a sharp accent on the violins could drown it. It would blend better with light pizzicato accompaniment or with string harmonics, or with very soft flutes in the middle register.

It sounds at written pitch. It has a range of scarcely more than two octaves. Any note above *e'''* is almost inaudible, and those below *d'* have very poor sound, even weaker than the rest of the range. This difficulty could perhaps be resolved if the low notes were given thicker plates of glass than the rest. It is normally piano manufacturers who undertake to build this lovely and too little known instrument. Like the glockenspiel it is written on two staves, but with two treble clefs.

I need hardly add that the method of playing both these little keyboards is exactly the same as for the piano. Within their respective ranges one can write all the figures, arpeggios and chords one would write for a very small piano.

The instrument Berlioz describes here is different from the musical glasses (or glass harmonica) famous from their association with Benjamin Franklin and Mozart and a highly fashionable instrument in the late eighteenth century. Nor is it the harmonica-glockenspiel found in Berlioz's music of 1828–30 (see 'Glockenspiel' above), which evidently had steel not glass plates. Kastner gave it a much wider range from *F* up to *g'''*.[27] It has been overlooked by most histories of musical instruments and there appear to be no surviving specimens. No compositions for this instrument are known.

THE ANTIQUE CYMBALS

These are extremely small and their pitch gets higher the thicker and smaller they are. I saw some in the Pompeii Museum near Naples which were no bigger than a piastre. Their sound is so high and soft that one would scarcely hear them unless every other instrument were silent. In ancient times these instruments were used to mark the rhythm of certain dances, rather like our modern castanets.

In the fairy scherzo of my symphony *Roméo et Juliette* I used two pairs of them, larger than those at Pompeii, that is to say a little smaller than a

[27] Georges Kastner, *Traité général d'instrumentation* (Paris, 1837), p. 29.

hand's breadth and tuned a fifth apart. The lower one sounds bb'' and the upper one f'''. To make them vibrate properly the players must not clash the two cymbals full face against each other but simply strike them edge to edge. Any bell foundry can make these little cymbals which are first cast in copper or brass and then turned to adjust them to the desired pitch. They should be at least eight millimetres thick. It is again a delicate instrument, like the keyboard harmonica, but its tone is stronger and it can easily be heard above a whole orchestra playing *piano* or *mezzo-forte*.

Berlioz visited Pompeii in October 1831 and wrote to his family: 'This morning at the museum I saw the ancient musical instruments found beneath the ashes at Herculaneum. I tried two pairs of little cymbals. As for the wind instruments, they are all incomplete.'[28] One of the pairs of cymbals Berlioz saw, now in the Museo Archeologico Nazionale in Naples, is described as having a diameter of 11 cm, being made of 'two circular sheets of bronze, each concave internally and surrounded by a broad flange, linked from the centres by a loose chain'.[29] Nothing is known of the second pair.

The published full score of *Roméo et Juliette* includes, under the heading 'Observations' (*NBE* 18: 3), the information that pairs of antique cymbals could be hired from the publishers, Brandus. These 'Observations' insist that the little cymbals should be placed near the conductor and not at a great distance with the other percussion, to prevent them from getting behind. Berlioz had learnt this lesson after being forced to abandon a performance of the *Reine Mab* scherzo at the Opéra in 1840.[30] The same precaution was offered in a letter to Hiller in 1840.[31] For a performance of the work in Weimar in 1852 Berlioz sent Liszt two pairs of little cymbals, which cost 100 sous a pair,[32] and in 1868 he gave his original pair to the Russian Musical Society in St Petersburg.

In St Petersburg in 1847 the two local kapellmeisters Romberg and Maurer were recruited to play the antique cymbals for Berlioz.[33] William Ganz records that when he and Eduard Silas played the little cymbals for a performance of the *Reine Mab* scherzo in London in 1852, Berlioz provided the instruments himself, insisted on a sectional rehearsal for the percussion, and had the cymbals placed near him. Berlioz evidently told Ganz that this was to prevent the sound being lost, but his real purpose was surely to maintain a good ensemble.[34]

Berlioz called for the antique cymbals again in Act IV of *Les Troyens* for the *Pas d'esclaves nubiennes* (*NBE* 2b: 536). This time they are pitched on e'' and f'', much lower than those in *Roméo et Juliette*. Later composers such as Ravel referred to these little cymbals as 'crotales'.

[28] *Cg*, 1, p. 493.
[29] John Ward-Perkins and Amanda Claridge, *Pompeii A.D. 79* (Boston, 1978), p. 182. The Inventory number is 76943.
[30] *Memoirs*, chapter 51.   [31] *Cg*, 3, pp. 733–4.
[32] *Cg*, 4, p. 193. In March 1853 Liszt sent a pair to Gustav Schmidt in Frankfurt, probably in preparation for the Karlsruhe festival in October of that year (Sotheby's Sale Catalogue, London, 9 December 1999).
[33] *Memoirs*, 'Travels in Russia'.   [34] A. W. Ganz, *Berlioz in London* (London, 1950), p. 124.

12

Unpitched percussion

THE BASS DRUM

Of all percussion instruments of indeterminate pitch it is surely the bass drum which has caused the most devastation and led to the worst abuses and excesses of modern music. None of the great composers of the last century thought to include it in the orchestra. Spontini was the first to use it, in the triumphal march in *La vestale*, and then a little later in several scenes in *Fernand Cortez*, where it is fittingly used. But to write for it in the fashion of the last fifteen years in every ensemble, every finale, every little chorus, in ballets, even in cavatinas, is the ultimate in absurdity and – let's call things by their name – in brutality. It's not as though composers even had the excuse of an original rhythm which they might be supposed to be emphasising in contrast to subsidiary rhythms. No, they bash the strong beats of every bar, they drown the orchestra and obliterate the voices. No melody or harmony or phrase or expression survives. Even the key can be drowned. Then they imagine they have devised a forceful style of instrumentation and created something beautiful!

I need hardly add that in this way of doing things the bass drum is almost always accompanied by the cymbals, as if the two instruments were inseparable by nature. In some orchestras they are both played by the same player: with one of the cymbals attached to the bass drum he can strike the other against it with his left hand while wielding the bass drum stick with his right. This economical practice is intolerable. The cymbals lose all their resonance that way and just make a noise like dropping a bag of scrap iron and broken glass. It's a vulgar trick, lacking all dignity and distinction. At the very best it would do for monkeys to dance to and for accompanying thimbleriggers, acrobats, sword-swallowers and snake-eaters in public places and the grubbiest city squares.

When sensibly used, however, the bass drum is admirably effective. For example, it can join in an ensemble as part of a large orchestra with the function of gradually reinforcing a broad rhythm which has already been established, joined by groups of louder instruments one by one. Its entry can be miraculous on such occasions; the orchestral pendulum assumes infinite resonance. Noise, thus harnessed, becomes music. *Pianissimo* notes on the bass drum together with cymbals in a slow tempo and struck at wide intervals are grand and solemn in character. The *pianissimo* of the bass drum on its own, on the other hand, is dark and menacing (if the instrument is large and well made), like distant cannonfire. In the *Dies iræ* of my *Requiem* I used the bass drum *forte* without cymbals and with two sticks. Striking with one stick on each side of the instrument, the player can execute a rapid succession of notes. Mingling (as it does in this work) with timpani rolls in several parts as part of an orchestration full of threatening effects, this can give an impression of the strange and terrifying noises that signal great natural catastrophes.

Elsewhere, in a symphony, when I wanted a muffled roll much lower in pitch than that of the lowest timpani I had a single bass drum placed upright like a side drum and played by two timpanists at once.

Berlioz's detestation of the abuse of the bass drum is to be found throughout his writings, from as early as 1823.[1] Let it suffice to recall that in *Les soirées de l'orchestre* one member of Berlioz's imaginary story-loving orchestra never strays from his task:

> A single member of this orchestra is never distracted. Devoted to his work, energetic, indefatigable, and with his eyes glued to the music and his arms in incessant movement, he would think it a disgrace to miss a single quaver or to allow any lapse in the quality of his sound. At the end of each act he is flushed, perspiring and exhausted, panting for breath. Yet he dare not seize the opportunity of a suspension of musical hostilities to have a glass of beer in a nearby bar. The fear alone of coming back late and missing the first few bars of the next act is enough to nail him to his post. One day the theatre manager, impressed by his zeal, sent him six bottles of wine by way of encouragement. Far from looking on this gift with gratitude, the player, conscious of his worth, sent it back to the manager with these proud words: 'I am not in need of encouragement!' It must be obvious that I am speaking of the bass drum player.[2]

In a feuilleton of 1835 Berlioz insisted that Weber never used the bass drum, that Beethoven used it only once, and that *Il barbiere di Siviglia* and other Rossini works have no bass drum at all.[3] He was wrong, though, in thinking that it had no place in the eighteenth-century orchestra, since it appears in a number of Gluck's scores as part of a 'Turkish' battery for exotic effects, as it does also in Mozart's *Die Entführung* and Haydn's Symphony no. 100. He later acknowledged that Gluck

---

[1] *Cm*, 1, p. 1.   [2] *Les soirées de l'orchestre*, pp. 21–2.
[3] *Jd*, 15 November 1835; *Cm*, 2, p. 348; Condé, p. 202.

had written for the bass drum in *Iphigénie en Aulide*[4] and rebuked Rossini for his excessive resort to the bass drum in *Le siège de Corinthe* and *Moïse*.[5]

For fear of the ubiquitous coupling of bass drum and cymbals Berlioz frequently marked his bass drum entries 'sans cymbales' (and the converse).

Perhaps Berlioz's most pointed attack on the abuse of the bass drum is found in his own music. The music for Pierrot/Pasquarello in *Benvenuto Cellini* satirises the worst in contemporary vulgarity by coupling an ophicleide solo with brutish thumps of the bass drum on the first beat of every bar (*NBE* 1b: 640).

In a more positive fashion Berlioz's scores amply illustrate his concern to use the bass drum for delicate *piano* effects as well as for irregular rhythmic counterpoint and for programmatic purposes. His favourite device of combining bass drum and cymbals for scenes of solemnity will be discussed in the section on the cymbals. On its own and played softly the bass drum can have an almost mystical grandeur, best illustrated by its *pianissimo* entries at bar 299 of the *Francs-juges* overture (*B&H* 4: 57), in the *Lacrimosa* in the *Requiem* (*NBE* 9: 74) and in Cellini's 'Seul pour lutter' (*NBE* 1c: 997), where the bass drum, marked '*mf presque p*', contributes to the awe with which Cellini awaits the judgment of the city of Rome.

There is a good example of the bass drum being used as a rhythmic counterpoint in the final scene of *Les Troyens* (*NBE* 2b: 723), where string tremolos and *piano* bass drum strokes supply a three-beat pulse against the prevailing 4/4 tempo, a disturbing element in the priestly solemnity of the scene. There is another example in the *Reine Mab* scherzo in *Roméo et Juliette* (*NBE* 18: 216); here, as often elsewhere, the bass drum carries a hint of distant battle.[6] In the *Marche hongroise* in *La damnation de Faust* the bass drum entry (*NBE* 8a: 67) evokes 'the thud of distant cannon'.[7] At bar 200 of *Le cinq mai* (*NBE* 12a: 387) a 'very large' bass drum has *piano* entries to suggest the sound of distant cannonfire marking the death of Napoleon.

A remarkable solo for bass drum is found in the last verse of *Hymne à la France* (*NBE* 12b: 148–57). Its intermittent majestic blows punctuate the music at decreasing intervals to create a feeling of intense patriotic fervour.

Twice in *Les Troyens* the bass drum is used to suggest the sound of breaking waves. The *Septuor* in Act IV (*NBE* 2b: 567) uses the bass drum, with low horns and low strings, to evoke the intermittent, rhythmically irregular sound of the 'slumbering sea'. Shortly after that, at the beginning of Act V (*NBE* 2b: 597), a single stroke of the bass drum accompanies a sudden surge of wind and tide before the last verse of Hylas's song.

Berlioz cites the *Dies iræ* from the *Requiem* and 'a symphony' (in fact the finale of the *Symphonie fantastique*) as examples of the two methods of striking rapid blows on the bass drum. In the first method the two drumheads are vertical and the player is free to strike both sides with left and right sticks (*NBE* 9: 32, 45). This is also found in the *Tempête* fantasy (*NBE* 7: 88) for an effect of distant thunder and in the last finale of *Benvenuto Cellini* (*NBE* 1c: 1168). The *Requiem*'s illustration of the noise accompanying 'great natural catastrophes' is echoed in later works. This rapid

[4] *A travers chants*, pp. 124, 195.   [5] *Ibid.*, pp. 125–6.
[6] Ian Kemp, 'Romeo and Juliet and Roméo et Juliette', in *Berlioz Studies*, ed. Peter Bloom (Cambridge, 1992), p. 69.
[7] *Memoirs*, 'Travels in Germany', II/3.

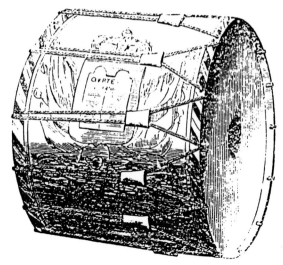

7 Bass drum.

reiteration of loud strokes is heard also in *Pandæmonium* in *La damnation de Faust* (*NBE* 8a: 420) and, more strikingly, in Act II of *Les Troyens* (*NBE* 2a: 212) for the 'bruit d'écroulement' that wakes the sleeping Aeneas.

In the second method the bass drum is set 'upright', implying that the head is horizontal, since the bass drum in Berlioz's time was often longer (deeper) than it was wide.[8] This was superseded by the shallower bass drum used today. In the *Symphonie fantastique* two drummers, both with sponge-headed sticks, play the same side of the drum (*NBE* 16: 115). Another example of this technique is found in the *Chœur d'ombres* in *Lélio* (*NBE* 7: 8). Both in the *Symphonie fantastique* and in *Lélio* Berlioz originally gave instructions to cover the head with a cloth as a form of mute.[9]

CYMBALS

Cymbals are very often used in conjunction with the bass drum, but as I have just observed of that instrument, they can often be used successfully on their own. Their high-pitched shimmering sound, with a noise that can be heard over every other noise in the orchestra, is ideal for various purposes, whether for extreme ferocity – in conjunction with the shrill whistling of piccolos and the thud of timpani or side drum – or for the feverish whirl of a bacchanale where joy turns to fury. Cymbals have never been used to so fine an effect as in the Scythians' Chorus 'Les dieux appaisent leur courroux' in Gluck's *Iphigénie en Tauride*.

[8] Peter H. Tanner, 'Timpani and percussion writing in the works of Hector Berlioz', p. 129.
[9] *NBE*, 16, p. xv, and 7, p. xvi.

A pronounced energetic rhythm in a large-scale chorus or orgiastic ballet gains greatly from being played not by a single pair of cymbals but by four, six, ten, or even more pairs, depending on the size of the building and the number of other instruments and voices.

The composer must always take care to specify the duration of cymbal notes, with a rest afterwards. If he wants the sound prolonged he must write long sustained notes as in Ex. 162a with the indication 'laissez vibrer'. In the opposite case he must write a quaver or semiquaver as in Ex. 162b, with the words 'étouffez le son', effected by pressing the cymbals to the player's chest as soon as he has clashed them.

Ex. 162

(a)

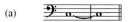

(b)

A sponge-headed timpani stick or a bass drum stick is sometimes used to set in vibration a cymbal suspended by its strap. This produces a metallic shimmering of quite long duration, sinister in effect but without the formidable impact of a blow on the tamtam.

For the use of cymbals in conjunction with piccolos to express ferocity, see above under 'Piccolo' (p. 147). There are many examples in his music. The 'feverish whirl of a bacchanale' is probably a reference to Spontini's ballet music for *Les Danaïdes*, also mentioned under 'Piccolo', although Berlioz never asked for such repetitive cymbal clashes as those in the Gluck example he cites.

He often requires more than a single pair of cymbals. Three pairs are needed in *La mort d'Orphée*, the *Sanctus* in the *Requiem*, and the *Symphonie funèbre et triomphale*. Some sources for the latter work suggest that nine or ten pairs were used in its original processional version.[10] The *Te deum* requires 'four or five' pairs. In the *Dies iræ* and the *Lacrimosa* of the *Requiem* he requires 'ten pairs', but since they are to be struck a single blow with a stick in each movement in support of the tamtams (*NBE* 9: 44, 94), ten cymbals rather than ten pairs are strictly the requirement. Yet the earliest sources of these entries specify 'six cymbals',[11] and when preparing his concert of 16 March 1845 at the Cirque Olympique, at which the *Dies iræ* from the *Requiem* was performed, Berlioz enquired about the price of 'twenty pairs of good cymbals'.[12]

In Act I of *Les Troyens* 'several pairs' of cymbals are heard offstage to simulate the sound of arms within the Wooden Horse (*NBE* 2a: 192), and in the carnival scene in *Benvenuto Cellini* there are to be 'fifteen or twenty tambourines and cymbals in the hands of the dancers and singers. The dancers who play these instruments should be dressed as satyrs and bacchantes' (*NBE* 1b: 572).

[10] *NBE*, 19, p. 109.   [11] *NBE*, 9, pp. 155–6.   [12] *Cg*, 3, p. 230.

Striking a suspended cymbal is a favourite device, always explained in full, as for example in *Roméo et Juliette* (*NBE* 18: 220), and the sponge-headed stick or bass drum stick is always specified. The instructions 'laissez vibrer' and 'étouffez le son' are common. In *Benvenuto Cellini* the indication 'sec' is used several times. At the moment in that opera when Pompeo receives a fatal swordthrust from Cellini the cymbals are given the following instructions: 'On this note the cymbals must not be struck one against the other but must be pulled sharply away from each other with a rapid rubbing motion after having brought them *silently* together in advance' (*NBE* 1b: 671), a device which anticipates the instruction 'zischend' in Strauss's *Ein Heldenleben*.

The *Sardanapale* fragment includes an early example of the two-plate roll (*NBE* 6: 217). A full orchestral climax is supported by 'the noise of cymbals one against the other', notated as a five-bar tremolo.

The cymbals are often to be clashed rapidly again and again. This is found, two notes at a time, in the overture to *Benvenuto Cellini* (*NBE* 1a: 24, 84), and at the end of the *Symphonie funèbre et triomphale* (*NBE* 19: 87–8) the cymbals have fast triplet clashes in the same rhythm as the melody. There is a run of twelve rapid clashes in the first version of the carnival scene in *Benvenuto Cellini* (*NBE* 1b: 605). This effect is often meant to suggest horror or catastrophe. Two examples, from *La damnation de Faust* and *Les Troyens*, have been mentioned in the section above on the bass drum, which has to execute the same figure.

The blending of soft cymbal clashes with soft bass drum strokes and chords from brass or harps creates a sound of impressive solemnity used more than once by Berlioz with telling effect. The pope's entrance in Tableau 3 of *Benvenuto Cellini* (*NBE* 1c: 853) provides an excellent example; another is Priam's blessing of Astyanax in Act I of *Les Troyens* (*NBE* 2a: 119). In the *Sanctus* of the *Requiem* the return of the opening section is profoundly intensified by the intermittent soft strokes of cymbals and bass drum (*NBE* 9: 120), and one could not overstate the poetic effect of the four strokes of cymbals and bass drum, marked progressively *p*, *pp*, *ppp* and *pppp*, at the end of *La captive* (*NBE* 13: 21–2).

Berlioz must often have played the percussion in his earlier concerts before he took to the podium. We have the authority of Jules Janin that he played the cymbals in his concert of 9 November 1834, which included *Le roi Lear* and the *Symphonie fantastique*,[13] and there must have been other occasions as well. This experience lies behind his pioneering exploration of new ways to play the cymbals and also behind his critical attention to the quality of the instruments themselves. In his report on German orchestras in 1843 he wrote:

Should I also mention the cymbals? Yes, if only to tell you that a whole and unblemished pair, neither cracked nor chipped, is extremely rare; I did not find one in Weimar, Leipzig, Dresden, Hamburg or Berlin. This always made me furious, and I have kept an orchestra waiting for half an hour and refused to start the rehearsal until they brought me two brand new cymbals, suitably vibrant and Turkish, to show the kapellmeister whether I was wrong to object so strongly to the ludicrous fragments of broken plate offered to me under that name.[14]

[13] Jules Janin in *Jd*, 24 November 1834.   [14] *Memoirs*, 'Travels in Germany', I/7.

THE TAMTAM

The tamtam, or gong, is used only for scenes of mourning or for the dramatic depiction of extreme horror. Played *forte* along with strident brass chords on trumpets and trombones, its tremor can be terrifying, and exposed *pianissimo* strokes on the tamtam, with their gloomy reverberations, are no less alarming. M. Meyerbeer has proved as much in the magnificent scene of the resurrection of the nuns in *Robert le diable*.

Gossec introduced the tamtam as an orchestral instrument in his *Marche lugubre* (1790), and it was later used by both Le Sueur and Spontini.[15] Berlioz used it occasionally throughout his career, from the *Messe solennelle* to *Les Troyens*. In the *Resurrexit* of the *Messe solennelle* the two important entries on the tamtam were taken out in later versions.[16] In the *Requiem* four tamtams are required, and in the *Symphonie funèbre et triomphale* two tamtams took part in the 1840 processional performances.[17] In *La damnation de Faust* Berlioz gives the following unusual instructions (*NBE* 8a: 416): 'Two timpanists roll with sponge-headed sticks on a tamtam suspended by its strap. Another person must hold the tamtam in the air while the timpanists do the roll.' It is as if Berlioz supposed that the tamtam, like a cymbal, was attached to its strap at the centre rather than at the edge. The third player's function can only be to steady the instrument, rather than to 'hold it in the air'.

A blow on the tamtam can have a portentous dramatic function. In *Benvenuto Cellini* a tamtam is struck at the moment when the cast of the statue explodes (in the Paris versions only; *NBE* 1c: 1172). In *La damnation de Faust* a tamtam and a bass drum, *pianissimo*, mark the moment when Faust signs away his soul (*NBE* 8a: 399). And in *Les Troyens* a tamtam hidden in Aeneas's shield gives out a 'long lugubrious sound' when struck by Mercury's caduceus (*NBE* 2b: 589). Here the marking ***mf*** recalls the unusual indication 'demifort' attached to the tamtam note in the *Resurrexit* (*NBE* 12a: 400).

At the first performance of the *Messe solennelle* in 1825 Berlioz himself took charge of the tamtam and was so moved by the occasion that at the climax of the *Resurrexit* 'I delivered such a mighty blow on the tamtam that the whole church shook. It was not my fault if the ladies failed to think that the end of the world was nigh.'[18]

THE TAMBOURINE

This is a favourite instrument with Italian peasants, always prominently heard at any festivity. It is very effective when several are used (like cymbals and together with them) to beat out a rhythm in a frenzied dance. It is not normally played solo in the orchestra except when the subject of the piece requires the depiction of the customs of those peoples who customarily use it, such as Gypsies, Basques, and Italians from Rome or the Abruzzi or Calabria.

---

[15] David Charlton, 'New sounds for old: tam-tam, tuba curva, buccin', *Soundings*, 3 (1973), p. 39.
[16] *NBE*, 23, p. xxx, and 12a, pp. x, 400.   [17] *NBE*, 19, p. 109.   [18] *Cg*, 1, p. 96.

It makes three quite different sounds. Simply struck with the hand its reverberation is very short. Unless there are many of them the tambourine struck in this way cannot really be heard unless the other instruments drop out. If the tambourine head is rubbed with the fingertips it produces a roll dominated by the sound of the little bells fixed round the edge; it is written as in Ex. 163a. But this roll must be very short because the fingers rubbing the head quickly reach the circumference and have to stop. A roll as in Ex. 163b, for instance, would be impossible.

Ex. 163

(a)

(b)

If on the other hand the head is rubbed with the flesh of the thumb, without stopping, the instrument makes a wild rattling sound. Ugly and grotesque though it is, it would not be absolutely impossible to make some use of it in certain types of masquerade.

True to his precept, Berlioz always wrote for two or more tambourines (with one exception), and always in an Italian setting. He heard it in Subiaco in 1831:

> Last night the children of the house danced a saltarello to the accompaniment of a tambourine played by the little girl from next door. [. . .] All the little peasant girls were wild with joy dancing with carefree abandon while the girl shook her tambourine and I flayed my fingers improvising saltarellos on the *chitarra francese!*[19]

Two months later he reported: 'The peasants never danced in my presence except to the sound of a tambourine; they adore that *melodious instrument.*'[20]

The *Orgie de brigands* in *Harold en Italie* was the appropriate setting for Berlioz's first use of the tambourine. In the autograph the 's' has been added to the entry 'tambour(s) de basque' throughout, although the number is not specified. At bar 157 (*NBE* 17: 145) there is found perhaps the first orchestral use of the finger-roll. Tambourines feature prominently in *Benvenuto Cellini*. In the *Chœur de masques* in the first Tableau both types of roll are found simultaneously (*NBE* 1a: 138): the first tambourine has a finger-roll while the second has a 'buzzing done by rubbing the thumb', as in Ex. 164. In the finale of the first Tableau the tambourine is used in a remarkable way: 'A timpanist plays a tambourine by striking it and rolling on it with his sticks; the tambourine must be placed on one of the timpani with the head upwards' (*NBE* 1a: 311). In the carnival scene, as we observed in the section on the cymbals, a group of fifteen or twenty singers and dancers play tambourines and cymbals, an effect described here in the *Treatise*, 'beating out the rhythm of a frenzied dance' (*NBE* 1b: 572).

[19] *Ibid.,* p. 473.   [20] *Ibid.,* p. 486.

Ex. 164

Tambourines are used in both *Roméo et Juliette* (*Fête chez Capulet*) and *Béatrice et Bénédict* to stress their Italian background. In the latter the chorus are directed to hold tambourines in their hands and 'shake them so as to make the little bells ring' (*NBE* 3: 44). The opening scene of Act II requires a single tambourine, probably intended to be played on stage.

Berlioz notated the tambourines, like most other percussion, on a bass clef.

THE SIDE DRUM

The side drum ('tambour', also known as 'caisse claire') is not often appropriate except in large wind bands. Its effect is better and nobler the more of them there are. A single side drum I always find feeble and vulgar, especially as part of a normal orchestra. I should acknowledge, however, that M. Meyerbeer succeeded in creating an especially awe-inspiring sound by pairing one side drum with the timpani for the famous crescendo roll in the *Bénédiction des poignards* in *Les huguenots*. But eight, ten, twelve or more side drums providing a rhythmic accompaniment or a crescendo roll can give magnificently powerful support to the wind. Simple rhythms which are without melody, harmony, tonality or anything that goes to make true music and which are intended simply to mark the pace of soldiers marching can be overwhelming when played by a body of forty or fifty side drums on their own.

It is worth pausing to mention the very real and special appeal of hearing a multiple unison: the simultaneous playing of an enormous number of kindred instruments, no matter what noise they make. This may perhaps be familiar from watching infantry drill: the little smack of the rifle band and the thud of the butt striking the ground on the commands 'slope arms!' and 'order arms!' has no significant impact when one, two, three or even ten or twenty men execute the command. But if the drill is done by a thousand men, those thousand unisons of a noise insignificant in itself will at once add up to a brilliant effect which cannot fail to catch your attention and hold you in thrall. It is a source of pleasure in which I find a certain vague, mysterious harmony.

Muffled drums are used as for the timpani, but instead of covering the skin with a piece of cloth players often just slacken the snares or slide a strap between the snares and the lower skin to prevent it vibrating. This gives the side drum a flat, dull sound rather like the noise made when the upper skin is covered. Muffled drums are suitable only for pieces conveying lamentation or terror.

Berlioz's instructions imply the existence of two kinds of side drum, which he does not explain in the *Treatise*. He usually calls for the plain 'tambour', but there are occasional demands for the 'tambour militaire', for example in the discarded *Prélude* of the *Te deum* (*NBE* 10: 174) where six military drums are required. There is a small part for a 'tambour militaire' in one version of Fieramosca's Air in *Benvenuto Cellini* (*NBE* 1b: 459). These may be references to the larger 'caisse roulante' described below under 'Tenor drum'. While the side drum in Berlioz's time was deeper and larger than it is today, there were certainly larger variants of the instrument with which Berlioz was probably familiar. A puzzling reference is found in a list of instruments playing the *Symphonie funèbre et triomphale* in 1840, where the two groups of side drums are described respectively as 'tambours' and 'tambours ordinaires'.[21]

Sometimes a single side drum is required, sometimes 'several'. Four are needed in the *Te deum* (apart from the six just mentioned in the *Prélude*), five in *L'impériale*, six in the *Hamlet* march, eight in the *Symphonie funèbre et triomphale* playing in two parts with four on each (some sources give numbers ranging from four to eighteen[22]). In the *Chanson de brigands* in *Lélio* there was originally a part for side drums, but this was later taken out (*NBE* 7: 199).

The side drums are frequently to be muffled, with the instruction 'voilés' or 'sans timbres' or both. This is cancelled by 'dévoilés' or 'avec les timbres', as in the *Marche* at the end of the *Te deum* (*NBE* 10: 141). As illustrations of the character of muffled side drums the *Hamlet* march falls into the category of lamentation, while the *Judex crederis* in the *Te deum* is clearly meant to inspire terror.

The side drum is another percussion instrument on which Berlioz may have had some passing experience as a player. Early in the *Memoirs* he mentions that he once played it, and in his account of the journey to Russia in 1847 he tells how he offered, facetiously no doubt, to play it again for the benefit of the Grand Marshal's wife.[23]

THE TENOR DRUM

The tenor drum ('caisse roulante') is a little longer than the side drum with a shell made of wood rather than copper. Its sound is dull, rather like a side drum muffled or without snares. It is very effective in military bands and its sombre roll acts like a half-tint to that of the side drum. It was a tenor drum that was used by Gluck to give such a barbaric rhythm striking the four repeated quavers in each bar of the Scythians' Chorus in *Iphigénie en Tauride*.

Unless the 'tambour militaire' mentioned in the previous section is the same as the tenor drum, Berlioz's only use of the latter is in the *Marche et Hymne* in Act I of *Les Troyens* (*NBE* 1a: 95) where its part is in unison with a side drum without

[21] *NBE*, 19, p. 109.   [22] *Ibid.*   [23] *Memoirs*, chapter 55.

snares. In the *Dies iræ* in the *Requiem* there is a part for a 'grosse caisse roulante en Si bémol', which is to be placed upright and played with two timpani sticks (*NBE* 9: 28). The problem of tuning an instrument that is traditionally unpitched is not easily resolved. It is always heard at the same time as timpani tuned to B♭.

THE TRIANGLE

Like the bass drum, like cymbals, like timpani, like trombones, like everything that booms, clangs or clatters, the triangle is deplorably abused these days. It has even greater difficulty than these other instruments in finding an appropriate role in the orchestra. Its metallic sound is only suitable for loud sections in extremely brilliant pieces, or for playing softly in strange, bizarre passages. Weber made the most felicitous use of it in his Gypsies' Chorus in *Preciosa* (Ex. 165a), and Gluck's use was even better in the *maggiore* section of the terrifying Scythians' Chorus in Act I of *Iphigénie en Tauride* (Ex. 165b).

Ex. 165

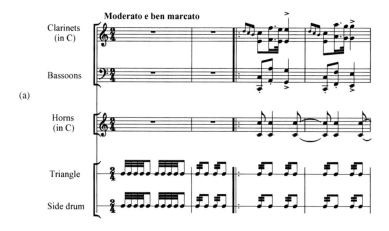

Berlioz treated the triangle, like the tambourine, as an Italian peasant instrument, even though it was found in the standard eighteenth-century Turkish percussion group. He did not use it before his trip to Italy, where he describes a serenade he heard in Subiaco which included 'a small iron instrument like a triangle which they call "stimbalo" '.[24] It is used (with great delicacy) in the opening section of *Harold en Italie* and several times in *Benvenuto Cellini*. It provides the metallic ting of Fieramosca's swordthrusts in his air 'Ah! qui pourrait me résister?' (*NBE* 1b: 459) and lends a brilliant urgency to the 'moccoli' chorus a little later in the same scene. Two unison triangles are heard in the *Fête chez Capulet* in *Roméo et Juliette*. It has a more general ethnic character in the *Marche marocaine* and the *Marche hongroise*.

In the *Marche et Hymne* in Act I of *Les Troyens* (*NBE* 2a: 95) there is a part for 'jeu de triangles' assigned to a series of seven pitches between f' and d''. Although triangles are traditionally regarded as unpitched percussion, Berlioz later, in the chapter on 'The orchestra' (p. 331), suggests that triangles may be tuned. Although no such instrument is known, the effect would doubtless be similar to that of the 'jeu de timbres'.[25]

Weber's *Preciosa*, which features a tambourine as well as a triangle, was first played in Paris in 1825, when Berlioz saw it more than ten times.[26] It was heard again in Paris in 1842 and 1858, when Berlioz praised its orchestration: 'Ah! you miserable disciples of the Parisian school, you ought to study this score night and day to learn how to write for the modern orchestra using all its resources without clumsiness, without cacophony, without crudity, without vulgarity and without losing an ounce of its energy.'[27]

[24] *Ibid.*, chapter 38.
[25] *NBE*, 2c, p. 757, is in error in suggesting that Berlioz did not imagine a set of tuned triangles.
[26] *Jd*, 23 April 1858; Condé, p. 346n. But according to Loewenberg, *Annals of Opera* (Totowa, 1978), col. 672, *Preciosa* was played one night only in 1825.
[27] *Jd*, 23 April 1858; Condé, p. 348.

Berlioz learned also from Rossini's use of the triangle in the overture to *Guillaume Tell*:

> The triangle is here extremely appropriate, with its little *pianissimo* ting sounding at intervals. It is the little bell attached to the sheep grazing quietly while their shepherds exchange their merry songs. 'Ah!' someone will say, 'so you see some dramatic purpose in this use of the triangle? In that case, kindly tell us, what do the violins or the violas or the cellos or the clarinets etc. represent?' To which I reply that the latter musical instruments are the fundamentals of the art, while the triangle, being merely a simple piece of iron whose sound does not belong with the recognisable sounds of the orchestra, should not be heard in the middle of a soft, gentle piece without very good reason, otherwise it will seem absurdly out of place.[28]

It is worth quoting a charming letter from Berlioz to Pohl of 28 August 1861: 'Liszt tells me you need a triangle: here's one made by Sax which has just been used here [in Baden-Baden] for the first time in the opening section of *Harold*. Like all triangles it's made in the image of God, but unlike most triangles (and unlike God) it plays true.'[29]

THE TURKISH CRESCENT

With its numerous little bells the Turkish crescent ('pavillon chinois') lends brilliance to noisy pieces like ceremonial marches for military band. It can only shake its sonorous mane at fairly wide intervals, that is to say about every half-bar at moderate tempo.

Known in French as 'pavillon chinois' or 'chapeau chinois' and in English as 'Turkish crescent' or 'jingling Johnny', this spectacular instrument had been adopted by European military bands since the middle of the eighteenth century. Unlike the other Turkish percussion instruments, the Turkish crescent was not absorbed by the classical orchestra, but Berlioz found occasion to use it in two of his compositions. It appears in the last movement of the *Symphonie funèbre et triomphale* and in the arrangement of Meyer's *Marche marocaine* of 1845. In both pieces it plays, as Berlioz recommends, no more than two notes to a bar. In the processional performances of the first of these in 1840 there were apparently four Turkish crescents taking part,[30] the same number envisaged by Berlioz in his ideal orchestra (see below, p. 330). In his description of the carnival he witnessed in Rome in 1832 a Turkish crescent is among the instruments playing on a small platform in the Piazza Navona.[31]

---

[28] *Gm*, 12 October 1834; Condé, p. 54; *Cm*, 1, p. 403.   [29] *Cg*, 6, p. 245.   [30] *NBE*, 19, p. 109.
[31] *Memoirs*, chapter 36; Brian Chenley, ' "Jingling Johnny": a note on the *pavillon chinois*', *Berlioz Society Bulletin*, 36 (1961), p. 4.

8   The *chapeau chinois.*

OTHER INSTRUMENTS

We will not here go into some little-known instruments of variable util-
ity such as the aéolidicon, the anémocorde, the acordéon, the poikilorgue, the antique sistrum etc., but merely refer the enquiring reader to
M. Kastner's excellent *Traité général d'instrumentation* for further information. Our purpose in the present work is simply to study instruments which
are used in modern music and to seek the laws which govern the setting up
of harmonious combinations and effective contrasts between them while
making special note of their expressive capabilities and of the character
appropriate to each.

The curious instruments Berlioz lists from Kastner's treatise were keyboard, not percussion, instruments, with the exception of the antique sistrum, for which Berlioz did later find a use. An unspecified number of sistra are heard on stage in the *Marche et Hymne* in Act I of *Les Troyens* (*NBE* 2a: 103) at the moment when Aeneas and his warriors make their first appearance. Kastner clarified the nature of the sistrum, which was Egyptian in origin, in his *Manuel général de musique militaire* (1848), where an illustration is given. The sistrum consists of a bronze frame through which metal rods pass. On the rods are rings and bells, which sound when the instrument is shaken.[32] Berlioz might well have seen the ancient sistra preserved at Pompeii on his visit there in 1831.

Berlioz used a few additional percussion instruments which are not mentioned in the *Treatise*. In addition to the sistra *Les Troyens* also requires a 'tarbuka' on stage for the *Pas d'esclaves nubiennes* in Act IV (*NBE* 2b: 536). The term is a variant of 'darabukkeh', 'tarabouki' and other spellings,[33] referring to a small goblet-shaped drum of Egyptian origin which the player strikes with his hand while sitting down. Berlioz has the part doubled by a 'tambourin' in the orchestra. This is a provençal drum with a long cylindrical body and a single snare, best known for its appearance in the *Farandole* in Bizet's *L'arlésienne*.

There is a part for castanets in the orchestral song *Zaïde*, clicking out a bolero rhythm. Since the castanets part is shown in the published piano reduction, the singer is probably intended to play the castanets herself in traditional Spanish style. A small anvil has a part in the chorus 'Bienheureux les matelots' in the last tableau of *Benvenuto Cellini* (*NBE* 1c: 1013). The anvil and two guitars keep up a persistent rhythm behind the plaintive choral melody based on a song Berlioz had heard in Italy. The anvil is to be struck with a small metalworker's hammer. Berlioz's use of the instrument had precedents in Kreutzer's *Abel* (1810), a work extravagantly admired by Berlioz;[34] Auber's *Le maçon* (1825); Spontini's *Alcidor* (1825); Pacini's *Il corsaro* (1831), which he may have heard in Rome; and Halévy's *La juive* (1835).[35]

These last two instruments come close to being sound effects, of which a number of examples are found in Berlioz's scores. In the opening scene of Act II in *Béatrice et Bénédict* there is a fully notated part for drinking glasses being banged on the table. A rumble of thunder is given a two-bar notation after Aeneas's departure in Act V of *Les Troyens* (*NBE* 2b: 678). The triple cannonade from the Castel Sant'Angelo is heard in the second tableau of *Benvenuto Cellini* (*NBE* 1b: 688), and at the climax of the *Marche pour la dernière scène d'Hamlet* a 'feu de peloton' is discharged in the distance, representing Shakespeare's 'peal of ordnance' (*NBE* 12b: 115). This category of instrumental effect recalls Berlioz's maxim stated in the introduction to the *Treatise* (see p. 5): 'Every sounding object employed by the composer is a musical instrument.'

In this connection we should quote Berlioz's words from an article in 1847:

---

[32] Ian Kemp, *Hector Berlioz: Les Troyens* (Cambridge, 1988), pp. 204–5.
[33] *Ibid.*, pp. 205–7.   [34] *Cg*, 1, pp. 70–1.
[35] *Les soirées de l'orchestre*, p. 221; David Charlton, 'Orchestration and orchestral practice in Paris, 1789–1810' (PhD diss., Cambridge, 1973), pp. 259–60. Mendelssohn's report on the anvil in *Il corsaro* is in his *Briefe aus den Jahren 1830 bis 1847* (Leipzig, 1899), p. 80.

In the field of percussion we have only poor quality instruments – useful no doubt for their purpose, but still of a lower order – such as timpani, cymbals, bass drum and triangle. All these sound machines, except the timpani, produce noises and not truly musical sounds. Furthermore they each play only one note, in which respect we are scarcely more advanced than the savages. We entirely lack a group of rich and varied percussion instruments with a precise sound, like the piano, but much more powerful. Blades, metal strips, gut strings, every size and shape of bell, glass vases and a host of sounding objects could be made into fine percussion instruments. It is just a question of discovering the system, and that will surely be done sooner or later. It is truly odd that despite the incredible proliferation of wind instruments for a hundred years or more and despite the wonderful advances that have transformed the harpsichord into the piano, no one has made any attempt to develop the orchestra in the direction I propose. In this area art has not taken a single step forward from the very beginning.[36]

[36] *Jd*, 12 October 1847.

13

New instruments

The author is doubtless under no sort of obligation to mention the multitude of experiments made daily by instrument manufacturers and their vaunted, mostly disastrous, inventions, nor to report the pointless individual specimens they would like to add to the race of instruments. But he should draw the attention of composers to the good advances made by inventive musicians, especially when their excellence is widely recognised and when they have already been adopted in the musical practice of a considerable part of Europe. These innovators are in any case few in number, and MM. Adolphe Sax and Edouard Alexandre stand at their head.

THE SAXOPHONE

We shall begin with M. Sax, who has made improvements to many well established instruments, as I have already indicated here and there in the course of the present study. He has filled many gaps in the family of brass instruments. His principal achievement in recent years, nonetheless, is the creation of a new family of instruments which use a single reed and a clarinet mouthpiece and are made of brass. These are the saxophones.

Berlioz played a crucial part in the early history of the saxophone and is generally credited with being the first to write about it. His support was critical in Sax's early success in Paris. Although this chapter of the *Treatise* was added for the 1855 edition, he first mentioned the saxophone in 1842 and wrote a brief section on it in the 1844 edition. For the sake of completeness I include here all Berlioz's writings on the saxophone in chronological order.

Sax first visited Paris in 1839, but it is not clear whether Berlioz met him then.[1] He visited the Paris Exhibition of that year, but did not exhibit, and Berlioz's

---

[1] 'Pleasant relationships were begun with Meyerbeer, Berlioz and Halévy, who listened with professional interest to Sax's demonstrations and discourse.' Wally Horwood, *Adolphe Sax 1814–1894: His Life and Legacy* (Baldock, 1983), p. 23.

account of the Exhibition does not mention him.[2] He returned to Paris in 1841, an opportune moment since Berlioz was then embarking on his extended study of instruments for the *Revue et gazette musicale*. In the article on the ophicleide of 13 March 1842 the saxophone was introduced to the world for the first time, though not by name:

> An invention notable for the beauty of sound it gives to the ophicleide is that of M. Sax of Brussels. He has replaced its mouthpiece with a clarinet mouthpiece. The ophicleide thus becomes a brass instrument with a reed. The difference in sound and tone quality resulting from this is so much to the instrument's benefit, according to all those in a position to judge, that the 'ophicléide à bec' will very probably come into general use in a few years' time.

This passage resolves the long dispute as to the origin of the saxophone, confirming that it was the application of a clarinet mouthpiece to an ophicleide that led to the invention, not the quest for a new kind of octave-overblowing clarinet, or any other factor. It also shows that the new instrument was to be a bass instrument designed to replace the ophicleide. Three months later, on 12 June 1842, before the series on instrumentation in the *Revue et gazette musicale* was complete, Berlioz again wrote about the saxophone, this time referring to it by name:

> The saxophon [*sic*], as the inventor calls it, is a brass instrument rather like the ophicleide in shape with nineteen keys. It is played with a bass clarinet mouthpiece, not with the kind of cup mouthpiece used by other brass instruments. The saxophon is designed to be the leading member of a new kind of family, that of brass with reeds. Its range is three octaves from Bb' upwards. Its fingering is similar to that of the flute or the second register of the clarinet. As for its sound, I know of no bass instrument in current use with which it can be compared. It is full, velvety, vibrant, enormously powerful but quite capable of playing softly. In my view it is far superior to the lower notes of the ophicleide for intonation and steadiness of tone. Its character is really quite new, with no resemblance to any of the sounds heard in the orchestra today with the possible exception of the bass clarinet's low *F*. Because it is fitted with a reed the saxophon can swell the sound up and down. At the top it produces notes with a vibrant, penetrating quality which could well be used for melodic expression. It will probably never be suited to rapid passages and complicated arpeggios, but low instruments were never intended for delicate manœuvres. Rather than complain about this, one should be thankful that the saxophon cannot therefore be abused and that its majestic character cannot be destroyed by having to play musical frivolities.

The instrument Berlioz describes corresponds to the bass saxophone, lower than any of the saxophones in regular use today. Its derivation from the ophicleide gave it the same low range and an upward-pointing bell. In the following year, 1843, Berlioz added a section on the saxophone in the proofs of the *Treatise* as an adjunct to the section on the clarinet (not the chapter on the ophicleide):

[2] *Jd*, 28 May 1839.

The saxophone is a large low-pitched brass instrument invented by Ad. Sax, who gave it its name. It is played not with a cup mouthpiece like an ophicleide (to which it bears no resemblance) but with a bass clarinet mouthpiece. We therefore class it unhesitatingly with the clarinet family.

The saxophone is a transposing instrument in B♭. Its range is from B' chromatically up to c'', sounding a tone lower, i.e. from A' up to bb'. Trills are possible throughout the range, but I believe they should be used with great circumspection.

The saxophone's tone is rather piercing and painful at the top, while its low notes, on the other hand, are grand and pontifical, so to speak. Like the clarinet it can swell up and down, which results in some unusual and unique effects especially at the bottom of its range. For pieces of mysterious and solemn character the saxophone is in my view the finest low voice ever heard. It resembles both the bass clarinet and the harmonium, this being sufficient indication surely that it should normally be used only at a slow tempo. It would also perform admirably as a solo instrument, supporting and colouring the harmony of a group of voices and wind instruments. Despite its extraordinary power it is unsuitable for the energetic, brilliant style of military music.

Berlioz's emphasis that the saxophone is not like an ophicleide suggests that he no longer regarded it as a potential replacement of the ophicleide at the bottom of the brass section, but more aptly as a relative of the clarinet. Yet it still had an ophicleide's shape and range; there is no mention here of a family of saxophones. Shortly before publication of the *Treatise* the saxophone was heard in public for the first time in Berlioz's concert of 3 February 1844. The *Hymne pour instruments de Sax* was an arrangement, now regrettably lost, of the *Chant sacré* for high E♭ cylinder trumpet, E♭ cylinder bugle, B♭ cylinder bugle, soprano clarinet, bass clarinet and saxophone with orchestral accompaniment.[3] Sax himself played the saxophone, the lowest member of the group.

In 1846 Sax took out a fifteen-year patent for a family of saxophones.[4] He had by now developed two members of the family: a 'tenor' in E♭, corresponding to the modern baritone saxophone, and a bass in B♭ or C. The latter still had the ophicleide form, but the 'tenor' saxophone had the characteristic forward tilt of the bell. The patent also includes sketches for six other sizes: two larger members, termed 'contrabass' and 'bourdon', and four smaller members shaped like bass clarinets and clarinets. Kastner published a *Méthode* for saxophone in the same year and a family of about six members was soon established. Although very little correspondence has survived, Berlioz became a close friend of Sax and was often using Sax's premises as a forwarding address and for rehearsals.

In the *Journal des débats* on 12 October 1847 Berlioz reported that the saxophone, 'that instrument thought to be purely mythical and commonly said not

---

[3] Horwood, *Adolphe Sax*, Appendix A; Holoman, *Catalogue*, p. 83.
[4] The patent is given in Horwood, *Adolphe Sax*, Appendix C, with illustrations.

to exist', had won a number of prizes at the Concours du Gymnase. The King had recently picked out the saxophone during a dinner and commended a band equipped with Sax instruments.

In the *Journal des débats* on 21 August 1849 he wrote again about the saxophone:

> The tone of the saxophone bridges the gap between the brass and the woodwind, but it also suggests, more remotely, the tone of the strings. In my view its principal advantage is the great variety and beauty of its different expressive capabilities. Sometimes low and calm, then passionate, dreamy or melancholy, sometimes tender like an echo, or like the vague plaintive sigh of the wind in the branches, or like the strange fading vibrations of a bell only after it has been struck. I know of no other instrument that possesses this particular capacity to reach the outer limits of audible sound. The only sounds that can give any idea of the saxophone's delicious half-tints and its suggestions of fading twilight are the *diminuendo* and *piano* of the cantors in the Russian Imperial Chapel, those wonderful singers who must make the good Lord envious of Tsar Nicholas. If they were applied to the skilful performance of some inspired poetic piece, these saxophone sounds would plunge the listener into an ecstatic state which I can imagine but cannot possibly attempt to describe.

Berlioz heaped more praise on the saxophone in the *Journal des débats* on 13 April 1851: 'It weeps, it sighs, it dreams, it can crescendo, it can fade gradually to the echo of an echo of an echo, to the very twilight of sound.'

Berlioz consistently praised Sax's instruments, especially at the Great Exhibition in 1851, and in 1852 he sprang to the defence of the saxophone when it was assailed by Scudo, critic of the *Revue des deux mondes*.[5] He was aware of the instrument's rapid development. When he came to reissue his *Treatise* in 1855, therefore, he had to rewrite the saxophone entry completely to read as follows:

> These new voices in the orchestra possess certain rare and precious qualities. Soft and penetrating in the upper register, full-bodied and smooth at the bottom, their middle range is somehow profoundly expressive. It is a tone quality *sui generis*, in short, vaguely comparable to that of the cello, the clarinet and the cor anglais, and endowed with a brassy colour which gives it its particular timbre.
>
> The body of the instrument is a parabolic cone made of brass equipped with keys. Being agile and almost as good at rapid figurations as at graceful cantilenas and dreamy or religious harmonic effects, saxophones can profitably feature in any kind of music, but especially in slow, soft movements.
>
> High notes on the bigger saxophones have a rather piercing and painful quality, while their low notes are grand and serene, almost pontifical. All of them, especially the bass and baritone saxophones, can swell up and down; this produces some unusual and unique effects especially at the bottom

[5] *Les grotesques de la musique*, pp. 91–2.

of the range which are entirely characteristic and somewhat resemble the harmonium. The tone of the higher saxophones is much more penetrating than that of clarinets in Bb or C, but without the piercing, often strident edge of the little Eb clarinet. This at least is the case with the soprano saxophone. One day some clever composer will do something marvellous with saxophones matched with the clarinet family or introduced in other combinations which it would be rash to attempt to predict.

This instrument is very easy to play, since the fingering is derived from the fingering of the flute and the oboe. Clarinettists, being already familiar with the embouchure, will master its mechanism in very little time.

Saxophones are six in number: sopranino ('aigu'), soprano, alto, tenor, baritone and bass. In fact M. Sax will shortly be producing a seventh, the contrabass saxophone. The range of each is about the same; according to the system proposed by M. Sax and already adopted by composers; each one is written on the treble clef, like clarinets. The range is chromatic throughout (see Table 11).

Table 11

	key	written range from	up to	sounding range from	up to
Sopranino	Eb	*b*	*d'''*	*d*	*f'''*
Soprano	C	*b*	*d'''*	*b*	*d'''*
	Bb	*b*	*d'''*	*a*	*c''*
Alto	F	*b*	*f'''*	*e*	*bb''*
	Eb	*b*	*f'''*	*d*	*ab''*
Tenor	C	*b*	*f'''*	*B*	*f''*
	Bb	*b*	*f'''*	*A*	*eb''*
Baritone	F	*b*	*f'''*	*E*	*bb'*
	Eb	*b*	*f'''*	*D*	*ab'*
Bass	C	*b*	*eb'''*	*B'*	*eb'*
	Bb	*b*	*eb'''*	*A'*	*db'*

Major and minor trills are possible on almost all the chromatic range of the saxophones. The following should be avoided:

$c\sharp' - d\sharp'$
$f\sharp' - g\sharp'$
$c'' - d''$
$c\sharp'' - d\sharp''$
$c''' - d'''$
$d''' - eb'''$
$d\sharp''' - e\sharp'''$
$e''' - f'''$

Despite the warmth of Berlioz's welcome to the new saxophone, it did not find a secure place in the orchestra and in the nineteenth century was mainly used in military bands, with occasional special appearances in the scores of Thomas, Bizet, Massenet and others. One reason for this was perhaps Berlioz's own reluctance to use it. In the 1840s Berlioz saw his career extending rapidly in Germany, England and elsewhere, where such instruments as the saxophone had few prospects of success. Yet it is hard not to speculate what the saxophone's subsequent career might have been if Berlioz had written freely for it in all his scores after 1844. The nearest he came to writing for it is in the autograph score of *La damnation de Faust*, composed in 1846. For the final movement, *Dans le ciel*, he originally pencilled the names 'tenor saxophone in Eb' and 'bass saxophone in Bb' against two staves which were left blank when the rest of the orchestration was filled in.[6] These would have been the instruments now known as baritone and bass saxophones, doubtless too heavy a sound for the ethereal atmosphere of heaven. When in 1848 Berlioz drew up his recommendations for new classes at the Paris Conservatoire he suggested the introduction of classes for the saxophone and the saxhorn (see below).[7]

Saxophones and saxhorns are mentioned in a document in Berlioz's hand of around 1851. These seem to be notes for a planned concert:

> 1 piccolo, 1 Eb clarinet, 6 clarinets, 10 saxhorns (two sets of the full family), 3 trombones, 2 cornets, 3 saxophones, 3 band double basses ('contrebasses à l'harmonie'), 2 side drums, 1 cymbal player. Have a carefully chosen programme of good pieces specially arranged for this orchestra by M. Bellon. M. Sax would have to get the necessary players in Paris or Brussels and have all the music copied before April 25th. M. M. Barnett has engaged a conductor for this project.

The document is signed by Berlioz and carries Sax's name and address (Rue St George 52) but is otherwise unidentified.[8]

SAXHORNS

M. Sax has also produced the families of saxhorns, saxotrombas and saxtubas, brass instruments with cup mouthpieces and a mechanism consisting of three, four or five valves.

The sound of saxhorns is round, pure, full, even, resonant and perfectly uniform throughout the range. Like cornets their various crooks range downwards from the standard little sopranino saxhorn ('petit saxhorn suraigu') in C, pitched an octave higher than the cornet in C. In France it has become standard practice to write all these instruments, including saxotrombas and saxtubas both high and low, on the treble clef, like horns, the only difference being that whereas the actual pitch of the horn in low

---

[6] *NBE*, 8b, p. 459 (where the two sizes of saxophone are wrongly identified).
[7] *Memoirs*, 'Travels in Germany', II/5.   [8] Unidentified facsimile in *NBE* files.

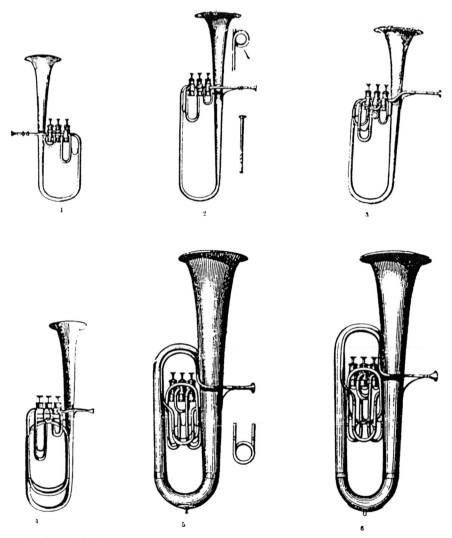

9   The family of saxhorns.

C is an octave below the written note on the treble clef, the actual pitch of some very low Sax instruments is two octaves below.

The ranges of the saxhorns are as in Table 12.

The little sopranino saxhorn's range also includes c, which on the sopranino saxhorn in C sounds c' and on the little sopranino saxhorn in B♭ sounds $b♭$. The lowest part of the range has rather poor tone quality and should not really be used below low a. But there is nothing more brilliant, more clear, or, despite its force, more unsoured than the whole top octave. The tone is, besides, so clear and penetrating that one can pick out a single sopranino saxhorn in a large group of wind instruments. The B♭

Table 12

	key	written range	sounding range
Sopranino	C	from $f\sharp$ to f''	from $f\sharp'$ to f'''
	B♭	from $f\sharp$ to f''	from e' to $e\flat'''$
Soprano	E♭	from $f\sharp$ to a''	from a to c'''
Alto	B♭	from $f\sharp$ to c'''	from e to $b\flat''$
Tenor	E♭	from $f\sharp$ to e'''	from A to g''
Baritone/Bass	B♭	from $f\sharp$ to e'''	from E to d''
Contrabass	E♭	from f to g'''	from $A\flat'$ to $b\flat'$
	B♭	from $f\sharp$ to c'''	from E' to $b\flat$
	low E♭	from f to g'''	from $A\flat''$ to $b\flat$
Bourdon	B♭	from $f\sharp$ to c'''	from E'' to $B\flat$

instrument is more usual than the C, and although it is a tone lower it is still difficult or at least very demanding on the player to reach the top two notes e'' and f'' (sounding d''' and $e\flat'''$). One should therefore be sparing with these precious notes and lead into them with care.

For the remaining saxhorns we do not list the first overtone, c; it is too poor to be used. We would simply warn composers that if they call for a four-valved instrument the chromatic range goes not just down to $f\sharp$ but all the way down to c.

The baritone and bass saxhorns both have the same range at the top. The baritone just has a slightly narrower bore while the bass, which nearly always has four valves, has a wider bore which allows it to go lower with greater ease.

Of the low contrabass saxhorn in E♭ and the bourdon saxhorn in B♭ pitched respectively an octave below the two previous saxhorns only the middle range should be used, and always in moderate tempo.

Sax patented the family of saxhorns in 1845. The instrument was derived from the valved bugle, and the resemblance of the saxhorn to existing instruments involved Sax in a long series of lawsuits. Yet by giving his instrument a new name and creating a uniform family of matched instruments he established the saxhorn as a principal section in French military bands and was successful too, with the help of the Distin family, in getting the saxhorn widely adopted by British brass bands. The saxhorns all retained the vertical format with the bell pointing upwards, but were built with a somewhat narrower bore than the tuba family. There were originally five sizes of saxhorn, extended in the 1850s to include the sopranino and the very large saxhorns shown in Berlioz's table.[9]

[9] A photograph of the six-foot-high bourdon saxhorn is shown in Horwood, *Adolphe Sax*, p. 120.

Berlioz warmly approved of the saxhorn from the beginning: 'Sax's new instruments, especially the cylinder bugles which he calls "saxhorns", have rare qualities of intonation and sound.'[10] The two cylinder bugles which took part in Berlioz's concert of 3 February 1844 (alongside the new saxophone) were probably saxhorns in all but name. In the account of his second tour of Germany published in 1848 he recommended the institution of a class in saxhorn at the Paris Conservatoire,[11] and unlike the saxophone the saxhorn found a place in Berlioz's scores.

In 1851 Sax added the smallest member to the family, the sopranino saxhorn ('saxhorn suraigu'), which prompted Berlioz to write to Sax:

> I paid you a visit to ask you to bring Arban to see me one day with a B♭ cornet and your little octave trumpet or saxhorn in B♭. I want to study the outer notes of their ranges and show you both a comparative table I have just made of the ranges of the four instruments based on the resonance of the tube which we were discussing this morning. There must be no uncertainty as to how to write for your little trumpet.[12]

Probably in the period 1851–3 Berlioz extended the *Te deum* by adding a *Marche* in which a sopranino saxhorn has a prominent part (*NBE* 10: 141–60, 187–91), and this, when played by Arban at the first performance in 1855, caused a sensation.[13] Since 1847 Sax had been in charge of the offstage band at the Opéra, where saxhorns were provided for Verdi's *Jérusalem* (1847), Meyerbeer's *Le prophète* (1849) and Halévy's *Le juif errant* (1852). Berlioz accordingly included a group of nine offstage saxhorns in *Les Troyens*, comprising one sopranino in high B♭, two sopranos in E♭, two altos in B♭, two tenors in E♭ and two contrabasses in E♭. Although he allowed conventional orchestral brass as alternatives to all of the saxhorns except the sopranino (for which no acceptable substitute existed), the characteristic tone-colour of saxhorns does (or should) dominate the elaborate orchestration of the finale of Act I, with the *Marche troyenne* accompanying the Trojan Horse into the city. They also have important parts in the *Chasse royale et orage*.[14]

For the performance of *L'impériale* at the Exposition Universelle in 1855 bass saxhorns doubled the ophicleides in the last few pages of the work.[15]

SAXOTROMBAS

These are brass instruments with a cup mouthpiece and three, four or five valves, like saxhorns. Their narrower bore gives the sound a more strident character, resembling the tone of both the trumpet and the bugle. The

---

[10] *Jd*, 1 April 1845.   [11] *Memoirs*, 'Travels in Germany', II/5.

[12] Letter from the period 1851–3, not in *Cg*; Metropolitan Opera House Archives, New York; *Nouvelles Lettres de Berlioz*, ed. Jacques Barzun (New York, 1954), p. 50.

[13] Théodore de Lajarte, *Instruments-Sax et fanfares civiles, étude pratique* (Paris, 1867), p. 13n.

[14] For Berlioz's use of saxhorns see Ian Kemp, *Hector Berlioz: Les Troyens* (Cambridge, 1988), pp. 208–12.

[15] *NBE*, 12b, p. 212.

family of saxotrombas has the same number of members as the saxhorn family. They are distributed in the same manner from high to low, with the same ranges.

The saxotrombas shared the saxhorns' vertical design and family homogeneity. Their bore was partly cylindrical, which gave them a more trumpet-like sound. But their success was short-lived and it is doubtful if Sax ever produced as many different sizes of saxotrombas as he did of saxhorns.[16] Berlioz never used a saxotromba.

SAXTUBAS

These are instruments with a cup mouthpiece and a three-valve mechanism. They make an enormous sound, audible from a great distance, and have an extraordinary effect in military bands in the open air. They should be treated just like saxhorns, except that there is no deep contrabass saxtuba in Eb and no bourdon saxtuba in Bb. Their elegantly rounded shape recalls the trumpets of antiquity on a much larger scale.

Sax designed the saxtubas for use on stage in Halévy's *Le juif errant* in 1852. They were constructed in a wide circular shape like the Roman buccina (to which Berlioz's comment refers) and were briefly successful as military instruments, especially on the occasion of the presentation of colours by Napoleon III in 1852, when it is said that twelve saxtubas dominated the entire massed bands of thirty regiments.[17]

THE CONCERTINA

This is a little instrument with brass tongues which are set in vibration by a current of air. In the accordion ('acordéon'), long regarded as a musical toy, lies the origin of the concertina and subsequently of the melodium. The concertina's sound is penetrating and soft at the same time; despite its weakness it carries quite far. It blends well with the tone of the harp or the piano, and it would go even better with the melodium, now the chief member of the family, except that there would be little point in such a pairing, since the melodium's tone is analogous to that of the concertina and it can produce the same effects, plus many others which the concertina does not have.

---

[16] For a photograph of four sizes of saxotromba see Horwood, *Adolphe Sax*, p. 61.
[17] Horwood, *Adolphe Sax*, p. 113.

The concertina is a kind of little elastic box held horizontally between the hands. It is played by means of buttons pressed by the fingertips, which lift a valve and allow the column of air, which is delivered by a pair of bellows located between the two ends of the box, to pass over the tongues or reeds of brass. The ends of the box consist of two plates bearing the keyboards of buttons on the outside and the vibrating tongues on the inside. Since the bellows have no valve, they cannot blow in or out unless the reed valves open and let the air needed to set the reeds in vibration alternately in and out.

The concertina has its own complete little family quite separate from its relative, the melodium. There are bass, alto and soprano concertinas. The bass concertina has the range of the cello, the alto that of the viola, the soprano that of the violin. The soprano is almost the only one in use. We will give as Ex. 166 the range of this concertina, known as the English concertina from its popularity in England.

Ex. 166

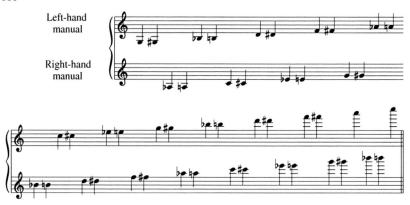

In the two chromatic scales shown in Ex. 166 – one representing the notes of the left-hand end, the other the right – it will be observed that the maker of the English concertina has introduced enharmonic intervals between Ab and G♯ and between Eb and D♯ in the lower three octaves, making Ab a bit higher than G♯ and Eb a bit higher than D♯ and conforming thus to acoustical doctrine, a doctrine entirely at variance with musical practice. This is a curious anomaly.

The concertina, having fixed pitches like the piano, organ and melodium, should clearly be tuned according to the principle of equal temperament. As it is, its enharmonic notes do not allow it to play with a piano or an organ or a melodium without striking discords when the musical phrase or the harmony requires unisons between the enharmonic Ab, G♯, Eb or D♯ on the concertina and the same notes, tempered, on the other instrument. This is because Ab and G♯ (or Eb and D♯) are identical on instruments with tempered tuning (unlike on the concertina) and because neither of the enharmonic notes A♭ and G♯ on the concertina will be in true unison with the A♭ or G♯ of the tempered instrument, which will fall between the concertina's two notes.

Furthermore the effect of this arrangement of part of its scale will be far worse if the concertina plays a duet with an instrument with adjustable pitch, like a violin, since musical practice, musical common sense, in fact the ears of all peoples who cultivate modern music all agree that in certain circumstances the notes called 'leading notes' are more or less subject to the attraction of the tonic above, and that minor sevenths and minor ninths are subject to the attraction of the note below on to which they resolve. Therefore the first of these, the leading note, can get a little sharper than it would be in the tempered scale, and the second a little flatter.

In Ex. 167a the flat *g♯′* on the concertina cannot thus be in tune with the violin's sharp *g♯′*, nor, in Ex. 167b, can the sharp *a♭′* on the one be in tune with the flat *a♭′* of the other, the two players subscribing to diametrically opposite laws, the *law of calculated vibrations* and the *musical law*, unless the violinist yields to the overriding need for a unison and plays in tune with the fixed-pitched instrument, in other words actually out of tune. On a small scale this can happen unconsciously without offending the ear when violinists play with the piano or other tempered instruments. But the extraordinary procedure which would reconcile the English concertina's system with the system of rising leading notes and falling sevenths in *music* would consist of taking the opposite line to the acousticians on the subject of enharmonics and using A♭ instead of G♯ and vice versa. The violinist who plays Ex. 167a musically would be more or less in tune with a concertina playing the same passage written out in the absurd way shown in Ex. 167c.

Ex. 167

The long-standing aspiration of acousticians to impose the results of their calculations on the practice of an art which is based above all on the study of the impressions made by sound upon the human ear can no longer be upheld today. For one thing, music rejects it utterly and can only survive if it does reject it. For another, the two-way modification of an interval between two notes which attract each other (in musical practice) is a very delicate nuance which solo instrumentalists and singers should use with immense care; orchestral players should normally do without it, and composers should anticipate its application and handle it accordingly. And for another thing, the great majority of musicians disregard it in harmonic textures, with the result that sounds which acousticians declare to be incompatible are perfectly well matched in musical practice, and intervals which should be discordant according to calculation are accepted as in tune by the ear, which pays no heed to imperceptible differences nor to mathematical logic. There is scarcely a single modern score where the composer has not written harmonic or melodic passages in sharps in one part of the orchestra (or chorus) and in flats in the other, either to facilitate performance or for any other reason, or for no reason at all. See Ex. 168a, and an example from a chorus from Meyerbeer's *Les huguenots*, Ex. 168b. Or, for a melodic example, Ex. 168c, where the two lines are in unison, or, for the impression of two different keys when just two notes are enharmonically related, see the passage from Weber's *Der Freischütz*, Ex. 168d. The cellos and basses here seem to be playing in G minor while the trombones seem to be in B♭ minor. If in this example the cellos and basses play their F♯ sharp and the trombones their G♭ flat, there would doubtless be audible discord. But in a good performance this must be avoided; then the two notes will be perfectly in tune, although each has a tendency to pull away from the other. On such occasions as this the orchestra becomes a large equal-tempered instrument. It does so also in a host of other cases without the musicians having any inkling at all.

Ex. 168

(c)

(d)

In the famous Demons' Chorus in his *Orphée* Gluck placed two parts in enharmonic relation in an indeterminate key. I refer to the passage on which Rousseau and others have written so much nonsense, based on the difference they thought they could perceive between G♭ and F♯ (Ex. 169). If it were true that in performance one noticed the difference between the chorus's F♯ and the G♭ of the cellos' and basses' pizzicato, this difference would, as I say, just produce an intolerable anti-musical discord. The ear would be offended, quite simply. Far from that being the case, the listener is profoundly moved by a feeling of majestic, deeply musical terror. In fact he does not know what key he is hearing; is it B♭ or is it G minor? He neither knows nor cares. But nothing in the ensemble of different vocal and instrumental lines causes him offence. The F♯ in the chorus and the second orchestra has the prodigious impact we know because of the unforeseen way it is introduced and because of the savage atmosphere arising from the indecisive tonality, not because of its supposedly monstrous discord with the G♭. One would have to be childishly ignorant of acoustics not to recognise that this discord could not possibly be the cause of the effect it has, since a few cellos and basses playing G♭, *piano* pizzicato, are bound to be covered, drowned in fact, by the sudden entry of fifty or sixty men's voices in unison and all the rest of the strings attacking the F♯ *furioso col arco.*

Ex. 169

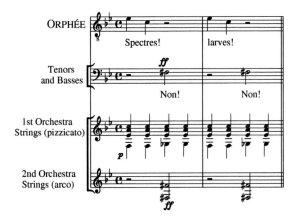

These preposterous arguments, the critics' ravings and the scientists' absurd theories, all of them obsessed with speaking and writing about an art of which they know nothing, have no effect except to make musicians laugh. But it is annoying. Knowledge, eloquence and genius should always remain girt about by the admiration and respect that are their due.

After this long digression I can return to the English concertina, whose barbarous scale is shown in Ex. 166. Despite the layout of this example the concertina is written on a single stave on the treble clef. Trills are possible on all degrees of the scale, though with less comfort at the bottom end. Double trills, in thirds, are easy. One may play diatonic, chromatic or arpeggiated passages on this instrument at considerable speeds. To the main voice one can add, if not several other complicated parts as on the piano or organ, at least a second voice moving almost parallel with the melody; it can also strike chords of four, six or more notes, as in Ex. 170.

Ex. 170

The German concertina, also very popular in England, is not constructed in the same way as the English model. Its scale goes down further, to *c* and *B♭*, and it contains no enharmonic intervals. It is thus designed for equal temperament. The range of concertinas varies according to the whim of the maker. Furthermore this instrument shares with the guitar the property that the composer should understand how it works and play it moderately well himself if he is to write for it to advantage.

Berlioz cannot have seen the concertina as an instrument with any potential place in the orchestra, yet he writes about it at length as an excuse to air his views on enharmonic intervals. The thought that Rousseau had dared to criticise Gluck for an imagined enharmonic offence (in his essay *Extrait d'un réponse du petit faiseur à son prête-nom, sur un morceau de l'Orphée de M. le chevalier Gluck*) was enough to arouse Berlioz's deepest passions.

He never wrote for the concertina himself and never wrote about it elsewhere. He probably encountered it in England, where it enjoyed great vogue in the years 1840–70. Introduced in Birmingham in 1837 by the scientist Charles Wheatstone, it attracted the attention of a number of Berlioz's London friends such as Molique, Benedict and Silas, all of whom wrote works for the instrument, usually for the concertina virtuoso Giulio Regondi; Silas even wrote an Adagio for eight concertinas.[18]

Berlioz's table of the concertina's available notes (Ex. 166) does not explain that the grouped pairs of notes indicate the push/pull alternatives for each button.

[18] For a full history of the English concertina, see Allan W. Atlas, *The Wheatstone English Concertina in Victorian England* (Oxford, 1996).

Up to four buttons in each hand may be pressed at once. He also seems to misstate the acoustical difference between D♯ and E♭, since the former is in fact higher than the latter, not lower.

Ex. 168a is an extract from his own *Te deum* (*NBE* 10: 121), which he does not identify.

ALEXANDRE'S MELODIUM

This is a keyboard instrument, like the pipe organ. Its sound is produced, as in the concertina, by the vibration of free metal tongues over which a current of air passes. This current is generated by bellows activated by the player's feet, and a greater or smaller volume of sound can be obtained depending on the way the feet propel the bellows mechanism and on the location of the instrument.

The melodium ('orgue-mélodium') has a crescendo and decrescendo; it is *expressive*. Hence the name 'expression register' given to its special mechanism. Fingering is the same as for the pipe organ. It is written on two, or sometimes three, staves, like the organ. Its compass is five octaves chromatically from *C* up to *c''''*, although this compass can be extended in melodiums with more than one stop. The number of stops varies considerably.

The simplest melodiums, which possess a single stop and the range given above, have two different types of tone: cor anglais tone from the left-hand half of the keyboard and flute tone from the right-hand half. Others can have bassoon, bugle, flute, clarinet, fife or oboe stops (so named from the analogy between the melodium's sound and that of the corresponding instrument) depending on the maker's inclination, also *grand jeu, forte* and *expression* stops. These stops give the melodium a range of seven octaves, even though its keyboard has only five. They are laid out for the player with an arrangement like that of the organ, on either side of the instrument's case. They are moved by drawing a wooden rod with either hand. Other stops are controlled by a similar mechanism placed beneath the case and activated by pressure from right to left or from left to right with the player's knees. These devices are called 'registers'.

The melodium does not have organ mutation stops, traditionally much admired by many people but in reality the creators of an appalling racket. They have just octave and two-octave stops, by means of which each key can sound the octave and fifteenth besides the note itself, or just the fifteenth without the octave, or even an octave above and an octave below at the same time.

Many ignorant players who love noise abuse these octave stops deplorably. The result is sheer barbarity, though less so, it is true, than that of organ mutation stops which give each note the simultaneous sound of the two other notes of its major triad, in other words its major third and fifth. Yet the barbarity is real, since besides the harmonic thickening they produce they inevitably cause terrible confusion in the harmony by forcing chords into inversions. Ninths thus make seconds and sevenths, seconds make sevenths and ninths, fifths make fourths, fourths fifths, and so on. To abide within truly musical bounds with such stops one would have to confine oneself to pieces written in counterpoint invertible at the octave, and this is never the case.

Ignorance in the Middle Ages, when they were searching for the laws of harmony, must be the reason why organs added these monstrosities, preserved and handed down by sheer habit; they will gradually disappear, it is to be hoped.

The melodium's sound is given out rather slowly, like a pipe organ, which makes it more suitable for a legato style than for any other, especially in sacred music and for soft, tender melodies at slow tempo. Agile pieces of a violent or fretful character played on the melodium attest simply, in my view, to the player's bad taste, to the composer's ignorance or to the ignorance *and* bad taste of both. The goal which M. Alexandre has set himself (and which he has attained) is to give the melodium a dreamy, religious character and to make it speak with all the inflexions of the human voice and of most instruments.

The melodium is an instrument for the church, the theatre, the salon and the concert hall all at the same time. It takes up little space and can be moved about. It is thus a servant of incontestable value to composers and music lovers. Since Meyerbeer, Halévy and Verdi have employed the organ in their operas, how many provincial theatres in France, even in Germany, have been too embarrassed to play these works when they have no organ? How many scores have been subjected to mutilation and adaptation of varying degrees of clumsiness because of this lack of an organ? Theatre managers today have no excuse for putting up with such misdeeds since for a modest outlay they can have a melodium almost as good as a pipe organ.

The same applies to small churches which music has still not reached. A melodium in the hands of a sensible musician can and should bring the civilisation of harmony and in due course dispel the horrible shouting still heard there in the service of religion.

The name 'harmonium' was patented in Paris in 1842 by Alexandre Debain for an instrument which had been the subject of experiment and development since the eighteenth century. His rivals devised their own names for multitudinous variations on what became a very popular domestic and church instrument in the nineteenth century. The firm of Alexandre père et fils in the persons of

Jacob Alexandre (1804–76) and his son Edouard (1824–88) named their version 'orgue-mélodium', introduced in 1844. They won Berlioz's support, leading to a close professional and personal relationship. From about 1856 until 1863 Berlioz received 2000 francs a year from the Alexandres in return, presumably, for regular promotion of Alexandre instruments in the press and perhaps personal endorsements of various kinds. Although very little correspondence between them has survived, Edouard Alexandre was a generous friend to Berlioz in his last years; he put up 50,000 francs for the production of *Les Troyens* and gave Berlioz a plot in the Cimetière Montmartre, in which both his wives and later Berlioz himself were buried, and on Berlioz's death Alexandre was an executor of the estate.

Berlioz, in his turn, was a tireless proponent of the Alexandre melodium. It was exhibited at the 1844 Exposition de l'Industrie, on which occasion Berlioz wrote warmly in its favour, drawing attention to its low price. His comments were issued by Alexandre in a pamphlet endorsing the instrument, *Notice sur les orgues mélodium d'Alexandre et fils.*[19] Later the same year Alexandre (probably Jacob) commissioned Berlioz to compose some music for the instrument, to which he responded with the *Sérénade agreste de la madone*, the *Toccata* and the *Hymne pour l'élévation*, three short pieces for melodium and Berlioz's only music for solo keyboard (*B&H* 6:33–40).

In private Berlioz expressed misgivings about the design of melodiums. He told Liszt: 'I cannot conceal the revulsion I feel at the sight of certain musical machines such as melodiums and small organs which resemble nothing so much as linen chests. If I love the harp its appearance has a lot to do with my affection for it.'[20] In public Berlioz's commendation of Alexandre instruments appeared regularly in the *Journal des débats*, almost always emphasising the melodium's low price and growing success: on its recent use at the Théâtre Italien and its usefulness in church and theatre (29 December 1844); on the 'percussion organ' (14 February 1847); on instruments at the 1855 Exposition Universelle (12 January 1856), reproducing the *Treatise*'s section on the melodium and describing the 'piano-Liszt' as well as a smaller version called the 'piano-organ'; on Thalberg's exquisite playing of the melodium (24 September 1856); on the success of this 'delicious instrument' in Russia (15 November 1856); on the success of the three-manual piano-organ at Baden-Baden (24 September 1857) and shortly after in Paris (14 December 1857); on the worldwide success of the melodium (27 February 1859); on its continuing success and the opening of the new Alexandre factory at Ivry (24 November 1860); the suggestion that every theatre ought to have an Alexandre melodium to keep offstage choruses in tune (28 January 1862); the admirable scheme for providing every commune in France with an Alexandre melodium for public use (14 May 1863). In *Les grotesques de la musique* Berlioz recounts an incident when a prospective buyer tries all the instruments in Alexandre's showroom but by failing to pump the bellows hears only the click of the percussion device which sets the reed in motion and walks out in fury.[21]

---

[19] *Jd*, 23 June 1844; Holoman, *Catalogue*, p. 434.   [20] *Cg*, 3, p. 283.
[21] *Les grotesques de la musique*, pp. 87–9.

It was through Berlioz's agency that Liszt commissioned from the Alexandres the giant 'piano-organ' delivered to Weimar in 1854, an instrument with three manuals, a pedal-board and eight registers designed to reproduce the sound of orchestral wind instruments.[22] In contrast, Berlioz devoted very little space to other Parisian manufacturers. He wrote only once about Debain's harmonium (in 1846) and, although he expressed approval of its adaptability and low price, he paid more attention to Debain's invention called 'antiphonel-harmonium', which enabled an organ or a harmonium to be played by people without musical skill. This used a board stuck with little pins, like the cylinder of a musical box.[23] Mustel's important development of the instrument in the 1850s was not reported at all.

As an illustration of the melodium's usefulness as support for offstage choruses Berlioz used a melodium at the end of the first part of *L'enfance du Christ* to accompany the chorus of invisible angels singing in an adjoining room (*NBE* 11:90). He specified 'orgue-mélodium ou physharmonica'. The latter was a similar instrument developed by Haeckl in Vienna in 1818 and introduced in France by Dietz, another Parisian builder. Berlioz heard it in Vienna in 1845.[24] The score gives such registration as 'jeu de flûtes' and 'céleste et tremblant doux'. The 1844 melodium pieces are marked 'musette', 'basson', 'flûte', 'cor anglais', 'clarinette' and 'grand jeu'.

ALEXANDRE PIANOS AND MELODIUMS
(WITH SUSTAINING DEVICE)

The sustaining device is the most important recent invention in the manufacture of keyboard instruments. This invention, now found on pianos and melodiums, allows the player to sustain a note, a chord or an arpeggio indefinitely in any part of the keyboard with a simple knee movement after the hands have been lifted from the keys. While several notes are being held in this way the player can use the freedom of his hands to strike new notes which are not part of the sustained chord and also those which are being sustained. It will be clear what a wide range of different attractive combinations this invention can make available on the melodium and the piano. These are truly orchestral effects, like string instruments playing four or five independent parts against a sustained chord in the wind (flutes, oboes and clarinets), or better still like the wind playing in several parts against sustained harmony on divided violins, or when the harmony and the melody move above or below a pedal. Furthermore the sustaining

[22] Alan Walker, *Franz Liszt, the Weimar Years 1848–1861* (New York, 1989), p. 77. The instrument itself is now in the Kunsthistorisches Museum, Vienna.
[23] *Jd*, 7 October 1846.   [24] *Memoirs*, chapter 56.

effect can have different degrees of intensity on the melodium depending on whether the so-called 'forte' stop at the side is open or shut.

Two knee-levers are located beneath the keyboard in such a way that they can easily be activated by light pressure from the player's knees. The one on the right sustains the right-hand half of the keyboard, the other the left-hand half. To sustain the sound the key and the knee-lever must both be pressed at the same time, as in Ex. 171a. To stop the sound being sustained a second knee pressure stops it at once, as in Ex. 171b. But if this second pressure on the lever terminates the first sustained chord, it replaces it immediately with a new sustaining effect if one or more new keys are then pressed, as in Ex. 171c. If after a short chord one wishes to sustain a single note of the chord, the knee lever must be pressed only after the keys for the notes which are not to be sustained have been released, while the finger still depresses the key of the note which is to be sustained. After that the hand is completely free. A series of these actions will change the sustained notes, with an extra pressure while the finger still holds down the key of the note to be sustained and the unwanted notes of the chord are released, as in Ex. 171d. This procedure works for both knee levers, on the piano as on the melodium.

Ex. 171

(a)

(b)

(c)

(d)

When writing for the piano or melodium with sustaining device, one must use at least three staves, often four. With four staves the top one is for high or middle sustaining, the bottom one for low sustaining. The two staves in the middle are then kept for the parts played by the two hands, as in Exx. 172a and 172b.

Ex. 172

(a)

sustaining

left knee

right knee

sustaining

(b)

   This section on the sustaining device appeared also in the *Journal des débats* of 12 January 1856. Edouard Alexandre introduced it in 1852 but, although Berlioz promised to write a feuilleton about it at that time, he evidently did not do so.[25] The sustaining pedal on the piano is usually credited to the blind piano maker Claude Montal in 1858, but Alexandre's invention evidently preceded this by six years.

   Ex. 172b is an extract from the slow movement of Beethoven's Fifth Symphony.

THE OCTOBASS

The Paris violin maker M. Vuillaume, whose excellent instruments are so sought after, has just enlarged the string family with a fine and powerful novelty, the octobass. This instrument is not, as many people imagine, an octave lower than the double bass. It is only an octave lower than the cello. Thus it goes a third lower than the four-string double bass's low E'. It has only three strings, tuned in a fifth and a fourth to C', G' and C. Since the fingers of the player's left hand are not long or strong enough to move comfortably up the strings, the dimensions of the octobass being enormous, M. Vuillaume has devised a system of movable keys which press the strings down firmly into grooves marked out on the fingerboard in tones and semitones. These keys are activated by levers gripped in the left

[25] *Cg*, 3, pp. 249, 268.

VUILLAUME'S OCTOBASSE, 1849

10   The octobass.

hand and pulled down behind the fingerboard and also by seven pedals moved by one of the player's feet.

This is enough to show that the octobass cannot perform any rapid passages and that it must be given a special part quite different from that of the double bass. Its range is only an octave and a fifth, from C' chromatically up to G.

This instrument makes a sound of remarkable beauty and power, full and loud without roughness. It would be admirable in a large orchestra; any festival orchestra with over 150 players ought to have at least three of them.

We will make no attempt here to dispute the opinion that the recent inventions of instrument makers can be fatal to the art of music. These inventions exercise in their own sphere the same influence as all other advances of civilisation; the misuse which can be – and undoubtedly is – made of them detracts nothing from their value.

When Vuillaume first exhibited his octobass at the Exposition de l'Industrie in 1849, Berlioz mentioned that it had already been heard at some German festivals.[26] It appeared again at the Great Exhibition in London in 1851 and at the Paris Exposition Universelle in 1855 and was applauded by Berlioz on both occasions.[27] This section of the *Treatise* is taken from the latter report, in which Berlioz also wrote lyrically about Vuillaume's mastery as a violin-maker and his skill at copying the finest Cremonese instruments. In his 1849 report of the octobass Berlioz added: 'I wish M. Vuillaume would produce the instrument I have often proposed to him: a percussion instrument with strings for producing fast low tremolos in several parts which double basses and timpani can do only imperfectly.'

Two specimens of the octobass are now known, one in the Musée de la Musique, Paris, the other in the Kunsthistorisches Museum, Vienna . Berlioz never wrote for the octobass. Sax also produced an outsize double bass going down to C' with four strings tuned in fifths.[28]

---

[26] *Jd*, 21 August 1849. For a full account of the octobass see Joël-Marie Fauquet, 'Deux lettres inédites d'Hector Berlioz', *Revue musicale de suisse romande*, 37/1 (1984), pp. 19–20; *Cg*, 5, p. 137.
[27] *Jd*, 27 November 1851 and 12 January 1856.
[28] Georges Kastner, *Traité général d'instrumentation, Supplément*, p. 10.

14

The orchestra

The orchestra may be regarded as a large instrument capable of making a great number of different sounds simultaneously or successively. Its power is limited or enormous depending on whether it involves all or only a part of the means of execution at the disposal of modern music and on whether these means are well or badly chosen and well or badly located in acoustical conditions of greater or lesser advantage.

The assortment of players whose coming together constitutes an orchestra could be regarded as its strings, tubes, chests and surfaces, made of wood or metal – machines bearing intelligence but subordinate to the action of an immense keyboard played by the conductor following the directions of the composer.

I think I have already said that one cannot show how beautiful orchestral effects are made and that this skill, which must clearly be developed by practice and reasoned observation, is like skill in melody, expression and even harmony: one of the precious gifts that the musician-poet, the inspired originator, can only be given by nature. But it is certainly straightforward to demonstrate with some precision the art of training orchestras to give faithful renderings of compositions of all shapes and sizes.

A distinction must be made between theatre orchestras and concert orchestras. The first are in general inferior to the second in many ways.

The space occupied by the musicians and their layout on a horizontal or terraced platform in an area enclosed on three sides or even in the centre of a hall, with resonators made of hard material designed to reflect sound, or of soft material which absorbs and breaks up vibrations close to the players or further away – these are all of great importance. Resonating surfaces are essential. Different arrangements are found in every enclosed building. The closer they are to the origin of the sound, the stronger their effect.

That is why open-air music *does not exist*. A gigantic orchestra playing in the middle of a vast open garden, like that of the Tuileries, will have no effect. Even if you play close to the palace walls their reflection is inadequate,

319

since the sound is immediately lost in every other direction. An orchestra of a thousand wind instruments and a chorus of two thousand voices in the middle of a plain will not have a twentieth of the musical impact of an ordinary orchestra of eighty players and a chorus of a hundred well arranged in the Conservatoire hall. The brilliant effect of military bands in certain city streets actually supports this view, though it seems to contradict it. The music is not in the *open* air then. The walls of tall houses bordering both sides of the street, the lines of trees, the façades of palaces and nearby monuments, all act as reflectors; the sound rebounds and circulates freely in the enclosed space between them before escaping through the gaps left open. But should the band march on still playing and emerge from such a resonant street into an open space without trees or buildings, the difference in sound is immediate. The band disappears and there is no more music.

> Berlioz's disdain for open-air music goes back at least to 1834:

> *No music is possible in the open air,* for a thousand and one reasons, the least of which is that you can't hear it. No, you can't hear it! You hear no detail, no nuance, not even a clean complete chord. Harmony is powerless, melody is expressionless and without its vital warmth, and any poetic idea is lost, unless it becomes an absurd jumble. An open-air orchestra will always end up as a rhythmic noise, with a few threads of melody audible here and there thanks to the piercing sound of a flageolet or a piccolo over the thud of the bass drum and the bull-roar of the ophicleide.[1]

On 28 July 1840 he had a critical experience of open-air music, conducting the first performance of his *Symphonie funèbre et triomphale* on the march through the boulevards of Paris to the Place de la Bastille for the inauguration of the Bastille monument.[2] He then observed that it was much easier to maintain the ensemble of his two hundred players in the boulevards than in the open squares, and after an open-air performance of the same work in the Hippodrome in 1846 his comment was: 'Open-air music is a chimera; 150 musicians in a closed building are more effective than 1800 in the Hippodrome scattering their harmonies to the winds.'[3]

The best way to arrange the performers in a hall of a size appropriate to their number is to build them up one behind the other on a series of risers, set out in such a way that each row can project its sound to the audience without any obstacle in the way.

Every well organised concert orchestra should be terraced in this fashion. In a theatre the stage will have to be completely closed off behind, to left, to right and above, with a wooden screen. But in a special hall or

[1] *Cm*, 1, p. 281.   [2] *NBE*, 19, p. viii.   [3] *Jd*, 29 July 1846.

at one end of a church where, as often happens, the back of the area is made of thick masonry reflecting nearby instruments too loudly and too harshly, one can easily soften the effect of the reflector and thus of its resonance by hanging drapes or placing suitable materials for breaking up the movement of sound waves.

Because of the design of our theatres and the requirements of staging, this amphitheatre arrangement is not possible for opera orchestras. Being relegated to the lowest point in the centre of the theatre, in front of the footlights and on a level floor, the players lack most of the advantages to be had from the concert arrangement I have just described. Numerous effects are lost and delicate nuances unnoticed in opera orchestras, however well they are played. The difference is so great that composers should be required to take this into account and not score their operas in the same way as symphonies, masses and oratorios designed for concert halls or churches.

Opera orchestras used always to consist of a number of strings in proportion to the rest of the orchestra. This has not been so for several years. An opéra-comique orchestra which used to have two flutes, two oboes, two clarinets, two horns, two bassoons, sometimes two trumpets and very occasionally some timpani, would have had nine first violins, eight seconds, six violas, seven cellos and six double basses. But you now find four horns, three trombones, two trumpets, bass drum and cymbals without any increase in the strings, so the balance is destroyed. The violins can hardly be heard and the total effect is horrible. An orchestra for grand opera which has, as well as the wind instruments I have listed, two cornets and an ophicleide, also percussion and sometimes six or eight harps, has no more than twelve first violins, eleven seconds, eight violas, ten cellos and eight double basses. It would need at least fifteen firsts, fourteen seconds, ten violas and twelve cellos to allow some reduction of their numbers in pieces requiring a very soft accompaniment.

An orchestra of opéra-comique size would suffice for a concert orchestra intending to play Haydn or Mozart symphonies. A large number of strings would usually be too loud for the delicate effects these two composers often give to flutes, oboes and bassoons on their own. But for Beethoven symphonies, Weber overtures and modern compositions in the grand romantic style the number of violins, violas, cellos and basses that I specified just now for grand opera is absolutely necessary.

The Opéra and the Opéra Comique at that time had precisely the numbers of strings that Berlioz lists here.[4] When Berlioz published the overture to *Benvenuto Cellini* in 1839 he prescribed a string strength of 15–15–10–12–9, a larger body

[4] *Agenda musical* (Paris, 1837; repr. Geneva, 1981), p. 48. The Opéra material for *Benvenuto Cellini* confirms these numbers.

than that which had played the opera in 1838 and approximately the same as that prescribed in most of his published scores. The *Symphonie fantastique*, for example, requires at least 15–15–10–11–9, the same as *Roméo et Juliette*; *La damnation de Faust* requires at least 15–15–10–10–9.

Yet for a hall hardly bigger than that at the Conservatoire, the finest, completest, loudest, most subtle, most varied, most majestic and most flexible concert orchestra would be made up as follows:

21 first violins	4 bassoons
20 second violins	4 cylinder horns
18 violas	2 cylinder trumpets
8 first cellos	2 cylinder or piston cornets
7 second cellos	3 trombones (1 alto and 2 tenors
10 double basses	or 3 tenors)
4 harps	1 bass trombone
2 piccolos	1 ophicleide in Bb (or tuba)
2 flutes	2 pairs of timpani and 4 timpanists
2 oboes	1 bass drum
1 cor anglais	1 pair of cymbals
2 clarinets	
1 basset horn or bass clarinet	

To perform a choral work such an orchestra would need:

46 sopranos (firsts and seconds)
40 tenors (firsts and seconds)
40 basses (firsts and seconds)

The *Rgm* text and the 1844 edition of the *Treatise* then have a section on the layout of the orchestra which was removed from the 1855 edition:

This body of 248 performers on a stage at one end of the hall would have five rows at the back each raised two and a half feet behind the next. Starting from the back at row 1, the highest and furthest from the audience, and listing from left to right, they should be divided as follows:

Row 1: bass drums, cymbals, two pairs of timpani, ophicleide, bass trombone.
Row 2: two double basses, two cellos, two cornets, two trumpets, three trombones.
Row 3: four double basses, eight cellos.
Row 4: two double basses, two cellos, four bassoons, four horns.
Row 5: two cellos, basset horn, two clarinets, cor anglais, two oboes, two piccolos, two flutes.

On the rest of the platform in the level space, which is much larger than the raised steps:

At the back just in front of Row 5 facing the audience in a single line if the stage is wide enough: eighteen violas.

In the middle and in front of the violas: one double bass, plus another double bass and a cello playing from the same stand leading the bass section.

At one side in front of the violas in three rows sideways to the audience: twenty-one first violins with the leader at the front of the first row.

On the other side of the platform, also in three rows: twenty second violins facing the firsts, with the leader of the seconds at the front of the first row.

In the empty space between these two groups of violins and in front of the cello and bass leaders' stand: four harps.

In front of the harps, close to the first desk of first violins and facing more or less directly the whole orchestra: the conductor.

The chorus would then be divided into three groups, each forming a complete choir. The smallest would be in the middle of the forestage, in front of the conductor and facing the audience. The other two on the left and right, sideways to the audience, would be raised on each side on three small risers of a foot and half to allow the easiest possible projection of their voices. On the front rows are the sopranos, behind them the tenors and finally, on the highest rows behind them, the basses.

The total of 248 players was given as 244 in the *Rgm* text, although the correct total is 246. The 1844 edition raised the number of piccolos from one to two, so the correct final total should be 247.

The layout of the orchestra, as given here, is so completely at variance with modern orchestral practice that its features need to be considered with some care. Firstly, Berlioz here emphasises the need for a steeply raked platform, rising to over twelve feet, to allow the sound to project, a degree of verticality that few halls offer and which required a great deal of temporary scaffolding for Berlioz's own concerts. For his big festival concert on 1 August 1844, for example, the platform had to be rebuilt after the final rehearsal in order to raise the back of the orchestra higher, since their sound was obscured by that of the large chorus placed in front.[5] German orchestras seem to have been happy to play on a more level platform, while public halls in England favoured a much steeper arrangement, as for example the Liverpool Philharmonic Hall, Birmingham Town Hall and the Royal Albert Hall, London.[6] Berlioz's concern that the percussion should not be too far from the conductor is expressed again here. The cellos and basses are all directed frontally at the audience, which has an important acoustic (and visual) impact. The principal cello and double bass share a stand – a traditional practice since the eighteenth century – and are brought prominently to the front with the harps. The first and second violins occupy the left and right

[5] *Memoirs*, chapter 53.
[6] Illustrations in *The New Grove Dictionary of Music and Musicians*, ed. Stanley Sadie (20 vols., London 1980), 2, p. 735, and 11, p. 93.

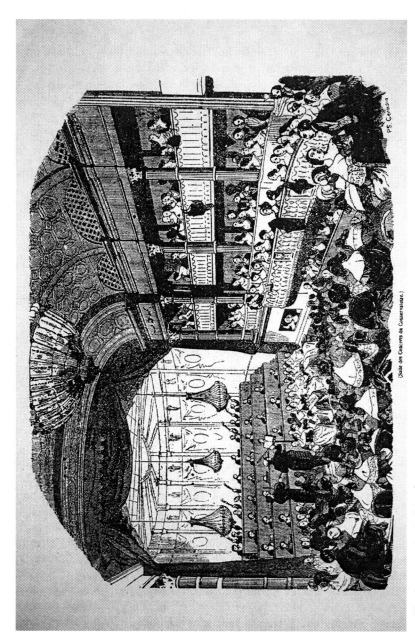

(Salle des Concerts du Conservatoire.)

P.S. Cerosia

11 The Conservatoire hall in 1843.

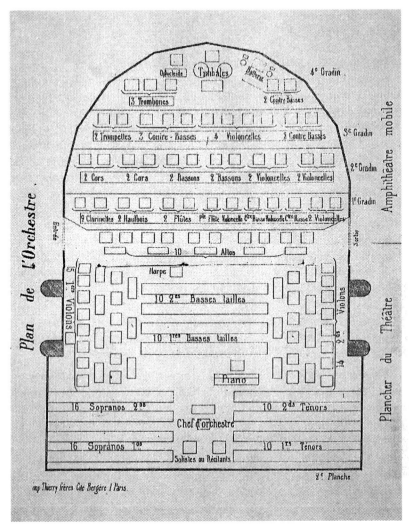

12   Layout of the Société des Concerts orchestra.

areas of the platform and face each other, an arrangement that was standard everywhere until the middle of the twentieth century. The chorus is placed between
the conductor and the audience, with obvious advantages of audibility and clarity that are lost when choruses have to sing over the heads of large orchestras,
as is usual today. Berlioz later shows how the problem of ensemble is resolved
by using sub-conductors. The chorus too must be on raked platforms to allow
their sound to project. In a letter of 9 March 1845 Berlioz drew a diagram to
show how the double chorus for *Roméo et Juliette* is to be set out in its terraced
seating.[7]

[7] *Cg*, 3, p. 233, where the diagram is incorrectly drawn. See *Le musicien errant*, ed. Julien Tiersot (Paris,
1927), p. 96.

An unpublished letter of 5 December 1850 to a musician in La Rochelle reiterates Berlioz's practice:

> For concerts I have given in the various theatres of Paris, London, Berlin, Prague, Vienna and St Petersburg, whatever the dimensions of the stage, I have always required the following arrangement: 1) Build a platform over the normal orchestra pit, the platform being a little lower than the stage. On the stage the orchestra is seated on risers in a semicircle. 2) On the platform in front of the stage and over the pit is placed the chorus, facing the audience, in the following order: at the front, first and second sopranos in two rows if there are very many or in one row if there are only thirty or forty. The tenors are behind the women and the basses are behind the tenors.
>
> In this way the audience can always hear the complete harmony wherever they are sitting. But since the chorus in this position have their backs to the conductor, who has to be on stage close to the orchestra, an assistant conductor must sit in front of the choir keeping his eye fixed on the conductor and conveying his indications to the singers.[8]

Finally, it was not by any means usual at that time to have the conductor face his players, as Berlioz does, rather than the audience.

The layout can be visualised from the diagram opposite.

The 'Observations' printed with the full score of *Roméo et Juliette* in 1847 (*NBE* 18: 3, 383) propose a similar layout of the orchestra. Then Berlioz omitted this whole passage from the 1855 edition of the *Treatise*, transferring his advice on seating to the chapter on the conductor (see below, pp. 358–9).[9]

Both editions of the *Treatise* continue thus:

> By doubling or tripling these numbers in proportion one would have a magnificent festival orchestra, without doubt. But it is a mistake to think that all orchestras should be made up on this pattern based on a predominance of strings; very good results can be had from the opposite approach. Being too weak to dominate the mass of clarinets and brass, the strings then become a harmonic bond with the strident sound of the wind band, sometimes tempering its noisiness and sometimes giving life to the tempo with tremolos that merge with side drum rolls and make musical sense of them.

When he wrote this (in 1842) Berlioz had recently added a body of strings to the *Symphonie funèbre et triomphale*, composed originally for wind and percussion only.

---

[8] Letter of 5 December 1850, kindly communicated by John Eliot Gardiner.
[9] For a full discussion of orchestral seating in Berlioz's time see Daniel J. Koury, *Orchestral Performance Practices in the Nineteenth Century* (Ann Arbor, 1986).

Their numbers are given as 20–20–15–15–10, while the wind are at about double the normal orchestral strength, with the exception of clarinets massed in much larger numbers. The blend of string tremolos and side drum rolls is illustrated at the end of the first movement (*NBE* 19: 36–8).

bass drum cymbals timpani timpani ophicleide bass trombone

d. bass d. bass cello cello cornet cornet trumpet trumpet tromb. tromb. tromb.

d. bass d. bass d. bass d. bass cello cello cello cello cello cello cello cello

d. bass d. bass cello cello bsn bsn bsn bsn horn horn horn horn

cello cello basset-horn clar. clar. cor anglais oboe oboe picc. picc. flute flute

vla vla vla vla vla vla vla vla vla vla vla vla vla vla vla vla vla vla

violin 1 violin 1 violin 1	d. bass cello	violin 2 violin 2
violin 1 violin 1 violin 1		violin 2 violin 2 violin 2
violin 1 violin 1 violin 1	harp harp	violin 2 violin 2 violin 2
violin 1 violin 1 violin 1	harp harp	violin 2 violin 2 violin 2
violin 1 violin 1 violin 1		violin 2 violin 2 violin 2
violin 1 violin 1 violin 1		violin 2 violin 2 violin 2
violin 1 violin 1 violin 1	CONDUCTOR	violin 2 violin 2 violin 2

	b	t	s	basses	s	t	b
	a	e	o		o	e	a
	s	n	p	tenors	p	n	s
	s	o	r	sopranos	r	o	s
	e	r	a		a	r	e
	s	s	n		n	s	s
			o		o		
			s		s		

Common sense suggests that unless he is obliged to accept this or that size of orchestra the composer should choose his combination of players to match the style and character of the work in hand and to achieve the main effects its subject-matter suggests. Thus in a *Requiem*, to give a musical representation of the great tableaux of the *Dies iræ*, I used four small brass bands (trumpets, trombones, cornets and ophicleides) set well apart from each other at the four corners of the main orchestra, which was made up of an impressive body of strings, with all the rest of the wind doubled or tripled, and ten timpanists playing eight pairs of timpani tuned in different keys. It is undeniable that the special effects achieved by this new kind of orchestra could not possibly be obtained in any other way.

This is the moment to mention the importance of the different points of origin of sound. Different sections of the orchestra are sometimes meant by the composer to give questions and answers, and this idea can only be clear and effective if the dialoguing sections are far enough apart. The composer should indicate in the score the sort of arrangement he thinks appropriate.

If, for example, the side drums, bass drums, cymbals and timpani are all used together to mark a certain rhythm, as is commonly done, they can stay all in one place. But if they play a dialoguing rhythm with one part marked by the bass drums and cymbals and the other by timpani and side drums, there is no question that the effect will be incomparably better, more interesting and more striking if the two groups of percussion are placed at the two sides of the orchestra and at a considerable distance from each other.

Berlioz had in mind not only his *Requiem* as an example of the purposeful separation of forces but also the *Symphonie funèbre et triomphale*, whose percussion are directed to be separated in exactly the fashion he suggests here. In that work eight side drums are placed on one side of the orchestra while the timpani, cymbals, bass drums and tamtam are at the other (*NBE* 19: 3).

This shows how great an obstacle to the composition of monumental and truly new works is the constant uniformity of performing forces. It is usually imposed on composers more from custom, routine, laziness and thoughtlessness than from economy. It is unfortunately true, though, that economy is all too good a reason, especially in France, where music is so remote from the national way of life, where the government does everything for the theatre but nothing for music itself, and where leading capitalists are prepared to pay 50,000 francs or more for an old master painting because it 'represents good value', but will not put so much as fifty francs towards an annual solemnity which would be worthy of a nation such as ours and would display the enormous musical resources it possesses but cannot properly use.

Yet it would be curious just once to attempt to bring together all the musical resources one could assemble in Paris in a specially written composition. Supposing that a composer had them at his command in a vast hall purpose-built by an architect who was both acoustician and musician, he would have to determine the precise layout of this immense orchestra before he began writing and have it all the time in mind when composing. With such an enormous body of musicians it is clearly of the highest importance to take account of the separation or proximity of its constituent groups. This requirement is quite indispensable in taking full advantage of them and in calculating the scale of effects with any accuracy. Until now, festival orchestras have been put together by quadrupling or quintupling each section of a normal orchestra and chorus depending on the number of available performers, but here we are discussing a quite different concept, and the composer who wished to bring out the prodigious, boundless resources of such an *instrument* would most certainly have to undertake a quite new task.

If the necessary time, effort and *money* were available, this is how it could be done in Paris. The layout of these groups is at the choice and the direction of the composer; the percussion, with their irresistible impact on the rhythm and their tendency to slow down when they are a long way from the conductor, should always, as I have said, be placed quite near him in order to be able to respond instantly and precisely to the slightest changes in tempo and pulse.

120	violins, divided into two, three or four parts
40	violas, perhaps divided into firsts and seconds; at least ten would play the viola d'amore if required
45	cellos, perhaps divided into first and seconds
18	double basses, three-stringed and tuned in fifths to G'–D–A
4	octobasses
15	more double basses, four-stringed and tuned in fourths to E'–A'–D–G
6	flutes
4	flutes in E♭ (incorrectly called 'in F')
2	piccolos
2	piccolos in D♭ (incorrectly called 'in E♭')
6	oboes
6	cors anglais
5	saxophones
4	tenoroons
12	bassoons
4	clarinets in E♭
8	clarinets in C, B♭ or A
3	bass clarinets in B♭
16	horns, 6 of them with valves
8	trumpets
6	cornets
4	alto trombones
6	tenor trombones
2	bass trombones
1	ophicleide in C
2	ophicleides in B♭
2	tubas

    30   harps
    30   pianos
     1   very deep organ, with at least 16-foot stops
     8   pairs of timpani, with 10 timpanists
     6   side drums
     3   bass drums
     4   pairs of cymbals
     6   triangles
     6   jeux de timbres
    12   pairs of antique cymbals at different pitches
     2   deep bells
     2   tamtams
     4   Turkish crescents

Total: 467 instrumentalists

    40   sopranos (children), firsts and seconds
   100   sopranos (women), firsts and seconds
   100   tenors, firsts and seconds
   120   basses, firsts and seconds

Total: 360 chorus

The two tubas were given in the *Rgm* text as two ophicleides in A♭ with the note 'These are now being manufactured'; this was revised in the 1843 proofs. The octobasses and saxophones were added in the 1855 edition of the *Treatise* and the total revised accordingly.

It will be seen that the chorus does not dominate this ensemble of 827 performers; in any case it would be very hard to find 360 decent voices in Paris, the art of singing being so little cultivated these days.

It would clearly be necessary to adopt a style of extraordinary breadth whenever the full tutti was engaged, saving delicate effects and light, rapid tempos for smaller orchestras which the composer could readily pick out and change around within this musical horde.

In addition to the kaleidoscopic variety of colours this mass of timbres could emit at any moment, there would be some unprecedented *harmonic* effects to exploit:

  1 by dividing the 120 violins and forty violas in a high register into eight or ten parts (for an angelic, airy *pianissimo*);
  2 by dividing the cellos and basses in a low register and in slow tempo (for a melancholy, religious *mezzo-forte*);

3   by grouping the bottom notes of the clarinet family as a small orchestra (for a sombre *forte* or *mezzo-forte*);
4   by grouping the lower notes of the oboes, cors anglais and tenoroons as a small orchestra with the flutes' low notes also (for a solemn, sad *piano*);
5   by grouping the low notes of the ophicleides, tubas and horns as a small orchestra, with the tenor trombones' pedal notes, the bass trombones' low notes and the organ's sixteen-foot open diapason (for a profoundly serious, solemn and calm *piano*);
6   by grouping the top notes of the E♭ clarinets, flutes and piccolos as a small orchestra (for a strident *forte*);
7   by grouping the horns, trumpets, cornets, trombones and ophicleides as a small orchestra (for a ceremonial, brassy *forte*);
8   by grouping the thirty harps with the full body of strings playing pizzicato (which would make a gigantic harp of 934 strings) as a large orchestra (for graceful, brilliant, sensuous sounds at any dynamic level);
9   by grouping the thirty pianos with the six jeux de timbres, the twelve pairs of antique cymbals, the six triangles (which could be tuned to different pitches, like the antique cymbals) and the four Turkish crescents as a metallic percussion orchestra (for a joyful, brilliant *mezzo-forte*);
10   by grouping the eight pairs of timpani with the six side drums and the three bass drums as a small percussion orchestra, almost entirely rhythmic (for a menacing effect at any dynamic level);
11   by combining the two tamtams, the two bells and the three large cymbals with certain trombone chords (for a lugubrious, sinister *mezzo-forte*).

   It would be hard to enumerate all the harmonic profiles each of these different groups could present when combined with other groups, whether they were kindred types or not. One could select the following:

1   a duet between the wind and the strings;
2   a duet between either of these and the chorus;
3   a duet between the chorus and the harps and pianos on their own;
4   a trio between the chorus (in unisons and octaves), the wind (in unisons and octaves) and the violins, violas and cellos (also in unisons and octaves);
5   the same trio, but accompanied by a rhythmic figure set down by all the percussion, double basses, harps and pianos;
6   a chorus unaccompanied, in three, six or nine parts;
7   a melody for unison violins, violas and cellos, or for unison woodwind, or for unison brass, accompanied by an orchestra of voices;

8   a melody for sopranos, tenors or basses, or for all voices in octaves, accompanied by an orchestra of instruments;
9   a semichorus accompanied by the full chorus and some instruments;
10   a small orchestra on the melody, accompanied by the full orchestra and some voices;
11   a broad, low melody played by all the cellos and basses, accompanied in the upper register by divided violins, harps and pianos;
12   a broad, low melody played by all the bass wind instruments and the organ, accompanied in the upper register by flutes, oboes, clarinets and divided violins;
13   etc., etc., etc.

Berlioz has often been accused of the wildest fantasy in imagining an orchestra of the size he suggests here. Yet he knew the resources of the capital better than anyone else and he had reason to believe that all these instruments and players, even ten violas d'amore and four octobasses, might be available if somehow they could be coordinated under a single direction. The problem was more political and financial than technical–persuading so many musicians to work for a single large project all at the same time, rather than the actual availability of instruments and players. Soon after drawing up this proposal he embarked on some concerts which drew on vast forces and quickly earned him a reputation for noisiness and megalomania which has been hard to dislodge, despite the very clear exposition here in the *Treatise* (and elsewhere) of his desire to enlarge the range of orchestral colour rather than simply to create a very large sound. The huge new structures of iron and glass popular in the 1840s similarly fired his imagination.

Chapter 53 of the *Memoirs* recounts the great Festival of Industry mounted in Paris in August 1844 and the concert in which 1022 performers took part. A handbill identified the performers as 140 sopranos, 130 tenors, 130 basses and an orchestra of 364, including 238 strings. There were evidently many children and additional wind players also.[10] The *Hymne à la France*, composed for the occasion (*NBE* 12b: 135), requires no harps and no pianos, nor any unusual instruments, but its strophic form illustrates the principle set out here of devising different combinations of large forces for cumulative effect. Four concerts which Berlioz conducted in the Cirque Olympique early in 1845 were similar attempts to display the splendours of the large modern orchestra with strong choral support. Concerts in which great numbers took part, with choral singers sometimes numbered in thousands, became a distinctive feature of the period 1850–70. Berlioz's concerts for the Exposition Universelle in 1855 were part of this movement.

When listing possible combinations of instruments, the composer's imagination is at work, and we can only regret that some of the sounds imagined here, particularly the combinations involving percussion, were not realised by Berlioz himself but had to wait until the twentieth century for others to claim as their own.

---

[10] *NBE*, 12b, pp. xii–xiii.

Without question the method of rehearsing this colossal orchestra must be the method that should be adopted for any large-scale work of complex structure with technical problems for individual parts or for the tutti: the system of sectional rehearsals.

This is how the conductor should proceed in breaking down his task. I presume that he knows the score he has to conduct *thoroughly and in the closest detail.* He will first appoint two assistant conductors for full rehearsals to give the beat, keeping their eyes on him throughout, to convey the tempo to the performers furthest from the centre. He will then select repetiteurs for each vocal and instrumental section, who will themselves be rehearsed in advance to get instructions in directing their part of the rehearsals. The first repetiteur will rehearse the first sopranos *on their own,* then the seconds, then the firsts and seconds together. The second repetiteur will take the first and second tenors in the same way, and the third will similarly take the basses. The full chorus is next divided into three, each a third of the whole, and finally the full chorus is rehearsed together. Choral rehearsals will be accompanied either by an organ or by a piano and some strings, perhaps violins and cellos.

The assistant conductors and orchestral repetiteurs will practise in separate sections in the same fashion:

1 first and second violins first separately then all together,
2 violas, cellos and basses separately then all together,
3 the full body of strings,
4 harps alone,
5 pianos alone,
6 harps and pianos together,
7 woodwind alone,
8 brass alone,
9 all the wind,
10 percussion alone, carefully instructing the timpanists to tune their drums properly,
11 percussion and wind together,
12 finally the full vocal and instrumental ensemble rehearsed by the conductor.

This schedule will produce an excellent standard of performance unobtainable by the old method of collective rehearsals and it will require no more than four rehearsals of each performer. Do not forget to put out a good number of tuning forks around the orchestra. This is the only way to keep such a wide range of different types of instrument properly in tune.

Berlioz seems to have picked up the idea of sectional rehearsals from Guillaume-Louis-Bocquillon Wilhem, founder of the Orphéon movement and a prominent choral conductor. Berlioz recommended sectional orchestral rehearsals as early as 1834, 'in the manner used daily in rehearsing choruses'.[11] Later, having warmly commended Wilhem's method of rehearsing in 1838,[12] he put it into practice soon afterwards when preparing *Roméo et Juliette* for performance.[13] Offering advice to Lecourt a few months later for a performance of *Le roi Lear*, Berlioz wrote: 'It's enormously difficult. When you do it again, do what I did for *Roméo et Juliette*: rehearse the first and second violins one day on their own, then the violas, cellos and basses the next day, then the wind, and then the whole ensemble. You will see how well that works. It's the only way to perform music of the present day.'[14] In his comments on Berlin musical life in 1843 Berlioz again recommended sectional rehearsals, this time for the chorus: 'Opera houses may flatly refuse to adopt it, for feeble reasons of economy and ingrained routine, but this sectional method is the only one that enables each part to be learned really thoroughly and sung with the requisite precision and subtlety of expression. I have said it before and I shall go on saying it.'[15] He described his rehearsals for the 1844 festival concert thus:

> I took separately, one after the other, violins, violas and cellos, basses, wood-wind, brass, harps, percussion, women and children of the chorus, and men. These nine rehearsals, of which no player took part in more than one, produced marvellous results – results which would certainly not have been obtained from as many as five full rehearsals. The session with the thirty-six double basses was particularly interesting. [. . .] That is the beauty of sectional rehearsals: you pass rapidly over anything that presents no problem to the particular section of chorus or orchestra in question, and contrariwise give all the time and concentration required to getting the awkward and difficult things right. The only disadvantage is that by the end the conductor is absolutely exhausted. However, as I think I have said before, in this sort of situation I become gifted with exceptional energy and rival a cart-horse in stamina.[16]

Berlioz returns to the topic of sectional rehearsals in the chapter on conducting (see p. 363).

Vulgar prejudice calls large orchestras *noisy*. If they are well constituted, well rehearsed and well conducted, and if they play real music, they should be called *powerful*. No two words are more different in meaning than these. A nasty little vaudeville orchestra can be *noisy*, while a large group of musicians appropriately used can be of extreme softness and can produce the most beautiful sound even in violent outbursts. Three ill-placed trombones can seem unbearably *noisy*, and a moment later, in the same hall, twelve trombones will leave the audience amazed at their noble and *powerful* harmony.

---

[11] *Cm*, 1, p. 368   [12] *Jd*, 6 July 1838; *Cm*, 3, pp. 489–93.   [13] *Cg*, 2, p. 599.   [14] *Ibid.*, p. 639.
[15] *Memoirs*, 'Travels in Germany', I/7.   [16] *Memoirs*, chapter 53.

I say more: unisons are truly effective only when multiplied above a certain number. Thus four first-class violins playing the same line together will produce a rather clumsy sound, perhaps even unpleasant, while fifteen violins of ordinary ability will be excellent. That is why small orchestras are so ineffective, no matter how good the players, and thus so weak.

But in the thousand combinations available to a monumental orchestra such as I have just described would reside a wealth of harmony, a variety of timbre and a series of contrasts comparable to nothing ever yet done in music, and, moreover, incalculable melodic, expressive and rhythmic power, an unequalled force of impact, and prodigious sensitivity in nuances of detail and ensemble. Its repose would be as majestic as the ocean's slumber; its agitation would suggest a tropical hurricane, its explosions the fury of a volcano. It would evoke lamentation, murmuring, the mysterious sounds of virgin forests, it would sound the clamours, the prayers, the hymns of triumph or mourning of a people whose soul is magnanimous, whose heart is ardent and whose passions are fiery. The very solemnity of its silences would inspire fear, and the most rebellious beings would tremble to watch its crescendo swell and roar like an enormous, sublime conflagration!

Thus ended the *Treatise* in its 1844 edition, with Berlioz's visionary evocation of the large modern orchestra. If it might be supposed that the disdain for small orchestras expressed here was contradicted by his now well-known orchestrations of songs, especially *Les nuits d'été*, it must be said that he never contemplated the reduction of the string body below a strength of about 10–10–8–8–6, the numbers specified for *La captive* (*NBE* 13: 11). These numbers are again suggested by surviving string parts for *Les nuits d'été*.[17] Berlioz remained unconvinced that a section of four violins (or fewer) made a viable musical unit.

The 1855 edition of the *Treatise* concludes with the following chapter, 'The conductor and his art'.

---

[17] *NBE*, 13, pp. 121–2.

15

The conductor and his art

Music may claim to be the most exacting of the arts. Of all the arts it is the hardest to cultivate and its creations are the most rarely presented in conditions which allow one to appreciate their true worth, to see their outline clearly and to learn their inner meaning and real character.

Of all creative artists the composer is almost the only one to depend on a host of intermediaries between him and his audience. These may be intelligent or stupid, devoted or hostile, energetic or lazy; from first to last they can contribute to the glory of his work, or they can spoil it, insult it, or even wreck it completely.

Singers are often accused of being the most dangerous of these intermediaries. That's wrong, in my view. The most to be feared, I believe, is the conductor. A poor singer can only spoil his own part; an incompetent or malevolent conductor can ruin everything. The composer who falls into the hands of a conductor who is neither incompetent nor malevolent must consider himself lucky, since the latter's pernicious influence can affect everything. The most magnificent orchestra becomes paralysed, the finest singers feel frustrated and benumbed, and the excitement and the ensemble vanish. Under such conducting the composer's boldest inventions seem like crassness, enthusiasm falters, inspiration is violently dragged down to earth, the angel loses its wings, the genius becomes a madman or a cretin, the god's statue is thrown from its plinth and dragged through the mud, and, worse still, the public, even the most musically gifted listeners, have no chance of knowing, when they are hearing a new work for the first time, what damage the conductor is doing and what follies, errors and crimes he is committing.

If any obvious mistakes are noticed in the performance, it's never him, it's his victims that get the blame. If he misses a choral entry in a final scene or movement, if he allows a jarring imbalance between chorus and orchestra or between the opposite sides of the orchestra, if he sets an absurdly fast tempo, if the tempo drags excessively, if he interrupts a singer before the end of a phrase, they say 'the chorus is appalling', 'the orchestra was lifeless', 'the violins wrecked the main theme', 'everyone was off form', 'the tenor got it wrong, he didn't know his part', 'the harmony is muddled', 'the composer can't write accompaniments for singers', etc., etc.

Even with well-known classics intelligent listeners can scarcely ever identify who is responsible for what. But the number of such people is so limited that their judgment carries little weight; bad conductors are free, in front of the same audience that would boo a good singer's 'vocal accident' without mercy, to indulge their own wickedness and incompetence with an untroubled conscience. Fortunately I am attacking an exception: malevolent conductors, whether competent or not, are pretty rare.

The conductor who is full of good will, but incompetent, is, on the other hand, extremely common, not to mention the innumerable feeble composers who can hardly be accused of conspiring against their own works but who conduct performers who are very often their superiors in every way. How many must there be who imagine they know how to conduct and then innocently ruin their own finest pieces!

Beethoven is said to have spoilt performances of his own symphonies on more than one occasion by trying to conduct them even when his deafness was almost total. In order to keep together, the players eventually agreed to follow the leader's discreet signals and not to watch Beethoven's baton at all. Conducting a symphony, an overture or any piece whose tempo stays the same for long periods without much variation or inflection is easy compared to conducting an opera or any work with recitatives, solo airs and frequent orchestral figures preceded by unmeasured rests. The case of Beethoven, which I have just mentioned, leads me to say at once that if I regard conducting an orchestra as extremely difficult for a blind man, it is certainly impossible for a deaf man, no matter how great his technical ability before he lost his sense of hearing.

The conductor must be able both to see and to hear; he must be agile and energetic; he must know the construction, principles and range of the instruments; he must be able to read a score and must have, besides the special talent whose ingredients we shall attempt to describe, other almost indefinable gifts without which an invisible bond cannot be struck between him and those whom he directs; without them the ability to convey his feelings to them is missing, and consequently the power, control and direction will slip from him completely. He is not then a leader and a director, but simply a time-beater – assuming that he can beat time and divide the bar into regular units.

The musicians must share his feelings, his perceptions and his emotions. His feelings and emotions will then pass to them, his inner flame will warm them, his electricity will charge them, his drive will propel them. He will radiate the vital spark of music. But if he is lifeless and cold he paralyses everything around him, like icebergs floating in polar waters which you can tell, from the sudden chill in the air, are not far away.

His task is a complex one. Not only must he interpret the composer's intentions in works which the players already know, he must also implant that knowledge when the work is new to them. He must correct everyone's errors and shortcomings in rehearsal and organise his available resources so as to get the maximum benefit as rapidly as possible. For in most European cities today music is so poorly supported, the players are so badly paid and the necessity for rehearsal is so little understood that the careful use of time must be regarded as one of the most pressing requirements of the conductor's art.

The rarity of good conductors and the perils of bad ones struck Berlioz very early in his career, to judge from his memory of his own first conducting experience. This was at St-Eustache in 1827, when he conducted the second performance of his *Messe solennelle*:

> How far I was from possessing the many varied qualities – precision, flexibility, sensitivity, intensity, presence of mind, combined with an indefinable instinct – that go to make a really good conductor, and how much time and experience and heart-searching have I since put into acquiring two or three of them! We often complain of there being so few good singers, but good conductors are rarer still and in the great majority of cases far more necessary and potentially dangerous to the composer.[1]

To this we should add the warning arising from Berlioz's impatience with Habeneck as conductor of *Benvenuto Cellini* in 1838: 'Unhappy composers! Learn to conduct yourselves (in both senses of the word); for conductors, never forget, are the most dangerous of all your interpreters.'[2]

Before Berlioz wrote the present chapter in 1855 to add to the second edition of the *Treatise*, his fullest essay on the art of conducting had appeared in the report of his travels to Prague published in 1848 and later incorporated in the *Memoirs*.[3] This should be regarded as a first draft of the present chapter.

Let us now consider the mechanical aspects of this art.

The ability to *beat time*, without considering any higher musical qualities, is none too easy to develop, and very few people do it properly. The gestures the conductor has to make, though simple in general terms, can be complicated by the division and sometimes the subdivision of the beats of the bar.

The conductor must above all have a clear idea of the main features and of the character of the work whose performance or rehearsal he is to direct, in order to be able to set at the outset, without hesitation or

---

[1] *Memoirs*, chapter 8.   [2] *Ibid.*, chapter 48.   [3] *Memoirs*, 'Travels in Germany', II/6.

error, the tempo the composer intended. If he is not in a position to have received instruction directly from the composer or if the tempos have not been handed down by tradition, he must refer to the metronome marks and study them carefully, since most composers today take the trouble to write them in at the beginning and in the course of their pieces.

I do not mean to imply that he must copy the metronome's mathematical regularity; any music done that way would be stiff and cold, and I doubt that one could maintain such level uniformity for many bars. But the metronome is, all the same, excellent to consult in order to establish the opening tempo and its main changes.

If the conductor has neither the composer's instructions nor tradition nor metronome marks, as often happens with early music written before the metronome was invented, there are no guides other than the vague terms used to convey tempo, his private instinct, and his feeling for the composer's style, as refined and accurate as that may be. Admittedly these guides are often inadequate and misleading. One has only to see modern performances of operas from the early repertoire in cities where the tradition of these works has disappeared to realise this. At least four out of ten different tempos will be taken at quite the wrong speed. I once heard a chorus in *Iphigénie en Tauride* played in a German theatre allegro assai in two instead of allegro non troppo in four, in other words exactly twice too fast. Examples of such disasters brought about by conductors' ignorance or heedlessness or by the real difficulty even the most gifted and careful people have in discovering the precise meaning of Italian tempo indications could be multiplied indefinitely.

Presumably no one would have any difficulty distinguishing a largo from a presto. If a presto is in two, any moderately intelligent conductor will be able to establish the speed the composer intended by studying phrases and themes in the piece. But if a largo is in four with a simple melodic outline and few notes in each bar, how can the unfortunate conductor discover the true tempo? In how many ways could he be wrong? The various degrees of slowness one might apply to such a largo are too numerous; the conductor's individual feeling will then be the only guide, even though it is the composer's feeling, not the conductor's, which is at issue. So composers must not neglect to give their works metronome marks, and conductors must undertake to study them carefully. For a conductor to neglect this study shows a lack of integrity.

Berlioz used the metronome all his life and inserted metronome marks in most of his scores.[4]

---

[4] For a study of Berlioz's metronome marks see Hugh Macdonald, 'Berlioz and the metronome', in *Berlioz Studies*, ed. Peter Bloom (Cambridge, 1992), pp. 17–36.

I will presume that the conductor is perfectly familiar with the tempos of the work he is to rehearse and perform. He wishes to convey his sense of rhythm to the musicians at his command, establish the duration of each bar and see that this duration is uniformly observed by all the performers. Now this precision and uniformity in a chorus and orchestra of whatever size will only be achieved by means of certain gestures made by the conductor.

These signs will show the main divisions, the *beats*, of the bar and often the subdivisions, or *sub-beats*. I do not need to explain what is meant by strong and weak beats; I presume I am speaking to musicians.

The conductor usually uses a small, light baton half a metre long and preferably white rather than dark (in order to be seen more easily), which he holds in the right hand. This is for making the beginning, the internal divisions and the end of each bar clearly understood. The bow used by some violinist-conductors is less suitable than the baton. It is rather too flexible; its lack of rigidity and the light air resistance caused by the bow hairs make its indications too imprecise.

The simplest of time-signatures, two in a bar, is very simple to beat. With the conductor's arm and baton raised so that the hand is level with his head, he marks the first beat by lowering the point of the baton vertically downwards (as far as possible by bending the wrist rather than lowering the whole arm) and the second beat by raising the baton vertically with the opposite movement, as in Fig. 1.

Fig. 1

One-in-a-bar should be beaten in the same way since it is really just an extremely rapid two-in-a-bar, especially for the conductor. Having to raise the point of the stick after lowering it forcibly divides the bar into two.

With four beats in the bar the first downward gesture (Fig. 2a) is universally adopted to mark the first strong beat at the beginning of the bar. The second gesture upwards from right to left (Fig. 2b) shows the second beat (the first weak beat). A third gesture, across from left to right (Fig. 2c) shows the third beat (second strong beat), and a fourth, obliquely upwards, indicates the fourth beat (second weak beat). The complete four gestures can be shown as in Fig. 2d.

It is important that the conductor does not move his arm much in all these changes of directions and does not make the baton cover too large an area, since each of these movements must be completed almost instantaneously or at least take no more than a barely measurable moment. But if

Fig. 2

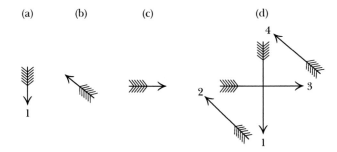

the instant is measurable, when multiplied by the number of times the gesture is repeated it ends by making the conductor fall behind the tempo he
is supposed to be setting and by giving his direction an irritating heaviness.
Furthermore this fault fatigues the conductor unnecessarily and produces
exaggerated, almost ridiculous, waving about, attracting the audience's
attention to the wrong thing and being most disagreeable to watch.

With three beats in the bar the first gesture, downwards, is again universally adopted to mark the first beat, but there are two ways of indicating the
second. Most conductors show it by going from left to right, as in Fig. 3a.
A number of German kapellmeisters do the opposite and move the stick
from right to left, as in Fig. 3b.

Fig. 3

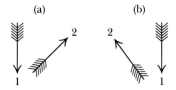

When the conductor turns his back to the orchestra, as is the practice
in the theatre, this method has the disadvantage of concealing the all-
important second beat from all but a very few of the players since the
conductor's body then hides the movement of his arm. The other procedure is better, since the conductor extends his arm outwards away from
the chest; if he is careful to raise his baton a little above shoulder level it
will be perfectly visible to all.

When the conductor faces the players it does not matter whether he
marks the second beat to the right or to the left. In any case the third beat
of a three-beat bar is always shown like the last beat of a four-beat bar, with
an oblique upward movement, as in Fig. 4a or 4b.

Five- and seven-beat bars will be better understood by the players if,
rather than indicating them with a special sequence of gestures, one treats

Fig. 4

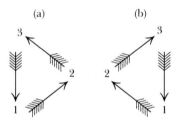

them as made up of three-beat and two-beat bars, or in the second case, four-beat and three-beat bars. The beats will thus be as in Fig. 5a in five-time and as in Fig. 5b in seven-time.

Fig. 5

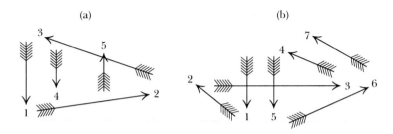

To be divided in this way it is assumed that these various time-signatures are at a moderate tempo. It would no longer apply if the tempo were extremely fast or slow.

Some conductors in Berlioz's time felt it was uncivil to turn their backs to the audience and therefore faced their listeners, in the manner of a vocal soloist. In the theatre the conductor sometimes stood between the orchestra and the stage and faced the singers, thus showing his back to the orchestra.

Berlioz never wrote a time-signature in five or seven beats without showing how the bar is to be subdivided. The *Combat de ceste* in Act I of *Les Troyens* (*NBE* 2a: 110) has dotted barlines to divide its five beats into three-plus-two, and the 'évolutions cabalistiques' in *L'enfance du Christ* (*NBE* 11: 49) are notated with alternating bars of three and four beats, never permitting a true seven-beat bar. There are two more examples among the sketches for *Les Troyens* (*NBE* 2c: 935, 938).

Two-in-a-bar, as I have explained, can only be done in the way I indicated just now, however fast the tempo. But if, exceptionally, it is very slow, the conductor will have to subdivide it. An extremely fast four-in-a-bar, on the other hand, must be beaten in two; the four strokes indicated in a moderate tempo become so hasty that they give the eye no clear lead and worry the player when they should reassure him. In addition – and this is more serious – by making these four pointless movements at a precipitate

speed the conductor destroys the flow of the rhythm and loses the freedom
of movement which the simple division of the bar in half would afford him.

In such cases, in general, composers are wrong to indicate a time-
signature in four. When the tempo is extremely fast they should only write
the signature ¢, never C, which can lead the conductor astray.

It is precisely the same for extremely fast triple tempos in 3/4 or 3/8.
The second gesture must then be omitted, so that the baton rests an extra
beat in the position of the first downbeat and rises only on the third beat,
as in Fig. 6. It would be absurd to try to beat three in a Beethoven scherzo.

Fig. 6

The converse applies to both these time-signatures, as it does for two-
beat bars. If the tempo is extremely slow each beat must be divided, making
eight movements in a four-beat bar and six in a three-beat bar. Each of the
main gestures we have just explained is repeated in shortened form. A slow
four-in-a-bar is done as in Fig. 7a, and a slow three-in-a-bar as in Fig. 7b.
The arm should play no part in the little extra movement shown for the
subdivision of the beat and the baton should be moved only with the wrist.

Fig. 7

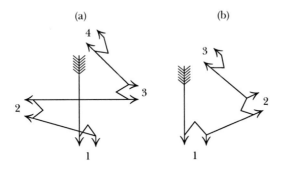

This division of the beats is designed to prevent the dislocation of rhythm
between players which can easily happen in the gap between one beat and
the next. If the conductor gives no indication in these gaps (which are very
lengthy owing to the extremely slow tempo) the players are left entirely
to themselves, *without a conductor*; and, since rhythmic feeling is never
the same for everyone, some will press forward while others pull back
and the ensemble is quickly destroyed. The only exception to this rule
would be if one were conducting a first-rank orchestra made up of great

players who know each other, play together often and know the work they are playing almost by heart. Even in those circumstances just one wayward musician can cause an accident. Why risk it? I am aware that certain players feel their pride slighted when they are kept on leading-strings in this way ('like children', they say), but to a conductor whose only concern is the excellence of the result this consideration carries no weight. Even in a string quartet it is rare for the individual feelings of the players to be free to express themselves fully; in a symphony it is the conductor's feeling which is at issue. The quality of the performance resides in the art of understanding and reflecting that feeling with unanimity, and individual inclinations – which, besides, cannot all coincide – should not be allowed to show.

Once this is understood it is clear why subdivision is even more essential in extremely slow compound time-signatures such as 6/4, 6/8, 9/8, 12/8 etc. But in these bars, in which triple rhythms are so important, there are several ways to break down the beat.

If the tempo is quick or moderate one need only mark the main beats of these bars in the manner shown for the analogous simple time-signatures. A 6/8 allegretto or a 6/4 allegro will thus be beaten as two-beat bars with a time-signature of ¢ or 2 or 2/4; a 9/8 allegro will be beaten as a 3/4 moderato or a 3/8 andantino, and a 12/8 moderato or allegro as a simple four-beat bar. But if the tempo is adagio, or particularly largo assai or andante maestoso, one must indicate either every quaver or a crotchet followed by a quaver for each beat, depending on the shape of the melody or the leading motive. In the triple time-signature shown in Ex. 173, for example, it is not necessary to mark every quaver; beating a crotchet and a quaver within each beat will do. The little gesture for the subdivision would then be done as in simple time-signatures, except that it subdivides each beat into two unequal parts, since it has to give a visual indication of a crotchet followed by a quaver.

Ex. 173

Larghetto grazioso

If the tempo is any slower there is no question. One will be properly in charge of the ensemble only by marking every quaver, whatever kind of compound bar it may be, as in Ex. 174a–c. In these three different time-signatures, with the tempos as shown, the conductor will mark three quavers in each beat, three below and three above for a 6/8 bar as in Fig. 8a, three below, three to the right and three above for a 9/8 bar as in Fig. 8b, and three below, three to the left, three to the right and three above for a 12/8 bar as in Fig. 8c.

Ex. 174

(a)

(b)

(c)

Fig. 8

    (a)   (b)   (c)

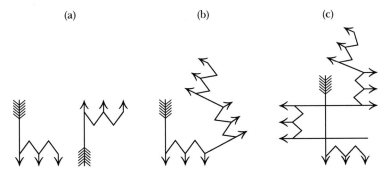

    The relatively few instructions to conductors given by Berlioz in his own scores are nearly all concerned with subdivision of the beat, confirming his fear that conductors may give too few beats and lose the ensemble. Examples are found in *La captive* (*NBE* 13: 20), *Roméo et Juliette* (*NBE* 18: 67), *Les Troyens* (*NBE* 2a: 35 and 2b: 589) and three times in *La damnation de Faust* (*NBE* 8a: 56, 80, 383). In the last of these, for 'Nature immense', the instruction is: 'Throughout this piece the conductor must beat the nine quavers of every bar, otherwise he will not get the desired rhythmic nuances with any precision.' In practice most conductors shirk the 144 beats a minute that this instruction implies and beat three, not nine, in this movement.

    Berlioz's recommendation to divide certain triple beats into two uneven subdivisions is a curious idea not endorsed by traditional conducting practice, although it is not unknown. His scores contain no instructions of this kind.

    Ex. 174c is a reduction of part of the *Chœur d'ombres* in *Lélio*.

    A difficult situation sometimes arises when certain parts of the score are in triple pulse while the rest retain a duple pulse in order to provide contrast, as in Ex. 175. If the wind parts in this example are played by true

musicians there is really no need to change the way of beating: the conductor can continue to subdivide into six or simply beat two. But if most of
the players seem to hesitate at the point where the triple rhythm is superimposed in syncopated form on the duple rhythm and mixed with it, this is
how to assist them. The anxiety caused by this sudden appearance of an unexpected rhythm in conflict with the rest of the orchestra always leads the
players to glance at the conductor to seek his aid. He should then meet their
eye, turn a little towards them, and show them the triple rhythm as if the
bar had three actual beats, using tiny movements so that the violins and the
other instruments playing the duple rhythm do not notice the change –
which would distract them completely. With this compromise the new triple
rhythm, secretly indicated by the conductor, can be played with complete
assurance while the duple rhythm, which was already firmly established,
continues without difficulty, even though the conductor is not marking it.

Ex. 175

On the other hand there is nothing more reprehensible and more unmusical, in my view, than the application of this technique to passages where
there is no superimposition of two contrary rhythms but merely syncopa-
tion. If the conductor divides the bar into the number of stresses it contains,
he will destroy the effect of the syncopations for all those audience who
are watching and replace a rhythmic concept of highly piquant character
with a dull change of time-signature. This is what happens when one marks
the accents rather than the beats in the passage from Beethoven's Pastoral
Symphony shown in Ex. 176a. This shows six gestures instead of the four
already established, which allow the syncopations to be felt and perceived
more fully, as in Ex. 176b. This wilful emphasis on a rhythmic shape *which
the composer meant to be contradicted* is one of the grossest faults of style that
a time-beater can commit.

Ex. 176

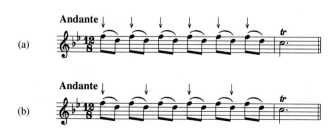

There is another daunting problem for the conductor which requires all his presence of mind, and that is the superimposition of different time-signatures. It is straightforward to conduct a time-signature of two duple beats above or below another time-signature of two triple beats if both are in the same tempo. The bars are then of equal duration and it is merely a matter of dividing them in two and beating the two main beats, as in Ex. 177.

Ex. 177

But if in the course of a slow movement a new idea is brought in whose tempo is quick, and if the composer has given this new tempo the short bars which it requires – either to make the quick passage easier to play or because it is impossible to write it any other way – there can then be two or even three short bars superimposed on one slow bar, as in Ex. 178. The conductor's task is to get these different time-signatures, unequal in length and tempo, to go correctly and to stay together. In this example it is done by starting to divide the beat at bar 1 (in the andante) before the entry of the 6/8 allegro and continuing to divide it thereafter, though making sure to make the division even clearer. Those playing the 6/8 allegro will then understand that the conductor's two movements show the two beats of their short bars, while those playing the andante know that these same two movements show no more than the division of a single beat of their long bar. Bar 1 will be indicated as in Fig. 9a and bars 2, 3 etc. as in Fig. 9b. This is basically very straightforward, since the division of the short bar and the subdivisions of the long bar coincide.

Ex. 178

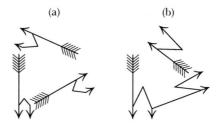

The following example, Ex. 179, where a slow bar is superimposed on two short bars without the same correspondence, is rather more tricky. Here the three bars of allegro assai before the allegretto are beaten in two simple beats as usual. When the allegretto begins, with its bar twice the length of the preceding bars and of those continued by the violas, the conductor beats two subdivided beats for the long bar, with two unequal strokes at the bottom and two more at the top, as in Fig. 10. The two main strokes divide the long bar in the middle and convey its pulse to the oboes without disturbing the violas who still maintain the quick tempo, since the little subdividing stroke also divides their short bar in the middle. At bar 3 of the allegretto he stops dividing the long bar into four because the triple rhythm of the 6/8 melody goes against it. So he then simply beats the two beats of the long bar and the violas, who are already launched on their rapid rhythm, keep going without difficulty, recognising that each stroke of the baton simply marks the beginning of one of their short bars.

Ex. 179

Fig. 10

This last example shows how careful one must be to subdivide the beats of a bar when any of the instruments or voices have triplets on those beats. If the subdivision falls in the middle of the second note of the triplet, it will disrupt the performance and could cause it to break down altogether. One should in fact stop subdividing the beat into two a little before the rhythmic or melodic shape divides it into three in order not to give the players the feeling of a contrary rhythm before they have to play it.

In Ex. 180 subdividing the bar into six, or the beat into two, is helpful and it presents no problem in bar 1. One beats it as in Fig. 11a. But one should abandon this in bar 2 and simply do the plain strokes of Fig. 11b because of the triplet on the third beat and the one after, which double strokes would contradict.

Ex. 180

Fig. 11

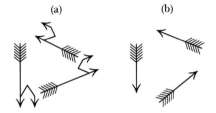

Ex. 178 is from the Sylphs' scene in *La damnation de Faust* (*NBE* 8a: 191), where a similar directive is supplied for the conductor as that given here. Ex. 179 is from the third movement of *Harold en Italie* (*NBE* 17: 118–20), and Ex. 180 is from the first movement of the same work (*NBE* 17: 6–7).

In the famous ballroom scene in Mozart's *Don Giovanni* the problem of keeping the three orchestras together, all written in different time-signatures, is less severe than one would suppose. It is sufficient to keep beating each beat of the *tempo di minuetto* as a downbeat, as in Ex. 181. Once it has joined the ensemble the little 3/8 allegretto, whose whole bar equals a third (or a beat) of that of the minuetto, and the other 2/4 allegro, whose whole bar equals two thirds (or two beats) of it, go perfectly with each other and with the main theme, and it all proceeds without any mishap. The crucial thing is to get them to come in right.

Ex. 181

Berlioz seems to be quoting *Don Giovanni* from memory. At first, in the *Treatise*, he printed Ex. 181 in the wrong key, F, then corrected it for the English edition and the separate publication of *Le chef d'orchestre*. He then gives the three separate orchestras in the wrong order, since the 3/8 allegretto comes in last of the three. In the separate publication of *Le chef d'orchestre* the time-signature of the remaining orchestra is given incorrectly as 3/4, not 2/4.

A bad fault I've seen committed is to broaden a two-beat bar when the composer introduces triplet minims, as in Ex. 182a. In this instance the third minim adds nothing to the duration of the bar, as some conductors seem to think. If the tempo is slow or moderate you can if you like beat these passages by treating the bar as if it were in three, but the duration of the full bar must stay exactly the same. When these triplets occur in a rapid time-signature in two (allegro assai), the three strokes just cause confusion; no more than two should be made, a downbeat on the first minim and an upbeat on the third. Because of the quick tempo these beats will look almost the same as two strokes in a bar with two equal beats and will not interfere with those parts of the orchestra which have no triplets (see Ex. 182b).

Ex. 182

(a)

(b)

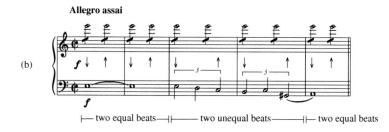

├— two equal beats —┤├——— two unequal beats ———┤├— two equal beats

Ex. 182b is similar to a passage in the overture *Le roi Lear* (*NBE* 20: 106). At the end of *Harold en Italie*, where triplet minims occur in a two-beat bar, Berlioz instructs the conductor to beat three (*NBE* 17: 200).

Let us now discuss the conductor's role in recitative. Since the singer or solo instrument is not subject to a regular division of the bar, it is a matter of following him closely and bringing in the orchestra accurately and together on the chords or instrumental figures which intersperse the recitative. In accompanied recitative one must get the harmony to change at the right moment, whether the accompaniment consists of held notes or of a tremolo in several parts, the least obvious of which is often the one the conductor should most concern himself with since it has the move which gives a change of harmony, as in Ex. 183.

Ex. 183

In this example the conductor must follow the unmeasured recitative but must at the same time be especially concerned with the viola part and get it to move exactly from the first beat to the second, from *f* to *e* at the beginning of the second bar. Otherwise, since this part is played by several instrumentalists in unison, some will hold the *f* longer than the rest and a momentary discord will be heard.

When conducting an orchestra in recitative many conductors customarily take no notice of the written divisions of the bar and give an upbeat before the beat on which a short chord occurs in the orchestra, even when the chord is on a weak beat (Ex. 184).

Ex. 184

In such a passage they raise their arms on the rest at the beginning of the bar and lower it on the beat with the chord. I cannot condone this practice, which is unjustifiable and liable to cause a mistake in performance. Besides, I see no reason why in recitative one should cease to divide the bar regularly or to beat the actual beats in the correct place, as one should in measured music. So for the above example my advice would be to beat the first beat downwards in the ordinary way and to move the baton to the left to bring in the chord on the second beat, and so on for other analogous cases, always dividing the bar into regular beats. It is also very important to divide it in accordance with the tempo previously indicated by the composer and not to forget, if this tempo is allegro or maestoso and if the solo part has been in recitative without accompaniment for some time, to give each beat an allegro or maestoso value when the orchestra comes in again. For when the orchestra is playing on its own it is normally measured; it plays out of tempo only when it is accompanying the voice or instrument which has the recitative. In the exceptional case when the recitative is for the orchestra itself, or for chorus, or even for part of the orchestra or chorus, since it is a matter of making a certain number of players or singers play or sing together, perhaps in unison, perhaps in harmony, but out of tempo, it is then the conductor who has the recitative, giving each beat of the bar the duration he feels he wants. As he follows the outline of the phrase he will sometimes divide and subdivide the beat, sometimes mark accents, sometimes he will conduct semiquavers if there are any: in sum he outlines the melodic shape of the recitative with his baton. It need hardly be said that the performers must know their notes almost by heart and will have their eyes fixed on him, otherwise there can be no confidence or ensemble.

In general, when the music is in tempo the conductor should require his performers to watch him as closely as possible. An orchestra that does not watch the stick is as if it had no conductor. Often, for example after a pause, the conductor must wait for all eyes to be fixed on him before giving the firm beat for the orchestra's attack. It is up to the conductor in rehearsal to train them all to watch at the crucial moment. In Ex. 185a, with a pause on the first beat held perhaps indefinitely, the figure shown as Ex. 185b cannot be played confidently and together unless the rule stated here is observed, since musicians who do not watch the beat cannot know when the conductor gives the second beat and resumes the pulse interrupted by the pause.

Ex. 185

Allegretto

(a)

(b)

Ex. 185 is from the 'évolutions cabalistiques' in Part I of *L'enfance du Christ* (*NBE* 11: 52). Ex. 184 is very similar to Polydorus's entry 'Seigneur!' a little earlier in the same work (*NBE* 11: 43). In Berlioz's scores there are almost no special instructions for the conductor, apart from the suggestions for subdividing the beat mentioned above. A single case at what might be considered an awkward moment for the conductor is found in the Finale of *Roméo et Juliette* (*NBE* 18: 337), where Berlioz suggests beating the first beat (which carries a pause) twice.

If the players have to watch the conductor, it follows that he must be sure to be seen by them. Whatever the layout of the orchestra, whether they are on terraced steps or on a level platform, he must place himself at the centre of all sight-lines. To raise himself up into full view the conductor needs a special rostrum, its height dependent on the number of performers and the size of the space they occupy. See that the stand is not so high that the score hides his face, for his facial expression counts for much in conveying his wishes. If the conductor does not exist for orchestras that will not watch him, he is no more likely to exist if he cannot be seen.

As for the practice of making a noise by striking the baton on the stand or stamping on the rostrum, it must be condemned unreservedly. It is worse than a poor trick, it's barbarism. In opera, however, when complex staging prevents the chorus from seeing the conductor, the conductor will have to be sure to get good choral attack after a rest by marking the preceding beat with a light tap on his stand with the baton. This exceptional case is the only one that justifies an audible beat; even then it's a pity to have to do it.

On the subject of opera choruses, I should add that chorus masters often take the liberty of beating time in the wings without being able to see the conductor's baton and often without being able to hear the orchestra. The effect of this arbitrary beat, badly done and unrelated to the conductor's, is to set up an inevitable rhythmic discord between the chorus and the orchestra and to destroy the ensemble instead of consolidating it.

There is another traditional barbarism which the intelligent, energetic conductor must set himself to eradicate. If a choral or instrumental piece is played offstage without the main orchestra, another conductor is absolutely necessary to conduct it. If the orchestra accompanies this group, the main conductor must listen to the music in the distance and allow himself to be strictly led by the second conductor and follow his tempo by ear. But if the sound of the main orchestra prevents the first conductor from hearing what is being played a long way away, as often happens in modern music, a special mechanical rhythm-transmitter is essential to communicate instantaneously between him and his distant forces. Some quite ingenious experiments have been done in this regard, with unexpected results in some cases. The one at Covent Garden, London, operated by the conductor's foot, works quite well. The only one to leave nothing to be desired is the 'electric metronome' set up by M. Verbrugghe in the theatre in Brussels. It consists of a set of copper wires connecting a battery underneath the stage to the conductor's stand and then on to a moving baton pivoted at one end on a board *at any distance* from the conductor. On the

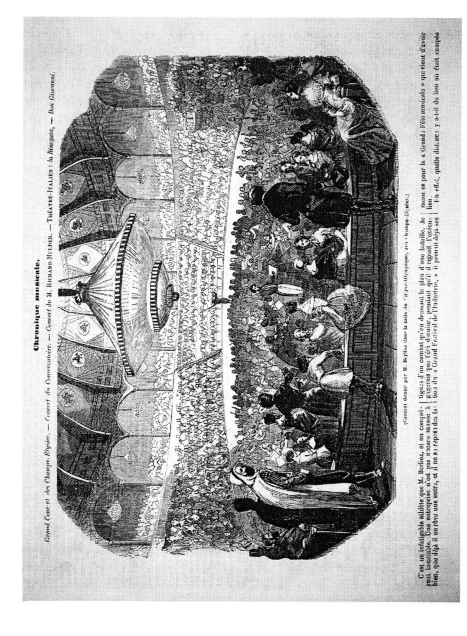

13   A Berlioz concert in 1844, showing a sub-conductor.

conductor's stand is fixed a copper key rather like a piano key, springy to the touch, with a pin about seven or eight millimetres long underneath. Immediately beneath the pin is a little cup, also copper, filled with mercury. As the conductor presses the copper key with his left index finger (his right hand is holding the baton), the key goes down, the pin goes into the cup of mercury, a weak electric spark is given off, and the baton at the other end of the copper wire oscillates on its board. Communication through the fluid to the moving baton is completely instantaneous, however far it has to travel. Performers in a group backstage with their eyes on the electric metronome's baton are thus directly in touch with the conductor's indications; if he needed to he could conduct a piece played at Versailles from the middle of the orchestra of the Paris Opéra. But it is important to fix in advance with the chorus (or their sub-conductor, if they have one) the manner in which the conductor will beat time, whether he is to beat all the main beats or just the first of each bar; the oscillations of the baton activated by electricity are always forward and back, so it gives no clear indications of this sort.

When I first used the precious device which I have tried to describe, in Brussels, a problem was encountered. Each time the copper key on my stand was pressed by my left index finger it struck another piece of copper underneath. Despite the lightness of the contact it made a little tapping noise which could distract the audience during the orchestra's rests to the detriment of the music. I brought this fault to the attention of M. Verbrugghe, who replaced the lower copper plate with the cup of mercury I have described, so that when the pin dips into it to complete the electric circuit it makes no noise. The only remaining problem with this machine is the crack of the spark when the mechanism disconnects, though the crack is too soft to be heard by the audience.

This metronome is not expensive to set up; it costs 400 francs at the most. Opera houses, churches and concert halls should have had one long ago. In the huge concerts I conducted last year (1855) in the grand Palais for the Exposition Universelle de l'Industrie, concerts involving over a thousand musicians, the effectiveness of M. Verbrugghe's invention was so obvious that three Paris opera houses (the Théâtre Italien, the Opéra Comique and the Théâtre Lyrique) all immediately acquired electric metronomes. Even in pieces of very rapid tempo, precision was astonishing and ensemble faultless.

Berlioz first encountered Verbrugghe's (or Verbrugghen's) electric metronome when he conducted *L'enfance du Christ* in Brussels in March 1855.[5] The choir of invisible angels at the end of Part I were singing offstage with the help of the device, which he recommends in a note at the beginning of the score. Berlioz

---

[5] *Cg*, 5, pp. 36–7.

hoped to use it for coordinating the organ in the first performance of the *Te deum* the following April, although this did not happen. In the first version of this passage, in the second edition of the *Treatise*, this last paragraph read as follows:

This metronome is not expensive to set up; it costs 400 francs at the most. Opera houses, churches and concert halls should have had one long ago. There are none anywhere except in the Brussels theatre. That would be hard to believe were it not for the apathy of the directors of most institutions where music is exploited, their instinctive hostility to anything which might disturb their fixed routine, their indifference to the interests of the arts, their meanness when it comes to spending money, and the complete ignorance of the basic principles of our art shown by nearly everyone in charge of its destiny.

In November 1855, however, Verbrugghe came to Paris to assist with the Exposition Universelle concerts Berlioz mentions, on which occasion the five sub-conductors – Tilmant, Bottesini, Hellmesberger, Vautrot and Hurand – were all equipped with electric metronomes at some distance from Berlioz's beat. A cartoon by Cham in *Le charivari* of 2 December 1855 imagined Berlioz wired to performers all over the globe. The three theatre managers were impressed by the machine, but the Opéra alone of Paris opera houses held out against installing an electric metronome until 1861 when Berlioz had it set up there for Gluck's *Alceste*.[6]

When he first saw the electric metronome Berlioz, with justifiable pride, pointed out that he had imagined such an invention over ten years before. In his story *Euphonia*, published in 1844, he described

an ingenious mechanism which would have been discovered five or six centuries earlier if anyone had troubled to think about it. It picks up the conductor's movements without being seen by the audience and conveys them directly *before the very eyes* of each player. It gives the beats of the bar and the various degrees of loud and soft with great precision. The players are thus in instant and immediate communication with the feelings of their conductor and can respond as rapidly as piano keys do to the pressure of the fingers, and the conductor can then truly claim to be *playing* the orchestra.[7]

Berlioz's vision was perhaps nearer to closed-circuit television than to the electric metronome.

I have not yet said all I have to say about those dangerous supernumeraries known as chorus masters. Very few of them are in fact competent to conduct a musical performance to a standard that the conductor can rely on. He cannot really keep a close eye on them when he has to work with them. The most formidable are those bereft by old age of all agility and vigour. Keeping any quickish tempo going is beyond them. Whatever

[6] *Memoirs*, 'Postface'.   [7] *Les soirées de l'orchestre*, p. 366.

speed is printed at the beginning of a piece they gradually slow down until the rhythm sinks into a medium crawl evidently in keeping with the flow of their bloodstream and the general decay of their organism. I should add that old men are not the only ones who can expose composers to this danger. There are men in the prime of life who have lymphatic temperaments and blood which seems to circulate moderato. Should they be conducting an allegro assai they slow it down gradually to moderato. If, on the other hand, it is a largo or an andante sostenuto they get progressively faster and reach a moderato long before the end, no matter how short the piece is. Moderato is their natural pace and they come back to it as infallibly as a pendulum goes back to its own pace when its oscillations have been hurried or held back.

Such people are natural foes of music with any character and are the greatest levellers of style. May the conductor be spared their assistance at any price!

One day, in a city which will be nameless, a very simple offstage chorus in allegretto 6/8 was to be performed. The chorus master's assistance was required; he was an old man . . . Since the tempo was first set by the orchestra our Nestor followed more or less correctly for the first few bars. But the slowing down was soon so bad that there was no way of continuing without making the whole thing ridiculous. They started again, twice, three times, four times; a full half-hour was spent getting more and more irritated, always with the same result. Keeping up the allegretto tempo was quite beyond this worthy man's powers. Eventually the conductor, losing patience, asked him not to beat time at all. He had found a way out: he demonstrated a marching movement to the chorus, lifting each foot in turn without moving. Since this tempo exactly fitted the duple rhythm of the 6/8 allegretto, the chorus immediately performed their piece as if they were singing on the march, with ensemble and precision and without slowing down, no longer obstructed by their sub-conductor.

Yet I realise that many chorus masters and orchestral sub-conductors are often truly useful, indispensable, in fact, for keeping large bodies of performers together. When these groups are arranged so that part of the chorus or orchestra have to turn their backs to the conductor, he will then need a number of sub-conductors in front of those who cannot see him to pass on his every movement. To get this transmission accurate the sub-conductors must take care not to take their eyes off the conductor's baton for an instant. Even if they stop watching him for just three bars to look at their score a disparity will arise between their beat and his and all will be lost.

In a festival concert in Paris in 1844 when I had 1200 performers under my direction, I had to employ five chorus conductors all round the choral body and two orchestral sub-conductors, one leading the wind and the other the percussion. I had carefully instructed them to watch me all the time; they did not fail to do so; and our eight batons, rising and falling without the slightest rhythmic variation, obtained from our 1200 musicians the most perfect ensemble ever known. By using one or more electric metronomes it may not seem necessary to resort to that solution now. One can of course conduct a chorus who have their backs to the conductor without any difficulty that way, but attentive, intelligent sub-conductors will always be preferable to a machine on such occasions.

Besides beating time, as the metronome's arm does, they have also to alert their nearby groups to expression marks and get their attention for entries after rests.

In a hall shaped like a semi-circular amphitheatre the conductor can control a large number of performers on his own, since all eyes will be able to see him without difficulty. Using a certain number of sub-conductors still seems better to me than concentrating on a single individual because of the great distance between the conductor and the far extremes of the chorus and orchestra. The further the conductor is from his musicians the weaker his control over them. Best of all would be to have several sub-conductors with several electric metronomes beating the main beats of the bar in front of them. That is how I directed the concerts in the Palais de l'Industrie in 1855.

Now should the conductor be standing or seated? Playing enormously long opera scores it is hard to avoid fatigue if you stand the whole evening. It is equally a fact that the sitting conductor loses some of his authority and cannot give full rein to his vivacity, if he has any. Should he conduct from a full score or from a cued-in first-violin part, as is practised in some theatres? He will surely have a full score in front of him. To conduct from a part which contains only the main instrumental cues, the bass line and the melody puts an unnecessary burden on the conductor's memory, and if he presumes to tell a player he has made a mistake when he cannot check his part he also runs the risk of getting the reply 'How do you know?'

The placing and grouping of instrumentalists and chorus fall within the conductor's province, especially in the concert hall. The best grouping of performers in a theatre or a concert hall cannot be definitively fixed, since the shape and layout of the hall's interior has an obvious bearing on deciding what to do. It depends also on the number of performers involved and sometimes on the type of composition they are performing. For concerts, in general, an amphitheatre on eight or at least five levels is essential.

A semicircular plan is the best for this amphitheatre. If it is wide enough to contain the whole orchestra the full body of players can be set out on different levels with the first violins at the front on the right; the seconds at the front on the left; the violas in the middle between the two sets of violins; the flutes, oboes, clarinets, horns and bassoons behind the first violins; a double row of cellos and basses behind the second violins; the trumpets, cornets, trombones and tubas behind the violas; the rest of the cellos and basses behind the woodwind; the harps at the front close to the conductor; the timpani and other percussion behind the brass; and the conductor near the front desks of first and second violins with his back to the audience at the bottom of the amphitheatre.

Extending forward from the lowest level of the amphitheatre there should be a horizontal platform or fairly large stage. Here will be the chorus, laid out in the shape of a fan, three-quarters facing the audience but still able to see the conductor without difficulty. The grouping of the chorus in voices will depend on whether the composer wrote in three, four or six parts. In any event, the women, both sopranos and contraltos, will be at the front, sitting down; the tenors will be standing behind the contraltos, the basses standing behind the sopranos.

Soloists will occupy the centre of the forestage, at the back, and will be placed so that they can always see the conductor's beat by turning the head a little.

Again I must repeat that these suggestions are only approximate; they can be altered in any number of ways for a variety of reasons.

At the Paris Conservatoire, where the amphitheatre consists of only four or five non-circular levels and cannot therefore accommodate the whole orchestra, the violins and violas go on the stage, with the cellos, basses and wind on the terraced levels. The chorus sits on the forestage facing the audience, but the entire section of female voices – sopranos and contraltos – cannot possibly see the conductor's beat since they are sitting with their backs to him. This layout is extremely awkward for that part of the chorus.

It is most important that the chorus on the forestage should always be on a level below that of the violins, whose sound will otherwise be seriously impaired. For the same reason, if there are no more steps down for the chorus in front of the orchestra, the women must definitely be seated and the men standing, so that the tenors' and basses' voices are freely projected, coming from a higher point than the sopranos' and contraltos', and are not muffled or blocked.

When the chorus's presence in front of the orchestra is not required, the conductor must remember to see that they go out, since this large number of human bodies interferes with the instruments' sound. A symphony played by an orchestra which is dampened in this way can be badly spoilt.

This section on the layout of the orchestra and chorus served as a replacement for the similar passage in the chapter 'The orchestra' dating from thirteen years earlier (see above, pp. 322–7). The suggestion that the chorus should leave the hall when they are not singing is embodied in the score of *Roméo et Juliette*, where the chorus is instructed not to enter until the fifth movement, the *Convoi funèbre*, since they are not heard (except offstage) before that point (*NBE* 18: 3).

There are other precautions relating solely to the instrumentalists that the conductor can take to avoid certain performance problems.

When placed on one of the furthest levels of the amphitheatre, percussion instruments, as I have said, tend to drag the rhythm and slow down. A series of bass drum notes struck at regular intervals at a fast tempo, as in Ex. 186, can completely wreck a finely set rhythm, break the orchestra's momentum and destroy the ensemble. From not watching the conductor's first beat the bass drum player nearly always comes in a bit late on his first entry. Multiplying this time-lapse by the number of notes that follow, one can easily see how quickly it can cause a horrible rhythmic discord.

Ex. 186

On such occasions the conductor's efforts to restore the ensemble are in vain; he can do only one thing, and that is demand that the bass drum player memorise the number of drum-strokes in that particular passage and keep his eyes fixed on the beat without looking at his part; he will instantly be able to follow the beat without the least error. Another type of delay, which happens for a different reason, is often to be observed in the trumpets when their part includes passages at quick tempo like that in Ex. 187a. Instead of breathing *before* the first of these three bars, the trumpeter breathes at the beginning, during the quaver rest. Making no allowance for the brief time he has for breathing, he takes the full time and adds another quaver rest to the first bar, as in Ex. 187b. The result is all the worse since the final accent, which is struck at the beginning of the third bar by the rest of the orchestra, arrives in the trumpets a third of a beat late, destroying the ensemble and the attack on the last chord.

Ex. 187

To avoid this the conductor must first warn his players in advance that they are almost all prone to inaccuracy without noticing it, and then, when conducting, glance at them at the critical moment and give the first beat of the bar in which they enter *slightly early*. It is hard to credit how difficult it is to stop trumpets doubling the value of a quaver rest in such places.

Ex. 187a is a passage that recurs several times in the overture *Le carnaval romain.*

When a long *accelerando a poco a poco* is marked by the composer for a transition from allegro moderato to presto, most conductors, instead of speeding the tempo up evenly and imperceptibly, push it forward in jerks. This must be carefully avoided. The same applies to the reverse process. It is even more difficult to broaden a fast tempo gently without lurching and transform it gradually into a slow tempo.

A conductor who wants to prove his enthusiasm, or who lacks any re-fined musical feeling, often asks his players to exaggerate the markings. He understands neither the character nor the style of the music. Expression marks become blemishes, accents become shrieks; the poor composer's in-tentions, no matter how honourable they may seem, are as misconceived as the affections of the donkey (in the fable) that smothered his master with kisses.

Let me now mention a few deplorable habits encountered in almost every orchestra in Europe; these are the despair of composers, and it is the duty of conductors to get rid of them whenever they can.

String players can rarely be bothered to do a tremolo. In place of this very striking effect they repeat the note at half, often less than half, the pace which produces a proper tremolo; instead of hemidemisemiquavers they play demisemiquavers; instead of sixty-four notes in an Adagio four-beat bar they play thirty-two or even sixteen. The agitation of the arm required for a true tremolo evidently calls for too much effort! This laziness is intolerable.

Out of laziness, similarly, or for fear of not being able to manage difficult passages, a good many double bass players take the liberty of simplifying their parts. The simplifier-school, much respected forty years ago, should be dead and buried. In early music double bass parts are very simple; there's no reason to impoverish them any further. In modern scores they are rather harder, true, but with very rare exceptions there is nothing unplayable: composers who know their business write them with care, in the way they should be written. If laziness causes simplifiers to deform their parts, the conscientious conductor has the authority to make them do it correctly. If it is from incompetence, he should dismiss them. It is fully in his interest to get rid of players who cannot play their instruments.

Flautists, being accustomed to dominating the rest of the wind, of-ten refuse to acknowledge that their part can be written below clarinet or oboe parts, so they transpose whole passages up an octave. Conduc-tors who cannot read scores properly, who do not know the work thor-oughly or who do not have a good ear will not notice this peculiar liberty flautists take. Yet it is common enough, and one should see that it does not happen.

Everywhere – and I don't mean just in some orchestras – I repeat, every-where, you will find that when ten, fifteen or twenty violinists have the same part to play in unison, they will never count their bars' rests, again from laziness, but leave the task to others. So scarcely half the section come in when they should, while the rest still have their instruments under their left arms and their gaze in the air. The entry is weak, if not missed altogether. I draw this intolerable habit to the attention and stern notice of conductors. Yet it is so deeply ingrained that it will not be rooted out except by making a great many violinists liable for the mistakes of one; for example, by fining a whole row if one of them misses his entry. If the fine were just three francs, I believe that when it can be imposed five or six times on the same individual in a session each player will count his rests and see that his neighbour does so too.

Berlioz seems once again to confuse left and right: violinists traditionally rest with the fiddle under their right arm.

An orchestra whose instruments are out of tune with themselves and with each other is a monstrosity. The conductor must therefore take the greatest care to see that the players tune up. This operation should not be done in public. Moreover, the noise of instruments warming up and playing during the interval is deeply offensive to sensitive listeners. One may measure an orchestra's poor training and musical mediocrity from the intrusive noises made during breaks in an opera or a concert.

It is also the imperative duty of the conductor to see that clarinettists do not use the same instrument (the B♭ clarinet) all the time, regardless of what the composer asks for, as if the various clarinets, especially those in D and A, did not have a special individuality fully appreciated by well-informed composers, and as if the A clarinet did not have an extra semitone below the B♭ clarinet, the excellent sounding c♯ produced by written *e*, a note which only gives *d* on the B♭ clarinet.

An even more corrupt and pernicious habit has arisen in many orchestras from the use of valve horns: that of playing as open notes (using the new mechanism fitted to the instrument) those notes which were intended by the composer to be played as stopped notes, with the right hand placed in the bell. Horn players nowadays, furthermore, use only the horn in F, no matter what was marked by the composer, as a result of the ease with which pistons and cylinders put their instrument into different keys. This custom leads to a host of abuses from which the conductor must take every care to protect the works of composers *who know how to compose*. For those who don't, it must be admitted, the problem is much less serious.

One must also resist the parsimonious habit practised in certain opera houses of having the cymbals and bass drum played by a single player. The sound of cymbals fixed to a bass drum (which has to be done to make the economy possible) is a vulgar noise, fit only for suburban ballroom orchestras. This practice also leads mediocre composers into the habit of never using either instrument separately and of treating them as uniquely suitable for the heavy accentuation of the strong beats of the bar, an idea that breeds noisy platitudes and has brought us the ridiculous extravagance beneath which dramatic music will sooner or later expire if a stop is not put to it.

I must finally express my regret at seeing choral and orchestral rehearsals everywhere still so badly run. The practice of massed rehearsals for big choral and instrumental works persists everywhere. The whole chorus is rehearsed at the same time, so are the instrumentalists.

Dreadful mistakes and countless howlers are made, especially in inner parts unnoticed by the chorus-master and the conductor. Once established, these mistakes degenerate into regular practice and survive right through to the performance.

Of all the performers the unfortunate chorus is much the worst treated during rehearsals, such as they are. Instead of getting a *good conductor*, who knows how to beat time and who knows about singing, to give the beat and make comments, a *good pianist* playing from a *well arranged vocal score* on a *good piano*, and a *good violinist* to play in unison or an octave above each vocal part as they are learnt separately – instead of these three indispensable musicians they are entrusted, in two thirds of the opera houses of Europe, to just one man who has no more idea how to conduct than to sing, not much of a musician, picked from the worst pianists they can find, or, more likely, who does not play the piano at all, a miserable specimen sitting at a broken down, out-of-tune instrument, trying to read a jumbled up score he does not know, striking wrong chords, major for minor and vice versa, and, because he must conduct and accompany both at the same time, using his right hand to give the chorus the wrong rhythm and his left hand to give them the wrong notes.

When you see such barbarous parsimony you would think we were back in the Middle Ages...

A faithful, well shaped, inspired interpretation of a modern work, even in the hands of artists of a high order, can only be obtained, I firmly believe, from sectional rehearsals. Each choral part must be rehearsed on its own until it is well learnt before joining the ensemble. The same procedure is to be followed for an orchestra learning a quite complicated symphony. The violins should be rehearsed alone first; then the violas, cellos and basses, then the woodwind (with a small group of strings to fill the gaps and cue the wind for their entries), then the brass in the same way. It is very often necessary to rehearse the percussion on their own, even the harps, if there is a group of them. Full rehearsals are then much more productive and more efficient, and one may pride oneself on thus achieving a fidelity of interpretation whose rarity is alas all too well attested.

Performances rehearsed in the old way are only approximate, which is fatal for most masterpieces. When the conductor has massacred a classic he still puts down his baton with a satisfied smile. And if he still harbours any doubts about the way in which he has carried out his duties, since no one, in the final analysis, is charged with monitoring his performance of them, he can mutter to himself: 'Bah! Woe to the vanquished!'

Berlioz concludes with one of his favourite phrases, 'Vae victis!', which he left in Latin in the *Treatise* but translated into French in the separate edition of *Le chef d'orchestre*. Whether or not he knew that it comes from Livy (attributed to the Gallic king Brennus on capturing Rome in 390 BC), he sprinkled it around in his correspondence with the resignation that marks his later years.[8]

When Berlioz first went to Germany in 1843 he was shocked by the low standard of chorus-masters:

Most of them are poor pianists. I met one who could not play the piano at all, and who gave the notes by striking the keyboard with two fingers of the right hand. Moreover, in Germany, as here, they still rehearse all the voices together in the same place under one conductor, instead of having three practice rooms and three chorus-masters for the preliminary rehearsals.[9]

Little need be said about Berlioz's competence and authority as an exponent of the art of conducting. Both in Paris and abroad he established a reputation as one of the first specialist conductors of the modern kind, a reputation that was at its height in the 1850s when he was in great demand in London and Germany and when he wrote this essay. This was not the first textbook on conducting, but he did set down the basic elements of stick technique and these are still in general use today.[10]

There is no finer tribute to Berlioz's conducting than V. V. Stasov's account of Berlioz conducting in St Petersburg in 1847:

Probably no one else has ever delved so deeply into the art of musical performance as he has; no one else has ever experienced the joy he does when 'playing the orchestra' (as he himself puts it). His amazing ear catches every nuance, even the most elusive. He never permits a single one to slip by; he can pick each one out through the thunder of the entire orchestra. Under Berlioz's direction the orchestra is like a steed that feels the full power of its rider. Leading it, Berlioz is a veritable general, adored by all his forces, inspiring them by some kind of extraordinary power to accomplish unprecedented feats. Under him, they do things it would have seemed no one on earth could have made them do. It is as though the musicians seated before him were not men but a row of keys; he plays on them with his ten fingers, and each one produces just the sound, just the degree of tone that is needed.

[8] For example, *Cg*, 4, p. 119. [9] *Memoirs*, 'Travels in Germany', I/1.
[10] For Berlioz's career and style as a conductor see Adam Carse, *The Orchestra from Beethoven to Berlioz* (Cambridge, 1948), pp. 373–6; Elliott W. Galkin, 'Berlioz as conductor', *Journal of the American Liszt Society*, 9 (1981), pp. 19–30; and Holoman, *Berlioz*, pp. 348–53.

Berlioz arrives in a city. He gathers together musicians of all kinds and calibres. He seldom has more than two or three rehearsals, sometimes (very rarely) four. Then suddenly this group is transformed into an orchestra; it becomes one man, one instrument, and plays as though all its members were finished artists. Berlioz's concerts come to an end. He leaves, and everything is as it was before: each man for himself. The mighty spirit that had inspired everyone for a moment is gone.[11]

[11] Vladimir Vasilevich Stasov, *Selected Essays on Music,* translated by Florence Jonas (London, 1968), p. 25.

Appendix

Berlioz's writings on instruments

Instruments and instrumentation were frequently the subject of Berlioz's feuilletons in the press. The *Treatise* started life as a series of articles on instrumentation in the *Revue et gazette musicale* in 1841–2, but there were many earlier and later articles in which the subject was his main concern. The following list includes Berlioz's principal writings on instruments. References in the form 'C 455' are to the catalogue of Berlioz's feuilletons found in Holoman, *Catalogue*, pp. 435–88. Page numbers indicate where an article has been quoted in this book.

Article	Published	Holoman	Page
'De l'instrumentation de Robert-le-diable'	*Gm*, 12 July 1835 *Cm*, 2, pp. 209–15	C 146	(59, 172)
'Musique religieuse. *Rachel, Noëmi, Ruth et Booz*, oratorios de M. Lesueur' (Le Sueur's orchestration)	*Jd*, 21 November 1835 *Cm*, 2, pp. 353–9 Condé, pp. 156–7, 159	C 175	
'Gymnase musical, soirée de valses de Strauss'	*Rgm*, 5 November 1837 *Cm*, 3, pp. 327–8 Condé, pp. 123–4	C 288	(213)
'Strauss, son orchestre, ses valses. De l'avenir du rythme'	*Jd*, 10 November 1837 *Cm*, 3, pp. 329–35 Condé, pp. 122–8	C 289	(xvii, 4, 208, 276)
'Nouveaux pianos de M. Pape' (Pape's 'piano sans cordes')	*Jd*, 6 July 1838 *Cm*, 3, pp. 493–4	C 320	(277)
'Instrumens de musique. Exposition des produits de l'industrie' (Boehm's new flute; Erard's and Pape's new pianos; inventions by Roller, Le Père, Boisselot and Leclerc; the melophone used in Halévy's *Guido et Ginevra*; Paris's 'harmoniphon' or keyboard-oboe; recent organs)	*Jd*, 28 May 1839	C 350	(108, 159–61)

(cont.)

'*Cours d'instrumentation considérée sous les rapports poétiques et philosophiques de l'art* par M. Georges Kastner'	*Jd*, 2 October 1839	C 358	(xvii)
'Orgue de Saint-Denis'	*Jd*, 19 October 1841	C 452	(161)
'De l'instrumentation' (1) (introduction, harp, mandolin, guitar)	*Rgm*, 21 October 1841	C 455	(5, 74, 77, 89)
'De l'instrumentation' (2) (piano, violin)	*Rgm*, 28 November 1841	C 456	(14, 27, 97)
'De l'instrumentation' (3) (viola, cello, double bass)	*Rgm*, 5 December 1841	C 457	(45, 53–4, 59, 63)
'De l'instrumentation' (4) (oboe, bassoon, contrabassoon)	*Rgm*, 12 December 1841	C 458	(100, 103, 111, 117)
'De l'instrumentation' (5) (clarinet, basset horn, bass clarinet)	*Rgm*, 19 December 1841	C 461	(124, 134–5)
'De l'instrumentation' (6) (flute)	*Rgm*, 2 January 1842	C 463	(145, 151–2)
'De l'instrumentation' (7) (horn, piston horn)	*Rgm*, 9 January 1842	C 464	(166, 182–3)
'De l'instrumentation' (8) (trumpet)	*Rgm*, 16 January 1842	C 465	
'De l'instrumentation' (9) (cornet)	*Rgm*, 23 January 1842	C 467	(193–5, 205)
'De l'instrumentation' (10) (trombone)	*Rgm*, 6 March 1842	C 476	(210, 224)
'De l'instrumentation' (11) (bugle, ophicleide, serpent)	*Rgm*, 13 March 1842	C 478	(231–2, 234–5, 239, 243, 297)
'De l'instrumentation' (12) (organ)	*Rgm*, 24 April 1842	C 490	(157)
'Instrumens de musique. M. Ad. Sax' (new Sax instruments, including the saxophone)	*Jd*, 12 June 1842	C 497	(135)
'De l'instrumentation' (13) (voices)	*Rgm*, 26 June 1842	C 499	
'De l'instrumentation' (14) (percussion)	*Rgm*, 3 July 1842	C 502	(276)
'De l'instrumentation' (15) (the orchestra, 1)	*Rgm*, 10 July 1842	C 504	
'De l'instrumentation' (16) (the orchestra, 2)	*Rgm*, 17 July 1842	C 507	

(*cont.*)

'Exposition de l'industrie. Instrumens de musique. Orgues-mélodium' (pianos by Erard, Pape, Pleyel and Herz; inventions by Boisselot; the 'piano sans cordes'; the 'piano octavié'; Barthélémy's tuning system, organs, melodiums; Sax's new instruments)	*Jd*, 23 June 1844	C 577	
'*Méthode de violon*, par M. Alard. *Méthode de cornet à trois pistons*, par Forestier'	*Jd*, 23 November 1844	C 584	
'L'orgue de Saint-Eustache et l'orgue–mélodium'	*Jd*, 29 December 1844	C 588	(313)
'De la réorganisation des musiques militaires' (the excellence of Prussian military bands and of Sax's new instruments, especially the saxhorn)	*Jd*, 1 April 1845	C 591	(304)
'Réorganisation de la musique militaire en France'	*Jd*, 12 September 1845	C 599	
'Antiphonel-harmonium de M. Debain'	*Jd*, 7 October 1846 *Rgm*, 11 October 1846	C 613	(314)
'Orgue à percussion de MM. Alexandre'	*Jd*, 14 February 1847	C 618	
'Sax et ses instruments' (Sax instruments; shortcomings in percussion instruments)	*Jd*, 12 October 1847	C 624	(295, 298–9)
'Exposition de l'industrie. Instrumens de musique. MM. Erard, Boisselot, Weulfel, Sax, Vuillaume'	*Jd*, 21 August 1849	C 670	(299)
'M. Gouffé et sa méthode de contre-basse'	*Jd*, 27 August 1850	C 684	
'*Manuel de musique militaire*, par M. Georges Kastner'	*Jd*, 17 January 1851	C 691	
'Le saxophone. Nabich, son trombone'	*Jd*, 13 April 1851	C 695	
'Les instruments indiens' (Chinese and Indian instruments)	*Jd*, 31 May 1851 *Les soirées de l'orchestre*, pp. 316–21	C 697	

(*cont.*)

'*Méthode de saxhorn*, par Sax' (the success of French makers at the Great Exhibition in London)	*Jd*, 27 November 1851	C 706	(318)
'Les jurys de l'Exposition universelle et les facteurs d'instrumens de musique'	*Jd*, 30 December 1851	C 709	
'Brochure sur les corps de musique militaire. Les orgues de Cologne'	*Jd*, 7 January 1852	C 710	
'Erreur du public au sujet de la trompette marine'	*Jd*, 13 January 1852 *Les grotesques de la musique*, pp. 91–2	C 711	
'Les instrumens de musique à l'Exposition universelle (1)'	*Jd*, 9 January 1856 *Les grotesques de la musique*, pp. 71–80	C 769	
'Les instrumens de musique à l'Exposition universelle (2)' (Boehm, Cavaillé-Coll, Sax, Vuillaume, Alexandre)	*Jd*, 12 January 1856	C 770	(138, 161, 313, 318)
'Les instrumens de musique à l'Exposition universelle (3)' (the concertina, enharmonics, acoustics, pianos, oboes)	*Jd*, 15 January 1856	C 772	
'Début de Thalberg sur l'orgue Alexandre'	*Jd*, 24 September 1856	C 791	(313)
'L'orgue Alexandre en Russie'	*Jd*, 15 November 1856	C 792	(313)
'*Méthode de trompette*, par M. Dauverné'	*Jd*, 3 February 1857	C 796	
'Le piano-orgue d'Alexandre'	*Jd*, 24 September 1857	C 807	(313)
'Le piano-orgue d'Alexandre'	*Jd*, 14 December 1857	C 811	(313)
'*Méthode théorique et pratique d'orgue-Alexandre à l'usage des pianistes*, par MM. d'Aubel et A. Durand, organiste du grand orgue de Saint-Roch'	*Jd*, 19 June 1858	C 822	
'La trompette marine'	*Rgm*, 27 February 1859 *Les grotesques de la musique*, pp. 91–2	C 853	(313)
'L'accord des instruments sans le secours de l'oreille; la musique enseignée avec le secours de cet organe exigeant. Moyen d'accorder les instrumens à cordes sans le secours de l'oreille, trouvé par F. Delsarte'	*Jd*, 30 December 1859 *A travers chants*, pp. 271–2	C 879	

(*cont.*)

'La *méthode d'orgue* de M. Engel. M. Sax; ses procès. Alexandre; sa bataille d'Ivry'	*Jd*, 24 September 1860	C 891	
'L'anex-piano'	*Jd*, 29 December 1860	C 892	
'L'orgue Alexandre'	*Jd*, 28 January 1862	C 917	(313)
'Orgues d'Alexandre. Leur introduction dans toutes le communes de France'	*Jd*, 14 May 1863	C 933	(313)

Bibliography

Principal editions of the *Treatise*

a) in French:

Grand traité d'instrumentation et d'orchestration modernes, contenant le tableau exact de l'étendue, un apperçu du mécanisme et l'étude du timbre et du caractère expressif des divers instrumens, accompagné d'un grand nombre d'exemples en partition, tirés des œuvres des plus grands maîtres, et de quelques ouvrages inédits de l'auteur, dédié à sa majesté Frédéric Guillaume IV, roi de Prusse, par Hector Berlioz. Œuvre 10me
Paris, Schonenberger, [1844]. 239 pp. Plate no. S.996
Hopkinson 30A. Holoman, *Catalogue*, p. 431

[The same title, then:] *Nouvelle édition revue, corrigée, augmentée de plusieurs chapitres sur les instruments récemment inventés, et suivies de l'Art du chef d'orchestre*

Paris, Schonenberger, [1855]. 312 pp. Plate no. S.996
Hopkinson 30B. Holoman, *Catalogue*, pp. 431–2

[The same]
Paris, Lemoine et fils, [1876]. 312 pp. Plate no. S.996, with a second plate number 14518H on the first four pages
Hopkinson 30B(a). Holoman, *Catalogue*, p. 432

[The same.]
Paris, Lemoine et fils, 1925

[The same.]
Farnborough, Gregg International, 1970

Le traité d'orchestration d'Hector Berlioz
Paris, Fischbacher, 1909. With translations of Strauss's additions by E. Closson
Hopkinson 30B(c)

b) in German:

Die Moderne Instrumentation und Orchestration
Berlin, Schlesinger, [1844]. 332 pp. Plate no. S.3000. Trans. J. C. Grünbaum from the first French edn
Hopkinson 30A(a). Holoman, *Catalogue*, p. 431

[The same], 2te Ausgabe
Berlin, Schlesinger, [1856]. 329 pp. Plate no. S.3000. The same as the first Schlesinger
    edn with translations of the new chapters
Hopkinson 30B(d). Holoman, *Catalogue*, p. 432

Instrumentationslehre. Autorisirte deutsche Ausgabe von Alfred Dörffel
Leipzig, Gustav Heinze, 1864. 285 pp. + 70 pp. musical examples
Hopkinson 30B(f). Holoman, *Catalogue*, p. 432

Instrumentationslehre. Ergänzt und revidiert von Richard Strauss
Leipzig, C.F. Peters, [1904–5]. Dörffel's translation with Strauss's additions
Hopkinson 30B(i)

Grosse Instrumentationslehre. Herausgegeben von Felix Weingartner
Leipzig, Breitkopf & Härtel, 1904. 307 pp. Trans. Detlef Schultz. This edition omitted
    the examples in full score. Weingartner contributed a two-page preface
Hopkinson 30B(j)

c) in Italian:

Grande trattato di stromentazione e d'orchestrazione moderne
Milan, Ricordi, [1844]. 307 pp. Plate no. 15081-7. Trans. Alberto Mazzucato from the
    first French edn
Hopkinson 30A(d). Holoman, *Catalogue*, p. 431

[The same, second issue]
Milan, Ricordi, 1864. 307 pp. Plate no. 15081-7

[The same,] *Edizione seconda.*
Milan, Ricordi, n.d. 309 pp. Plate no. 15081-7

[The same] *Con appendice di Ettore Panizza*
Milan, Ricordi, [1912]. 3 vols. Plate no. 113600-2. The appendix contains examples by
    Strauss, Verdi, Puccini, Sinding, Chabrier, Boito, et al.
Hopkinson 30B(1)

d) in English:

A Treatise upon Modern Instrumentation and Orchestration
London, Novello, 1856. 257 pp. Trans. Mary Cowden Clarke
Hopkinson 30B(o). Holoman, *Catalogue*, p. 432

[The same,] 2nd edn
London, Novello, 1858. 257 pp.
Hopkinson 30B(p). Holoman, *Catalogue*, p. 432

[The same,] *revised and edited by Joseph Bennett*
London, Novello, Ewer & Co., 1882
Hopkinson 30B(r)

[The same]
London, Novello & Co, 1904
Hopkinson 30B(s)

[The same]
Ann Arbor, UMI, 1973

Treatise on Instrumentation
New York, Edwin F. Kalmus, 1948. 424 pages. Trans. Theodore Front from Strauss's
German edn

[The same]
New York, Dover Publications, 1991

e) in Spanish:

Gran tratado de Instrumentación y Orquestración. Para uso de los compositores españoles
Madrid, Minuesa, 1860. 240 pp. Trans. Oscar Camps y Soler
Hopkinson 30A(f). Holoman, *Catalogue*, p. 432

f) in Russian:

Bolshoy traktat o sovremennoy instrumentovke i orkestrovke
Moscow, Musïka, 1972. Translation of Strauss's version by S. P. Gorchakov

Separate editions of *Le chef d'orchestre*

a) in French:

Le chef d'orchestre: Théorie de son Art
Paris, Schonenberger, 1856. 47 pp.
Hopkinson 30C. Holoman, *Catalogue*, p. 432

[The same,] *Deuxième édition*
Paris, Lemoine et fils, n.d. 47 pp.
Hopkinson 30C(a). Holoman, *Catalogue*, p. 432

There were at least ten editions of this publication.

b) in German:

Der Orchester-Dirigent
Berlin, Schlesinger, [1856]. 40 pp. Trans. J. C. Grünbaum and including the chapter
'Die neuen Instrumente'. Text in both French and German
Hopkinson 30C(b). Holoman, *Catalogue*, p. 432

Der Orchester-Dirigent.
Leipzig, Heinze, 1864. 48 pp. Trans. Alfred Dörffel
Holoman, *Catalogue*, p. 432

[The same]
Leipzig, Leuckart, 1877. 48 pp. Trans. Alfred Dörffel
Die Kunst des Dirigierens
Heilbronn, Schmidt, 1902. Ed. C. Frhr. v. Schwerin
Hopkinson 30C(c)

c) in English:

The Art of Conducting
Boston, White, 1888. 46 pp.
Hopkinson 30C(e)

How to Conduct an Orchestra
Philadelphia and Chicago, J. W. Pepper. 30 pp. Ed. Thomas a' Becket
Hopkinson 30C(f)

The Orchestral Conductor: Theory of his Art
New York, Carl Fischer, 1902. 21 pp. Adapted from Mary Cowden Clarke's translation
Hopkinson 30C(g)

The Conductor: The Theory of his Art
London, William Reeves, [1917]. 63 pp. Trans. John Broadhouse
Hopkinson 30C(d)

The Orchestral Conductor
London, J. R. Lafleur & Son, n.d. 16 pp. Ed. Roy Cathcart

d) in Russian:

Dirizher orkestra
Moscow, 3rd edition, 1912. Trans. P. Shchurovsky

Separate editions of the *RGM* articles

a) In French:

De l'instrumentation
Paris, *Revue et gazette musicale*, 21 November 1841 to 17 July 1842 (see Appendix I)

De l'instrumentation
Paris, Bègles, Le Castor Astral, 1994. 171 pp. Ed. Joël-Marie Fauquet

b) in German:

Die Kunst der Instrumentirung
Leipzig, Breitkopf und Härtel, 1843. 112 pp. Trans. J. A. Leibrock
Holoman, *Catalogue*, p. 431

On the *Treatise*

H. Kling, 'Le grand traité d'instrumentation et d'orchestration modernes', in *Le livre d'Or du centenaire d'Hector Berlioz* (Paris, [1903]), pp. 122–4
Camille Saint-Saëns, *Portraits et Souvenirs* (Paris, 1909), pp. 4–6
Ernest Closson, 'Richard Strauss et le *Traité d'orchestration* d'Hector Berlioz', *Le guide musical*, 55 (1909), pp. 591–4, 607–11
Hans Bartenstein, *Hector Berlioz's Instrumentationskunst und ihre geschichtlichen Grundlagen: ein Beitrag zur Geschichte des Orchesters* (Strasbourg, 1939); 2nd, expanded, edn (Baden-Baden, 1974)

Edward Lockspeiser, 'The Berlioz–Strauss treatise on instrumentation', *Music and Letters*, 50/1 (1969), pp. 37–44
Joseph-Marc Bailbé, 'L'orchestre et *Le traité d'orchestration*', in *Berlioz artiste et écrivain dans les 'mémoires'* (Paris, 1972), pp. 87–104
Frédéric de La Grandville, *Recueil complémentaire des exemples d'orchestration cités dans le texte du grand traité d'instrumentation d'Hector Berlioz* (Faculté des Lettres et Sciences humaines, Reims, 1978)
Alastair Bruce, 'Berlioz's treatise on instrumentation', *Berlioz Society Bulletin*, 104 (Summer 1979), pp. 2–13
Joël-Marie Fauquet, 'The *Grand Traité d'instrumentation*', in *The Cambridge Companion to Berlioz*, ed. Peter Bloom (Cambridge, 2000), pp. 164–70

On Berlioz's Orchestration

H. Lavoix fils, *Histoire de l'instrumentation depuis le seizième siècle jusqu'à nos jours* (Paris, 1878)
Adam Carse, *The History of Orchestration* (London, 1925)
Tom S. Wotton, 'Orchestration', in *Hector Berlioz* (London, 1935), pp. 99–121
Adam Carse, *The Orchestra from Beethoven to Berlioz* (Cambridge, 1948)
Jacques Barzun, 'Structure and harmony through timbre', in *Berlioz and the Romantic Century* (2 vols, Boston, 1950), 1, pp. 448–69
Hugh Macdonald, 'Berlioz's orchestration: human or divine?', *Musical Times*, 110 (1969), pp. 255–8
Pierre Boulez, 'L'imaginaire chez Berlioz', in *Points de repère* (Paris, 1981), pp. 239–47; published in English as 'Berlioz and the realm of the imaginary', *High Fidelity Magazine*, 19/3 (1969), pp. 47–54
Benjamin Perl, 'L'orchestre dans les opéras de Berlioz' (thesis, Ecole Pratique des Hautes Etudes, 1983)
Performance Practice: Music After 1600, ed. Howard Mayer Brown and Stanley Sadie (London, 1989)
Joël-Marie Fauquet, 'L'innovation instrumentale devant l'Académie (1803–1851)', in *Musique et médiations*, ed. Dufont et Fauquet (Paris, 1994), pp. 197–249

Guitar:

Philip James Bone, *The Guitar and Mandolin* (London, 1914), pp. 36–40
Joseph Zuth, 'Die Gitarre des Berlioz', *Zeitschrift für die Gitarre*, 1 (1922), pp. 8–11
Victor Kolon, 'Die Pariser Gitarre von Paganini–Berlioz', *Zeitschrift für die Gitarre*, 5 (1926), pp. 50–3
Paul Jerald Dallman, 'Influence and use of the guitar in the music of Hector Berlioz' (MMus thesis, University of Maryland, 1972)

Wind:

Anthony Baines, *Woodwind Instruments and their History* (London, 1957)
Cecil B. Wilson, 'Berlioz's use of brass instruments' (Ph.D. dissertation, Case Western Reserve, 1971)
Hugh Macdonald, 'An ophicleide you cannot refuse', *Berlioz Society Bulletin*, 101 (1978), pp. 3–5
Jürgen Eppelsheim, 'Berlioz' "Petit Saxhorn Suraigu"', in *Gesellschaft für Musikforschung. Bericht über den internationalen Musikwissenschaftlichen Kongreß. Berlin 1974*, ed. Hellmut Kühn and Peter Nitsche (Kassel, 1980), pp. 586–91

Anthony Baines, *Brass Instruments: Their History and Development* (New York, 1981)
Benjamin Perl, 'Les cuivres dans les opéras de Berlioz', *Brass Bulletin*, 45 (1984), pp. 18–30
E. P. Sandor, 'Development and use of the chromatic trumpet in the nineteenth century orchestra', *NACWPI Journal*, 33/4 (1985), pp. 4–12
Ernest H. Gross III, 'The influence of Berlioz on contemporary nineteenth century use of brass instruments', *Brass Bulletin* (in 4 parts): 67/3 (1989), p. 20; 68/4 (1989), p. 34; 69/1 (1990), p. 88; 70/2 (1990), p. 62
Edward H. Tarr, 'The romantic trumpet', *Historic Brass Society Journal*, 5 (1993), pp. 213–61
Diana Bickley, 'The trumpet shall sound', *Historic Brass Society Journal*, 6 (1994), pp. 61–83
David Whitwell, 'Berlioz – his music for winds', *The Instrumentalist*, 20 (1996), pp. 71–5

Organ:

D. Batigan Verne, 'Berlioz *versus* the organ', *The Organ*, 6 (1927), pp. 171–8
Guy Warrack, 'Hector, thou sleep'st', *Musical Times*, 104 (1963), pp. 896–7
Denis McCaldin, 'Berlioz and the organ', *The Organ Yearbook*, 4 (1973), pp. 3–17

Voices:

Geneviève Duval-Wirth, 'Berlioz et la voix', *Silex*, 17 (1980), pp. 87–94

Percussion:

Tom S. Wotton, 'The roll of the drums', *Musical Opinion*, 25 (1902), p. 366
Peter Hyde Tanner, 'Timpani and percussion writing in the works of Hector Berlioz' (PhD dissertation, Catholic University of America, 1967)
Nancy Benvenga, 'The use of the percussion in the symphonies of Berlioz' (typescript, Boston, 1969)
James Blades, *Percussion Instruments and their History* (London, 1970)
Cecil B. Wilson, 'Some remarks about multiple timpani and Berlioz', *The Instrumentalist*, 28 (1973), pp. 55–6
John Crabbe, 'Hell's bells and Hector Berlioz', *Hi-Fi News and Record Review* (1978), pp. 91–3
Nancy Benvenga, 'Berlioz and sponge timpani sticks', *Berlioz Society Bulletin*, 100 (Summer 1978), pp. 5–9

Conducting:

Michael Paul Matesky, 'Berlioz on conducting' (DMA dissertation, University of Washington, 1974)
Elliott W. Galkin, 'Berlioz as conductor', *Journal of the American Liszt Society*, 9 (1981), pp. 19–30
Donald L. Appert, 'Berlioz, the conductor' (DMA dissertation, University of Kansas, 1985)

Bibliographies

Michael G. H. Wright, *A Berlioz Bibliography* (Farnborough, n.d.)
Cecil Hopkinson, *A Bibliography of the Musical and Literary Works of Hector Berlioz 1803–1869*, 2nd edn, ed. Richard Macnutt (Tunbridge Wells, 1980)
D. Kern Holoman, *Catalogue of the Works of Hector Berlioz* (Kassel, 1987)
Jeffrey Langford and Jane Denker Graves, *Hector Berlioz: a Guide to Research* (New York, 1989)

For further sources used in this book, see 'Abbreviations' (p. xxxviii).

General index

377

Index of Berlioz's works

Printed in the United Kingdom
by Lightning Source UK Ltd.
121128UK00001B/13-14